For Bob
With gratitude.
Erika
6/14

State-Building and Multilingual Education in Africa

How do governments in Africa make decisions about language? What does language have to do with state-building, and what impact might it have on democracy? This book provides a longue durée explanation for policies toward language in Africa, taking the reader through colonial, independence, and contemporary periods. It explains the growing trend toward the use of multiple languages in education as a result of new opportunities and incentives. The opportunities incorporate ideational relationships with former colonizers as well as the work of language NGOs on the ground. The incentives relate to the current requirements of democratic institutions and the strategies leaders devise to win elections within these constraints. By contrasting the environment faced by African leaders with that faced by European state-builders, it explains the weakness of education and limited spread of standard languages on the continent. The work combines constructivist understanding about changing preferences with realist insights about the strategies leaders employ to maintain power.

Ericka A. Albaugh is an assistant professor in the Department of Government and Legal Studies at Bowdoin College. She received her Ph.D. in Political Science from Duke University and her M.A. from the Fletcher School of Law and Diplomacy at Tufts University. Her B.A. in International Relations is from Pepperdine University. Her articles have been published in the *Journal of Modern African Studies*, *International Studies Quarterly*, and *Democratization*. She has received major fellowships from the Pew Foundation, the Social Science Research Council, and the Spencer Foundation. She has conducted extensive field research in Cameroon, Senegal, and Ghana. Prior to graduate study, she worked for World Vision.

State-Building and Multilingual Education in Africa

ERICKA A. ALBAUGH

Bowdoin College

CAMBRIDGE
UNIVERSITY PRESS

CAMBRIDGE
UNIVERSITY PRESS

32 Avenue of the Americas, New York, NY 10013-2473, USA

Cambridge University Press is part of the University of Cambridge.

It furthers the University's mission by disseminating knowledge in the pursuit of education, learning, and research at the highest international levels of excellence.

www.cambridge.org
Information on this title: www.cambridge.org/9781107042087

© Ericka A. Albaugh 2014

First published 2014

A catalog record for this publication is available from the British Library.

Library of Congress Cataloging in Publication Data
Albaugh, Ericka A.
State-building and multilingual education in Africa / Ericka A. Albaugh.
    pages   cm
Includes bibliographical references and index.
ISBN 978-1-107-04208-7 (hardback)
1. Multilingualism – Africa.   2. Language and education – Africa.   3. Education and state – Africa.   4. Education, Bilingual – Africa.   5. Language and languages – Study and teaching – Africa.   I. Title.
P115.5.A35A43   2014
306.44'96–dc23   2013027345

ISBN 978-1-107-04208-7 Hardback

Contents

List of Tables and Figures

Preface

This book originated as a query of a simple, yet controversial, assertion by Lamin Sanneh, author of *Translating the Message* (1989). He wrote that missionaries had preserved culture in Africa by translating its languages, and therefore should be lauded rather than maligned as often they were in modern Africanist scholarship. As a person of faith, I was intrigued. Yet as a budding Africanist, aware of the many sins committed on the continent in the name of saving it, I was wary. And so I set out to look with objective eyes at the impact of language transcription in Africa. This topic was too big, of course, and it had to be shaped into a *political* question. Fortunate to travel to Cameroon with a predissertation fellowship, I found that a question crystallized. In a country of enormous diversity that had tried to subdue its difference since independence, why was the government suddenly deciding to use a multitude of its languages in its education system? Exploring this question and its corollary – "What has been the impact of this policy?" – has taken several years and several trips to Africa.

The predissertation trip to Cameroon took place between January and June 2001, with three months spent in Ngaoundere learning Fulfulde, and the remaining three months traveling to make contacts in eight of the country's ten regions. The "real" field research occurred during the academic year 2002–2003: July and August in Paris, September to December in Cameroon, January to March in Senegal, and March to May in Ghana. In March 2004, I conducted two weeks of interviews in Paris and Marseille/Aix-en-Provence. Though the dissertation was completed in May 2005, my research continued with follow-up trips to Cameroon and Senegal in the summer of 2009 and to Cameroon in the summer of 2011. In all, I have spent more than fourteen months in Cameroon, four months in Senegal, two months in Ghana, and three months at various points interviewing in France.

The original manuscript would not have begun or concluded without the training and encouragement I received from my dissertation committee members. Through several years of working as his research assistant and profiting from his advising, my consideration for Donald L. Horowitz, my Chair, has grown from initial trepidation to sincere intellectual respect and personal appreciation. His insistence on high academic standards and a fearless ability to speak his mind have emboldened me with increasing courage to present my own views with confidence. Robert O. Keohane is truly a gifted mentor, and he, more than anyone, has guided my development as a scholar. I prize his skill for taking a tangle of ideas and organizing them from his broad vantage point into a coherent research project. I appreciate above all his unflagging belief in me. Steven I. Wilkinson, fresh from his own field research, but already with the perspective of an established scholar, provided invaluable practical and theoretical suggestions. He also exhorted me continually to write more clearly, more directly, and more boldly, and the dissertation has improved as a result. Finally, I thank Catharine Newbury for agreeing (with some pleading) to accept a student from Duke who hoped to benefit from the strengths in African politics that she offered her students at the University of North Carolina at Chapel Hill. Graciously, she consented not only to my presence in several of her classes at UNC, but to serving as an outside adviser, even when she moved an even greater distance to Smith College.

These advisers, as well as other faculty and graduate student colleagues in the Department of Political Science at Duke University, provided a stimulating and rigorous environment to incubate this project. Since graduating, I have begun teaching at Bowdoin College, where I continue to find support. My colleagues have heard or read various iterations of my chapters. Students in my courses on African Politics and on State-Building in Comparative Perspective have challenged and inspired my thoughts on these issues. Chase Taylor helped me greatly with maps. I also am deeply indebted to the generosity of Lauren MacLean, Pierre Englebert, and two anonymous reviewers for their immeasurably helpful comments on the manuscript. Of course they are not to blame for mistakes that remain.

I have been exceedingly fortunate to receive financial support from many sources. The Pew Foundation funded three years of my graduate study at Duke. The extraordinary Predissertation Fellowship offered by the Social Science Research Council allowed me a year in which I could study African language (Hausa and Fulfulde) and African history, as well as enjoy a six-month exploratory tour of Cameroon. The U.S. Education Department's Foreign Language and Area Studies program provided for intensive French language study in Paris and field research using the French language in Cameroon and Senegal. Duke University's Graduate School supplied the funds for my research in Ghana. The Spencer Foundation made my final year of writing immeasurably more peaceful by granting me a Dissertation Fellowship for Research Related to Education. Bowdoin College allocated research funds for me to return to Cameroon and Senegal twice, along with summer research assistants through the Gibbons Fellowship program to help with GIS mapping. And a Bowdoin Faculty grant allowed me to draw all of the pieces together in the final write-up during my junior sabbatical year, 2011–2012. I am grateful to all of these institutions for their belief in my work and their truly generous financial support.

I also want to thank the publishers of three journals for permission to reuse portions of the following articles: Some of the material in Chapter 4 appeared as "The Colonial Image Reversed: Language Preferences and Policy Outcomes" in *International Studies Quarterly* 53, 2 (June 2009): 389–420; much of the material in Chapter 6 appeared as "An Autocrat's Toolkit: Adaptation and Manipulation in 'Democratic' Cameroon" in *Democratization* 18: 2 (April 2011): 388–414; and many ideas about bargaining and preferences sprinkled through Chapters 5 and 6 were previously published as "Language Choice in Education: A Politics of Persuasion" in the *Journal of Modern African Studies* 45, 1 (2007): 1–32.

To the many people in Cameroon, Senegal, Ghana, France, Britain, and the United States who responded to interviews, letters, e-mails, or phone calls, I am indebted. Any presentation of research findings is an interpretation, and I am aware that many of the people who contributed their thoughts and experiences will not necessarily agree with my analysis. I have endeavored to keep their voices and faces in my mind as I write, and to be true to their stories. I am thankful for the many research assistants who agreed to help me, particularly Usman Ahmadu in Cameroon, and for the organizations and people who allowed me to live in each country: SIL, Jim and Karen Noss, Professor Teddy Ako, and especially Solomon and Alice Tatah in Cameroon; the Tekpo family in Accra; and famille Mbaye in Dakar, who offered much more than a comfortable home and the best restaurant in Senegal.

Finally, I want to thank my husband, Jason, who, if truth be told, should be a coauthor of this manuscript. When we married, we agreed that I would support him first through his schooling, and then he would support me through mine. I got by far the better part of the bargain. He has been patient through school-inspired moves from California to Massachusetts and then to North Carolina and to Maine, stable through coursework, encouraging through exams, and amazingly enthusiastic through eighteen months of field research. In the three African countries, he accompanied me (not only because I was pregnant, but because he was genuinely interested) on nearly every interview in that year of dissertation research, except when he was too sick to venture out. This man who prefers cool climes and familiar food sacrificed many of his comforts to support my dream of becoming an Africanist scholar. The discovery was sweeter, and the trials bearable because he was with me. And in the write-up stage, he continued to prove his dedication, juggling an accountant's work schedule to help care for our children and even initiating an absurdly early wake-up regimen to make sure we both had time to work and share evenings together as a family. He built my database, helped with formatting, and proofread each chapter. Most importantly, he reminded me continually that life is more than work and study. I know now more than ever why I married him.

The finished book will never do justice to all of its contributors. But if the final product is anything of quality, it derives from the nurturing setting in which it grew.

I

Introduction

Political cohesion seems to require a standard language. As historical state-builders monopolized violence, collected regular taxes, expanded bureaucratic reach, constructed centralizing roads, and mapped territory and population, they viewed language rationalization as a critical component of their interventions. Moving from ruling indirectly through intermediaries to interfacing directly with citizens required the ability to communicate with this population. Mass conscription and universal compulsory education aided greatly in this endeavor, and while it took until the early twentieth century before linguistic reality began to approximate visions of uniformity in Europe, the two centuries prior demonstrated vigorous and conscious efforts by rulers toward this goal of language standardization.

These hard-fought efforts at linguistic unity reached their apex just as African states were achieving independence, and most new leaders adopted the nation-building goals of language standardization. Recently, however, many states appear to be ignoring these historical models, and across Africa, governments are endorsing the use of more local languages as media of instruction in primary schools. Whereas less than 40 percent of states used African languages in education at independence, nearly 80 percent do presently. Rather than a deliberate movement toward monolingualism, perpetual multilingualism appears to be their vision and not just an inconvenient reality. Especially on a continent where high ethnolinguistic diversity is a standard explanation for poor growth, weak governance, and conflict, why are governments highlighting, rather than attempting to diminish, their linguistic diversity?

Democracy promotion has replaced nation-building as the appropriate goal for African states, but even in the latter, a common language is central to providing the communicative resources that allow citizens to participate and to hold their rulers accountable. Hobsbawm notes that a national language only became important when ordinary citizens became a significant component of the state: "The original case for a standard language was entirely democratic, not cultural. How could citizens understand, let alone take part in, the government of their country if it was conducted in an incomprehensible language?" (1996, 1067). Green argues that a cohesive civic nation is the best guarantor of democracy, and drawing on the traditions of Durkheim[1] lauds a centralized education that helps individuals forge broader loyalties and construct participatory skills that can sustain democracy (Green 1997, 170, 186). Particularly after the spectacular dissolution of the Soviet Union and Yugoslavia, states that strayed furthest from the homogenizing model to institutionalize nationhood on a subnational level (Brubaker 1996, 29), the dangers to states of institutionalizing difference seem acute. Brubaker notes that unlike European nationalisms that conceived states as belonging to a particular group, African nationalism purposely was framed in a supraethnic rather than ethnonational idiom (Brubaker 1996, 64, fn13). The importance of a common, neutral language in holding together such a polity is self-evident. It is even more puzzling, then, that this supraethnic façade should be deliberately pulled away with a focus on subnational language units.

This book explains the increasing recognition of language in education as a combination of material and ideational opportunities, along with electoral incentives for current rulers. The environment that produces this policy choice is vastly different from that faced by state-builders in Europe, an important acknowledgment that opens the possibility for differing trajectories of state development. While the majority of the book explains the causes, the final chapter begins to explore the consequences of multilingual education for national cohesion and political mobilization, which are much more benign than the previous paragraph implies.

This introductory chapter is divided into three parts. The first lays a framework to explain the empirical increase in mother tongue education across the African continent, juxtaposing my own theory about the causes of these policy choices with alternative explanations. The second discusses the policy of mother tongue education generally – its rationale and current scholarly debates. The third part of the introduction describes more fully the differences in contexts faced by historical European state-builders – from whence we derive our monolingual model – and contemporary African states – where we see the multilingual option taking precedence. The chapter ends with a plan of the book.

THEORETICAL FRAMEWORK

In explaining the causes of multilingual education policy, three alternative accounts could compete with my own: norm-based, rational choice, and sociostructural. First, it may be simply part of the rise of identity politics that began in

---

[1] "Society can survive only if there exists among its members a sufficient degree of homogeneity; education perpetuates and reinforces this homogeneity by fixing in the child, from the beginning, the essential similarities that collective life demands" (Durkheim 1922/1956, 70).

the 1960s and 1970s, and the norm of multiculturalism and linguistic rights has finally penetrated across the globe. As international human rights activists have persuaded governments to acknowledge the rights of minority language groups within their borders, widespread multilingual education thus may simply reflect a growing international norm that favors protecting minority languages. Second, multilingual policies could reflect leaders aiming to prevent potential conflict by granting concessions to groups that demand special or equal treatment. This would be a rationalist bargaining explanation that assumes governments respond to language group pressures led by elites. The spread of democracy gives more voice to organized groups, which is why we see more policies promoting their particular interests. Third, adding nuance to the bargaining explanation with a sociostructural perspective, it might be that more cohesive, hierarchical groups would demonstrate a greater ability to hold on to their cultural identities than dispersed, "stateless" groups. Where stronger, hierarchical subunits exist, one may expect to see more attention to their languages. While I draw elements from each of these explanations, none can by itself explain the outcomes we see.

The increase in the use of local languages indeed results from both internal and external pressures, but they are different from those commonly assumed. I argue that African governments enacting mother tongue education policies are responding to two different forces – one a "push" and the other a "pull." The push comes not from language groups or their representatives demanding rights to use their languages in education – indeed, many speakers explicitly do not want this right – but from an alliance of indigenous linguists and foreign nongovernmental organizations (NGOs), who use a recent accumulation of written languages and evidence of their success as media of instruction to offer an alternative to African governments facing failing education systems. Their pressure, however, has been building for a long time, and it might not have been accepted officially if another factor had not provided a moment of opportunity.

This opportunity, the pull, is provided by the new discourse of a former colonizer, France. Rather than a vague call by the entire international community to promote languages in support of diversity, a specific, new message began to emanate from France in the 1990s. Reversing its long-standing preference for French-only as the medium of instruction in African primary schools, France began to communicate its support for initial schooling in local languages. This was not because France had suddenly decided to care about local languages, but because its foreign policy leadership had been convinced by a group of strategic scholars that learning initially in a local language helps a child to learn French.

These forces meet to influence a person – a policy maker. Why would such a policy maker see the benefit of multilingualism? Current African leaders can be compared with historical state-builders as we assess their preferences, along with those of other social actors. I argue that their preferences are different from those of past rulers. They emerge as a result of the opportunities described previously, but their preferences also evolve as leaders adapt new strategies for maintaining power. As they survey their states, I suggest that the context they face – the need to consolidate their power within electoral institutions – is different from the context faced by historical state-builders prior to the late twentieth century.

Why should we compare African trajectories to historical state-building episodes? The comparison is useful because political leaders, no matter what the historical period, aim to stay in power by extending their control over opposition, and all must adapt to material and institutional constraints. African states are notoriously weak – as measured by governments' abilities to control violence, spur economic growth, invest in infrastructure, and care for populations[2] – and the harm that their citizens have endured spurs questioning of causes. The recognition of Africa's weakness prompted many studies to probe reasons for it. One obvious candidate is the continent's tremendous ethnolinguistic fragmentation.[3]

Language is the strongest marker of ethnic identity. Usually a familial given, it is also changeable, susceptible to individual choice and social planning. No wonder, then, that it has been an object of tremendous scholarly interest and political intervention. But African state leaders have not shown as much concern for linguistic cohesiveness as we might expect. This is because of a unique context.

Jeffrey Herbst (2000) has highlighted ably many differences between contemporary Africa and the Europe where "war made states" (Tilly 1990). Protected by the Organization of African Unity (OAU) agreement on sacrosanct borders and sustained by foreign aid and taxes on primary commodities, African leaders have not needed to build up bureaucracies for internal taxation as did prior state-builders. And geographic barriers made this penetration even more daunting (Herbst 2000, chapter 5). While stable borders had momentous impact by creating permanent citizens and foreigners, Herbst observes the relatively weak effect of African citizenship laws in establishing a strong national bond between state and citizen. But like other theorists, he assumes that leaders *want* to establish a common national identity.[4] That states want to control the allocation of citizenship is not disputed. That they care about deepening national identification is what I contest.

First, without the demands of war, mass conscription is not necessary. This reduces the value of large populations. Second, income taxation is rendered

---

[2] African states make up 22 of the 29 slots in the bottom quintile in the *Index of State Weakness in the Developing World*. None but island states of Mauritius, Seychelles, and Cape Verde are in the top quintile (Rice and Patrick 2008, 39–42).

[3] Easterly and Levine 1997; Alesina Baqir, Easterly 1999; Collier and Gunning 1999; Rodrik 1999; Keefer and Knack 2002. Even studies using more nuanced fractionalization measures concur that linguistic fractionalization (Alesina et al 2003: 167) and politicized ethnic diversity (Posner 2004) harm growth.

[4] He argues that states requiring a more demanding citizenship based on descent, rather than place of birth, "may actually make the job of establishing a common identity more difficult" (Herbst 2000, 243) – implying that establishing a common identity is a goal.

relatively unnecessary by reliance on trade taxes, commodity sales, and foreign aid. This reduces the value of productive populations. Both of these factors dilute the need of African leaders to induce compliance and productivity by protecting citizenship rights. A recent development paradoxically has weakened incentives for rulers to connect with their citizens even more: pressure toward electoral institutions. Whereas the Cold War era African leaders grew progressively weaker in an environment that lacked external war and muted internal competition, current leaders have similar protected borders, but they are facing potential competition through the ballot box.

Thus, three periods of state-building can be compared: First, the classic European state-building era of the eighteenth and nineteenth centuries provided a context of interstate war, where leaders invested in national unity to augment their power. This was in order to quell rebellion and to raise funds and fighting men. Second, during the Cold War era in Africa, without the threats of war, leaders invested less in unity. Because African leaders did not have to make societal bargains to borrow for war making, they could retain their authoritarian rule, appeasing potential rivals more selectively through patronage. Third, in contemporary Africa, without the threats of war, but with shrinking resources and demands of democratization, current leaders may find *dis*unity an attractive strategy.

What did this have to do with language? Seeking to bypass the mediating role of local elites, centralizing European rulers sought national unity through a standard language. African independence leaders, in contrast, did not require conscripts or rely on direct taxation, so they demonstrated ambivalence regarding national unity through language. Believing such policies irrelevant to their goals of maintaining power, they retained whatever language policies they inherited from their colonial predecessor. But as electoral competition is added to the context, the push and pull forces described earlier encourage leaders to rethink their strategies. Striving always to enhance their internal authority, leaders agree to multilingual policies because they begin to see in them long-term possibilities for entrenching their power. Table 1.1 shows these three periods and linguistic outcomes.

State-building in Europe eventually led to forms of democracy, but it was not a smooth transition. Forced to offer rights and protection to the wealthy and landed citizens from whom they borrowed, autocrats found their authority restrained. Landlords wanted military positions, capital holders required property rights, merchants wanted infrastructure. Later, the raising of national armies also created claims on the state for welfare and benefits. Through this process, governments began intervening more in food distribution, health, and education of workers to improve productivity. Tilly shows that state expenditure in Norway grew from 3 percent of gross domestic product (GDP) in 1875 to 24 percent in 1975, and that social service provision as a percentage of GDP in Denmark grew from 1 percent in 1900 to 25 percent in 1975 (Tilly 1992, 121). Restraint, constitutionalism, and provision of welfare were part and parcel of

TABLE 1.1. *Language Policy in Three Periods*

Ruler Environment	External Context	Political Context	Language Policy
18th/19th-century European	Threat of war	Restrained autocracy	*Proactive monolingual*
Cold War African	No threat of war	Patronage autocracy	*Language ambivalence*
Post–Cold War African	No threat of war	Electoral autocracy	*Proactive multilingual*

militarization. The elements of value to citizens – democracy and services – came with a high price.

Scholars have mined the successful European experience for clues about what produces a deep democracy. National cohesion and dense networks of trust top the list. Both would seem compromised by linguistic fragmentation, which is the motivation for this study. The bulk of the book is dedicated to explaining the causes of the shift from monolingual to multilingual state-building, and the final chapter begins to look at its effects on these valued outcomes.

To observe these trends empirically, I created an original database of language policies in all African states, using a composite measure called "Intensity of Local Language Use in Education" or ILLED. This measure refines my previous coding (Albaugh 2005, 2009) to capture both depth and extent of language use in each country. I first assign a number from 0 to 5 to show the proportion of local languages that are used in each country, and then multiply that number by 1, 1.2, 1.5, 1.8, or 2 to show how extensively the languages are used across the primary curriculum.[5] This yields a composite score between 0 and 10, 0 indicating exclusive use of a European language and 10 indicating exclusive use of African languages through the entire primary cycle.

This way of coding enables one to compare small, homogeneous countries with large, multilingual countries, looking not at the raw number of languages used but at the proportion of possible languages used overall. Appendix A provides narrative information supporting the coding and lists the languages used in education and their proportions within each country.

Figure 1.1 compares the intensity of local language use in education at independence with the intensity in 2010. Whereas at the time of independence,

---

[5] ILLED = (Proportion of Languages) × (Extent of Use). **Proportion of Languages:** 0 = None (European Only); 1 = Classical Arabic; 2 = Single Minority Language (<50%); 3 = Few Languages/One Major Language (50–70%); 4 = Several Languages/One Dominant Language (70–85%); 5 = All Languages/One Overwhelmingly Dominant (>85%). **Extent of Use:** 1 = Experimental; 1.2 = Moderate; 1.5 = Extensive; 1.8 = Generalized; 2 = Exclusive.

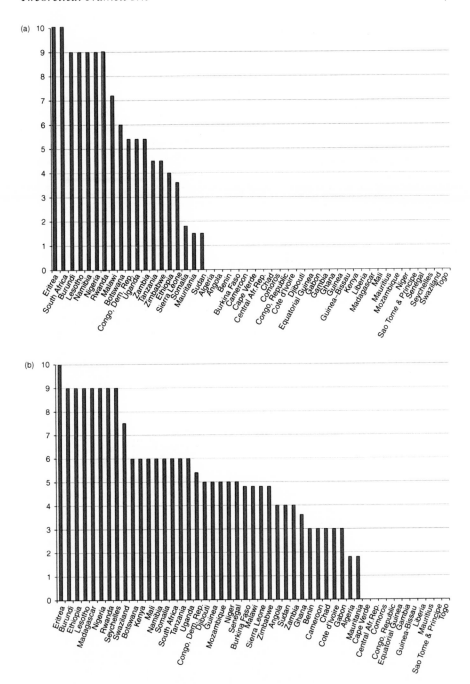

FIGURE 1.1. Intensity of Local Language Use in Education (a) at Independence or in 1960 and (b) in 2010. Note that I coded states that were not colonized (Liberia, Ethiopia) or that were independent much earlier (South Africa) in 1960.

only nineteen out of forty-nine African states (39 percent) were using local languages in primary education, the number has doubled to thirty-eight states (78 percent) doing so currently.

Clearly, the use of local languages in education has increased over time. Scholars familiar with African colonial history quickly will note that virtually all of those countries using local languages at independence were former British colonies. It is customary to point out the differences in ruling practices between France and Britain in Africa. While scholars have challenged the neat dichotomy in recent years, a stark distinction does hold true in the two colonizers' approaches to education. British colonial educational policy favored initial teaching in the medium of the vernacular and then a switch to English-only in the later primary grades. French administrators insisted on the French language as medium from the outset of schooling. As one would expect, this practice carried over to independence, with Anglophone countries maintaining their inherited method of mother tongue education and Francophone countries preferring French-medium education.

Though a few Francophone African countries experimented briefly with local languages in the interim, the medium of instruction policies three decades after independence were remarkably stable. In its landmark 1988 report, *Education in Sub-Saharan Africa*, the World Bank devoted a few pages to assessing language medium in education in African countries. The bank observed that of the fifteen former British colonies in their sample, thirteen of them (87 percent) were using one or more African languages in education (World Bank 1988, 44, 154–156). Of the fifteen former French colonies surveyed, only four were using one or more African languages in their primary education. The weight of historical precedent continued to prevail until about 1990.

At this date, most Anglophone countries were using local languages, and only a few Francophone countries were experimenting with local languages. The dramatic changes occurred after 1990, when fourteen out of eighteen former French territories began or expanded local language use in their schools, compared with only one country doing so at independence.

Such a trend could point to a convergence toward high levels of local language use across the continent, which would be consistent with the competing explanation that international norms of minority rights are stimulating mother tongue education everywhere. But when we look at the direction of changes from 1990 to the present, as we will in Chapter 4, it becomes clear that the overwhelming upward trend is concentrated in Francophone Africa. In contrast, Anglophone Africa is making policy changes in both directions. And if we examine international norms on this issue, they are actually not consistent.

THE POLICY OF MOTHER TONGUE EDUCATION

Unlike scholars who urge government support of languages to stall their unprecedented death rate, this study is concerned with the factors beyond a fear of language extinction that motivate states to alter their policies. While I believe that the choice of mother tongue education is more political than pedagogical, one such motivation could be the educational benefits such a policy purports to provide. Therefore, we should look first at the scholarly history around mother tongue education.

Works that discuss medium of instruction policy in developing countries usually refer to a 1953 UNESCO document as the landmark statement supporting such a method.[6] The benefits of local language use were only a theoretical assumption at that point, however, rather than an assertion backed with research. Dakin et al. (1968, 27), summarizing an edited volume that assessed the use of the mother tongue in developing countries, wrote:

The evidence about the difficulties of a foreign medium at the school stage thus seems inconclusive. The superiority of the mother tongue has not been everywhere demonstrated.... The practical arguments for the mother tongue in schools seem to rest more on the attitudes to language of the pupils, and the deficiencies of the teachers, than on any positive benefits of such instruction.

The most important early experiment in Africa, and the one cited most frequently, was the Ife Six-Year Primary Project undertaken in Nigeria from 1970 to 1976.[7] It is widely upheld as the most conclusive evidence for the vigorous use of the mother tongue in education, though later assessments have cautioned that several nonlanguage factors – preparation of the teachers, new materials, additional attention – in fact may have accounted for the success of the students (Akinnaso 1993, 274). Another Nigerian experiment was the River Readers Project, which also began in 1970 (Williamson 1980). This project produced inexpensive primers in all twenty-eight of the state's languages, which were used in the first year of primary school. The River Readers Project did not have the same level of evaluation as the Ife Project, but it clearly showed the feasibility of using several small languages, rather than only a large regional language, in the first years of education.

Other analyses have been mixed. Experts evaluating mother tongue teaching in Kenya were unconvinced about the superiority of mother tongue classrooms over English-only (Cleghorn et al. 1989). As with the Ife Project, the major problem with the comparisons is that mother tongue experimental classrooms have many other factors that contribute to their success. Nonetheless, there is widespread agreement among international educators that, in principle, teaching in the mother tongue is the best method.

---

[6] It recommended mother tongue education for its psychological, sociological, and educational benefits (1953, 11).

[7] Description by Afolayan (1976); positive assessment by Fafunwa, Macauley, and Sokoya, eds. (1989); cautionary assessment by Akinnaso (1993).

General language rights and specific rights to education in local languages have been a theme of UNESCO declarations and major international conferences for decades. The organization has sponsored several conferences on the theme of promoting African languages (Yaounde 1983, Lagos 1989, Accra 1994). Many believe that UNESCO is behind the recent wave of mother tongue experimentation in Africa:

The effect of UNESCO's relentless advocacy is that member states of the Organization have been under pressure to re-examine their policies. Those already engaged in the practice of mother tongue education have felt justified, and those that have not had such a policy have made statements supporting it or have actually embarked on experiments and pilot projects. In effect, conducting initial literacy or lower primary education in an imported official language is no longer fashionable. (Bamgbose 2004, 7)

A *norm-based* explanation would attribute such a change to the diffusion of human rights norms: "After 1985, we can say that the world began a process of genuine international 'norms cascade,' as the influence of international human rights norms spread rapidly" (Risse, Ropp and Sikkink 1999, 21).

One can indeed observe such an international norm of preserving minority cultures has been gaining strength for the past fifty years, with the last two decades being the most significant. The modern principle can be traced most concretely to the 1966 International Covenant on Civil and Political Rights, the beginning of a consensus on the necessity to protect minorities. But protection does not necessarily equal promotion. The 1990 Convention on the Rights of the Child guaranteed children the right to use their language and the right to education, but it did not connect the two rights. Only recently has the 1992 UN Declaration on the Rights of Persons Belonging to National or Ethnic Religious and Linguistic Minorities explicitly promoted mother tongues in education. The principle of nondiscrimination has grown to active *promotion* of minority identities. The declaration "unambiguously requires the State to allow private language use in private, public and collective action" (König 1999, 404).

Several events at the international level demonstrate accelerated attention to minority rights in recent years. The UN created a High Commissioner for Human Rights in 1993, and a UN Working Group on Minorities was set up in 1995 (Wright 2004, 192). A Universal Declaration of Linguistic Rights (UDLR) was proclaimed on June 6, 1996, at the University of Barcelona. The Council of Europe adopted a Framework Convention for the Protection of National Minorities 1998 – a "legally binding multilateral instrument for the protection of national minorities in Europe" – and in the same year the European Charter for Regional or Minority Languages promoted the "use of regional or minority languages in education and the media and urged their use in judicial and administrative settings, economic and social life and cultural activities" (Wright 2004, 192–193).

Despite the appearance of normative convergence, however, education policies continue to diverge. In 1990, UNESCO, UNDP, UNICEF, and the World Bank sponsored the World Conference on Education for All in Jomtien, Thailand. Linguist Shirley Brice Heath led a session on the need for consideration of language in education. Article 5 of the ensuing Jomtien Declaration's "Framework of Action to Meet Basic Needs" includes a rather vague statement that "literacy in the mother-tongue strengthens cultural identity and heritage." The International Conference on Education, convened by UNESCO in 1992, affirmed the "cultural importance of introducing mother tongues and national languages into educational systems" because language "is the most evident and pervasive manifestation of culture and is often the central point in establishing and maintaining the cultural identity of a people" (Section I. D. 14). Yet participants agreed only that "the choice of one or more languages, the mother tongue or a national or foreign language, as a separate subject or as a medium for studying other subjects *is determined by the educational and cultural policy of each country*."[8] At the 2000 World Education Forum held in Dakar, Senegal, mother tongue education was cited as one of nine good practices and successful policies for the African context.[9] Nadine Dutcher, former World Bank consultant, called for greater leadership by international organizations such as UNESCO to follow rhetoric with action. "Over the past decade, there has been a striking lack of leadership on language at the international level" (2004, 47).

In sum, rhetoric in favor of local languages abounds, but forceful recommendations and consistent rationales are lacking. I argue it is instead bilateral messages that are much more important. The trend in local language policy changes reflects the pull of confluent ideas within French-speaking industrialized countries, contrasted with indecisiveness within English-speaking industrialized countries regarding language use in education. A recent consensus in the Francophone world has led to a new and clear message communicated to the African countries in its sphere of influence, whereas the persistent divisions within the Anglophone community have resulted in a muted and ambivalent message conveyed to Anglophone Africa. Within African states, bureaucrats are persuaded by the rhetoric of language NGOs and external permissiveness, while rulers are influenced more by their own personal interests. Their changing preferences are central to the explanation of this policy change.

If a first competing explanation is international norms emerging from scientific studies of the educational benefits of mother tongue education, a second competing explanation rests on rationalist bargaining. As will be explained in

---

[8] Italics added. 43rd International Conference on Education [Geneva, 14–19 Sept 1992]. Paris, Jan. 1993. (Section IV.14).

[9] Preamble: A Framework for Action in sub-Saharan Africa, first adopted in Johannesburg, South Africa, Dec. 1999.

Chapter 3, this explanation is incorrect because it does not accurately capture the preferences of major social actors. But it is also faulty because it rests on an understanding of bargaining between holders of power that derives ultimately from a European context. As Bratton and van de Walle have argued, African politics is marked by persistent neopatrimonialism (1997, chapter 2). Big men dominate the system and stand above its laws. The state has low extractive capacity, and therefore state offices are distributed and public resources privatized (Bratton and van de Walle 1997, 66). Scholars have described this phenomenon and discussed its effects primarily on outcomes such as democratic transition or economic growth. The origins of neopatrimonial behavior are not well theorized. But for this present study, the lack of need for rulers to bargain with populations for resources is at the root of this distinction,[10] and it helps to explain why the traditional bargaining models do not apply.

A more nuanced view of bargaining is found in the work of Catherine Boone (1995, 2003), who looks at subnational variation in the strength of groups in relation to the state, which could present a third alternative explanation. She argues that in West Africa, where "hierarchies were strong and rural elites had economic autonomy, indigenous elites were in a position to contest the state's claims on rural surplus.... In the absence of social hierarchy, regimes were far less constrained" (Boone 1995, 17). Though Boone focuses on economic policy rather than language policy, extrapolating from her schematic gives the expectation that rulers should have had much more ease in spreading a single language – their own or a foreign one – where competing local authorities were weak. And where local authorities were strong, one would expect more promotion of minority languages. We will look at this potential explanation for variation in language policies in Chapter 4.

To set the stage, however, for discussing how bargaining over language is different in Africa, I paint a picture of how this bargaining unfolded in Europe. Using France and Britain as representative European cases, I elaborate the preferences of major actors regarding language standardization during these states' consolidating years.

EUROPEAN LANGUAGE AND EDUCATION: STATE-BUILDING IN FRANCE AND BRITAIN

Most scholars conceive of nationalism as a modern phenomenon, revolving around memory, writing, and literacy. And it is widely accepted that a standardization of language within compulsory primary education eventually

---

[10] See Jane Guyer (1992) for an excellent study of this phenomenon in Nigeria. She writes: "familiar phenomena such as clientage, prebendalism, withdrawal from the state, and unproductive investment may be seen as interrelated processes in a struggle to create a polity based on representation without (or before) taxation" (46).

contributed to the cohesiveness of European nation-states. This section probes the incentives of early state-builders who made decisions about language and education within the territory they controlled. It concludes that their motivations to build linguistic unity through standard education depended at root on a competitive and dynamic environment: constant threats of war and need for fighting men, internal ideological and religious rivalries, and populations that were mobile, communicating and shifting in relative strength. These conditions differ markedly from the context faced by African leaders, a distinction that explains in large part the difference in their language strategies as well.

European state-builders needed fighters, workers, taxpayers, and later voters. They had three major reasons for wanting to spread a single language across the territory they ruled: control, loyalty, and extraction. First, building states meant breaking the mediating position of local power holders and wresting from them direct power over the bodies and resources of the population within a given territory.[11] As it related to language, this meant penetrating local leaders' communication monopoly. Second, rulers aimed to secure the loyalty of populations, which could be facilitated by teaching unifying myths and symbols in a common language. These first two goals coincided with the transition from mercenary to citizen armies. A common language allowed for better coordination between officers and troops, and the patriotism that could be instilled through standard education helped produce loyal fighters. Finally, a common language throughout the territory facilitated opportunities for trade and economic linkages, improving productivity and deepening rulers' potential tax base. It was the innovation of technology for mass literacy that made possible this control, loyalty, and extraction.

Benedict Anderson points to a dramatic shift in the role of language that followed the dethronement of Latin beginning in the sixteenth century. Following Luther's provocation of the Protestant Reformation in 1517, material printed in the German vernacular increased threefold in twenty years (Anderson 1991, 40). For the first time, there was mass readership for Luther's Bible translations. The French language similarly began to replace Latin in publication frequency.[12] Anderson explains that the stratum of Latin readers was so slim that the market for books written in Latin was saturated quickly. After the seventeenth century, therefore, printers sought new markets in vernacular readership. These print capitalists – printers of books and newspapers – provided a new basis for national consciousness in certain dominant languages. Anderson argues that print languages served to widen fields of exchange and fix official versions of languages, which often meant elevating

---

[11] Tilly (1992, chapter 2) argues that before the era of the French Revolution, all states used some form of indirect rule. The transition to direct rule gave rulers direct access to citizens and the resources they controlled through household taxation, mass conscription, censuses, and police systems.

[12] Anderson 1991, 18; citing Febvre and Martin 1958, 321. See also Stone 1969, 78–79.

a language of power at the expense of weaker languages or dialects. From the sixteenth to the eighteenth century, the spread of official languages by would-be monarchs was relatively accidental, spurred by the printing press, capitalists, and pragmatic rulers seeking administrative efficiency. There was no concern for mass literacy, however, given small state bureaucracies and limited scope of state activities.

By the eighteenth century, the ascendance of popular novels and daily newspapers gave people who never saw each other face to face the ability to imagine themselves as a community (Anderson 1991, 77). Rather than a thin stratum of elites, with only Latin and marriage ties in common, the bourgeoisie was deepening and dividing along linguistic lines. And this is when rulers also began to see the advantages of deliberate language rationalization.

Unlike the sixteenth century spread of language, which was largely unselfconscious, nineteenth century official nationalisms purposely used language as a central marker. Leaders began to see mass public education as a means of building integrated national polities. But this recognition of education's role happened in a particular context: one of competition. France demonstrates the singular importance of war, while Britain highlights the contributions of religious rivalries and industrial dynamism. In each instance, standard-language education allowed for greater control, loyalty, and extraction.

The eighteenth century began the transformation across Europe from mercenary to standing armies (Tilly 1992, 29). This followed a change in military technology: a shift toward the proliferation of gunpowder weapons, which disadvantaged smaller fighting units and advantaged large standing armies. Because of its size and population, France could excel, and Porter (1994, 110) attributes the French rise to dominance to its unparalleled military. Large armies required discipline, control, and logistical coordination. Raising more troops also required greater coercion and stronger justification for manpower demands. As the century went on, troops became permanent across Europe, and absolutist states spent 80–90 percent of their revenues on funding the army, requiring unprecedented levels of taxation (Porter 1994, 110). Reaching deep into rural areas, bypassing reluctant nobles, the king had to convince the masses in his language.

The French Revolution was caused in part by the difficulty raising enough funds to pay this growing military. During the revolution and after, France continued to wage war on neighbors, and the Convention introduced the *levée en masse* (Porter 1994, 130). Through the course of the fighting, as the bulk of the nobles fled, they were replaced by more bourgeoisie and peasant classes. Recruitment drives gathered even more, until 68 percent of soldiers were peasants. The new Assembly discharged foreigners and passed a law conscripting men eighteen to twenty-five years old. Though resisted, the law eventually incorporated 300,000 new members in the army (Porter 1994, 130). The army became a center of nationalism, where a common language, myths, and symbols could spread.

The ideology of the revolution, of course, was central. France's state-organized primary schools had the "vocation not only to transmit knowledge but also to form the new citizens of the republic" (Chafer 2007, 439). They aimed to counter church schools and the influence of monarchist ideas with a secular French republicanism, which "embraced defending the principles of 1789 and inculcating notions of patriotism, civic responsibility and respect for order" (Chafer 2007, 439). The Convention Speech in 1792 emphasized the importance of linguistic unity. Eugen Weber, in his masterful *Peasants into Frenchmen*, summarizes:

Linguistic diversity had been irrelevant to administrative unity. But it became significant when it was perceived as a threat to political – that is, ideological – unity. All citizens had to understand what the interests of the Republic were and what the Republic was up to.... Otherwise, they could not participate, were not equipped to participate in it.... A didactic and integrative regime needed an effective vehicle for information and propaganda.... The ideal of the Revolution lay in uniformity and the extinction of particularisms. (1976, 72)

The Convention acted to abolish dialects and replace them with French, decreeing that everywhere "instruction should take place only in French" (Weber 1976, 72). Though the policy foundered initially, the principle survived (Bell 1995, 1406). A unified language was part of civilizing the peasantry.

In the aftermath of the revolution, Napoleon expended most of his energy on elitist military academies as a place for indoctrination of state-induced nationalism (Porter 1994, 132). He unified the legal code, created a centrally appointed and regulated bureaucracy, and continued the secularization of education to break the influence of the Catholic Church. The strict military discipline and military curriculum in his lycées derived from the "inexorable calculus of the military state" (Porter 1994, 134).

The July Monarchy from 1830 was openly anticlerical and "counted on elementary education to raise a generation of citizens that would support liberal, bourgeois democracy" (de Swaan 1988, 96). The Loi Guizot (1833) marked the first effective law to enact universal, compulsory education, and though the state did not achieve the universalization of the French language it envisioned until the 1880s, this was certainly its intent. Despite many shortcomings, "from 1833 onward the government, supported by a steadily growing vested interest, bent itself to advance and develop public education" (Weber 1976, 308). For all of the nineteenth century, then, the French state was deeply involved in standard language education as a state-building tool.

The French Revolution and its aftermath provided a model for this deliberate literacy promotion, as its success raising citizen armies and spreading a nationalist ideology became well known. Anderson argues that the simple existence of mass produced texts made the French Revolution a blueprint for future revolutionaries and state-builders to follow. Universal education in Prussia, for example, gained acceptance in the nineteenth century, as the state viewed it as a tool to gain direct access to the lower ranks as taxpayers, recruits, and later voters. De Swaan describes Prussia's efforts to educate civic mindedness and loyalty and to improve tax flows by promoting trade and industry. As rural lords were not always forthcoming with military recruits for the king's army, breaking their mediating position gave rulers more direct access to these fighting resources. "Part of the effort to free the country's human and economic resources from feudal bonds was the drive for mass education which would instill loyalty toward the Prussian state" (de Swaan 1988, 89, 91).

In France, the rationalization of eighty-eight patois into one single, standard language was a long-term process of creating French citizens. Weber argues that "patriotic feelings on the national level, far from instinctive, had to be learned" (Weber 1976, 114). Schools became much more effective after the 1880s, with the Jules Ferry Laws (Ozouf 1984, 400–415), accompanied by the practical improvements in roads and increase in teachers and facilities. By 1881, most classrooms had wall maps – a physical image of the national hexagon. And public schools did ultimately achieve integration around national symbols, history, and a standard language (Weber 1976, 337).

Through the lens of war and revolution, then, France shows competition inducing a standard language education. Its official embrace of spreading a single language derived from its militarization and revolutionary ideology. The process happened later in England, and through a different route. Aside from the competition of warfare, the mechanisms of religious rivalries and industrial dynamism produced the same outcome. Examining this process allows us to move below the sole desires of rulers to examine the preferences of other actors in society. In Europe as a whole, the other significant actors were the church hierarchy and the landed gentry. In England particularly, it also included an emerging merchant and entrepreneurial class.

Certainly the state in England was less interventionist and more decentralized than that in France, but it too saw the utility of a standard language in its state-building project.[13] It simply had to wait for forces other than revolution to tip the balance of competing social forces toward its preferences. While it made sense for rulers and their bureaucrats to desire a standard language to facilitate their administration, the gentry distrusted mass education, and the clergy were ambivalent.

Schools prior to the nineteenth century were primarily a means of religious instruction for commoners. Wealthy families hired tutors for their children, while the rest of the population had the option of parish schools charging minimal fees. Teaching people to read carried a tension. It might induce citizens to absorb ideas about order and hierarchy, or it might release them to challenge

---

[13] Unlike in France, educational efforts in England were aimed primarily at increasing literacy in a tongue that most people spoke. Britain's "periphery," however, much more resembled France, where the state favored the spread English and intervened to exclude Irish, Gaelic, and Welsh from national schools from the 1830s. See Grillo 1989.

the status quo. It might propagate beliefs and inculcate morals, but it might also incite rebellion (de Swaan 1988, 57). Therefore, ambivalence reigned prior to the nineteenth century. It was rivalry between the state-sponsored Anglican Church and the dissenting churches that stimulated the widespread provision of education for the poor (Stone 1969, 81). The Anglican Church had not seen literacy as a high priority, while Dissenters viewed personal familiarity with the Bible as necessary for spiritual growth and saw education as a means to instill obedience and industry. Competition "for the minds and loyalties of the poor" meant that the Anglican Church was drawn into providing similar educational services (Stone 1969, 82). The result was a population broadly able to read, even if not deeply literate, as England entered its industrializing years.[14]

Ernest Gellner (1983, chapter 3) insists on the functional need of industrial society for general, mass education: "The level of literacy and technical competence, in a standardized medium, a common conceptual currency ... can only be provided by something resembling a modern 'national' education system" (33). This linear thesis has been scrutinized, partly with the assertion that while England was first to industrialize, it was later than other continental European states to legislate mass education. Yet the competition between Anglicans and Dissenters had produced a population that was indeed broadly literate, many able to read pamphlets and newspapers that could prove destabilizing.

England demonstrates that the link between public schools and industrialization is more nuanced. Governments saw schools first as spaces for *control* and then later as sites for improving worker productivity. Early industrialization in England had drawn people to the cities, creating a large, urban working class. The latent unrest contained in this population made public education's methods of discipline and potential for reducing crime attractive to the government as well as to employers. And in the later years of industrialization came a recognition of education's potential to train more qualified workers for skilled tasks (de Swaan 1988, 106; Stone 1969, 137).

Industrial growth also meant that more members of the state bureaucracy began to depend on trade for their well-being, and the entrepreneurial class was growing. These swelling ranks of the middle class stood to gain from a national network of communication to broaden their avenues for trade. At the same time, as England's dynamic industrialization improved the speed of the printing press, print capitalists continually competed for readership. They held a critical interest in promoting literacy among potential readers. This commercial middle class then joined metropolitan bureaucrats who supported educational renewal, particularly the teaching in a standard language. Half a century after France, in 1870, an Elementary Education Act gradually produced compulsory, state-funded education in England.

---

[14] Stone (1969, 119) estimated an adult male literacy rate in England of more than 50 percent in 1750, and more than 80 percent in Scotland. The rate had jumped to more than 80 percent in England by 1850.

TABLE 1.2. *Preferences of Actors Regarding Language of Instruction: Europe* (de Swaan)

Ruler	Bureaucrats	Regional Elites	Clergy	Entrepreneurs/ Business	*Outcome*
Standard	*Standard*	*Local*	*Local*	*Standard*	**Standard language**

Abram de Swaan carefully investigates the expansion of state functions in Europe in order to generalize about the actor preferences that converged on universal elementary education in a standard language. I have distilled his findings into Table 1.2.

First, rulers wanted a standard lingua franca, a national language that would help them to break the mediation privilege of either local gentry or church leaders. If all citizens spoke a common language, the ruler's own paid bureaucrats could communicate directly with citizens, without relying on the translation of local leaders. The "state apparatus would tend to promote knowledge in central code ... for the entire territory, since this would enable its officials to approach the citizens directly – that is, without local mediation" (de Swaan 1988, 73). The level of language competency was intended to be relatively low, in order not to foment rebellion. Therefore, the goal was to provide enough education in a standard language to make communication possible, but not so much as to make citizens think about disloyalty. Bureaucrats, similarly, would want a standard language, in order to make their administration easier. Processing documents in multiple languages or attempting to communicate laws to speakers of multiple languages would be cumbersome. A standard language obviously would facilitate their work.

Regional elites, however, would resist. Landed nobility explicitly did *not* want a standard language because of their concern about losing their mediating role. Clergy members, another local group, also resisted the usurpation of their sole responsibility for education. It was "inherent in the position of local and regional elites to oppose the spread of the standard code in their sphere of influence so as to safeguard the allegiance of their clientele and maintain their advantages of monopolistic mediation" (de Swaan 1988, 73–74). The nineteenth century was especially important, since entrepreneurs, especially traders and publishers, were becoming more and more involved with commerce over wider distances. As they began to grasp the potential of a standard language to extend their markets, they saw the benefits of universal education. Those "involved in supraregional commerce [would] support the promulgation of national codes of communication, of the standard language, of standard measures and currencies, of elementary arithmetic and geography, so as to facilitate exchange" (de Swaan 1988, 73). With this constellation of preferences, the balance tipped toward support of universal education in the nineteenth century, and eventually a standard language curriculum prevailed throughout Europe.

From this brief historical survey, it is clear that the reasons for imposing a standard language depended on a competitive environment. First, in the context of mass war, where rulers desperately sought fighters and taxes to pay them, they would look to break mediation monopoly of regional elites and aim for direct control. A single language allowed the state and its agents to communicate directly with citizens without relying on local intermediaries. A single language in schools and militaries also provided a means for patriotic inculcation and ideological engineering, so central to the revolutionary project. Alternatively, religious competition for the loyalty of the masses drew the state more deeply into education. Church rivalry in England meant that basic literacy expanded before the state officially appropriated education. Finally, within the dynamics of industrialization, control of mobile, restive populations and their productivity grew in importance. The merchants and entrepreneurs on whom the government depended for resources also began to favor a wider network of communication and literate workers. Competitive environments therefore shifted preferences in a way that led major actors to agree ultimately on the provision of mass, standard education in both France and England.

The focus on France and Britain was deliberate, as these European powers had the greatest influence in Africa. Looking beyond their borders at the populations and resources they might control, language was an important component in their calculation. In the colorful words of Anderson, imperialism aimed to stretch "the short, tight, skin of the nation over the gigantic body of the empire," to dress "Empire in national drag" (Anderson 1991, 86). Was this, in fact, the aim of the French and British colonizers in Africa? While it may have been so for the czarist Russian imperialism that was the subject of his remark, Chapter 2 will argue that in fact, nation building was not the goal of European colonizers in Africa. They only needed a few administrative intermediaries and soldiers because of their superior firepower, secure borders, and limited plans for industrialization. This contributed to the neopatrimonial tendencies in the African context. British and French colonial policy, along with accompanying missionary impacts on language, will be examined in Cameroon, Senegal, and Ghana. No matter the colonial policy, each case demonstrates linguistic bifurcation, with a small stratum of elites speaking a European language – an incomplete penetration of a standard language and necessary maintenance of multilingualism.

Chapter 3 then looks at independence leaders in Africa, finding that their incentives had not much changed from those of their colonial predecessors. Since African independence was achieved at the height of monolingual hegemony in Europe, it was expected that leaders of new African states would be similarly devoted to linguistic nationalism. Yet most of them struggled with the reality that their most viable "national" language was a foreign one. Others have explained the resulting multilingual outcome as a rational bargain between leaders and regional elites. I argue in this chapter that their policies in fact reflected apathy, as they discovered declining incentives to invest in a standard language. Colonial precedent continued. And yet, behind the scenes, movement away from these legacies was gaining force. The "push" of language NGOs and the "pull" of international discourse were changing language opportunities and incentives for African leaders.

Chapter 4 describes these opportunities, contrasting international ideas within Anglophone and Francophone communities, and it brings these theoretical insights to bear on the cases of Senegal and Ghana. This chapter confronts the *international norms* alternative explanation. It provides empirical evidence of the importance of language transcription in Francophone states, along with the differing international messages received by governments considering local language education. As Francophone bureaucrats in charge of education were persuaded, politicians needed a real incentive. This came in the form of elections.

Chapter 5 discusses this post-1990s environment. The wave of protests calling for immediate elections, international pressures for the same, and development policies that favored bypassing of government coffers made leaders' positions initially precarious. Discourse about minority rights, decentralization, and power sharing ascended. Facing pressure, "desperate democratizers" scoured their toolkits for strategies that would keep them in power. They began to discover that language and citizenship laws could be turned to their advantage. This chapter incorporates elements of the rival explanation that *subnational variation* influences leaders' strategies for maintaining power.

Chapter 6 describes the specific case of Cameroon, where President Paul Biya, facing real electoral competition for the first time in 1992, worked adeptly within the constraints prescribed by democratic institutions to increase his own control. Boundary changes and targeted disenfranchisement marginalized the opposition. More subtly, constitutional decentralization and minority rights provisions, including mother tongue education, are believed by authorities to fragment opposition and secure government control. This chapter serves as the bridge between the *causes* of multilingual policies and their *consequences*.

Chapter 7 asks whether there might be a silver lining to the cynical view that language concessions are being used only to augment the power of autocrats. Drawing from the rich literature on democratization, it assesses the impact of mother tongue education on groups' likelihood of political participation. Though evidence is only preliminary, it appears that groups possessing a written language and learning it in school may be more likely in the long run to oppose autocratic states.

The book as a whole contributes several important pieces of new knowledge. First, it provides a tool for comparing African states' treatment of local languages in education systems over time. Second, it presents a concise historical picture of the development of education in colonial Africa and the central role played by language. Third, it offers a general model for continuity and change in language policy in independent Africa. Fourth, it begins to assess whether changes in policies benefit or harm the states enacting them, concluding that local language policies may in the long run be of greater service to citizens than to rulers attempting to entrench their power. Finally, it places all of these findings in the comparative context of state-building, a process that has unfolded very differently in Africa than elsewhere.

2

Language and Education in Africa under Mission and Colonial Influence

Let us look on education as a precious gift that we distribute with great care . . . and let us reserve its benefits for qualified recipients.

French colonial Governor-General Carde[1]

The premature teaching of English inevitably leads to utter disrespect for British and native ideals alike, and to a denationalized and disorganized population.

British High Commissioner in Northern Nigeria, Lord Lugard[2]

The nineteenth century saw the consolidation of European states around single languages. The most powerful of these states extended their reach to Africa. Preceded virtually always by missionaries, these evolving colonial administrations had to negotiate their aims for subject populations within the strong influence of mission activities. Foremost among mission activities was education, with its necessary decision regarding language of instruction. This chapter will show that future French territories diverged even initially from other regions, and this trajectory became even more distinct in the seventy-five years of formal colonial rule.

Despite this discrepancy, however, the goals of actors in all territories can be categorized similarly. Missionaries aimed to save lost souls and diffuse morality. Administrators needed indigenous auxiliaries to help them control and extract from vast populations. Africans wanted access to jobs through education. The main argument of this chapter is that these combined desires led to no strong preferences on the part of any actors for a linguistically unified population.

This chapter begins with a continental scope, and then narrows to a focus on the three cases of Senegal, Ghana, and Cameroon. It first addresses the question of languages and their transcription from the perspective of the missions that

---

[1] Arrêté fixant l'organisation générale de l'Enseignement en Afrique occidentale française, 1 May 1924, printed in the *Journal Officiel de l'A.O.F.*, No. 1024, 10 May 1924, p. 327.
[2] Later Governor-General of Nigeria. F.D. Lugard, *Annual Reports*, Northern Nigeria 1900–1911, 646. (Cited in Coleman 1963, 137).

were central to this work. The location and duration of these missions differed, as did their methods, explaining a large portion of the distinction that would evolve within French territories. The chapter then addresses the impact of different colonial ruling practices, specifically relating to education. It will show that France's territories differed from others not only in the lower percentage of the population with their languages in written form but their lower attainment of education in general, despite French colonists' more direct attempts at controlling it. The colonial period ended with higher enrollment rates generally in Anglophone Africa, largely because of the more expansive presence of missions.

Nonetheless, government interest in expanding education beyond a restricted group of beneficiaries arose very late in the colonial period, and enrollments across the continent were not nearly enough to diffuse a single language in any territory. Regardless of their treatment of African languages, colonial administrators had no intention of creating a broadly educated society. Containment of education in a European language to only a few suited their purposes of rule. Literacy rates on the eve of independence showed the success of their policies. No matter the policy, outcomes converged across colonial territories: a small percentage of children enrolled in schools and lack of effort to spread mass, standard education in a single language. The visions of the administrators in the introductory quotations were achieved.

MISSIONS AND THE TRANSCRIPTION OF AFRICAN LANGUAGES

Before the arrival of missions and colonizers, languages across the African continent had begun to consolidate through common historical mechanisms: trade and conquest. Certainly these were not always peaceful processes, but the rationalization of a ruling group's language within a corresponding state or empire was largely halted by the countervailing forces of missions and colonizers. Mansour (1993), for example, describes the early spread of the Manding language within the Mali Empire, a homogenizing process that was in some measure arrested with the arrival of Europeans, and their creation of the bounded territories of Mali, Senegal, Gambia, and Niger.

Overall, the writing[3] of African languages depended initially on geography and location of mission stations – first established in southern Africa and along the West African coasts. As formal colonization enclosed missionary work within specific boundaries, a patterned divergence emerged. As early as 1900, French territories boasted noticeably fewer languages with a written form. By

---

[3] This is not meant to discount a deep history of indigenous writing in Africa. For the purposes of this study, when I say written language, I am referring primarily to one written in Latin script. I use the date of first written Bible portions as a proxy for when an accessible literature might begin to spread. Certainly, there is a longer tradition of writing African languages such as Soninke, Songhay, Wolof, Fulfulde, and Hausa in Arabic (Ajami script), or Amharic (in Ge'ez). The reach of these writings was so small, however – only among a minuscule cadre of religious scholars – that they would not be implicated in the educational and state-building processes that are examined here.

1950, this distinction had magnified so that less than 60 percent of populations under French administration had their languages in written form, compared to close to 80 percent in all other territories. This was a result of the duration of missionary presence in the various territories, as well as differing colonial attitudes toward African languages, and it would have enormous consequences for the education policies chosen by these independent African states.

It is impossible to say with precision how many languages existed in Africa prior to European penetration. In order to present a picture of continental scope, I have extrapolated backward from present population figures, a gross simplification given careful scholarship regarding language transformation over time.[4] Certainly the encounter with traders, missionaries, educators, and administrators altered the size and stretch of language groups. I provide figures for comparative purposes, rather than precision, knowing full well that this static picture contradicts a more accurate historical process of fluidity. Nonetheless, it allows for revealing comparison.

Missionaries usually preceded colonizers in Africa, their modern wave beginning early in the nineteenth century. They clustered in coastal settlements, on trade routes, and particularly in areas with favorable climates, often densely populated regions for these same reasons (Johnson 1967, 171–172). Clayton Mackenzie provides a synthesis of the vitriol directed against mission collaboration with colonial rule or the praise directed toward their emancipating work in Africa (Mackenzie 1993, 46–48). Rather than condemning or justifying missionaries, I want to discern their specific effects on language.

By tracing their presence by their written legacies,[5] it becomes apparent where these missionaries clustered. In southern Africa, the Tswana language was written by 1830, Nama by 1831, Xhosa by 1833, Sotho by 1839, and Zulu by 1848. On the West Coast, Mandinka (Gambia) had a written form by 1837,

---

[4] The most serious danger to this method is misrepresenting the size of language groups in British possessions, as the missionary policy of choosing certain languages likely spread them farther than their "natural" boundaries, thus making it seem that a higher proportion of populations in these territories had their language in written form. To give more credibility to these figures, I offer two observations. First, *Ethnologue* (Lewis 2009), the source from which these language numbers are drawn, has been criticized for creating too fine divisions among groups speaking essentially similar dialects. *Ethnologue* linguists counter by showing their careful attention to testing interlanguage intelligibility, only reporting as separate those languages whose groups profess to understand neighboring languages below a certain threshold. In any case, by relying on this source, I capture distinctions among languages that early missions likely did not care to highlight, and so I am erring on the side of fewer speakers than more. Second, I consulted Bruk's *Atlas Nirodov Mira* (1964) (with helpful translations shared by Dan Posner), a widely cited source that provides population estimates around 1960 for major groups. The fact that the sizes of "my" groups are consistently smaller than those in the Atlas gives me greater confidence that I am not overcounting in British territories. As will be shown in the text, the major expansion of education in these languages occurred after 1940, and so the bulk of linguistic consolidation would have happened after this date.

[5] I use the year a Bible portion was transcribed as a proxy for a written language. These dates were compiled from Grimes (1996, 2000) and Lewis (2009).

Grebo (Liberia) by 1838, Ga (Ghana) by 1843, Bassa (Liberia) by 1844, Duala (Cameroon) by 1848, and Bube (Equatorial Guinea) by 1849. The island of Madagascar had its Malagasy written as early as 1828, while Amharic and Oromo in Ethiopia had early written form for unique reasons.[6]

In 1850, extrapolating from current figures for these mother tongue speakers, about 14 percent of the continent's[7] population had their languages in written form. Though they were not yet formally colonized, the future distinction of French territories was already foreshadowed. Only five languages had been put to writing in future French territories, and if Madagascar is excluded, only 1 percent of the populations that would be under French control had potential access to a written language. In future British territories, by contrast, missionaries had committed to writing the languages of 15 percent of these populations.

As colonial boundaries began to demarcate territories within the continent, language treatment diverged. By 1900, more than 60 languages had been written in British territories, compared with only 20 in French territories. In every single one of the seventeen future British territories,[8] transcription for multiple languages was taking place – eleven in Nigeria and six in Kenya, for example. In contrast, transcription was taking place in only eight of the eighteen future French territories, and never for more than three languages (e.g. for Gabon, where American missionaries were prevalent) per territory. Certainly, part of the number discrepancy is explained by a difference in population – British territory would include more than twice the number of people in French territory, so there were simply more languages to transcribe. But in fact, the language distribution is not nearly as uneven as one might expect: British territories had 693 languages, while French had 579.[9] In British territories, more than 9 percent of those languages were transcribed by the turn of the twentieth century, while in French territories, it was less than 4 percent. The number of *people* covered with that transcription in 1900 was nearly 50 percent in British territories and only 31 percent in French, the latter driven upward by the near-universal coverage of Algerians with the transcription of Algerian Spoken Arabic and the earlier-mentioned transcription of Malagasy for Madagascar. In continental, sub-

---

[6] Amharic had religious writings as early as the fourteenth century, but its elevation as an imperial language in the nineteenth century ensured its domination, and a Bible transcription was completed in 1824. Oromo, a widespread trade language, appeared in written form in the seventeenth century and had a Bible transcription by 1841.

[7] This is sub-Saharan Africa and the Horn, plus Algeria because of its historical significance to France. It does not include Egypt, Tunisia, Libya, or Morocco.

[8] "British territories" and "French territories" include original German territories in East Africa (Tanganyika, Ruanda-Urundi) and in West Africa (Togo and Cameroon), all redistributed to victorious powers after World War I.

[9] These numbers are drawn from Lewis (2009), which counts the number of mother-tongue speakers of all languages currently spoken in each country. While the size of groups certainly was influenced by the history of their language transcription, the actual *number* of languages probably was not appreciably different in the mid-nineteenth century.

Saharan Africa, the percentage of the French-colonized population covered with a written language in 1900 was only 7 percent.[10]

The first half of the twentieth century saw the continued work of missionaries, particularly in British territories, where more than 130 languages were written over those fifty years, raising the total portion of the population whose mother tongue had written form to more than 75 percent. During these years, sixty-five additional languages were written in French possessions as well. But still the population covered with a written language did not reach 60 percent.

In 1900, most languages in Belgian territory[11] were not written, with the exception of five languages covering 6 percent of the population in the Congo. But early in the twentieth century, Burundi and Rwanda each gained a single written language that covered virtually the entirety of their populations. The Congo had forty-six more languages transcribed in this period, covering 73 percent of its population. Of the Portuguese territories, Angola had its major languages written prior to the turn of the century, and most of its remaining languages written before 1950; Mozambique had written languages for 78 percent of its population by 1950, and Cape Verde had its near-universal Kabuverdian written by then as well. Only Guinea-Bissau and the islands Sao Tome and Principe had no written form for most of their populations' languages. In the "other" category, Spanish Equatorial Guinea had its largest language, Fang, written in 1894, while Italian/ British Somalia had Somali written in 1915. Ethiopia had 75 percent of its population covered with a written language by 1950, and Eritrea had 84 percent. Liberia's five major languages were written in the first part of the century, making its population that had a written language 69 percent by 1950.

In sum, French territories differed from *all* others. Missionaries in British, Belgian, Portuguese, and "other" territories had transcribed enough languages to cover between 76 and 81 percent of these populations by 1950. In contrast, only 58 percent of the population within French territories had the same. Table 2.1 shows this discrepancy. It also reveals a potential *effect* of this difference. French territories have the smallest number of speakers per language by far. Other territories, whose major languages were transcribed much earlier, have many more speakers per language. This likely demonstrates the language consolidation that took place as a result of these early transcriptions. As scholars have noted (Posner 2003; Vail 1989), early missionaries were pragmatic. Seeking to reach as many people as possible through one translation of the Bible, they combined related language groups by teaching standard orthography to neighboring areas. This served to expand the size of dominant groups, as speakers learned these languages and often adopted them as their own mother tongue. In French territory, as will be explored in Chapter 3, more recent transcription efforts are having

---

[10] Even this figure is too high, as it includes the German territories Cameroon and Togo, major portions of which were only transferred to France after 1919.

[11] Again, former German colonies transferred to Belgium are included.

TABLE 2.1. *Population with a Written Language – 1850, 1900, 1950*

Territory*	2010 Estimated Population	Percentage of Population with a Written Language**				Number Written by 1950/Number of Languages**	Average Number of Speakers per Language
		1850	1900	1950			
British	428,242,787	15	47	76	196/698 (28%)	615,291
French	178,165,784	6	31	58	85/579 (15%)	307,713
Belgian	80,559,463	0	6	79	52/147 (35%)	548,024
Portuguese	41,044,650	.4	51	80	34/84 (40%)	488,627
Other (Eq. Guinea, Eritrea, Ethiopia, Liberia, Somalia)	100,313,940	40	53	76	26/103 (25%)	973,922
TOTAL	828,326,624	14	41	73	397/1609 (25%)	514,808

* Early German territories (Tanzania, Rwanda, Burundi, Cameroon, Namibia, and Togo) are not included separately to make the table less cumbersome, as each was transferred to another power after World War I.

** Percentage of the population with a written language is a cumulative measure of the groups with Bible portions transcribed in each period. The number of languages counts only those with more than 10,000 speakers. These data come from the *Ethnologue* (Lewis 2009) and those recorded from earlier census dates are adjusted to obtain 2010 population estimates. Admittedly, this does not capture the fact that the spread of languages that have survived depends much on their transcription history.

TABLE 2.2. *Mission Density (1950s) and Percentage School-Aged Children Enrolled circa 1960*

	Missions per Million	Percentage Children Enrolled
British territories		
South Africa (incl. Botswana, Lesotho, Swaziland)	1666	50
Zambia	1248	36
Zimbabwe	1166	48
Ghana	775	34
Malawi	759	28
Kenya	634	33
Uganda	527	28
Tanzania*	420	15
Sierra Leone	347	14
Nigeria	225	22
Mauritius	58	65
Sudan	42	12
AVERAGE:	656	32
Belgian territories		
Belgian Congo (incl. Rwanda and Burundi)	1348	35
Noncolonized territories		
Liberia	397	20
Ethiopia	43	4

	Missions per Million	Percentage Children Enrolled
French territories		
Madagascar	1259	31
Cameroon*	771	36
Togo*	271	23
Cote d'Ivoire	233	23
French Equatorial Africa (CAR, Chad, Congo Rep., Gabon)[12]	216	22
French Soudan (Mali)[13]	163	4
Benin	159	14
Algeria	6	25
Niger	6	3
Guinea	3	10
Senegal	1	15
AVERAGE:	281	19
Portuguese territories		
Angola	745	7
Mozambique	257	18

* Transferred from Germany after World War I.

Source: Mission data calculated from Bingle and Grubb (1957); enrollment data calculated from Mitchell (2007).

[12] The missions per million figures for Republic of Congo and Gabon are diluted by the inclusion of Chad and Central African Republic, which had virtually no missionary presence. Republic of Congo and Gabon had enrollment rates in 1960 that were near 40%, whereas Chad and Central African Republic had 11 to 15%.

[13] The boundaries of French Soudan do not coincide exactly with present-day Mali and included portions of territories with higher enrollments.

the opposite effect. With so many missionary linguists "competing" for popula-tions, ever-smaller groups are receiving their own transcriptions.

Some of this historical difference depends on the distinction between Catholic and Protestant missions, both in their methods and in their relationship with their states of origin.[14] In French Africa, education early on was in the hands of Catholic missionaries "who had inherited from the Roman Empire a strong tendency toward linguistic and cultural centrism. This inclination, coupled with France's strong propensity for cultural imperialism, led to schooling that was virtually entirely in French" (Michelman 1995, 219). Protestant missions were deeply concerned with individual conversion above outward ceremony, which often was thought to require understanding of the gospel in one's mother tongue. "Unlike the spiritual and institutional centrism of the Catholic Church, Protestantism, with its emphasis on the individual's direct relationship to God, was intensified in Britain by that nation's tradition of individual rights and parliamentary democracy" (Michelman 1995, 218). Aside from their general opposing treatment of indigenous languages, there was a clear difference in state control of these missions.

In Catholic colonizing countries such as France and Portugal, church-state pacts barred religious competition and asserted state control much earlier than where Protestant missions dominated. In French Africa, private (mission) educa-tion gradually expanded from its initial purposes of teaching catechism and train-ing African priests. Early Catholic missions had a large share of grants from the French government's development arm because the Catholic Church had men in leading positions in the French government (Moumouni 1964, 81). By contrast, in mainly Protestant countries such as Britain (and the United States, which also sent a large number of missionaries to Africa), there was much less state oversight of missions and therefore education. This led to variable relationships between colonizers and missions. MacKenzie, in his comparison of Protestant missions in Zimbabwe and Zambia, found "an image of inconsistency rather than of co-ordinated conspiracy." Missionary-colonist association was usually a "pragmatic collusion, and one born out of the political and military vulnerability of mission-aries in the face of colonial might" (1993, 54, 62–63).

Ali Mazrui summarizes forcefully that "Protestantism encouraged religious decentralization, and sometimes religious apartheid....The trend under Protestantism was not only toward individualism but also toward national com-partmentalization." In contrast, the Roman Catholic Church, "like the French empire, has been substantially centralized. The Church has illustrated religious centralization within a multiracial religious community" (Mazrui 1983, 41). Certainly there is truth to the stylized distinctions, but as will be shown in the

---

[14] On missions in Africa see Groves 1964; Albert Gérard 1981, 177–182. See David Bell (1995) for an important discussion of early Catholic priests in France using local languages other than French for evangelization. Unlike Protestant missionaries, however, their goal was not to translate religious works to be read directly by the peasants, only to make it easier for fellow priests to "transmit the words orally to their flocks, as they always had" (1428).

case studies, this dichotomy is not always so neat. Nonetheless, Protestant missions did dominate in southern Africa, southern and central Nigeria, and the Kenya highlands, while Catholic missions were prominent in French West Africa, and these regions are where the sharpest distinctions hold. Central Africa and former German territories were split between both types of missions and variations within them, which are often where the ambiguities arise.

No matter the type of missions, their contribution to education is unambiguous. Table 2.2 shows the number of missionaries per million in the 1950s and the territories' enrollment rates around 1960. It is clear that British Africa's much higher density of missions produced much higher enrollment rates. Francophone Africa follows a similar pattern of more missions resulting in higher enrollment rates, though Algeria and Senegal have higher enrollments than would be expected, and French Soudan (Mali) lower. As in Portuguese Africa, where Catholic missions predominated, this discrepancy underscores the fact that these missions were not as singularly responsible for education as in the British and Belgian territories.

COLONIAL EDUCATION POLICY – DIVERGENT IDEOLOGIES

The types of missions interacted with different colonial methods of rule. Scholars have often divided colonial rule into stylized categories similar to the Catholic-Protestant distinction. As earlier, there are truths to the distinctions. French colonial policy was based on a "belief that the political and cultural destinies of their subjects would eventually coincide with their own" (Michelman 1995, 218) – an attitude of *assimilation* or gradual integration into the French way of life.

The British, on the other hand, envisioned separate development for Africans. The classification of indirect rule has its origin in (British) Lord Lugard's 1922 treatise about how to rule in British Africa (1922/1965, 193–229). The idea was to use existing authorities to improve effciency. All of Britain's crown colonies were administered as separate units, each with its own governor, who reported to the Secretary of State for the Colonies. But central to the policy were finding the most appropriate local authority, demarcating his territory accurately, and giving him "guidance" in line with British objectives.

French direct rule was much more centralized, implemented through two federations (West African – AOF, and Central African – AEF), each of these with a governor-general, a governor for each colony below him, and a *commandant de cercle* for smaller regions. While they recognized a need to use African intermediaries, the ideal was to find loyal, competent men, rather than search out traditional authorities.[15] According to Cumming, it was France's revolutionary

---

[15] Georges Hardy, however, a director of education in the AOF, discusses the utility of education for reinforcing traditional elites (1917, 19), a pragmatic concession that was made because of limited means and particularly in Muslim areas. A shift from "assimilation" to "association" in French policy has been noted by many, beginning with Betts (1961); Peter Geschiere (1993) clearly traces the French change in strategy toward traditional elites in Cameroon.

ideals that "set her apart from other European colonizing powers, which were essentially conservative monarchies." This meant that direct rule ideally was designed to erase feudal aristocracies, undermine hereditary chiefs, and promote instead francophile elites. And unlike other European powers, "who saw themselves as trustees, [France] was working to integrate her colonies into a Greater French Republic" (Cumming 2005, 234).

This dichotomous distinction has been challenged since its articulation, most importantly for implying too much cohesiveness to ruling practices that were often worked out differently on the ground (Firmin-Sellers 2000, 254 notes 7–10). Regardless of their intentions, administrators had to adjust to the strength of the groups they encountered. This book argues, however, that even if administrative techniques and outcomes were altered on the basis of local circumstances, there was a clear distinction in education methods between French and British colonizers. This grew more pronounced through the colonial period and continued through independence and into the present, with a stronger, more singular influence from metropolitan France and a weaker, more fragmented influence from Britain. Missionaries in British territories handled education independently of colonial oversight much longer than their counterparts under French administration, while the latter attempted to control education centrally as early as 1903.

As indicated, education in British Africa began as the domain of missionaries, primarily Protestant. Despite assumptions to the contrary, not all of these Protestant missionaries saw the utility of local languages. Enough of them did, however, that the colonial office considered it important to articulate its goals. Initially, in 1847, long before its official annexation of territories, the Education Committee of the Privy Council (to the Colonial Administration) argued for the diffusion "of grammatical knowledge of the English language as the most important agent of civilization" (Ofori-Attah 2006, 416). An Education Ordinance in 1882 set the ground rules for church-state partnership. The vernacular was only to be used during specific periods, and English would be the medium of instruction in all public schools. Only mission schools teaching in English would receive grants-in-aid from the government. But many missions operated outside the control of the British administration, which seemed content to allow them to handle education as they saw fit.

Prior to 1920, education was "generally considered a matter for local initiative and voluntary effort" (Whitehead 2005, 441). "Aside from encouraging mission education as a first step toward 'civilizing' Africa, [British] governmental efforts to bring Western education to Africans were at first weak and laggard" (Sutton 1965, 62). The education of all but the tiniest minority was left in the hands of mission schools. British interest in the control of education began late and was of relatively short duration: from the 1920s to the 1950s.

As it began consolidating more direct control of education in its colonies after World War I, the British government was influenced by the recommendation of the Phelps-Stokes Commission, which had visited various territories in Africa in 1920/21. The commission itself had been motivated by a conference held in Cambridge in 1910, where mission groups had "strongly urged colonial governments to take a more active and responsible part in the development of education in their African territories" (Rukare 1969, 124). The resulting report recommended that schools adapt to local realities, including using local languages, stating (Jones 1925, 26):

The elements to be considered in determining the languages of instruction are (1) that every people have an inherent right to their Native tongue; (2) that the multiplicity of tongues shall not be such as to develop misunderstandings and distrust among people who should be friendly and cooperative; (3) that every group shall be able to communicate directly with those to whom the government is entrusted; and (4) that an increasing number of Native people shall know at least one of the languages of the civilized nations. ... The following recommendations are offered as suggestions to guide governments and educators in determining the usual procedures in most African colonies:

1. The tribal language should be used in the lower elementary standards or grades.
2. A *lingua franca* of African origin should be introduced in the middle classes of the school if the area is occupied by large Native groups speaking diverse languages.
3. The language of the European nation in control should be taught in the upper standards.

As will be shown at the end of this section, the third recommendation did not have very widespread effects, since only a very few pupils made it to this level.

In 1923, the Colonial Office established the Advisory Committee on Native Education in British Tropical Africa, and in 1925, this committee produced a "Memorandum on Education Policy in British Tropical Africa," a document outlining decentralized education with restricted aims. It took up several themes that had been advocated by the missionaries at the core of the British education structure in Africa: Schools should be concerned with religion and character training; attention to the vernacular would have primary importance; government should control education but cooperate with missions; education should be adapted to meet local needs and conditions (White 1996, 13).

The Colonial Office in the 1930s adopted a purposely indefinite policy: "With few assumptions and a statement of general principles" it would not be surprising "if these principles in their local application [were] adapted with the utmost elasticity to local conditions" (Whitehead 2005, 443). And this variability indeed marked British policy. A doctoral study comparing education policy in the Gambia and Malawi from 1925 to 1945 claimed there was no central policy emanating from the Colonial Office, "only general guidelines ... and these guidelines were worked on, very much like raw material, by local factors, forces and pressure groups to produce systems of education that while bearing a superficial similarity to one another were, in reality, often quite different."[16]

Before moving to the French contrast, it is important to consider briefly the German and Belgian policies (Portuguese policy was very similar to the French). The German model, though ending after World War I, must be acknowledged for its impact on language. Like the British, missionaries from Germany were mostly Protestant, though Catholic missions were also involved.[17] German missionaries and colonizers carried with them romanticist ideas about natural nations, along with a Weberian confidence, as Hashim puts it, that "rational institutions could force even the most 'irrational' men, or 'races,' to behave rationally" (Hashim 2009, 73). German colonial rule thus elevated African languages – but a limited number – and had more direct and earlier oversight of missions than did the British. The German West African territories of Togo and Cameroon therefore had much earlier experience with indigenous language education than other French territories, and East African Tanzania was also more systematically "penetrated" with Swahili than other British territories.

Belgian colonizers have been chastised for their extreme paternalist views (Young 1994b, 254). Their method was to use local chiefs integrated into a strict hierarchy to assure control. Pierre Alexandre observes that among the Belgians, "the exclusive use of African languages for education and administration resulted incontestably from the desire to keep the Africans in a kind of linguistic prison or, if one prefers, to shelter them and keep them sheltered from dangerous reading (neither Voltaire nor Marx has been translated into 'government' Kikongo)" (Alexandre 1972, 79). As "indispensable auxiliaries" (Young 1994b, 255), Catholic missions completed a triad with colonial administration and private companies. The colonial government ceded land to missions, who agreed to handle education (Fabian 1983, 169). The "integral state had not the least desire to transform its 'empire of silence' into a true civil society," and missionaries desired to "mould ... purified rural communities protected from what they perceived as the corruption of Western commercial and industrial life" (Young 1994b, 255). Contradictory linguistic policies arose largely because of Belgium's own complicated language conflict. There was thus in Belgian colonies early attention to African languages, but always a ranked view of European over African languages, a hierarchy, according to Fabian, that fit with Catholic ideology (1983, 171).

French colonial policy differed from all of these in its refusal to use African languages. Missionaries, primarily Catholic, operated under the assumption that the French language was part of the civilizing package they offered

---

[16] J. C. E. Grieg 1978, 5, cited in Whitehead 2005, 448.
[17] See Dah (1983, 61) for a discussion of the Protestant-Catholic controversies at a Missionary Society conference in Bremen in October 1885.

Africans.[18] The French government also insisted on control over mission education much earlier, working in partnership with mission schools to achieve its goals. Anticlerical legislation in France between 1901 and 1904 culminated in a separation of church and state in 1905 (Gardinier 1985, 335). Between 1903 and 1924, the French government took deliberate steps to acquire complete control over all schools in Africa (White 1996, 11). As early as 1903, France had organized a single, homogeneous service of teaching in French West Africa,[19] replacing religious with lay teachers in state schools, cutting off support to mission schools in West Africa, and diminishing it in Equatorial Africa.[20]

By 1912, Governor-General of French West Africa William Ponty formalized the language policy in a decree: "The goal of elementary teaching is the diffusion among the indigenous people of spoken French. *The French language is the only one to be used in schools. It is forbidden for teachers to use local speech with their students.*"[21] In 1922, France limited missionary activity by declaring that any new school required government permission, government-certified teachers, a government curriculum, and the exclusive use of French as the language of instruction (White 1996, 11). Monsieur André Davesne, inspector of primary education in Senegal under the colonial authorities and author of the textbook *Mamadou et Binéta*, which was used across Africa in primary schools, wrote in 1933 of the French goal in West Africa:

We have the ambition – which does not seem at all "utopian"– to *franciser* [Frenchify] all of the A.O.F., in the linguistic and scholarly sense of the word, as well as in the "humane" sense. Even more, we do not believe it possible to dissociate these two preoccupations: teaching French, leading African peoples to live a more humane life; the French language appears to be an incomparable instrument of civilization.[22]

Pragmatism, however, resulted in elitism: "We can get to only a tiny minority of our native children, and our very concern for the people placed under our guardianship imposes upon us the need for selection on a rational basis. It makes it imperative that we reserve the all too rare openings in our schools for those who are able to profit by our instruction," declared French Governor-General of

---

[18] Though the majority used French, Catholic missions also were not monolithic. Mission schools in Gabon – American Protestants and French Roman Catholics – both taught their own foreign languages, but the main instructional medium was Mpongwe and other indigenous languages (Gardinier 1985, 335).

[19] Arrêté No. 806 Organisant le service de l'Enseignement dans les colonies et Territoires de l'Afrique occidentale française, 24 Nov. 1903, reproduced in Turcotte 1983, 40–43.

[20] The only real difference between the AOF and AEF was the involvement of missions in education. By 1935, more than 80 percent of children in West Africa were attending public schools, while missions continued to educate the majority of children in Equatorial Africa (Gardinier 1985, 336).

[21] Underlined in original text. Arrêté No. 1633 Réorganisant le service de l'Enseignement dans la colonie du Haut-Sénégal et Niger, 2 Nov. 1912, *Journal Officiel de l'A.O.F.*, No. 413, 9 Nov. 1912, 712.

[22] André Davesne 1933, 4 (cited in Blonde 1979, 22, my translation).

French Equatorial Africa Raphael Antonetti in 1925.[23] This echoed Carde's senti-ment quoted at the beginning of the chapter.[24] Therefore, a "very limited number of African children were exposed to a simplified curriculum designed to train a small cadre of loyal, mainly low-level subordinates to assist the colonial admin-istration" (Michelman 1995, 220).[25]

It is clear that French and British colonial policy differed significantly with regard to language. While the methods differed, the ultimate outcome was the same: a lack of linguistic unification. For the French, this was the result of an elitist education. For the British, "adapted" education was the cause.

This was because colonizers had the same goals. As the following section will elaborate, these were, first, to train a few elites to help them administer; second, to ensure that the masses were controlled; and, third, to restrain potentially restive elites from challenging their rule. Early, this was evident by restrictions on access; later, even with expanding enrollment after World War II as a result of heightened demands by returning African veterans and metropolitan parlia-ments pressing for "development" in the colonies, the extremely low literacy rates in a European language reflected the lack of genuine effort to transform the masses with universal education. Whether the language choice was indigenous or foreign, the result was the same – a tiny cadre of elites that was linguistically separated from the general population.

SELECTIVE TRAINING AND RESTRICTION OF THE "MASSES"

The essential aim of the colonial powers through education was to train person-nel to aid in administration (Moumouni 1968, 38). Education was explicitly *not* for the masses. Sons of chiefs were chosen first, then those of notables and civil servants. In 1924, the French hoped that secondary school graduates would number about thirty-five for all of French West Africa, or about four or five per colony (Moumouni 1968, 48). Only two lycées – postsecondary schools – existed in French West Africa before 1958, in Senegal's Dakar and St. Louis. This restricted education seemed to be motivated partially by the need to control the birth of nationalist, restive sentiment. As early as the 1870s, in the important territory of Algeria, General Tirman, a French governor, wrote, "The hostility of the native is measured by his level of education" (cited in Benrabah 2007b, 204, my translation).

---

[23] Circular No. 8 Concerning the Organization of Public Education, 8 May 1925, reproduced in Cowan et al. 1965, 54.

[24] See a careful study by Alice Goheneix-Minisini (2011) that lays out the central contradiction in French colonial language policy: promising the French language as an instrument for emancipa-tion and limiting education out of fear of rebellion.

[25] B. W. White (1996, 11–12) explains that one of the main features of French colonial education, aside from the use of the French language, was enrollment limitation, based on estimates of job availability, in order to prevent disillusion and disorientation of unemployed youth.

Gardinier reports that in 1935, French West Africa had 62,300 pupils in primary schools and French Equatorial Africa had 15,877 (1985, 334). Given the population at the time, this meant that less than half a percent of the residents in the two federations was attending school. Though French rhetoric spoke of providing basic education for masses, the resources were not forthcoming. "Although the assimilationist goal persisted as an ideal, in practice it was only seriously applied in education after World War II" (Michelman 1995, 220). And even then, "only some 5 percent of the population of French West Africa had received any French education by the end of the Second World War" (Chafer 2007, 441).

The policy of assimilation led to the introduction of metropolitan curriculum and continued use of French language: "At least half of the program in the primary school was devoted to the French language and culture" (Gardinier 1985, 339–340). Moumouni notes that statistics for 1945–1960 "do not contain any reference to literacy campaigns in Black Africa. The reason is that despite all the grand propaganda about achievements in this field, the battle against illiteracy was never, *per se*, a real interest of the French colonial administration" (Moumouni 1964, 80).

Enrollment in secondary education remained "practically stationary" until 1957 (Moumouni 1964, 76). After the 1956 *loi cadre*, primary and secondary enrollment nearly doubled in two years. But this development had its drawbacks. Given the dearth of existing qualified secondary teachers, this meant that a large number of unqualified teachers were hired. "The manifest desire of the various governments to expand education was translated mainly by an increase in the number of primary school students, and by hiring teachers with dubious qualifications because of the huge increase in enrollment, so that the general level of education tended to drop" (Moumouni 1964, 78–79). Elementary classes were crowded (a class of seventy-five pupils was not unusual), with poorly qualified teachers in the majority: Only 7 percent of primary teachers had graduated from teacher training courses in 1957–1958 (Gardinier 1985, 340). Gail Kelly, expert on French colonial education policy, concurs that their aims for education in West Africa were explicitly elitest, ascriptive, and restricted (1984, 11).

The British also worried about creating too many educated Africans, but rather than curbing numbers, they chose to restrict the masses through an adapted education. Their experience in India showed them that educated elites could be dangerous (Yamada 2009, 34). "What colonial governors were keen to avoid at all costs was responsibility for the creation of an intellectual proletariat or 'babu' class such as had bedeviled India" (Whitehead 2005, 442). Combined with growing criticism of mission education's denationalization and uprooting of Africans, the idea of adapting the curriculum gained currency as a way to "offset the danger of excessive exposure to Western values" (Yamada 2009, 35). Emphasis would be on developing primary vernacular education and "limiting the spread of English secondary education in line with genuine employment opportunities" (Whitehead 2005, 442).

In 1944, the Advisory Committee published "Mass Education in African Society," which advocated much more spending on education, but retained the adaptive model. It was only after this date that enrollment expanded significantly. In Nigeria, for example, before World War II, colonial government expenditure on education ranged from 1 to 4.3 percent; after the war, the figure rose to 10 percent and above (Ogunsheye 1965, 125). In the early 1940s, only 18 percent of school-aged children attended school in Southern Nigeria, and this was high if compared to the less than 2 percent in the North (Ogunsheye 1965, 127). After the war, the Southern colonial government subsequently poured nearly 50 percent of its budget into education. While this raised the southern portion of Nigeria to near-universal enrollment by 1958, almost three-quarters of primary teachers were uncertified or probationers (Ogunsheye 1965, 129).

As did state-builders in early Europe, colonizers had to walk a fine line between creating capable administrators and restraining their ambition. Moumouni decries the ideological conditioning with its psychological consequences – elites trained to defend and propagate the myths of white superiority and "congenital incapacity" of blacks, "treated handsomely as long as they were 'loyal' and 'cooperative.'" It was an education just sufficient to make "good but blind officials" (Moumouni 1964, 49). Universities were not established until the late 1940s in British Africa – the University College at Ibadan (1947–1948) and the Nigerian College of Technology. Institutions for higher education appeared even later in French Africa with Dakar's Institut des Hautes Études established only in 1950 (Gardinier 1985, 334). The "birth and expansion [of university education] was originally connected with the desire to control the amount of higher education received by Africans" (Moumouni 1964, 67).

Whatever the language policy in primary education, secondary education virtually always used the language of the colonizer. But secondary education barely reached 3 percent of Africa's school-aged population at independence. Comparisons are difficult before 1940 because of inconsistent reporting of primary and secondary enrollments separately. What can be said with certainty is that while secondary education began somewhat earlier in the British territories, it remained extremely limited. In the 1930s, there were only about 3,000 secondary school students in French Africa outside Algeria and Madagascar. British Africa had more – 33,000 plus any secondary students in South Africa (whose secondary figures are not reported separately). By 1960, the number of secondary students had grown in French Africa to 150,000, though half of these were in Algeria and Madagascar. British Africa had more than 500,000, plus those in South Africa (Mitchell 2007, 119–131). But the fact that fewer than 700,000 students were attending secondary school in 1960 out of a population of more than 223 million shows that a restricted education was practiced in general across the continent.

Two points are clear from Table 2.3. First, British territories had a head start in educating their populations. As early as the 1930s, average enrollment in these territories was three to six times higher than in other regions. Belgians caught up

TABLE 2.3. *Primary and Secondary Enrollment in Africa, 1930–1960*

	Circa 1930		Circa 1940		Circa 1950		Circa 1960		
	Number Students Enrolled	Percentage School-Aged Population	Number Students Enrolled	Percentage School-Aged Population	Number Students Enrolled	Percentage School-Aged Population	Number Students Enrolled	Percentage School-Aged Population	Dates Recorded
British territories									
Ghana	54,400	6	80,100	7	307,000	21	680,000	34	1931, 1938, 1950, 1959
Kenya	101,000	10	140,800	13	372,100	19	801,000	33	1930, 1938, 1950, 1960
Malawi	136,000	26	197,000	35	227,100	25	292,100	28	1930, 1940, 1950, 1960
Mauritius	35,900	26	41,000	29	58,100	37	128,000	65	1930, 1940, 1950, 1960
Nigeria	186,000	3	329,000	5	999,000	9	3,048,000	22	1930, 1938, 1950, 1960
Sierra Leone	15,000	3	23,000	4	29,900	5	93,500	14	1930, 1940, 1950, 1960
South Africa	736,000	26	1,043,000	31	1,553,000	38	2,625,000	50	1930, 1940, 1950, 1960
Sudan			67,000	3	132,000	4	420,000	12	1940, 1950, 1961
Tanzania	130,000	8	119,100	7	224,900	8	466,000	15	1930, 1945, 1951, 1960
Uganda	17,200	1	55,400	4	235,000	14	563,500	28	1930, 1939, 1950, 1960
Zambia	18,000	4	59,000	12	143,000	24	328,600	36	1930, 1940, 1950, 1960
Zimbabwe	117,600	32	124,000	26	256,000	36	541,100	48	1930, 1940, 1950, 1960
Average		13		15		20		32	
French territories									
Algeria	197,000	9	286,000	11	374,000	13	814,000	25	1931, 1940, 1950, 1960
Benin	14,000	3	15,000	3	35,080	6	102,100	14	1936, 1938, 1951, 1961
Burkina Faso					14,400	1	58,500	4	1950, 1960
Cameroon*	107,000	14	126,000	14	159,400	10	604,000	36	1937, 1944, 1950, 1962
Central Afr. Rep.					19,200	5	69,600	15	1950, 1960
Chad					8,100	1	96,700	11	1950, 1961
Congo Rep.					41,900	15	119,800	39	1950, 1960

Territory									Dates
Cote d'Ivoire	12,000	1	14,000	1	33,300	4	250,000	23	1936, 1940, 1950, 1960
Gabon					21,500	14	59,200	41	1950, 1960
Guinea	8,400	1	8,700	1	18,400	2	103,800	10	1936, 1938, 1951, 1960
Madagascar			189,800	15	249,000	18	475,000	31	1938, 1950, 1960
Mali	13,600	1	13,500	1	25,900	2	68,150	4	1936, 1938, 1951, 1960
Mauritania			0		2,400	1	15,800	6	1951, 1961
Niger	1,800	0.3	3,200	0	6,200	1	24,900	3	1936, 1948, 1951, 1960
Senegal	15,000	3	17,000	3	38,000	5	138,500	15	1936, 1938, 1950, 1960
Togo	5,600	2	13,000	5	41,800	10	107,900	23	1931, 1941, 1950, 1960
Average	**4**		**5**		**7**		**19**		
Belgian territories									
Congo, Dem. Rep.**	156,100	4	292,600	6	897,800	18	1,666,000	35	1931, 1943, 1950, 1961
Burundi**							103,400	12	1961
Rwanda**							262,400	31	1961
Average	**4**		**6**		**18**		**26**		
Portuguese territories									
Angola	4,100	0.4	6,900	1	16,300	1	111,500	7	1931, 1940, 1950, 1960
Mozambique	47,300	4	93,500	6	160,900	8	418,800	18	1930, 1940, 1950, 1960
Average	**2**		**3**		**5**		**13**		
Other territories									
Ethiopia***					56,100	1	249,700	4	1950, 1960
Liberia					25,000	10	67,000	20	1950, 1961
Somalia							24,200	3	1960

* French only to 1950 (no separate figures given for British Cameroons prior to 1948).

** Rwanda and Burundi are included with DRC figures prior to 1960.

*** Public schools only for 1950 figure.

Source: Mitchell (2007). Population figures taken from table A1 where available. If not, estimations from table A5 were used. In the few cases where neither was available, a figure was extrapolated using the closest date and 1960 population growth rate from the World Bank WDI. School-Aged Population calculated by multiplying the total population by .33, the average percentage of children aged 5–19 in several populations reported by Mitchell (table A2) for various dates.

in the late 1940s, while the French and Portuguese lagged until the late 1950s. This means that even though the French (and Portuguese) had a centralized policy of using a single language in both primary and secondary education, this language was in no way diffused across their colonial populations as they claimed their assimilation policy intended.

Second, because the British relied so heavily on Protestant missions, which usually preferred vernacular education, and themselves advocated this policy after the 1920s, the vast majority of pupils educated in British territories were also not learning a single language. While the British, like other colonizers, did indeed prescribe English in secondary and higher education, only a small minority of students achieved this level, even in the terminal colonial period.

The bottom line is that in no way can it be said that colonizers genuinely tried to spread a single language among the masses. Protestant missions, much more active in British Africa, where education was spreading more widely, generally preferred vernacular education as the most effective method of conversion. And African elites themselves, once having experienced the benefits of selective education, had little desire to expand this education to potential competitors. The following section will elaborate in the cases of Senegal, Ghana, and Cameroon the differences in mission and colonial methods, but similar lack of strong pressure for mass standard language education.

MISSION AND COLONIAL LANGUAGE INFLUENCE IN SENEGAL, GHANA, AND CAMEROON

Senegal and Ghana represent archetypical French and British applications of standard policy. Cameroon, because of its mixed colonial history and because of its high concentration of missionaries, had more experience with local languages than other French territories. This section will highlight the education policies and progress within each territory, particularly as they relate to language. It will show much variation in mission and colonial activities, a more complicated picture than the simplified dichotomies described previously. Relatively significant primary education began much earlier in Ghana and Cameroon than in Senegal, and the colonial period ended with a stark distinction that would continue through independence to the present.

Regular French contact with Senegal began very early, with seventeenth century traders who established a post on the uninhabited "island" of St. Louis at the mouth of the Senegal River. The French language began to spread primarily through the *signares* – women who provided these traders with many services and often grew wealthy as a result. Local interpreters and military recruits for protection and conquest also contributed to the spread of French (Hale 2009).

But the story of Senegalese colonial education and its relationship to language starts with French Catholic teacher Jean Dard, who opened the first primary school at St. Louis in 1817 (Seck 1993, 25, 100). He taught students using a method of translating from mother tongue to French, and he used gifted and accomplished older students to train younger pupils – the *école mutuelle*, one of two methods practiced in metropolitan France. The other was direct instruction by religious orders (Johnson 2004, 142). Dard maintained that students who learned through the Wolof medium would perform better than students who had not first learned their mother tongue. In a letter to the (French) governor of Senegal, Dard writes: "I think that one can better cultivate the intelligence of students and more surely attain the goal of their instruction if one begins with the study of their mother tongue" (Dumont 1983, 196). But Dard was not interested primarily in the instrumental use of Wolof for French acquisition. Wolof was "instrumental" for a more effective spiritual penetration of the Senegalese. And he also had a strong linguistic curiosity (Dumont 1983, 261–262).

As a Catholic educator in Senegal, Dard was unique in privileging an African language. Abbé Guidicelli, apostolic prefect of Senegal, explains that, aside from Dard's incompetence, one of the reasons the children were deserting his school was that Mr. Dard, "to teach himself the language of the country (informal jargon), instead of the French language taught and continually spoke yolof (sic) to his students" (Seck 1993, 35). A "commission scolaire" was sent by Governor Jubelin to Dard's school on March 25, 1829, and found students poorly assimilated and with only a superficial knowledge of French. The "fundamental vice" of Dard's system was "the use of the indigenous language, spoken but not written, as the medium of instruction" (Dumont 1983, 262). By 1830, French officials had summoned Dard back to the metropole, and his method was abandoned for French immersion. From then to the turn of the century, teaching was done by religious orders – brotherhoods such as the Frères de Ploërmel and sisterhoods such as the Soeurs de l'Immaculée Conception – using the same manuals that they used in metropolitan France, instructing exclusively in French (Johnson 2004, 144).

Louis Faidherbe, governor of Senegal from 1854, believed the French language should be the primary medium "through which French civilization would be transmitted" (Kuenzi 2011, 58). It is estimated that the religious orders had taught a total of 25,000 to 30,000 students by 1903 (Kuenzi 2011, 59, citing Doria-Hausser 1989, 83). The secularization of the school system after this date brought more schools under direct government control. Following Dard's brief overture toward local languages, stories of "Le Symbole" abound, in which the speaking of the mother tongue in African schools under French control became a punishable offense (Johnson 2004, 144). This directly mirrored the method of erasing patois in France, where a "token of shame" was displayed by children caught using their native tongue (Weber 1976, 313).

In 1913, approximately 4,500 students were enrolled in Senegal's primary schools (Kuenzi 2011, 59, citing Conklin 1989), a number that rose to 15,000 by 1936, or 2.5 percent of the school-aged population. This had doubled to 30,000 by 1948, which, however, was less than 4 percent of the school-aged population. Not until 1951 are secondary school students even enumerated – 2,300 of them – while primary enrollment had increased to 43,000. On the eve of independence, France's most important colony could boast only 107,000 students in primary school and 8,700 students in secondary out of a population of more than three million. This was less than 12 percent of the school-aged population (Mitchell 2007, 1023, 1029).

Despite these low figures, the goal of creating a small indigenous elite was relatively successful in Senegal. The nearly nine thousand secondary school students was a comparatively high proportion of all educated students, when evaluated against other French territories. A postgraduate teacher training college that began in St. Louis in 1903, the École William Ponty, drew students from all over French West Africa, producing about fifty graduates per year for forty years – a total of two thousand at the end of World War II (Chafer 2007, 441). It trained teachers, medical assistants, and interpreters and clerks for the colonial service. The rhetoric of *assimilation*, however, was not seriously applied until after World War II. Though selective, "the education provided at Ponty was not even recognised as equivalent to that provided by similar post-primary schools in the metropole." It was only after the war that Pontins were allowed to study for the *baccalauréat*, a prerequisite for French university (Chafer 2007, 442).

As for Senegalese languages, while Wolof was written early, it was largely abandoned in schools, and other languages received little attention.[26] None of the other major languages in Senegal was written until after independence. Senegal thus ended the colonial period with low primary enrollment, relatively high secondary enrollment, and no use of local languages in education. It clearly displayed a French policy that placed a high premium on education of a very few elites in the metropolitan language.

In Ghana, then the Gold Coast, the earliest schools were "castle schools" in the forts of Elmina, Christiansborg, Accra, and Cape Coast, founded to train African elites' children and those born of unions between British traders and locals (Sackey 1996, 127). These were not mission-affiliated, even if many of their teachers had trained in religious schools themselves. Jesse Jones reports that as early as 1751, the castle schools had educated twelve hundred pupils (1925, 140). These pupils learned English through "repeated readings of primers and spelling books" (Sackey 1996, 127).

The Reverend Thomas Thompson of the Society for the Propagation of the Gospel (SPG) established the first official Anglican Mission on the Gold Coast in 1752 (Andrews 2009, 668). He complained about the "strange kind of Jargon"

---

[26] The Mandinka language, spoken by 6.6% of Senegal's population, was also written very early (1837), but this was because of its transcription for British-colonized Gambia, with 43% of the latter's population speaking this language. Jalunga, a language primarily of Mali, spoken by less than 1% of Senegal's population, was written in 1907. Pular or Fuuta Jalon, spoken by 1.5% of the population and considered a language of Guinea, was written in 1929. Calculated from Lewis 2009.

that he found in West Africa and relied on an interpreter to speak with locals. Parliament had approved SPG's charter but could not officially direct its work, as the mission depended on private funds. Teachers were religious chaplains, famous among them one of Thompson's students, the Reverend Philip Quaque (1747–1816), first African to be ordained a Church of England minister. He, like the other chaplains, instructed pupils in English, as he had not retained any fluency in his native Fetu, and he used an interpreter for his messages to local parishioners (Andrews 2009, 679–680). The SPG clearly was frustrated by this: "If Quaque could not speak the language, the SPG had forfeited the major benefit of investing so much money to train him in the first place." The body urged Quaque "to endeavor to recover his own language" (Andrews 2009, 680–681).

After 1821, the British government pursued more direct involvement in administering the Gold Coast territory, including some oversight of education. Governor Charles McCarthy between 1822 and 1824 showed his concern with the proper teaching of English, ordering English textbooks for the schools (Sackey 1996, 129).

From the 1830s, missionary methods in the Gold Coast diverged. Workers of the German Basel Mission settled first among the coastal Ga around Accra and in 1835 moved inland to work among the Twi in Akuapim, located on a healthier climate ridge (Coe 2005, 34). Wesleyan Methodists settled among the coastal Fante in 1835, while Bremen missionaries arrived in 1847, settling at Peki, Ho, and coastal Anlo among the Ewe on the eastern side of the River Volta (Isichei 1995, 169).

These missions represented two different approaches to language. Like the Anglicans, the Wesleyan Methodists endeavored to transmit English through church and school (Anyidoho and Kropp-Dakubu 2008, 147–148). Methodist superintendant, the Reverend Thomas Birch Freeman, in 1841 envisioned a time "when the English language will become the classical language of all the tribes and people . . . and thus enjoy a direct introduction to its extensive literature" (cited in Sackey 1997, 130). He saw advantages for Methodist youth to acquire English in order to gain jobs in the government sector. In contrast, the German Basel and Bremen Missions saw the utility of indigenous languages. This was largely inspired by German romanticist ideas about unique nations and cultures (Meyer 2002; Coe 2005, 30–35). Another reason was that these German missionaries did not want to teach English so as not to encourage the language of their Wesleyan and Anglican competitors (Anyidoho and Kropp-Dakubu 2008, 148).

Coe illustrates in wonderful detail the work of the Basel Mission in Akuapem (2005, chapter 1). She describes the Reverend J. G. Christaller's efforts in translating the Bible into the Twi language, quoting his views of the relationship between vernacular language and nationhood in the 1890s: "I do not believe that all the Tshi [Twi] tribes will ever exchange their vernacular for the English language; I doubt whether the Ga people will do so, and if they did, it would be unnatural. A nation's best home is its own language. . . . [Men] should not deprive their own people of their peculiar nature in order to make them members of an other nation that had a different growth and history" (Coe 2005, 41–42). These missionaries and their African converts were instrumental in collecting histories about particular language groups and the construction of more tangible, bounded identities with their writing and objectification. The nationalism of local Gold Coast elites was inspired by the writing of history, and the selective revival of custom (Coe 2005, 47).

This mission history laid a foundation for language development in the colony. *Akan* is an umbrella term for mutually intelligible varieties of languages: Twi (Akuapem, Asante, Akyem, Akwamu, Wassa) and Fante (Borebore, Agona, Gomoa, Bono).[27] After the arrival of the missionaries, the Akuapem-based orthography originating in the Basel Mission spread through Twi-speaking areas. The Fante-speaking area, because it was settled by different missionaries, used a different orthography. And, from the 1960s, Asante linguists and writers developed their own orthography. The result is that Akan exists as three languages, Twi, Fante, and Asante, though recent missionaries have begun to use the term *Akan* to cover the whole group.[28] Ewe has a single standard version, developed by Bremen missionaries. A crucial factor to the cohesion of this ethnic group, according to Lawrance (2005, 223), is that education was vigorously pursued in the Ewe-speaking areas by German missionaries operating in both the German territory (Togo) and the British territory (Ghana): "This led to widespread literacy in and acceptance of the standard language throughout the Ewe-speaking lands, and it was the focus of an emerging Ewe nationalism" (Anyidoho and Kropp-Dakubu 2008, 153). After Togoland divided in 1914, emphasis on Ewe declined, especially in the French-mandated area. In the British area, though neglected, it still served as a rallying point for southern regional nationalism. According to Anyidoh and Kropp-Dakubu, the Ewe language remains in active use to an extent not found for other Ghanaian languages (2008, 154).[29]

By 1874, when the British government gained administrative control over the colony, there were more than one hundred mission schools throughout the territory. Even by 1881, of the 139 schools in the Gold Coast, only 3 were under direct colonial management (Ministry of Education, Ghana 2000). In order to strengthen its oversight of education throughout the territory, the British government drew up in 1887 an "Ordinance for the Promotion and Assistance of Education in the Gold Coast Colony." This ordinance required

---

[27] Lewis (2009): http://www.ethnologue.com/show_language.asp?code=aka.

[28] The 2009 edition of *Ethnologue* has one entry for the Akan group as a whole (though noting numbers of speakers of these various subgroups), whereas the 2000 edition had separate entries for Asante Twi, Akuapem Twi, and Fante.

[29] The Ga language, whose people are from the capital, Accra, has not been a similar rallying point. There are many fewer speakers to begin, plus a large number of other immigrant speakers diluted its influence in Accra, making the role of the Ga language mainly symbolic: "Apart from a few individuals, the Ga show little interest in their language as a written medium."

teaching of and in English (Sackey 1996, 129). Schools that used indigenous languages as medium of instruction could not qualify for grants-in-aid from the government. Lord Derby in the London Colonial Office explained that "instruction in the native language may safely be left to the stimulus of self interest and government subsidies are not required for its encouragement" (Sackey 1996, 129–130).

Nonetheless, the Basel and Bremen Missions continued to use local languages, and though they were expelled from both Togo and Ghana after Germany's defeat in 1917 (later reinstated), the report of the Phelps-Stokes Commission in 1920/21 validated their method. Ghana introduced "16 provisions designed to align the curriculum to local needs and interests," and Governor Guggisberg reversed the English-only policy with a decree in 1925 that required the vernacular as the medium for primary school (Ofori-Attah 2006, 418). This shift in attitude that romanticized African life as "equal, pastoral, and communal" led to an emphasis on "adapted education" that, while fraught with ambiguities (Coe 2005), would prevail until independence nearly thirty years later.

Comparing Ghana's experience with that of Senegal, relatively widespread primary schooling began much earlier in the former, virtually all because of the missions. Recall that in 1881, Ghana already had 139 schools, whereas Senegal had only 48 by 1913. By 1901, Ghana had 12,000 primary students enrolled, or 2.5 percent of the school-aged population. Senegal did not reach this percentage until 1936. By 1938, Ghana had 80,000 students enrolled overall, and this jumped to 680,000 in 1959, or 31 percent of the school-aged population,[30] compared with Senegal's less than 12 percent.

On the secondary level, Ghana also excelled. Coe's comprehensive investigation of Achimota secondary school, the first to be established by the government in the Gold Coast, reveals that the administrators intended through secondary education to "create a new elite that was not 'denationalized' but could serve as appropriate brokers between 'civilization and the masses'" (Coe 2002, 31; see also Ofori-Attah 2006: 414). Though she paints an appropriate parallel between the goal of creating cultural "brokers" in both colonial Algeria and Ghana, it could be argued that the scale of the project was much broader in Ghana than in the other French territories outside Algeria. Whereas Ghana had 153,000 secondary students enrolled in 1957, its year of independence, Senegal had only 9,500 in 1960, when it gained independence.[31]

Importantly, southern Ghanaian languages were taught at Achimota, thus continuing students' interface with these major languages. "The most important work of Achimota in the area of vernacular language was producing textbooks

---

[30] Coe attributes this to a mass education project promoted by Nkrumah's government under Gold Coast "self-rule" from 1951 (2002, 25).

[31] Mitchell 2007, 1,027 for Ghana; 1,029 for Senegal. Ghana had a little less than twice Senegal's overall population.

and convincing the Cambridge Exams council in the 1930s that four languages from the south (Ewe, Fante, Ga, Twi) should be recognized as subjects for the School Leaving Certificate examination" (Coe 2003, 32, citing Agbodeka 1977). While this process fixed and "schematized" these languages in artificial ways, it simultaneously indicated their importance, evidence of the ambiguity with which Ghanaian "culture" was taught at Achimota (Coe 2002, 33). Coe states that Achimota aroused passionate feelings and criticism within the Gold Coast. Many educated Africans "suspected that the reason for teaching local arts, language, and customs was to keep Africans in inferior positions. Thus, they pushed for an academic education and a focus on the English language." This resulted by the 1950s in a retraction of some of the school's emphasis on Ghanaian languages, as Achimota became "ordinary" and "went western" like other (secondary) schools (Coe 2002, 38–40).

Nonetheless, Ghana's primary schools through the terminal colonial period continued to use its local languages. Six languages had been written by independence (eight if the variations in Akan are separated, as they were at the time), covering 63 percent of the population. Primary education had spread much further than in Senegal (31 percent vs. 11.5 percent of the school-aged population), largely because of the foundation laid by missions, and the ratio of secondary students to primary was more than three times as high in Ghana,[32] even though Senegal was favored in secondary education compared to other French territories outside Algeria.

Senegal and Ghana are fairly straightforward, compared to the territory that would become Cameroon. Cameroon experienced German colonization (1884–1917), followed by French and British trusteeship (1919–1960). Because of the early German mission activity, as well as that of American and British mission societies, it had a more widespread experience with missions than other French territories. Languages were transcribed early and used widely in education, until the French administration moved to restrict them in its (larger) portion of the territory. Though schools in the British section continued to use the vernacular, this also declined in the terminal colonial period.

As in Ghana, missionaries preceded colonists, and their education and evangelistic efforts shaped much of the country's language development. Most Protestant missions aligned more closely with the Basel and Bremen Mission ideas than the Methodist or Anglican, emphasizing the use of vernacular languages. The first to arrive were Jamaican members of the London Baptist Society, who encountered Isubu speakers in the coastal town of Bimbia in 1844. A mission and school were established, and a year later, these missionaries were joined by British members of the same mission society, who settled in King Atwa Town, or Douala. Both groups set to work immediately on Scriptures in their respective groups' language. American Presbyterians began working

[32] Secondary enrollment in Senegal was 7% of total, versus 24% of the total enrollment in Ghana (Mitchell 2007).

among Bulu speakers around Baganta in 1879; their compatriots to the south on the coast were working among the Fang, the major language for what would be Equatorial Guinea, with many speakers on the Cameroonian side of the future border as well. Though these English-speaking missionaries might have previewed British colonization, it was actually Germany that made treaties with Douala chiefs to acquire the territory of Kamerun as a protectorate in 1884. English had already begun to spread, as a result of trade with British and these early missionary societies, so one of the primary goals of the German colonizers was to replace English with German.

With the arrival of the Germans, the Basel Mission (with its headquarters already established in the Gold Coast) replaced the British Baptists in the Douala area in 1886 (Dah 1983, 114). They had been invited through the All-German Missionary Conference that met in 1885 to take over the work of the London Baptist Missionary Society. Initially hesitant, seeing Kamerun as a "region of death," they only agreed if the colonial government would give "free scope" to their missionary work (Dah 1983, 68–69).

Two of their major goals were to establish schools that allowed children to read Scripture and to protect the "national particularities of the people," including their languages (Dah 1983, 111). These early German missionaries were particularly influenced by Theodor Oehler, theologian and professor at the mission seminary, and Inspector of the Basel Mission. He viewed mission schools as central to the mission's efforts. Children had to be shown the Word of God. "In order to preserve good national customs, teaching and preaching must be done in the native language" (Dah 1983, 111).

These Basel missionaries inherited the Baptist translation of the Bible into Duala. The Baptists had not been as interested in schools as in congregations, having left only 268 pupils enrolled in Baptist schools (Dah 1983, 127, 114). As described previously, the Basel missionaries were convinced of the importance of evangelization in the vernacular. But they were also practical. Hearing many different tongues, they saw the difficulty of using all of them. "During the first stage in the Cameroons, the colonial government supported the Duala and helped to strengthen its exercise of power by using its language and imposing this as the lingua franca for the whole colony" (Halden 1968, 87). This was a result of the Basel Mission's exclusive focus on Duala. "Naturally the Basel Mission found itself at odds with tribes not belonging to Duala and unwilling to speak its language, but on the other hand it was nevertheless understood that an African language was closer to another African language than to the alien European tongue" (Halden 1968, 90). From 1886 to 1896, the Basel Mission opened nine schools along the coast, consolidating them over the next six years. By 1900, three major languages had been transcribed, Duala, Bulu, and Fang, which covered approximately 9 percent of the population.[33]

---

[33] Bamun had an indigenous script created by King Njoya in 1896.

Efficient German roads, rail, and military presence provided a way for missionaries to expand their presence to the interior, penetrating the "hinterlands" at the turn of the century. From 1903 to 1914 they moved inland. First, they reached the Grassfields areas of Northwest Cameroon, encountering the Fon[34] of Bali in 1903. Believing this group to be more influential than it was, the missionaries chose this language as the inland language of instruction and religious literacy. In Bali, Chief Fonyonga "used his soldiers to collect children to fill the empty school house which he had ordered the natives to build." Later it was discovered that most of these children were not natives of Bali but of subject tribes (Dah 1983, 128). Nonetheless, Bali (Mungaka) was used in the Northwest, while Duala remained the mission's language of choice for the southern forest regions.

The American Presbyterians who had settled among the Bulu were allowed to stay after German occupation, if they agreed to teach German (Mokosso 1987, 35). They did so, reluctantly, and only as a subject. They primarily used the Bulu language for instruction, and then neighboring Bassa after World War I. With their own printing press, they produced monthly vernacular newspapers, quarterly publications of Sunday school lessons, along with medical, industrial, and financial news (Mokosso 1987, 55). Bonuses given to schools on the basis of success in the German language exam, however, pressured schools to abandon vernacular teaching (Vernon-Jackson 1967, 45).

German Catholics of the Pallotine order had arrived in 1890, establishing stations in fifteen coastal towns in the lower central regions of the territory (Dah 1983, 11). Unlike the Basel and Presbyterian Mission schools, the Catholics "taught more secular subjects in direct preparation of the children for use by the colonial administration. For that they received considerable financial aid from the Government" (Dah 1983, 154).

In 1907, a conference between missions and the German colonial government had established the ground rules for education. Much of this had to do with language policy, particularly as raised by the Basel Mission. The colonial administration was worried about the mission's promotion of only two languages (Duala and Bali), fearing that it could cause larger group solidarity or smaller group resentment. The conference articulated an education policy aimed to "supplant English with German" and reemphasized the goal of "limiting the teaching of vernaculars outside their tribal areas, particularly Bali and Duala" (Fonlon 1969, 34). A 1910 school reform policy proposed using the mother tongue for the first three years and then switching to German only in subsequent years. The colonial government wanted the missionaries to use the language of *each* local community along with German. Catholics and Baptists had no problem with this, but the Basel Mission balked (Dah 1983, 135). It was the topic of discussion at a missionary conference in Duala in April 1912, and Oehler raised the issue with the colonial office in 1913, "trying to convince them that it was impossible for BM

---

[34] The Fons are royal leaders of cultural groupings in the Grassfield areas of Cameroon.

[Basel Mission] missionaries to learn the many Cameroonian languages and that the BM was prepared to introduce German in the fourth year of schools" (Dah 1983, 133). A negative reply was returned, and Basel Mission finally did accept government aid, implying that it was shifting its views of schools not just as centers of religious instruction but toward more secular aims. The war began, however, and the German government reform was never implemented.

By 1913, on the eve of World War I, missionaries provided nearly all of the education in Cameroon. Certain languages were being used widely: Duala, Bali/ Mungaka, Bulu, and Fang. In that year, there were 45,000 mission students, compared to 844 pupils in four government schools.[35] This represented about 6 percent of school-aged children, and it was much closer to the situation in the Gold Coast/Ghana than Senegal.

All mission schools closed, however, from 1914 to 1916. With its defeat, Germany had to give up its territories, and German Kamerun was divided unevenly between the British and the French for administration, France gaining about four-fifths of the territory. The German language "vanished almost overnight from the Government offices, from the commercial houses, from the churches, from the schools" (Fonlon 1969, 36). Basel missionaries were expelled in 1917, and French missionary replacements did not arrive until 1919.[36] France allowed the American Presbyterians to stay (Gardinier 1985, 338), but French missionaries would need to take over approximately four hundred missions in Cameroon (Dah 1983, 116). The Mill Hill Catholics arrived in the British Cameroons, introducing the use of Pidgin to schools and churches, as they had done in Nigeria.

Most of the Islamized north remained closed to missionary activity until after World War I, with the exception of one school at Garoua established in 1906. Norwegians obtained permission from French administrator to work in Ngaoundere in 1925 (Dronen 2009, 61). Their purpose was to work among the "pagan" Mbum, not the Muslim Fulbe. They quickly realized, however, that the Mbum were more Islamized than they thought and therefore expanded north among the Dii people (Dronen 2009, 62). In general, powerful Muslim *lamidos* closed their territories to Christian missionaries.

After its transfer from German administration, Cameroon experienced differing language policies in British and French zones. British policy was relatively more consistent with German precedent, but it was applied with even more laxity than in their other possessions. They administered the "Cameroons" as a province of neighboring Nigeria, and because of its distance from Lagos, this

---

[35] The Basel mission had 16 main stations and taught about half of those 45,000 students in its many schools (Dah 1983, 34). Presbyterians had 9,564 pupils in 125 boarding schools (Mokosso 1987, 41). Baptists and Catholics taught the remaining mission pupils.

[36] In 1925, the Basel Mission was allowed back in the British portion of the territory (Stumpf 1979, 117).

area was "virtually abandoned as far as government action regarding schools was concerned" (Vernon-Jackson 1967, 16).

As in Ghana, the British administrators were influenced by the Phelps-Stokes Commission, which had recommended that schools adapt to local realities, including using local languages (King 1971, 56). Still, the government's participation was slight. Even as late as 1947, there were only 7 government schools out of a total of 250 schools in British Cameroons (Report by His Majesty's Government 1948, 17). The vast majority were mission schools, which saw the inherent utility of using local languages in their evangelization efforts. In 1958/59, there were eighty-four mission stations engaged in education work in British Cameroons: fifty Catholic, twenty-two Basel, and twelve Cameroon Baptist; this was an increase from twenty-three mission stations in 1947 (Great Britain, Colonial Office, 1958, 381). The number of schools in British Cameroons at that time was 527, more than doubled from ten years earlier (Great Britain, Colonial Office, 1958, 375), enrolling about 10 percent of school-aged children. Though the British were not very involved and did not put forward an official language policy until 1953, most missions were practicing what would be prescribed: The local language should be used where the majority spoke it; a "dominant vernacular" was to be used in mixed areas; and English was to be used where there was no common language.

In contrast, from the beginning of its administration (1919) in French Cameroun, the French required the use of French in government schools. Fonlon notes that "the French zone ... developed a well-organized, though very selective, educational system using French as the official language" (1969, 38). A decree by the French governor in 1920 granted missions three years within which to dismantle vernacular education, tolerating it only for religious subjects. In 1946 the teaching of vernaculars was banned completely (Gardinier 1963, 31). A few missions maintained the practice, however, despite the ban. This could have been significant, given the proportion of mission to government schools. In 1947, only 16 percent of students attended public schools. In general, however, the French language increased noticeably in importance.

On both sides, there was a gradual reduction in attention to vernacular languages, even by missions, partly in response to preferences of the population (Mokosso 1987, 46). The Basel Mission (on the British side), for example, reduced the number of its vernacular schools from 351 in 1943 to 93 in 1952 (Stumpf 1979, 127). In 1956, a conference of the British colonial administration and missions called for a decrease in the use of Pidgin and the vernacular in favor of English, and by 1958, the government required that only English be used in education (Stumpf 1979, 128).

To summarize, until the very end of its administration, British colonial policy in Cameroon favored the use of the vernacular as a medium of instruction for the first few years of school. French colonial policy tried to curb the use of vernaculars in schools from the outset, though some mission schools continued the practice. The commonality was a lack of government attention to mass education. The French government was much more actively involved, but even as late as 1958, in French Cameroun, there were only 330,893 students in primary school, nearly 70 percent of them in private schools (Le Vine 1964, 78). There was not much in the way of secondary provision, even in a territory with a relatively large missionary presence. In 1925, only 72 students attended one secondary school. By 1958, this had jumped to 7,590 secondary students – half government, half private (Le Vine 1964, 78). But enrollment said little about retention. Only one-fifth of those who began primary school received their secondary school leaving certificate. Half of those dropped out by the end of the first year. Le Vine calculates that only 0.1 percent of children who began primary school finished secondary school (1964, 76–77).[37] There were no schools of higher education until 1960.

The French side was more successful at educating its population, not because of more active government policy, but because of the continued work of missions. In 1950, French Cameroun had 12 percent of its school-aged children enrolled compared to 9 percent in British Cameroons; in 1958, the French attention and British neglect showed more clearly, with 20 percent of school-aged students enrolled in the French side versus 10 percent in the British side. In 1959, just before independence, the combined territory had 24 percent of its school-aged population enrolled – 435,000 students in primary and 9,300 students in secondary school (Mitchell 2007). Secondary enrollment was thus only 2 percent of the total.

Cameroon's mixed colonial and mission influence produced a relatively widespread primary education (as in Ghana) but highly restricted secondary (as in Senegal). As independence approached, several of Cameroon's languages had written form, as a result of the long mission presence. In 1960, thirteen more languages had been added to the three that had been transcribed at the turn of the century.

CONCLUSION

Senegal reveals the lack of interest paid by primarily Catholic missionaries and administrators to indigenous languages for evangelization or education. Its major language, Wolof, was written early, and though it was a mother tongue for nearly 40 percent of its population, it explicitly was not used in schools. Senegal entered independence with this sole major indigenous language written. Ghana shows the variations among Protestant missionaries but an eventual convergence upon a vernacular-based education policy, and it entered independence with eight of its languages written for 63 percent of its population, the major ones being used in school. Cameroon's history reveals both impulses at

---

[37] He cites a UNESCO Cameroonian Educational Planning Group Preliminary report that traced a group of 60,231 children who began education in 1947. Only 2,157 finished the primary cycle, and only 82 finished secondary.

work, which left Cameroon at independence with sixteen written languages, covering 44 percent of its population, but a reduction in their use in schools across the territory.

It should be clear that the policies and interactions between missions and colonial administrators were far from neat. Missions varied considerably, particularly among Protestants (Wesleyan vs. Bremen, for example). British policy was from the start much more laissez-faire, though in British Cameroons this was more evident than in Ghana. French administrators aimed to take earlier control in Senegal and demonstrated this also in Cameroon. In 1959, Ghana and Cameroon had relatively high percentages of school-aged students enrolled, but Ghana had much higher secondary enrollment as well. Senegal, with less than half of the other territories' numbers enrolled overall, paid more attention to secondary students as a proportion than did Cameroon.

Even in these three territories with more than usual missionary penetration (Cameroon and Ghana) or metropolitan interest (Senegal), the colonial aim was explicitly *not* a rationalized linguistic environment. Education in the European language was for a tiny cohort until World War II. Only with the inducement of the wars did colonial administrations change their lax attitudes, spurred by conscription needs, metropolitan insistence on "developmental" aims for the colonies, and returning veterans. But even after the push, enrollment in secondary school across Africa was minuscule at independence. Apart from Ghana and Mauritius, with 19 percent and 22 percent, respectively, no other sub-Saharan African country had more than 6 percent gross secondary enrollment in 1960; more than half had gross secondary enrollment of 2 percent or less (World Bank 1988, table A-8, 132).

This chapter has shown the sharp variation in French and British colonial policy and the strong influence of missionaries as agents of education and language transcription. It revealed that colonial administrators, unlike state-builders in Europe, were not interested in mass education, content with the production of only a few elites to aid in their administration. Therefore, the standardization of language across an entire population did not have a high priority. In short, regardless of the style of rule, it resulted in societies fragmented vertically by differing access to education.

3

Language Choices in Independent African States

At independence, new African leaders had a choice as to the language policy they would pursue in education. To promote education in general was not in question; this was part of the bargain they had struck with an expectant population. As the medium of instruction, they could choose either a former colonial language or local language(s) exclusively, or they could combine the two at different points in the curriculum. Other scholars have noted that while many leaders rhetorically lauded the virtues of African languages in populist campaigns, most settled into the pragmatic comfort of continuing to use imported languages in official domains, including education (Laitin 1992; Mansour 1993, 119; Simpson 2008, 4–8; Mazrui and Mazrui 1998). Motivations for this choice are imputed to be either operational efficiency, lack of political will, or self-serving separation from the masses (Mazrui and Mazrui 1998; Fishman 1971; Mansour 1993, 122). This chapter examines reasons behind these motivations and explores how they differed from the motivations of leaders forming nations in earlier contexts. It argues that in an environment of stable borders and low direct taxation, African leaders were motivated *neither* to spread a common language widely throughout their territories *nor* to elevate local languages out of a sense of nationalist pride. This resulted in little attention to education in general and the maintenance of colonial precedent in the specifics of language medium, except in unusual ideologically driven instances.

The passage to independence did not mark a clean break with the colonial past, and this is especially true among French colonies. This chapter will explain why this is so and discuss how this contributed to choices leaders made about the languages used in education. It will begin by surveying the range of literacy levels across Africa at independence and highlight education policies enacted by new governments. It will show that these bore little relationship to demographic distinctions but were almost uniformly continuations from the colonial period. Even up to 1990, with only a few exceptions, all countries maintained the policies begun by their colonizer. And unlike earlier nation builders, they were ambivalent about enforcing a single lingua franca, whether indigenous or foreign. Though school enrollment figures continued to increase, literacy levels in any unifying language remained relatively low. Therefore, virtually all African countries remained multilingual by default. Unlike other scholars who attribute this multilingual character to the force of subnational language elites opposing a rationalizing center, this analysis sees no such strong opposing preferences in either direction. Inertia and neglect, rather than attention, is the rule. Policies did become more deliberate however, in the 1990s, at which time multilingualism took center stage as a conscious policy in many new states. The next two chapters will take up the reason for that shift.

EDUCATION AND LITERACY AT INDEPENDENCE

In the waning years of colonial rule, education had become a priority. Pushed by international development norms and voting publics who needed justification for continuing colonial involvement, Britain, France, and Belgium had begun to invest heavily in education (Young 1994a, 208–213). Rather than entrusting it entirely to missions, colonial administrators had begun asserting operational control over budgets and literacy outcomes. Similarly, leaders of newly independent states faced publics that demanded immediate modernization and greater equality, which were seen to flow from universal access to primary education. Independence leaders presided over populations at different educational starting points. Enrollments in former British colonies were relatively high (32 percent), followed by former Belgian colonies (26 percent), while average rates in French (19 percent) and "other" territories (10 percent) were especially low. As noted in the previous chapter, this can largely be explained by the fact that British and Belgian colonies had much earlier and more widespread missions, deeply involved in education. Figure 3.1 shows this distinction.

The variation within these groupings is also notable. While some of it has to do with size of territories and the easier spread of schools within small, densely populated areas, much can also be attributed to mission presence. Within the French colonies, Gabon, Congo, Cameroon, and Madagascar had much higher mission presence than other territories. This is also true of the Belgian Congo and Liberia. Not surprisingly, these variations in enrollments translated into differing literacy rates at independence. Figure 3.2 plots literacy rates around 1960.

Average literacy rates in French Africa were clearly the worst overall. Without the tiny islands of Comoros, the average would be only 10 percent. On the continent, Cameroon, Algeria, Congo-Brazzaville, and Gabon hovered around 15 percent literate. Mauritania's figure is slightly misleading, since it counts literate population eleven and older, rather than fifteen and older, as do other states. British Africa had average literacy rates of 31 percent, more than twice as high as the French territories. This distinction is markedly stronger than the difference in enrollments in the same period and again reflects the much longer

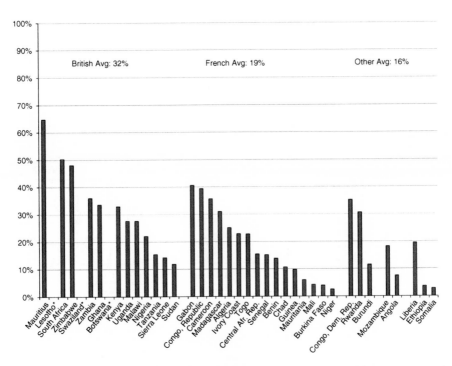

FIGURE 3.1. Percentage of School-Aged Children Enrolled in 1960. The percentage of population aged 5–19 in school. *Source:* Calculated from Mitchell (2007). *Unfortunately, several small countries were not included. It is evident from other sources (e.g., World Bank 1988), however, that Lesotho, Swaziland, and Botswana had high enrollment rates at independence. They are inserted approximately where they would fall in comparison to other British territories, but actual percentages are not indicated (nor included in the average), because they are based on less reliable data.

history of mission presence in British Africa. The drive toward higher enrollment at the end of the colonial period pushed the averages closer, but the head start in the British Africa was appreciable and provided those states with a wider base of literacy at the beginning of independence.

With most new states below 30 percent literate, however, one of the strongest public demands at independence was for universal primary education (Sutton 1965, 72). Coleman agreed that leaders felt palpable pressure from the public for expansion of enrollments. Education was a "requisite" for the "badge of modernity" (Coleman 1965, 39). Having won the right to govern, new leaders had to provide more services and require less of their citizens. Abernethy's study of Nigeria attributes this expansion to the new political elite's need for a "dramatic welfare scheme to win popular support" (Abernethy 1969, 133–136). Indeed, by 1970, the earliest year that comparable calculations are available, African states

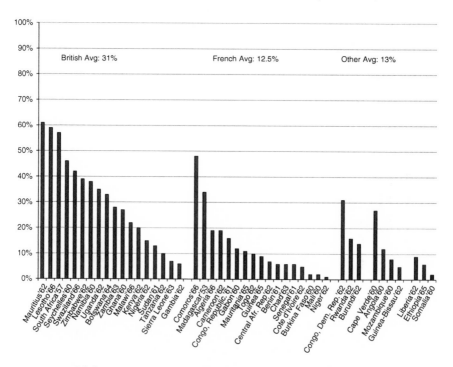

FIGURE 3.2. Adult Literacy circa 1960. *Source:* Drawn from UNESCO 1977 and 1988. Djibouti, Sao Tome and Principe, Equatorial Guinea, and Eritrea are not included, because their earliest available dates were after 1980.

were allocating an average of 17 percent of government expenditures on education (ADEA 1999). This spending varied widely. Perhaps not surprisingly, given their relatively larger task, former French colonies were not especially stingy when it came to educational spending. Though outpaced by the three former Belgian colonies, which spent an average of 24 percent, former French colonies allocated an average of 19 percent, with some, such as Mali, at 31 percent and Burkina Faso and Congo-Brazzaville allocating 26 percent and 24 percent, respectively. Anglophone states averaged less (15 percent), none allocating more than 20 percent. Ghana spent relatively generously, while a few, such as Zambia, spent only 8 percent of government revenue on education. Likely this was because of the continuing high number of private or mission schools.

On average, former British colonies had 36 percent of their primary education provided privately as of 1970 – Ghana, Kenya, and Tanzania occupied the low end of the spectrum with only 2 to 5 percent of their primary schools private; Zambia, Mauritius, Nigeria, Sudan, Botswana, and Gambia were at a middle level (27–38 percent); and Swaziland, Sierra Leone, Zimbabwe, and Lesotho had virtually all of their primary education provided by private schools (76–100 percent) (World Bank 1988, 137). This is in contrast to the average in former

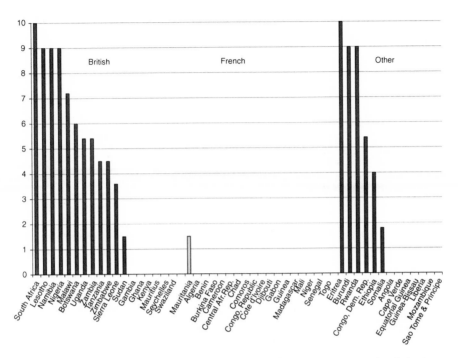

FIGURE 3.3. Intensity of Local Language Use at Independence or 1960, by Colonizer. *Source:* See Appendix A. South Africa, Liberia, and Ethiopia coded at 1960; all others coded at their independence year.

French colonies of only 17 percent private primary schools, this figure driven upward by Gabon (49 percent) and Cameroon (54 percent), central African states that had much higher percentages of missions in their territories than other Francophone states during the colonial period.

For most governments, however, education initially was a spending priority. They had options, however, about what *type* of education they would pursue. Would the medium of instruction be a European language or an African language? Most opted to follow the pattern established by their colonial predecessors. Figure 3.3 illustrates the choices made upon independence about the medium of instruction. As explained in the Introduction, I scored states on a scale of 0 to 10, capturing both the proportion of existing language groups affected and the extent of language use across the curriculum.

Clearly, former British and other territories were maintaining their use of local languages that began under colonial rule, while Francophone states were not. Only Mauritania had introduced Arabic as a comedium with French. The specifics of each country's policies are discussed in Appendix A.

To test whether indeed the colonial precedent is playing the strong role I attribute to it, I run a simple OLS regression with the Independence ILLED score

TABLE 3.1. *Regression: Determinants of Intensity of Language Use at Independence.* Outcome: Intensity of Local Language Use in Education *(0–10)*

	Model 1	Model 2	Model 3	Model 4
Constant	11.49	15.03	15.73	11.87
French	2.21**	1.77*	1.87*	1.45
	(1.07)	(1.07)	(1.07)	(1.06)
British	1.29	.71	.23	.60
	(1.03)	(1.05)	(1.17)	(1.0)
Population (log)[a]	2.59**	2.93**	2.91**	2.09**
	(.78)	(.78)	(.81)	(.91)
Linguistic Fractionalization[b]	3.5**	3.05*	3.25*	2.45
	(1.67)	(1.64)	(1.65)	(1.65)
Literacy rate[c]		4.45*	4.02*	4.33*
		(2.42)	(2.43)	(2.37)
Democracy[d]			.76	
			(.56)	
Percentage population with a written language, 1960[e]				2.68*
				(1.60)
N	49	49	49	49
Adj R^2	.37	.40	.415	.422

Standard errors in parentheses.

*Significant at .1 level.

**Significant at .05 level.

[a] World Bank, WDI.

[b] Scale: 0 to 1. Language speakers calculated from Lewis 2009. I created a linguistic fractionalization index using Rae's formula: $1 - \Sigma g_i^2$, where g_i is the proportion of the population in language group i. Adapted from Gary Cox (1997, 205).

[c] Scale: 0 to 1. At or near year of independence. South Africa, Liberia, and Ethiopia recorded at 1960. Drawn primarily from UNESCO 1977 and UNESCO 1988 but supplemented with ADEA 1999 and World Bank figures.

[d] Autocracy = 1, Intermediate = 2, Democracy = 3 (adapted from Marshall and Jaggers's *Polity IV* database); Cape Verde, Sao Tome and Principe, and Seychelles assigned comparable scores from Freedom House.

[e] Date of Bible portion as proxy for written language. Drawn from Grimes 1996 and 2000.

as the outcome (Table 3.1). Though it is with an admittedly small group of cases (forty-nine), the findings are suggestive. Consistent with my explanation, being a former French territory is significantly associated with less intense use of local languages as media of instruction. British identification is in the predicted direction, but it remains insignificant because the "other" category also includes several states using local languages (Rwanda, Burundi, Democratic Republic of Congo, and Ethiopia). Also, as will be explained further in the chapter, a few Anglophone states (Ghana and Kenya, for example) undertook early experiments with "Straight to English," and the independence snapshot captures this period.

It is clear that large populations correspond with more intense use of local languages in education. Language fractionalization is negatively associated with intensity of use in the first three models, suggesting that extremely fractionalized states may have difficulty using all of their languages. I will look more closely at this later in the chapter. Higher literacy rates also correspond with intense use of local languages in education. Of course, as seen previously, literacy was much lower in former French colonies, but the fact that the French group remains significant even when literacy rates enter the equation strengthens my argument that there is something else going on within this subset of cases. Democracy is strongly correlated (.49) with former British colonies in that period, though it does not contribute to explaining the intensity of local language use. Scholars such as Liu (2011) have suggested that democracies are more likely to enact minority-language-supportive policies, but this regression does not support that view. Finally, I include the percentage of the population that had a written language in 1960. As discussed in the last chapter, missions were much less active in transcription in the French colonies. The fact that this variable reduces the significance of the French dummy and the language fractionalization variable lends support to the role of transcription as a causal mechanism that I describe in the following chapter.

Overall, the regression supports Figure 3.3, reiterating the strong role played by colonial history in explaining the policies adopted by African states at independence. This path dependence belies the abundance of rhetoric about language that agitated the independence period.

INDEPENDENCE POLICIES – THEORY AND PRACTICE

African states achieved independence "precisely at the moment that mono-lingualism in Europe and the US reached its zenith" (de Swaan 2001, 64). The modernization paradigm dominated development discourse, expecting that African citizens would shed their parochial attachments and transfer their loyalty to the central state. The congruence of state and nation was to be achieved through the integrating force of universal education. In early independent Ghana, Nkrumah spoke of liberation as freedom from particularisms, erasing of tribalism (Verlet 1986, 72). At this time, influential scholars such as Deutsch drew on the European unitary model when envisioning the beneficial nationalism that would derive from increased social communication through higher levels of education (Deutsch 1953/1966).[1] Lerner envisioned the combined forces of urbanization, literacy, and media growth that would propel the transition to an integrated, participative society (Lerner 1958, 60).

---

[1] See also Connor (1972) for a nuanced critique of Deutsch's equivocation about the unproblematic benefits of mobilized populations.

Africanists such as James Coleman also contemplated the socializing and integrative roles of education. He noted in 1963 that the "knotty problem of how to create nations out of heterogeneous cultural materials" (Coleman 1963, 409) was similar in Africa to that in other regions. Though initially it might intensify divisions among ethnic, regional, or parochial groups, he concluded that in the "long run it will be education and the changes it stimulates which will bridge or reduce these gaps" (Coleman 1965, 30). He and others identified the potential short-term imbalances created if mass education produced too many school leavers for the economy to absorb, and a potential climate of elitism (Coleman 1965, 29, 527, 354; Abernethy 1969). Yet they continued to hold to the long-run "integrative role of education in nation building and political development" (Coleman 1965, 30). Education systems "can be powerful instruments in forging national unity, in developing a common language of political communication, and in providing exposure to, if not inculcating a positive affect for, national symbols and goals" (Coleman 1965, 227). Clearly, for these scholars, the language of education was naturally to be a single, unifying one.

Other scholars, drawing primarily on the Indian experience, recognized that the medium of education might not necessarily be singular. The germ of the formal idea that languages could be used as the building blocks of states rather than trying to erase them in favor of monolingualism can be traced to early language planners in the 1960s, and a field of inquiry called Language Policy and Language Planning (LPLP).[2] A major point of agreement with modernization scholars was the inherent changeability of languages and their use, and thus the potential for altering outcomes through planning. Though these scholars conceded that much language change is not planned, they were confident that deliberate attempts to influence the social use and status of language would be successful (Ferguson 1977, 9). Charles Ferguson argued that "the functional change which is most often the focus of political pressure and governmental policy making at the national level is probably the choice of medium of instruction in the education system" (Ferguson 1977, 12). As they readily admitted, the new states of Africa and Asia became a laboratory for language planning.[3]

These LPLP theorists shared assumptions of how linguistically plural states would arise. Das Gupta describes the Indian progression of policies concerning language, which had influenced his vision of the potential in other developing states: First, voluntary organizations (associations, parties, movements) express language demands, creating the impulse for a change in language policy. Second, the impulses are processed by the legislatures, which "treat them in the context of other competing demands emerging from the general political scene." Finally,

---

[2] The seminal work in the field was Fishman, Ferguson and Das Gupta, eds. 1968. See also Fishman 1974 and Rubin et al. 1977.

[3] "The language problems of developing nations present sociolinguistics with a virtually inexhaustible and untouched field for the exploration of its central hypotheses and concerns" (Fishman 1968, 13).

"once an ordered ranking of the values has been reached, obviously in terms of the political ordering of the leading group in the legislature, the relative place of the language policy area is established and appropriate legislation is sought" (Das Gupta 1976, 197).

Brian Weinstein added a nuance between mass and elite sentiment about language. He pointed out that, historically, the language issue could remain dormant until it was mobilized by "language strategists" – cultural elites who could transform language into "a symbol for new community frontiers" (Weinstein 1982, 62). Once these elites converted language into a form of capital that yielded tangible benefits, "Africans, Asians, and Latin Americans in particular called for the expansion of educational systems and then began to appeal for instruction through the mother tongue. Change in education policy has thus been one of the most popular promises of revolutionaries and nationalist leaders in these parts of the world" (Weinstein 1982, 100).

But was it? In fact, reported Coleman in 1965, "post-colonial political elites have shown surprising restraint on the issue of indigenization of the school curriculum" (Coleman 1965, 45). Certainly in Francophone Africa the French system of education went virtually unchallenged (Debeauvais 1965, 88), and the rhetoric of early Francophone African presidents reflected the French model. Debeauvais noted that "all leaders gave priority to the task of strengthening national unity within the boundaries drawn by the colonial powers at the end of the nineteenth century" (1965, 86). According to this scholar, these leaders saw education "as a political factor of overriding importance" and for this reason "French has been chosen as a national language wherever linguistic plurality might have favored one group over another" (Debeauvais 1965, 88). Cameroon's President Ahidjo promoted the idea of an essentially French fatherland, "implying cultural unity and even homogeneity" (Stark 1980, 279). In a 1962 speech, he claimed that "leaders ... should search very diligently for those characteristics most calculated to help in integrating the tribes one into the other, in merging them together, in order to hasten national unity."[4] Similarly, Cote d'Ivoire's first president, Houphouët-Boigny, claimed the unifying force of French in an early speech to Ivoirians (Knutsen 2008, 165).

In Senegal, President Senghor's attachment was more subtle. He promoted the idea of Negritude – a vein of thought that emerged in the inter-War period from African and Caribbean intellectuals based in Paris (see Wilder 2005) – which celebrated essential African characteristics that were opposed to European. Senghor did not advocate separation from the metropole, however, but described a process of assimilation that would incorporate this essentiality, leading to a hybrid, elevated black and European culture in Africa (Cumming 2005, 236). Any initial radical tendencies in his ideas were swiftly moderated. Refusing to challenge French dominance, "Senghor's Negritude has been, above all, a bridge to the colonial establishment" (Markovitz 1969, 41). As to language, Senghor initially

---

[4] Ahidjo speech to a Party Congress in July 1962, cited in Stark 1980, 279.

advocated bilingualism – scientific works written in French, with poetry, theater, tales written in indigenous languages. But after 1958, his ideas began to shift (Ndao 2008; Senghor 1962), and, according to a biographer, in 1963 Senghor explicitly rejected his rhetoric supporting indigenous languages: "He not only dropped his advocacy of self-expression in an indigenous tongue but became a foremost exponent of the utility and aesthetic necessity of French" (Markovitz 1969, 62). While the African school must "not uproot the student from his milieu ... but integrate the African values of civilization,"[5] it would still do it in French.

In addition to providing unity, the French language was upheld as central to maintaining new states' linkages to international commerce and diplomacy. Pragmatic reasons for keeping French were the desire to facilitate technical cooperation with France and fears of downgrading the academic level, "which therefore prevailed over practical considerations that might have led to primary school teaching in the vernacular" (Debeauvais 1965, 87). Coleman concludes that "most of the former French colonies display a virtually uncritical adherence to the French school curriculum" (Coleman 1965, 46). He attributes this, first, to the socialization and self-interestedness of the educated class: Having been educated entirely in the French system, "they know no other, and as a product of that system, they have a vested interest in it," and, second, to their practical dependence on the metropole for teachers and aid (Coleman 1965, 46).

Guinea was the only country to attempt to sever its ties with France at independence, a unique refutation of continued French hegemony, and this was evident in its decision to use several languages in education. President Sékou Touré argued that the "African elite is not to be recognized by its diplomas, or by its theoretical or practical knowledge, or by its wealth, but only by its devotion to the evolution of Africa" (Coleman 1965, 38). Even Guinea, however, did not implement its radical education measures until ten years after declaring independence, and these ended with the death of their ideological founder. And while North African Francophone states – Algeria and Mauritania (as well as Morocco and Tunisia, which are not included in this study) – did increase their use of Arabic after independence, across sub-Saharan Francophone Africa there were no early attempts to question the primacy of French in official and educational domains.

Anglophone Africa demonstrated more early experimentation and somewhat more variation in policy. Though one might have expected language elites to be more invested in thoroughgoing mother tongue education in Anglophone Africa, many states in fact initially attempted a "straight to English" model. Gambia, Ghana, Kenya, and Zambia experimented with English-only schools in the first few years of independence. Within Anglophone Africa, only in Tanzania and Malawi were there early, determined efforts to introduce a single indigenous language nationwide. Mazrui and Mazrui note that it took extraordinary

---

[5] Senghor speech to the National Assembly 1963, cited in Markovitz 1969, 79.

measures by quasi-autocratic states to enact such radical language nationalization policies (Mazrui and Mazrui 1998, 96). But only Gambia and Zambia continued their English-only experiments, while the other two early experimenters and the rest of the former British colonies quickly returned to the familiar habit of using several local languages as the basis of the primary curriculum with a transition to English in later grades. The variation at the local level and high percentage of private schools in Anglophone Africa continued to reflect a legacy of British decentralization.

Whether their rhetoric supported European or African languages, the fact is that very few leaders genuinely tried to spread a standard language broadly among their citizens. Instead, leaders continued the colonial practice of restricting schooling of the masses to low-level vocational training. Many writing on Africa have reasoned that the lack of motivation for the spread of English or French was "elite closure," so dubbed by Myers-Scotton (1993) – not wanting (themselves or their children) to compete for jobs with other entrants. In places where efforts to spread languages have been enforced, there may be alternate explanations: Benrabah argues that in Algeria, policy makers are implementing the Arabization language policy for the majority of the population "in order to enable their own children educated in French to have less competition for the well-paying jobs and prestigious career options (modern business and technology) which require competence in French" (Benrabah 2007, 204).

Throughout independence Africa, in all but a few instances, the colonial precedent prevailed. It is true that a wave of "indigenization" experiments swept across the continent in the 1970s – indigenous in content and in language. Mobutu's *authenticité* (1972) reinforced Congo/Zaire's four vehicular languages in the education system; Somalia's military regime (1972) introduced Somali's new script; Madagascar's *malgasization* (1972) brought Malagasy exclusively into the curriculum; Burundi's *Kirundization et ruralization* (1973) reinforced Kirundi; Amin in Uganda decreed that Swahili would be a national language (1973); Niger began experiments in Hausa and Zarma (1973); the Central Africa Republic's "Collective Promotion Schools" (1974) introduced Sango (1974); Togo's *authenticité* movement (1975) introduced Ewe and Kabiye in schools as subjects; Congo Republic envisioned "people's schools" (1977) that would use Lingala and Kituba; Cote d'Ivoire's government took up the rhetoric about reviving cultural heritage through languages (1977); Mali opened four schools teaching in Bambara (1978); Burkina Faso's revolution promised to introduce mother tongues in schools (1979); and the same year, Senegal began experimental classes in Wolof and Serer.

In the 1970s, it appeared that local languages might indeed be gaining ground. With the exception of North African Arabization initiatives, however, it was only *outside* Francophone Africa that new experiments "stuck." Congo/Zaire and Burundi were simply reinforcing the Belgian colonial system that had used a limited number of local languages. Experimental schools in Central African Republic, Togo, Congo-Brazzaville, Cote d'Ivoire, Burkina Faso,

Guinea, and Senegal had all ended after a few years. Rhetoric was not enough to overcome the deficiencies in materials and the continuing connection with the metropole. Virtually none of the former French colonies sustained their experiments in African language education.

CONTINUING EXTERNAL INFLUENCE – LA FRANCOPHONIE AND THE COMMONWEALTH

Why should France continue to exert such strong influence? This section will show that after the wave of independence in the 1960s, the relationship between France and its former colonies was different from that of Britain and its own. It was an attempt to control versus guide, ideology versus pragmatism – distinctions that were established at the start of the colonial period. I will first describe the relationship of France with its former colonies through the lens of la Francophonie, and then contrast this with Britain's connection to Africa via the Commonwealth. Looking at aims, organization, and budgets, it is clear that the linkages between France and its former colonies remained much closer and more hierarchical, facilitating easier communication of policy preferences, than those between Britain and its possessions, the latter permitting more leeway for local experimentation.

"Neither for historians nor for politicians does the moment of independence mark a clear dividing line in Francophone Africa," says Francophone Africa scholar Cruise O'Brien (1991, 150). He and others have written of the networks emanating from the French president's palace to Africa, showing convincingly that even after decolonization, the franc zone, military agreements, technical assistance, and private networks enabled France to maintain its historic mission in Africa (Hale 2009; LeVine 2004; Smith and Glaser 1997). The present study is particularly concerned with how the relationship influenced language policy, and for this, the central actor is la Francophonie. Michelman succinctly describes France's historical obsession with linguistic purity (1995, 217). He explains that as early as 1539, the Edict of Villers-Cotterêts was intended to make "language a tool for consolidating and extending royal power over peoples who lived outside the Ile de France and against clerics seeking to maintain the dominant role of Latin" (Michelman 1995, 176). French geographer Onésime Reclus first used the term "francophonie" in 1880 to designate the French-speaking world (Hagège 1996, 137). Today, "la Francophonie" comprises fifty-seven member states and governments, an outgrowth of the French colonial empire after the independence of Francophone Africa. With the advent of the Fifth Republic in 1958, France recognized a need to make changes to the original mission of "Greater France," talking of its *"besoin de rayonnement"* (a need to spread culture) and wish to be at the heart of a Franco-African "family." In so doing, the French political classes were able to retain a "longstanding emphasis on centralized states as the key to societal progress and a strong focus on the French language as the ideal vehicle for conveying Paris's universal values" (Cumming 2005, 238).

The modern idea of la francophonie originated with Léopold Senghor, Hamani Diori, and Habib Bourgiba, presidents of Senegal, Niger, and Tunisia, respectively, who proposed a "Commonwealth à la française" in order to ensure that broken administrative ties would not lead to severed cultural and economic linkages. La Francophonie's first manifestation was a conference of education ministers of French-speaking countries in 1960, followed by an association of universities in 1961, and of parliaments in 1967. Finally, in 1970 the Agence de Coopération Culturelle et Technique (ACCT) grew out of a loose grouping of former French colonies, becoming the Agence Intergouvernementale de la Francophonie (AIF) in 1995 and renamed the Organisation Internationale de la Francophonie (OIF) in 2005. I will refer to this institution as "The Francophone Agency."

This Francophone Agency, advocated initially by African states and Quebec, was envisioned as an association of countries and governments that shared the language of French in common and whose purpose was to promote its members' cultures and to ensure developmental cooperation among them. France originally did not favor the idea for two reasons. First, France preferred bilateral organs, which it could control entirely, to multilateral organizations, in which its voice would be one of many. And, second, France worried that visibly sponsoring the efforts for such an organization would appear neocolonial. African countries advanced the organization to ensure that they would continue to benefit from Northern cooperation, and Quebec supported it because becoming a member in its own right gave the province additional leverage against the federal government of Canada (Chaudenson 2000, 60). Twenty members founded ACCT in 1970; thirteen were newly independent African states. Another nineteen members had joined by the end of the 1980s, and again more than half of these were in Africa. The High Council of la Francophonie (described later) began publishing its yearly reports in 1985, which gave figures for French speakers within countries around the world. In strict population terms, by the end of the 1980s, Africa made up well over half of the community of la Francophonie. The cultural and linguistic center of the fold, France's population only accounted for 16 percent of the total. Financial contributions are assessed differently, as will be elaborated, but in strictly numerical terms, the heart of la Francophonie was in Africa.

The OIF is headquartered in Paris, and its role is to carry out decisions made at biennial summits in areas of cultural, scientific, technical, economic, and legal cooperation. France, while reluctant to appear at the helm of the organization when it first began, has embraced it wholeheartedly since the late 1980s, and concern with la Francophonie is woven tightly through the most important French bureaucratic structures.

Particularly after the debacle of Rwanda, argues Hale (2009), France had to shift from the earlier hard policies of military intervention, in which "*la françafrique"* acquired negative connotations, to a softer influence. The reorganization of the OIF in the mid-1990s was intended to project France's cleaner image. Hale argues that the OIF operates as an apparently international organization, but it is clearly aimed at extending France's influence. *"La Françafrique* and Francophonie are two sides of the same coin in the relationship between France and Francophone Africa" (Hale 2009, 196).

The Haut Conseil de la Francophonie,[6] chaired by the French president, assists the secretary-general of the OIF, currently the former Senegalese president Abdou Diouf. While members of this council hail from many countries outside France, they are chosen by the French president, and the budget of the High Council is provided by the French minister of foreign affairs. Since 1986, there has been a French minister appointed for la Francophonie and an office within the French Ministry of Foreign Affairs dedicated to overseeing French activities within la Francophonie. Therefore, la Francophonie is not simply a multilateral organization, separated from the center of the French government; it is deeply intertwined with all of the linguistic aspects of French foreign policy.

The overall budget for the OIF is nearly $300 million, and France pays about 60 percent of this amount.[7] Furthermore, contributions by France to *bilateral* Francophonie are much greater than these to multilateral Francophonie, much going directly to French language instruction around the world (such as through the Alliance Française program) and to Radio France International.[8]

In contrast to this ever-closer relationship between France and its former colonies through la Francophonie, the relationship of Britain with its territories has grown looser over time. When Canada gained self-governing "Dominion" status in 1867, the British Empire had to rethink its purpose, and after 1884, it became known as the "British Commonwealth of Nations" (McIntyre 2001, 8). With the Statute of Westminster (1931) formally recognizing the legislative sovereignty of the dominions, and the London Declaration (1950) allowing the coexistence of republican governments with recognition of the British monarch at the head of the Commonwealth, it was possible for most of Britain's newly independent colonies to join this loose affiliation after World War II.

Thus, unlike la Francophonie, which emerged in the wake of decolonization, the Commonwealth existed prior to the independence of most of its member states. Its leadership structure, however, underwent some changes after Africa gained independence. Prior to 1965, British civil servants managed Commonwealth affairs. But in the early 1960s, Ghana's first president, Kwame Nkrumah, "led the move to establish a neutral Commonwealth

---

[6] Changed to "Consultative Council" in the mid 2000s and then very recently to "Permanent Council."

[7] Budget figures from A.Wolff, Chargé de Mission, High Council of la Francophonie, pers. comm., March 24, 2005. French contribution from M. Vandepoorter, Chef du Bureau, Service de la Francophonie, pers. comm., April 4, 2005.

[8] M. Vandepoorter, Chef du Bureau, Service de la Francophonie, pers. comm., April 4, 2005.

Secretariat, which came into being in 1965" (McKinnon 2004, 1). The Secretariat was staffed and directed by representatives from all members of the Commonwealth. Currently, fifty-four countries make up the Commonwealth fold. Unlike la Francophonie, where Africa represents more than 50 percent of its population (and 65 percent of its member states), African countries constitute only 17 percent of the population within the Commonwealth. The United Kingdom itself only contributes 5 percent of the Commonwealth's population.[9]

The Commonwealth structure is looser, reflecting the British tradition and the original aims of the Secretariat: Its goal explicitly was *not* to become rigidly institutionalized (Commonwealth Secretariat 1966: 1). The Secretariat is based in London and housed within the same building is its principal operating arm, the Commonwealth Fund for Technical Cooperation (CFTC). This fund was created in 1971, and its purpose was "to provide technical assistance at minimal cost through expert advice, training schemes and specialist seminars" (Doxey 1989, 20). Within the CFTC are various programs, of which the Education Programme is one. Other intergovernmental program agencies include the Commonwealth Foundation, the Commonwealth Scholarship and Fellowship Plan, and the Commonwealth of Learning.

The Commonwealth Parliamentary Association (CPA), founded in 1911, is made up of all members of legislatures, including British offshore islands, central and provincial legislatures in federal states, and assemblies of some dependencies, totaling about fourteen thousand members in 142 branches (Doxey 1989, 165). The CPA holds annual conferences and conducts seminars on parliamentary procedure, the role of MPs, the role of the Opposition, how to manage executive/legislature interface, the independence of judiciary, and relationships with media.

Aside from these well-established links between governments and between professional associations, there are numerous decentralized networks among citizens of Commonwealth states in general. Known as the "People's Commonwealth," these are the several hundred nongovernmental organizations that work on inter-Commonwealth affairs, making the boundaries of the Commonwealth even more diffuse.

Unlike the French government's close links with la Francophonie, Britain has not taken a similar intense interest in the Commonwealth. Several reports on the Commonwealth in the 1990s chastise Britain for its indifference.[10] The Commonwealth Secretariat's budget is much smaller, $73 million for 2010–2011, and Britain contributes about 30 percent of the budget (DFID 2011, 1).

[9] Obviously, both are dwarfed by giant India, whose population makes up nearly 60 percent of the Commonwealth.

[10] E.g., House of Commons FAC, *The Future Role of the Commonwealth* (1996); Rob Jenkins, Paul Gready, Shaun Milton, *Reassessing the Commonwealth* (1997); Thomas Henry Bull Symons, *Learning from Each Other* (1997).

Compared with those of la Francophonie, the budget and goals of the Commonwealth are much more modest. Particularly after Mitterand came to power, the French government began to translate its exclusively bilateral vision of its relationship with former colonies to work through this multilateral organization. The first meeting of heads of state took place in 1986, at which time France set up a ministry for la Francophonie. "By the 1990s, the French government had come to see the Francophone movement as the framework for a useful bloc in the fight for markets and as an arm in the battle against English and American influence" (Wright 2004, 131). The point of impulse has slowly shifted from the South to the North, a transformation not unnoticed by African members, who see in this development a neocolonial cast.

According to Jacques Legendre, secretary-general of the Parliamentary Assembly of la Francophonie, the major orientations of la Francophonie are four: (1) affirmation and organization of a political Francophonie, (2) defense of cultural diversity, (3) respect for human rights and promotion of democracy, (4) engagement in favor of sustainable development (Legendre 2003, 18–23). Placed even before issues of democracy and development are aims of elevating la Francophonie as a political force and defending cultural diversity. A more skeptical description of the purposes of la Francophonie comes from Paulin Djité, analyzing French President Mitterand's announcement in 1989 that France had cancelled the public debt for thirty-five of the poorest countries in Africa, in order to reinforce the idea of the new economic orientation of la Francophonie: "for the African political elite, this new Francophonie is above all a new 'lender of funds' while, for their European and Canadian partners, it is another pragmatic strategy for the achievement of their cultural and linguistic aims" (Djité 1990, 25).

By comparison, the Mission Statement of the Commonwealth Secretariat reads: "We work as a trusted partner for all Commonwealth people as: a force for peace, democracy, equality and good governance; a catalyst for global consensus-building; and a source of assistance for sustainable development and poverty eradication" (Commonwealth Secretariat, iii). It lists as its fundamental values democracy, human rights, equality for women, universal access to primary education, and sustainable development and poverty alleviation. The two main long-term goals of the Secretariat's strategic plan are (1) "To support member countries to prevent or resolve conflicts, strengthen democracy and the rule of law and achieve greater respect for human rights," and (2) "To support pro-poor policies for economic growth and sustainable development in member countries" (Commonwealth Secretariat, 7). La Francophonie and the Commonwealth thus share concerns for peace, democracy, law and good governance, economic and social development, and human rights. But only la Francophonie includes language and cultural diversity within its primary issues of interest.

The relationship between France and la Francophonie and that between Great Britain and the Commonwealth are very different. Furthermore, the position of Africa in each grouping is not parallel. While la Francophonie was founded in emulation of the Commonwealth, it has surpassed the Commonwealth's example. The purposes of the organizations share much in common – peace, democracy, development – but la Francophonie has the added dimension of cultural preservation, which is much less pronounced in the Commonwealth. The structure of la Francophonie has centralized into a potent political force, and it is much more tightly integrated into the foreign policy of its metropole, France. The budgets, while difficult to compare because of greater decentralization in the Commonwealth, reinforce la Francophonie's higher profile. Furthermore, the additional support for la Francophonie by France bilaterally via its Cooperation arm is more seamless than the Commonwealth's overlapping efforts with the UK Department for International Development (DFID).

These institutional differences, undoubtedly arising from distinct French and British imperial legacies, have continued to inform relationships between the "metropole" and the "periphery." As will be further developed in Chapter 4, this has led to France's ideational imprint throughout la Francophonie, and particularly among its African members, whereas Britain remains in the role of "critical observer" to its counterparts in the Commonwealth, leaving its former colonies much more room for variation. Among Francophone states, previously bilateral France/Africa ties were most important in determining education policy; now, France reinforces this strong linkage with its increasingly important role at the center of la Francophonie.

In the language of institutionalism, where differing effects of institutions depend on their perceived legitimacy and the ability of actors to evade them (Firmin-Sellers 2000, 254), France has consistently put more resources into the institutions that monitor compliance with its preferred language policy. This results in much more uniform outcomes within Francophone Africa regarding language use in education.

POLICY INERTIA

By 1990, with only a very few exceptions, states continued the type of educational policies begun under colonial rule. Former French colonies maintained a French-only curriculum, and former British colonies used local languages much more frequently. Only a few Francophone countries were experimenting with local languages by this date. Algeria, Chad, and Mauritania were simply using Classical Arabic (which remained a foreign language for most pupils) along with French, and Madagascar is unique in that it had experienced both British and French rule and had a long history of local language transcription before independence. Only Mali and Niger had at this time begun innovative, small-scale mother tongue experimentation in primary schools. See Figure 3.4.

One could legitimately ask whether this array of policies is an appropriate default position, given the demographic constellation of each state. An

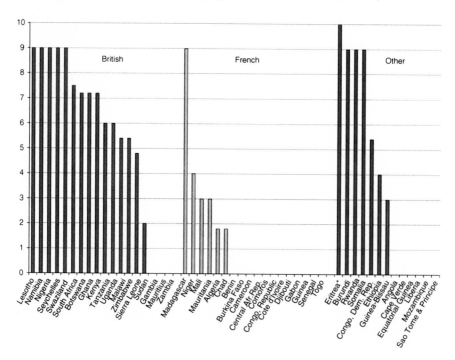

FIGURE 3.4. Intensity of Local Language Use in Education 1990, by Colonizer. *Source:*
See Appendix A.
*Eritrea is coded at 1993, year of its independence (previously part of Ethiopia).

alternative explanation to colonial legacy is a demographic one. The most
obvious factor that likely would influence the number of languages used in
schools is the number of languages that exist in a country. The *Ethnologue*
(Lewis 2009) puts the number of languages in the world at 6,809, of which 2,058
(30 percent) are in Africa. The countries under study contain enormous linguistic
diversity, and it would not be surprising if their language policies mapped closely
onto their demographic contours. After allowing time for colonial heritage to
dissipate, that is, one might expect that in countries with many languages,
multilingual policies would prevail.

At an extreme, however, it might be that existence of too many languages
would make the cost and logistical challenges of using them overwhelming. Thus
a country with many languages might be a likely candidate for maintaining a
European language as a neutral alternative to the expense of introducing all of its
languages in education. A World Bank publication observes: "It is typically
more difficult to adopt coherent policies promoting [local languages] in coastal
countries with hundreds of African languages than in interior or Sahelian
countries with a more limited number of tongues and a few predominant *lingua
franca*" (Easton, Nikiema and Essama 2002, 2).

The prevailing analytical assumption in the standard literature on growth and governance is that the presence of more groups creates more conflict.[11] Causally, this is often attributed to the difficult agreement over public goods. Relating to local language use in education, this would generate an expectation that having too many groups would make agreement over language medium difficult, and a neutral European language would remain the only reasonable alternative. These are opposite functional expectations: One expects that more languages result in greater use of them in education; the other expects that more languages lead to more conflict and less likelihood of agreeing to use them in education. The regression (Table 3.1) seemed initially to point to fractionalization reducing the intensity of language use, though Model 4 cast doubt on this view. To see which assumption is more accurate, one can visually examine the relationship between number of language groups and language use in education.

Though straight language counts are available, they are limited in that they cannot capture relative size and magnitude. Two other measures have been commonly used in measuring diversity in politics: ethnic fractionalization and number of effective ethnic groups (Ordeshook and Shvetsova 1994, 107–109). To correspond specifically with my outcome variable, I calculated my own measures of *linguistic* fractionalization and number of effective *languages*. These new measures utilize figures derived from *Ethnologue* (Lewis 2009), a source that specifies for each country the number of languages and its mother tongue speakers. The fractionalization index[12] (F) essentially shows the probability that two individuals drawn at random from a country will be from different language groups. "Effective number of languages" is a derivation of this index $[1/(1 - F)]$, which gives a more intuitive sense of the number of significant language groups that exist in a country. For example, in raw numbers, Zimbabwe has 14 languages with more than 10,000 speakers, and its fractionalization index is .54 out of 1. However, it has only 2.2 "effective number of languages." This seems to capture relatively well the fact that Zimbabwe has two major language groups – Shona (with more than 10 million speakers) and Ndebele (with 1.5 million) – and its remaining languages are smaller. Nigeria, known for its linguistic diversity, has 249 languages with more than 10,000 speakers. Yet, because only a few of these are extremely dominant – Yoruba, Hausa, and Ibo, with more than 22 million speakers each, and 14 other languages with more than a million speakers – its "effective number of languages" reduces to 8.8. This number is not intended to count the top languages numerically, but to evaluate their weight in the context of the remaining languages in the country. Figure 3.5 plots the intensity of language use in 1990 against the effective number of languages in each state.

[11] Easterly and Levine 1997; Alesina, Baqir, Easterly 1999; Collier and Gunning 1999. But see Habyarimana, Humphreys Posner and Weinstein 2007, discussed in the Conclusion.

[12] This is a derivation of Rae's index: $1 - \Sigma g_i^2$, where g_i is the proportion of the population in language group *i*. Adapted from Gary Cox (1997, 205).

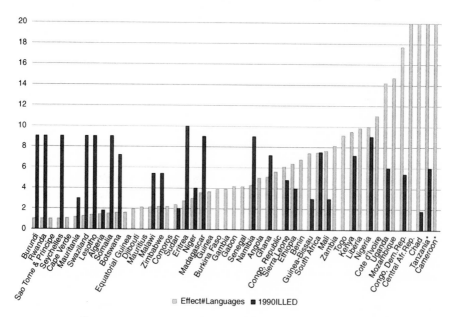

FIGURE 3.5. Effective Number of Languages and Their Intensity of Use in Education, 1990. *Tanzania and Cameroon are truncated at 20 for the sake of the graph; their actual "Effective Number of Languages" are 25 and 37, respectively. Again, Eritrea is coded for 1993.

We see, in fact, that the number of languages bears very little relationship to language policy. While those states with only one major language (Burundi, Rwanda, Seychelles) did seem inclined to use it in education, other states with only one language (Sao Tome and Principe and Cape Verde) did not. And states with similar constellations – Angola and Ghana, for example – had opposite policies. The states with the very highest effective number languages did seem to use them slightly less intensely, but many states with high effective number of languages – Nigeria, Kenya, Uganda – used them near the maximum intensity. Overall in 1990, as at independence, states continued to cluster where their colonial legacy left them.

But regardless of policy – local or foreign language instruction – the reality of low literacy rates in any language meant lack of standardization and de facto multilingualism. A common explanation for multilingualism is a bargaining one. Retaining the assumptions by early language planning theorists Das Gupta and Weinstein – that leaders will mobilize their followers to demand recognition of their languages in return for local support – Laitin (1992) explains the maintenance of multilingualism as a result of bargaining between rulers and regional elites.

He admits that the preferences of elites are normally assumed, rather than established: "The assumption that minority elites mobilize their followers is accepted wisdom in African studies. Yet, in regard to the issue of national language choice, we know very little about the role of leaders from minority language groups. ... The considerable negative power [to block the naming of a language from a different region as the official language of the state] and parochial preferences of regional groups in regard to language have been widely assumed in African political linguistics but not adequately demonstrated" (Laitin 1992, 96–97). Despite this admission, he follows the conventional wisdom and confers upon regional elites a strong preference for preserving their own language and mobilizing their followers to press for the same privilege.

Laitin also assumes that national leaders want to rationalize languages in the face of these opposing regional pulls. For administrative efficiency, national leaders want a standard language. And yet, they gain popularity by promising attention to local languages. At independence, he argues that "nationalist leaders and their parties were ... committed to the development of indigenous African languages and were opposed to the continued use of the language of colonial administration," and the promotion of African languages was "quite a popular political stance" (Laitin 1992, 112).

With this foundation of preferences, Laitin predicts several results: maintenance of a European language, diffuse support for an indigenous national language, growth in pidgins and urban lingua francas, and specific, regional support for vernaculars. All these contribute to a 3 ± 1 outcome. Generally, a person will need to be proficient in a European language, a language of wider communication, and his or her own regional language (three languages). If this regional language happens to be the language of wider communication, the number is reduced to two, and if the regional language is so small that it does not "count" as an official state language, the individual will know a fourth language. These individual repertoires are reflected and reinforced by language policies of the central government.

Though carefully equivocal, Laitin assigns regional elites preferences that implicitly (and necessarily) make them active advocates for language rights for their groups. He says that even where there is no obvious national language, regional elites will have an incentive to press for cultural autonomy: "The cost for the central bureaucracy of avoiding regional secession could well be agreement on language autonomy in the region" (Laitin 1992, 118). Table 3.2 organizes these preferences within a framework similar to Table 1.2 in Chapter 1.

Echoing de Swaan's model for Europe, Laitin argues that rulers desire a standard language for ease of administration, while regional elites prefer to retain their mediation monopoly by retaining local languages. The bargain between these important actors in Laitin's formulation results in a multilingual outcome – rulers exchanging language rights in return for political support from regional elites' language groups. Laitin commends de Swaan's "floral model" of

TABLE 3.2. *Preferences of Actors Regarding Language of Instruction:*
Africa (Laitin)

Ruler	Bureaucrats	Regional Elites	Clergy or Entrepreneurs	Parents	*Outcome*
Standard	*Standard*	*Local*	*N/A*	*Mixed*	***Multilingual***

communication and language choice for explaining incentives toward linguistic homogenization. He argues, however, that it is not sufficient to explain when regional languages might instead gain strength. For this, he models language choices as binary, depending heavily on ethnic entrepreneurs and reflecting individuals' perceptions of economic payoff, in-group status, and out-group acceptance of language shift (Laitin 2007, 32–33, 39–42, 55–56).

Such an interpretation rests on insights derived from European state-building and language planners observing the Indian and Soviet experience. I argue that in Africa at independence, leaders initially convinced of the necessity of a wide-spread standard language changed their minds rapidly. They did not in fact hold strong preferences for standardizing language. At the same time, the assumed presence of regional elites who advocate for their own languages in official domains is not reflected in reality on the ground, as I will show in the following chapters. In Table 3.2, then, there would be no important actor pressuring for local languages. Without this national push and regional pull, multilingualism prior to the 1990s is a default outcome, rather than a deliberate choice.

UNDERSTANDING LEADER PREFERENCES

New leaders perceived themselves in a relatively precarious position at independence. They did not know what the future would hold. Francophone states, with the sole exception of Guinea, were intent on maintaining their ties with the metropole. All recognized the potential for unrest in the masses and saw that the desire for education among the population was widespread and intense; it was a means for social advancement (Debeauvais 1965, 89). It is not surprising that leaders made initial efforts to pacify this potentially restless population with large expenditures on education.

And yet, many of the educational policies mobilized young people for participation in a modern economy that could not afford indefinitely to employ all of them. Efforts toward "practicality" and rural, manual education followed quickly (Debeauvais 1965, 73). The educational entitlement could not be retracted, but it is likely that those occupying leadership positions perceived little problem in the bifurcation created when only a few succeeded in earning spots in secondary school. A paternalist government requires only a minimum of downward communication. Education in the former colonial language ensures continuous replenishment in the ranks of the elites, while still separating it from the masses.

As the previous chapter pointed out, enrollment in secondary school across Africa at independence was minuscule. Even thirty years later, after massive external intervention to bolster education, secondary school enrollment rates remained low. Ten countries had less than 10 percent of students enrolled beyond the primary grades; eleven more had less than 15 percent; eleven more had less than 25 percent. Thus, thirty-two of the forty-five countries for which data are available had secondary enrollment rates of less than 25 percent in 1990 (World Bank WDI).[13] By this date, moreover, overall literacy rates remained very low. Half of the countries in sub-Saharan Africa had literacy rates of less than 50 percent by 1990; some, like Niger and Burkina Faso, were extremely low (11 percent and 16 percent, respectively). If one takes 75 percent as a marker for widespread literacy, only Seychelles, Namibia, Mauritius, Zimbabwe, and South Africa had achieved this by 1990.[14]

Coleman noted with surprise that there was not as much interest in political socialization as he would have expected in the early years of independence. It was a remarkable fact that "in only a few instances have schools been made agencies for manifest political socialization by governing elites" (Coleman 1965, 47). Only revolutionary-centralizing states (for example, Guinea) had taken explicit steps to politicize the school curriculum. He reasoned this was because of dependence on external staff, the outlook of the ruling elites, culturally fragmented societies, and lack of organizational capacity (Coleman 1965, 48). He also observed a devaluation of education, the "strong strain toward anti-intellectualism" (Coleman 1965, 38). Why should this be so? Political socialization and education in a single language serve the specific purpose of national unification. Beneath leaders' rhetoric, the reality was that the national unification that was supposed to result from political socialization and education in a single language was superfluous to their maintenance of power.

Initially, unity seemed an obvious imperative. None of the leaders could have known the consequences of their guaranteed sovereignty through protected borders. As Robert Jackson (1990) and later Jeffrey Herbst (2000) demonstrated admirably, borders in Africa were secure because of conscious decisions by African leaders, international norms, and Western patron protection.[15] As Lonsdale observed, "Nationalist history was ... rather short lived, little longer

---

[13] These figures are calculated by averaging the data provided for 1985 and 1990. This was done because in this period, enrollment figures did actually fall as a result of the debt crisis in many African countries, and it appears that some revision of unrealistically high enrollment data was undertaken.

[14] ADEA 1999, supplemented by UNESCO 1990 and UNESCO 1985 for Algeria and Angola, respectively, and by World Bank WDI for Eritrea (2002), Sao Tome and Principe (1991), and Seychelles (1987).

[15] Crawford Young (1983, 199) opens his essay on the secession claims of Biafra, Katanga, and Eritrea with the statement that "in the postcolonial state system in Africa, no principle has been

than the Black Star decade of Nkrumah's lease on power, 1957–1966" (1981, 150). With economic and political lifelines from abroad, leaders realized that selective patronage was a logical tool, since challenges to their rule would arise from internal competitors, rather than external threats. These internal competitors did not care about language rights. They cared about shares of the spoils.

According to Cooper, "One might even argue that the first generation of African leaders were inclined to dismantle the structures of civic participation precisely because they had witnessed and benefitted from its success in making claims against colonial rulers, claims that they realized might be even harder for them to fulfill than they were for colonial regimes" (Cooper 2008, 172). He explains that the "first generation of African leaders ... soon began to erode the horizontal politics of citizenship in favor of the vertical politics of patrimonialism, suppressing trade unions, farmers' organizations and other associations of civil society, eliminating rival political parties and rendering elections meaningless, stigmatizing dissent as an assault on national unity" (2008, 191).

While the rhetoric of Africa's new independence leaders such as Lumumba, Nkrumah, and Touré envisioned the comprehensive nationalist party as a weapon of liberation (Young 1994b, 258; Schmidt 2005), such radical populism could not sustain itself after the colonial enemy was removed. Crawford Young reveals that though Mobutu's regime initially used unifying symbols, "over time 'authentic Zairïan nationalism' was transformed and personalized, first as '*authenticité*', subsequently as 'Mobutism'" (Young 1994b, 261). Leaders realized they could not, and then that they *did not need to*, create true links with citizens because of access to extracted resources or external sources of funding.

Recalling the reasons for universal education in a standard language given in Chapter 1, it is perhaps surprising that education was pursued at all. The first reason given was so that leaders could break the mediation monopoly of elites in order to tax their citizens directly. In Africa at independence, there was little fiscal mediation preserved by regional elites that leaders had to infiltrate. The small amount of direct taxation collected by local chiefs was reduced still further as new elites tried to demonstrate a rupture with the onerous burdens imposed by the colonial administration.[16] If there is no need to bypass, there is no need to communicate directly.

Second, European states spread a standard language through universal education in order to raise citizen armies. Fighting requires discipline, communication, loyalty, patriotism – all usefully transmitted through a universal education system in a standard language. New states in Africa had agreed not to challenge each other's borders, and so mass armies were not on the horizon. Armies in

---

more fundamental than the sanctity of the existing sovereign units, within their current frontiers." Drawing from Young, Pierre Englebert (2009, chapter 6) shows that this principle has endured forcefully to the present, such that any current secessionist movement makes claims not on the basis of cultural distinction, but on the basis of a colonial border precedent.

[16] See Guyer (1992, 42, 55–56) for the explicit example of Nigeria. She cites Ekeh (1975) for this general phenomenon across Africa.

Africa are extremely small, relative to those of every other region in the world. Fourteen states have armed forces of fewer than ten thousand soldiers. This is not just a product of small populations; Central African Republic, with 4.3 million citizens, has an army of only three thousand; Liberia, with 3.7 million, has an army of only two thousand as it tries to rebuild itself from civil war. Simply looking at the number of armed forces as a percentage of the total labor force, Africa has about half the numbers of other developing regions (World Bank WDI).[17]

Finally, we saw that governments pursued language rationalization in the wake of industrialization in England in order to facilitate control and increase worker productivity Africa has failed to industrialize (Page 2012, ii86). The relative productivity of industry and manufacturing in Africa is far lower than in other regions; a sample of typical low-income African countries showed that in manufacturing as a sector, the value-added share and labor share are about half that of a benchmark middle-income country (Page 2012, ii89).

The outcome, then, has been expenditure on education to pacify potentially restive masses, with little interest in its real effects. Poor literacy scores have persisted overall, even with enrollment increases. Ink and effort have been expended on revealing gaps in literacy; eradicating it became an enormous international enterprise. Many of the gains in Africa's education can be attributed to donor energy and funding. But low literacy rates persisted to the 1990s. Anglophone Africa appeared to be doing relatively better, though much of this is a residue from the colonial period – existing facilities, secondary school leavers, and trained teachers to maintain the momentum.

In the former British colonies, enrollment at independence almost exactly predicted later literacy rates; the correlation between the two figures is .89. The difference between Anglophone and Francophone territories is still pronounced, with the former achieving 62 percent average adult literacy and the latter only 39 percent. Expenditures on education actually fell in more than half of the countries. Certainly this reflected a drying up of resources, which was punished with social mobilization in the late 1980s. It also reflected leaders' lack of motivation.

In 1990, for example, Ghana boasted a literacy rate twice as high as Senegal's: 58.5 percent to 28 percent (ADEA 1999). But it should have been even higher, since the difference at independence was 27 percent for Ghana versus 6 percent for Senegal. At the risk of cynicism, I would suggest that leaders simply were not serious about spreading mass education. Though Ghana's first president, Kwame Nkrumah, was a staunch nationalist and created the Bureau of

---

[17] Armed Forces as percentage of total labor force: Sub-Saharan Africa = .53%; Latin America = .97%; South Asia = 1.11%. Africa's figures do not include Eritrea, Djibouti, or Algeria, which are counted as Middle East/North Africa. It has exactly half of the percentage of citizens out of total population serving in the armed forces as do the other two regions. Armed forces as percentage of total population (calculated): Sub-Saharan Africa = .22%; Latin America and South Asia = .44% each.

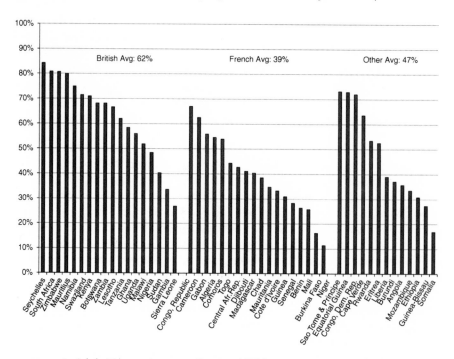

FIGURE 3.6. Adult Literacy in 1990. *Source:* ADEA 1999 except Angola and Somalia (recorded in 1985) from UNESCO 1990 and Seychelles, Sao Tome and Principe, and Eritrea (recorded in 1987, 1991, and 2002, respectively) from World Bank WDI.

Ghanaian Languages to ensure the preservation of African languages, he also instigated "Experimental Schools" in Accra, which used English-medium only, in contrast to the colonial practice of using vernacular medium. This ambivalent attitude translated into spotty application of the mother tongue policy ever since. A multiyear study funded by USAID in the 1990s looked at the quality of education in Ghana, and concluded that educational failure in public schools was caused by a lack of *application* of the mother tongue policy, rather than its presence.[18] On the other hand, teachers (particularly in rural areas) with weaker mastery of English circumvented the policy by continuing with mother tongue instruction long past the initial three years, with the result that children were never adequately exposed to English.[19] Thus, the policy in some settings was not applied and in others was overapplied – both lowering public school performance, according to the report.

[18] J. Dzinyela, Team Leader, IEQ Project, phone interview by author, Accra, April 18, 2003.
[19] C. Churcher, Minister for Basic, Secondary and Girl-Child Education, interview by author, Accra, April 17, 2003.

Nowhere, except in extreme ideological cases, was a unifying language achieved. Mazrui and Mazrui call it lack of political will (1998, chapter 7). Moumouni criticizes an expansion of primary education that was "based solely on demagoguery: a supposed conformity with the will of the people ... [which] explains the lack of seriousness with which problems relative to the opening of new classes are solved" (Moumouni 1968, 96). I argue that between 1960 and 1990, this lack of proactive language rationalization reflected the incentives of leaders facing a different environment than that faced by European state-builders. Comparing snapshots at independence and 1990, one would see little movement in educational language policy. Though there were some experiments in the interim, the vast majority of states reverted to colonial precedent. And virtually all neglected education in general. Only a very few states entered the 1990s with a widespread common language that had been promoted by deliberate government policy. The reason for this was a specific environment faced by leaders at the helm of new African states. Initially precarious in their positions, they uniformly invested in education, responding to demands from a restive public. But realizing quickly their relative security from external threats or mass mobilization, they began to concentrate their energies on securing the support of a few potential competitors. Rather than trying to break the mediation monopoly of these regional elites and reach citizens directly through widespread single language education, leaders were content to remain separated from the masses, needing them neither for direct taxation nor for war making. The standardization of language, then, was not of great concern. Ambivalence and continuation of colonial precedent were the natural responses.

The main intention of the chapter was to offer an explanation for the language-in-education policies through the independence period: a continuation of colonial precedent. Alternative explanations raised briefly were democracy, demographics, and bargaining. Democracy, in short supply across the continent, did not appear to play a role, as evidenced by the regression analysis. While extremely fragmented states seemed slightly less inclined to use all of their languages in education, demographics were not a consistent predictor of language policy. The bargaining explanation required strong preferences on the part of leaders and regional elites, and this chapter laid the foundation for why these were not evident in Africa. More will be said about all of these in coming chapters.

In contrast to the inertia of the independence period, the 1990s saw an upsurge in attention to local languages. Unlike the brief experiments of the 1970s, however, this round has persisted. The next two chapters propose an explanation for this policy shift, which is a combination of altered opportunities and incentives.

4

Opportunities for Policy Change

Ideas, Materials, and Advocacy Networks

Though foreign powers no longer govern Africa as they did during the colonial period, vestiges of this dependent relationship have remained in several areas since independence, foremost among them language policy. The increasing attention to local languages in Francophone states does not sever the metropole-periphery relationship, but extends it. It has its origin in a cultural connection between France and its former colonies. The strongest alternative explanation for widespread diffusion of a similar policy would be global norms prompted by advocacy networks and spread through the mechanism of a tipping model (Keck and Sikkink 1998; Risse-Kappen 1994). But the multilingual education policy has not been adopted everywhere evenly. My explanation for a particular idea adopted by specific countries and reflective of local opportunities details the phenomenon more precisely.

Policies tend toward inertia. To contemplate change, a leader must be presented with unusual opportunities and incentives. This chapter argues that the opportunities for using local languages in education have changed dramatically in the last two decades, reducing the costs of considering this option. The distinctive educational policies preferred by French and British colonial administrators carried over strongly into the first thirty years of independence, with most former British colonies using African languages for primary education and nearly all former French colonies using French as the only medium of instruction. And yet this colonial legacy has been reversed in the last two decades. This is a result of two new opportunities. One is a different international perspective, and the other is expanded domestic possibilities. First, France changed the message it was communicating to states in its sphere of influence, and, second, language transcription and networks of advocates grew exponentially in the same states. In contrast, Anglophone states received contradictory messages, and transcription activities were much more marginal. This chapter explores first the international context

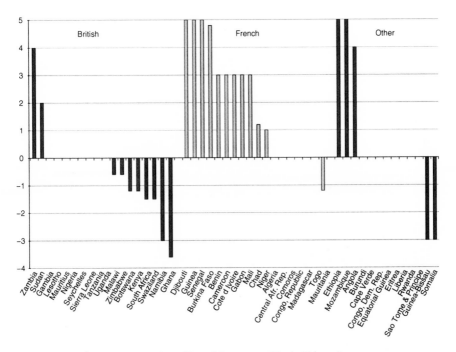

FIGURE 4.1. Change in Intensity of Local Language Use in Education, 1990–2010.

and then the domestic circumstances that combined to present African political leaders and bureaucrats with new opportunities to consider using local languages in education.

The chapter begins by showing the changes that have occurred since the 1990s – a significant increase in the use of local languages in education systems across Africa. The strongest competing explanation is one of global norms diffusion.[1] A norm of linguistic rights certainly has grown since UNESCO's 1953 publication of *The Use of Vernacular Languages in Education*. The majority of the chapter will show how the role of ideas is indeed central, but it is within a particular Francophone subset of cases. The chapter will demonstrate how the Anglophone influence differs. The final part of the chapter looks at this contrast within the cases of Senegal and Ghana.

First, let us see the changes that occurred. Recall that in 1990, nearly all states were maintaining the language policy they had inherited from their

---

[1] Johnson (2006, 692), for example, attributes Réunion's new official recognition of Creole to a general European directive on the status of minority languages. König (1999, 403–404) points to the role of international law in promoting the rights of linguistic minorities. Blommaert (1999) notes a continentwide trend favoring local languages from the 1970s.

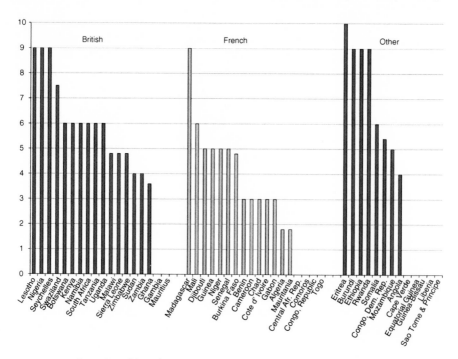

FIGURE 4.2. Intensity of Local Language Use in Education in 2010, by Colonizer.

colonizer. By the early 2000s, however, this had changed dramatically. Figure 4.1 shows the changes that occurred between 1990 and 2010.

Changes are indeed occurring across the continent, but it is only in former French territories that they are uniform.[2] Former British possessions and "other" territories are changing in both directions. Figure 4.2 shows the intensity of language use by 2010. Unlike the brief experiments in the 1970s, virtually all of these changes have persisted for at least a decade.

Francophone states are increasing their multilingual policies because of changed opportunities and incentives. This chapter will describe the two opportunities – a different message from France to its former colonies and the production of local language materials and advocacy by language NGOs – while the next will focus on the incentives.

---

[2] Mauritania is the only Francophone state that appears to have reduced its use of local languages since 1990. This is because of an anti-French phase of its educational history between 1982 and 1999, which replaced the French medium with mostly Arabic medium and a few experimental Pulaar, Soninke, and Wolof classes. According to one source, these experiments ended in 1999, when the government reintroduced French as a colanguage of instruction with Arabic. Other sources indicate that local languages probably remain in use in the south of the country, but this is difficult to confirm.

AN ALTERED INTERNATIONAL PERSPECTIVE

A plausible explanation for increased language use is the spreading of a norm of language rights. While I agree that idea change contributes to the outcome, the singularity of the idea is much more pronounced in the Francophone sphere. As explained in the prior two chapters, France's colonial policy regarding language in education was clear, and it continued well into its colonies' independence years. French was to be used as the sole medium of instruction. Rebel Guinea was the only Francophone state to undertake a significant experiment in local language medium education. The French ministry in charge of development aid maintained its belief in the priority of the French language in African education until about 1990, at which time it made a fundamental change. This dramatic reversal in the relationship of French with African languages reveals a shift in French policy makers' preferences, whose origin is a change in their causal ideas. Their altered preferences translated into different policy prescriptions toward the African states that receive French aid, transforming the environment in which African leaders made their policy decisions in the 1990s. The carrier for the idea was a strategic scholarly community. Epistemic community scholars have long recognized the importance of crisis for stimulating a search for new sources of policy advice (Haas 1992, 352–354). This builds on the insights of the literature on agenda setting in public policy, which asserts that crises provide opportunities for new solutions – solutions that may have long awaited their appropriate problems – to be considered (Walker 1977, 423–445; Kingdon 1984; Horowitz 1989, 249–288; Grindle and Thomas 1991). Historical institutionalists label these moments "critical junctures."

This story includes a crisis. It then departs from traditional accounts of epistemic communities by explicitly incorporating strategic agency. Ideas are not adopted as policy simply because they are good ideas. If these ideas are "floating" in the scientific community, why at a certain moment – aside from a crisis, which could be protracted – do policy makers suddenly believe them? The answer requires purposeful action on the part of influence agents – tactical scholars – who persist in their scholarly advocacy, making their ideas accessible and appealing to the appropriate policy makers. The entire story involves an idea as both an *effect* of a scholarly community's strategic action and a *cause* of changed policy. The idea is this: that education in a child's first language aids her acquisition of a second language. As will be shown, there is now consensus on this idea within the political leadership in the Francophone world, whereas in the Anglophone world, it continues to be the subject of contestation. The reason for this agreement can be traced to the strategic, well-positioned writing of a particular group of academics.

The majority of the chapter is devoted to tracing how this change of ideas percolated upward from linguists to policy makers. It was then communicated to Francophone African states, which remained linguistically and financially dependent on France. This differs markedly from the varying influences on

Anglophone Africa, bearing remarkable similarity to the laissez-faire attitude of British colonial rule. Education policy was left largely to local initiative, and outcomes then and in the present reveal much more variation.

As mentioned in the previous chapter, la Francophonie has consistently grown closer to the apex of French foreign policy. A network of linguists from France, Canada, Belgium, and Francophone Africa forms the Francophone scholarly community. This community has influenced French policy makers through the multilateral Francophone Agency, described in Chapter 3. It also influences French bilateral foreign policy through France's governmental aid organization, the Directorate-General for International Cooperation and Development (DGCID), formerly la Coopération Française. The DGCID currently is directed by the French Ministry of Foreign Affairs and funds a range of development initiatives, the majority in Africa.

Concerted activity by the community began in 1987. In that year, Robert Chaudenson, a French linguist who had specialized in Creole languages, answered a call for research from la Coopération Française. He proposed a research project looking at the relationship between African languages and development and received the funding to inaugurate a multiyear collaborative project, LAFDEF.[3] This funding from la Coopération Française linked Chaudenson's research directly to the bureaucrats responsible for implementing French foreign policy in Africa. The next year, Chaudenson was elected secretary of an existing language research body attached to the Francophone Agency, CIRELFA.[4] Chaudenson's position at the helm of CIRELFA gave him an official link to the Francophone Agency, France's most important multilateral influence in Africa. In 1989, Chaudenson proposed folding his LAFDEF into the more institutionalized CIRELFA, and the center of the scholarly community was born. There were forty-nine researchers at that time: thirty-four from thirteen African countries and fifteen from France, Belgium, and Canada.[5] CIRELFA was thus in a prime position – at the nexus of French bilateral and multilateral cooperation in Africa – to influence the opinion of Francophone policy makers.

The linguists in this community were inspired by a variety of motivations. Most cared genuinely about the languages they studied. Understandably, the native French speakers also cared deeply about the preservation of French.[6] They shared a major principled belief: Languages in the world, and French in particular, should be protected from domination by English. Through their research, they grew to share the causal beliefs that (1) children learn best in their first language, and (2) children learn a *second* language better if they

---

[3] Langues Africaines, Français et Développement.
[4] Centre International de Recherche et d'Étude en Linguistique Fondamentale et Appliquée.
[5] Members are named in Chaudenson (2000, 285).
[6] Of course these linguists have a variety of motivations, aside from the singular preservation of French. Their commonality is in the strategic packaging of their message for consumption by northern Francophone leaders.

begin in their first language. These were not new causal beliefs; the new element would be their packaging.

This community of experts found a niche in a previously underutilized research arm of la Francophonie. From here, it produced several writings in quick succession, "bombarding" Northern Francophone leadership with critiques of its inaction on matters of language in education. The unusual aspect of this community of scholars was the activism of Robert Chaudenson and his colleague Louis-Jean Calvet. When asked how they viewed their vocation, they said they saw it as political, and their audience primarily as political leaders.[7] Here is the strategic agency that cannot be downplayed in any study of the role of ideas. Because of a mounting crisis of French retreat, these critiques and suggestions found a more ready audience than in years past and resulted in changed French rhetoric, followed steadily by changed French action.

The French linguist and historian Claude Hagège cites the Treaty of Versailles (1919), translated into both French and English rather than only French, as the moment the French language began its retreat (Hagège 1996, 89). France faced a new need to defend its language. By 1965, Charles de Gaulle had established the "High Committee for the Defense and the Expansion of the French Language." In 1975, the French government passed the Loi Bas-Lauriol, stipulating that French must be used in all commercial transactions – publicity, instructions, advertising – and terminology commissions arose to find words for these activities if necessary. Yet English continued to creep into French communication. In 1992, France amended its constitution to state that the official language of the Republic was French, a clarification that had not previously seemed necessary (Hagège 1996, 89; Wright 2004, 122–125). In recent years, France has notoriously resisted what it considers *American* globalization, even translating the term into "mondialisation," instead of the anglicized "globalisation."[8] In France's view, the unwelcome result is a homogenization of culture, as English language and American culture dominate all others.

Three events marked France's reaction to the severity of the threat. First were the GATT negotiations between 1988 and 1993, specifically as they related to trade in culture (Frau-Meigs 2002). As the United States pushed for free trade in all areas, France and its allies fought to keep culture – represented by books, films, theater – exempt from the leveling forces of liberalization: the "cultural exception." According to la Francophonie's report of the year 1993, "The cultural exception represents the fight of the French or European David against the American Goliath" (Haut Conseil de la Francophonie 1994, 55). The second event was the Toubon Law. Introduced in August 1994 by Jacques Toubon, then French minister of culture and la Francophonie, this law was an attempt to keep

---

[7] R. Chaudenson, interview by author, Marseille, April 23, 2004; L. J. Calvet, phone interview by author, May 12, 2004.

[8] The biennial publication of the Francophonie for 2002–2003 titles its first section "La Francophonie: une autre mondialisation" (Conseil Consultatif de l'OIF 2003, 5).

Anglicisms out of French spoken and written communication. It demonstrated France's heightened perception of the English threat and its official goal of maintaining its own linguistic purity. The third event was the body of discussions concerning languages of the European Union in 1995 and 1996.[9] France pushed for "obligatory plurilingualism" in Europe: mother tongue plus two foreign languages. The rationale was that if only one foreign language were required, people would undoubtedly choose English, and French would be threatened even more.

The outcome of all of these events was that France clarified its strategy for advancing the French language against the threat of English: promote all European languages apart from English. This conveniently allowed France to identify itself with an "international ethic" of diversity. But how did this relate to African languages, which had always been subordinate to French? Africa contains nearly three-quarters of Francophones (real, occasional, and potential) in the world (Haut Conseil de la Francophonie 1990). As seen in the previous chapter, its French-only policy in African schools was nonnegotiable, even after its colonies' independence. France had steadily provided resources, technical assistance, and teachers to aid in this endeavor.[10]

Yet in 1985, only an estimated 19 percent of Africans were literate in French, and by 1994 the figure had fallen to 14 percent (Haut Conseil de la Francophonie 1994, 95). If France wanted to ensure that this vast reservoir of people continued to look to the "metropole" for linguistic and cultural products (textbooks, pleasure books, cinema, theater, radio, television), it simultaneously had to ensure better French language acquisition and protect against the invasion of the competitor, English. But it concerns more than economic gain. It is about French survival. If the French language had to rely only on France, Belgium, Switzerland, and Quebec to maintain its stature, it would be dwarfed by neighbors and have no claim to world prominence. Francophone Africa is the means to continued French global influence.[11]

Happily, Francophone academics had a solution. Promoting African languages did not compete with French, they promised. In fact, when children began education in their mother tongue, transition to a second language would be made easier. This was the key that reconciled France's multilingual rhetoric with its desire to save French.

Prior to the 1990s, in the absence of a strategic scholarly community, the Francophone Agency sponsored numerous African language description projects in the name of cultural preservation, but there was no link to a concurrent

---

[9] France did not sign the Council of Europe's Charter for Minority Languages until 1999 and still has not ratified it, being blocked constitutionally by the 1992 amendment enshrining French as the language of the Republic.

[10] Cumming (2005, 238–239) notes the "phenomenal number of French teachers being sent to Africa: some 11,000 in 1985, with around 3000 in Cote d'Ivoire alone."

[11] See Chafer 2002 for an insightful analysis of the explicit cultural motives of French imperialism.

goal of furthering French. These halfhearted programs were perceived rightly by African linguists as appeasement. With the arrival of the strategic scholarly community, one can discern a shift in the discourse of policy documents: from African language study to preserve culture toward African language study for its practical benefits to French.

The French justified their early lack of attention to African languages by blaming African governments for foot dragging (AIF 2001, 115). I would argue these supposedly reluctant African governments were simply pragmatic. Their preferences were heavily induced by the institutional possibilities. They knew that France – by far their countries' largest donor[12] – was unconvinced of the utility of African languages at this time. There was no point in making major changes to their education systems when they could little afford such innovation and knew they would receive no support from France.

Francophone discourse changed in 1989. After two Francophonie Summits held in the North (Paris and Quebec), the Francophone heads of state assembled in Dakar, Senegal, for their Biennial Summit. In preparation, the conference organizer Christian Valantin convened an expert session on languages and education, soliciting input from academics. Among them were members of the scholarly community, who thereby contributed greatly to the conference's contents. Robert Chaudenson hastily prepared a provocative book, *1989: Toward a Francophone Revolution?*, to be distributed to all participants at the summit. In it, he drew a parallel between the French Revolution of 1789 and the present moment of revolution within the French-speaking world. If the original French Revolution involved a crisis of language, and ended with the French language triumphing over other "patois," the present crisis of French, in contrast, actually *depended* on minority language for its resolution (Chaudenson 1989, preface). He wrote in colorful, nontechnical language: "If you throw 100 babies in a pool, it is likely that a few of them will find a way out and escape drowning ... but one doesn't deduce, in general, that this is the best way to teach them to swim," referring to the method of teaching children French from the beginning of primary school (Chaudenson 1989, 154).

The summit was a climactic event and inspired optimism on the part of those who believed in the use of African languages in education. It focused specifically on African languages and produced a Decennial Plan for Linguistic Management, which talked about French and African languages in terms of "functional complementarity" for the first time (Actes du Sommet de Dakar 1989, 203). The conference was particularly clear on the link between mother tongue learning and second language acquisition:

---

[12] Since 1960, between half and two-thirds of French bilateral development aid has gone to its former colonies in Africa (Chafer 2002, 12). Within French-speaking Africa, France was the top overall donor in virtually *every* country until very recently, giving more than the World Bank, the EC, or the United States each year. OECD, *International Development Statistics* (IDS) online: http://www.oecd.org/dataoecd/50/17/5037721.htm

We now recognize the inadequacy, in the context of French as a second language, of the methods conceived for the teaching of French, a foreign language, as those inspired from French as a mother tongue. ... One who does not master his mother tongue encounters difficulties with a second language. (Actes du Sommet de Dakar 1989, 214)

The Francophone Agency (with the participation of France, its most influential member) was finally demonstrating some real political will. The salutatory gestures toward cultural preservation through funding endless research gave way to a realization by the agency that partner languages were not only tolerable, but essential for the preservation of French.

Despite this rhetoric emanating from the conference, however, financial support for programs on African languages actually decreased in the following years. This was for two reasons: changed leadership and institutional reorganization. The new secretary-general of the Francophone Agency, Canadian Jean-Louis Roy, elected just after the 1989 summit, apparently was not bound to the decisions taken at Dakar, and he decided to reorient the linguistic focus of the organization. He favored a project called "Language Industries" – a term encompassing a variety of activity around information technology. In the reorganization, much of the financial responsibility for language research was transferred from the headquarters of the Francophone Agency to another "operator" of the OIF, the Association of Francophone Universities, also based in Canada. The only element of language research left untouched was CIRELFA. Paradoxically, this deficit of official activity provided the opening for CIRELFA to gain greater visibility with its critical writings.

For the 1991 Francophonie Summit in Chaillot, CIRELFA prepared a second book under the direction of Chaudenson (Chaudenson 1991). It was the result of the scholars' collaborative work on a "grille d'analyse" (analytic grid). This "grille" could be presented graphically, and it showed the radical inconsistency between official status and actual use of French in most of Francophone Africa. With this evidence, France could see clearly the reality of its failure in Africa. The book's conclusion makes transparent its goal:

Political decision makers ... rarely have the time to read a 200-page book; it is thus imperative, if one wants a chance to be heard, to present them with such realities in a more concise and striking form. This grid permits the presentation, in just one page, and thus the inclusion in just one glance, of all the actual situations of French in the entire Francophone sphere. (Chaudenson 1991, 191)

Between 1988 and 2000, CIRELFA published more than thirty books and disseminated a triennial bulletin to policy makers.[13] These continued to show, theoretically and through case studies, the weakness of French proficiency in Africa and the paradoxical necessity of local languages for the preservation of

---

[13] *Langues et Développement*, first published in 1988, was intended to provide quick information to policy makers. The book series, under the same title, was supposed to permit the "visibility and diffusion" of the best results of the program (AIF 2001, 121).

French. The framing connected the proposed solution to broader French goals, and, importantly, it magnified the crisis.[14] Louis-Jean Calvet stated starkly:

Currently only about 10% of Francophone Africa speaks French, and many have recognized quickly that if this rate continues, the international position of French will be changed dramatically. The future of French is linked to that of African languages. ... Without a linguistic policy playing on this complementarity, there will not be a future for French. (Calvet 1993, 490)

More hyperbolically, Chaudenson warned that "French may be wiped out of Africa in 30 years, maybe less. Five percent of Africans speak French, essentially the elite. If we lose Africa, French becomes a non-factor" (Nadeau 1999, 7). These linguists highlighted the feebleness of French in Africa and made a commonsense argument about pedagogy – children are not learning because they cannot understand the teacher. The use of African languages resolved both problems.

It was important that Chaudenson had his foot in both avenues of French influence. He could funnel his opinions both to the Francophone Agency and to the French Ministry for Cooperation at the same time. Furthermore, because AUPELF was not interested for the moment in languages and education, Chaudenson had a virtual monopoly to set the tone and direction of the research. The budget for CIRELFA was relatively small, compared to the funding given to prior language projects – about $150,000 annually. But this funded research and publication of at least two books per year. These were coordinated, pointed projects, and instead of being relegated to the shelves of academics, the work was intentionally distributed to policy makers. CIRELFA's advising role became more and more important.

The radical message preached by the strategic scholarly community – that *French* was in trouble and had to be rescued by national languages – was simply a repackaged version of linguistic research that had been circulating for a long time. Yet until about 1989, with the concerted, politically aimed writings of the strategic scholarly community, "it never entered anyone's mind to engage in reflection about the specific problems posed by the use of French as medium of education for students who used other languages when they arrived at school" (AIF 2001, 129). A Francophone African linguist observes that there is now virtual consensus on the idea that children learn writing best in a language they use outside school (Tréfault 2001, 227–228). Explicitly citing the Francophone Agency and DGCID, he observes that "rare are the voices that dare to go against the current of this dominant discourse" (Tréfault 2001, 228).

Thus, even with this lack of concrete action immediately following the Dakar Summit, the changed message emanating from the "Northern" members of la Francophonie after 1989 was heard loudly in Africa. In the 1990s, we see the

---

[14] Weingast (2005, 170) elaborates the microfoundations of critical junctures, in which proponents of a new idea find it rational to try to scare decision makers by exaggerating potential negative consequences.

start or expansion of several local language education initiatives in Francophone Africa, which would not have been attempted in the decades before.

La Francophonie at the start of the new millennium declared itself at the "center of a crusade in favor of plurilingualism" (Haut Conseil de la Francophonie 2001, 59). The transformation is evident in its regular report, *Etat de la Francophonie dans le monde*. The 1987 report contained no mention of African languages at all. In 1993, the publication recognized the importance of African "partner languages" and dedicated several paragraphs to the need for "complementarity" between these languages and French. The publication in 1997 demonstrated the most dramatic change, devoting an entire section to the benefits to French of schooling in the mother tongue, and subsequent publications continue to reinforce this changed strategy.

After the disappointing lull in activity following the rhetoric of the Dakar Summit, the 1997 Hanoi Summit represented the "decisive shift" toward real support of African languages in the eyes of experts (Renard 2002, 8). Connecting the crisis of French to globalization, the Charte de Hué (1997, 1) included the following statement:

Globalization is not beneficial for all. It is built on a general marketization that erases identities and imperils the existence of all languages ... the francophone movement confronts this challenge in proposing another way of thinking about the world.... French can be a vector of hope ... by making alliance, notably as a second language, with all of the languages in her bosom.

Demonstrating a changed understanding of the relationship between languages and education, in 1997 the Francophone Agency attached CIRELFA, which had previously been affiliated with the Office of Culture in the Francophone Agency, to the Office of Education and Training. African languages were now viewed as a route to educational improvement, rather than a tool of cultural preservation. Then, in January 1999, the Francophone Agency created for the first time an Office of Languages and Writing. This office sits at the heart of the Francophone Agency. Robert Chaudenson became a permanent consultant to this office in his capacity as director of the ongoing series Languages and Development.

Importantly, the Francophone Agency's strategy document states clearly that it expects to see education plans in Africa that include national languages:

The Agency will from now on concentrate on partner languages in states which, having chosen French as an official language..., encounter a critical problem of education for populations whose mother tongue is not French....Significant support will thus be given to countries that have chosen teaching in certain national languages in the first years of study, following the principles of convergent pedagogy, for which the effectiveness in the subsequent mastery of French has been demonstrated. (AIF 2000, 10–11)

"Convergent pedagogy" refers explicitly to the method of teaching French through local languages advocated by members of the scholarly community

(Wambach 1994; Poth 1997). The Francophone Agency links its interventions to the preexisting elaboration of national language policies by member states themselves. What may appear an independent decision on the part of African governments to implement a program that includes local languages in education is more likely an anticipation of significant support from the Francophone Agency.

Though France provides the majority of the Francophone Agency budget, the amount it spends multilaterally is only a small fraction of its bilateral spending on Africa. Similar rhetoric in support of mother tongue education is evident in program documents of the bilateral DGCID. The minister of foreign affairs' program document for 2002 devotes a special section to partner languages (Ministère des Affaires Étrangères). Since most bilateral funding is now sectoral (e.g., given to the education sector as a whole, rather than for individual projects), it is difficult to measure the amount contributed for language components of overall education plans. But the education strategies of virtually all Francophone African countries currently contain a mother tongue element, and France supports them through sectoral financing.

France's financial and institutional support has coalesced into a program called Écoles et Langues Nationales (ELAN), jointly funded by the French Ministry of Foreign Affairs and the Francophone Agency.[15] This program, launched in 2011, is targeting in particular eight Francophone states (Benin, Burkina Faso, Burundi, Cameroon, Democratic Republic of the Congo, Mali, Niger, and Senegal) and has two elements: first, to support the eight ministers of education in enacting the reforms necessary toward the concurrent use of African languages with French in primary education, and, second, to create an international disposition of support (exchange of information, expertise, and training) in the service of bilingual education in African states (Organisation Internationale de la Francophonie 2011, 7, my translation). The cost of this project is 9.1 million Euros (approximately US\$12.7 million) for the first four years, 4.5 million supplied by the French government, 2.6 million from OIF, and 2 million from the countries themselves (Agence Française de Développement 2011, 5). For the first goal, its interventions will include expanding existing experiments in using African languages; intensifying advocacy at the ministerial level to "experiment with, consolidate, and deploy the practice of bilingual education" throughout the country; holding international seminars; training specialists; sending missions of technical support; diffusing the results of research; and putting in place a Web site for countries to collaborate. For the second goal, interventions will include linguistic planning in each country,

---

[15] Specifically, it is a partnership between institutions of la Francophonie (OIF and AUF) and of the Coopération Française (the Ministry of Foreign Affairs and the French Agency for Development). After yet another restructuring of French Cooperation between 2004 and 2006, France's development interventions were split between DGCID, which took responsibility for governance, justice, police, security, cultural affairs, research, and higher education, and the French Agency for Development, which took responsibility for seven strategic sectors under the umbrella of economic and social development. The first of these sectors is education.

contributing to scholarly materials, training of teachers, reinforcing national advocacy, and contributing to on-the-ground evaluations (Agence Française de Développement 2011, 8). This is a full-press effort to use African languages to further French.

CHANGED CAUSAL IDEAS

Clearly, discourse changed regarding the utility of mother tongue languages in education: The Francophone Agency created a specialized office to manage this new priority, and funding was forthcoming from both the Francophone Agency and the Coopération Française to support mother tongue projects. A group of scholars had a new idea, a crisis existed, and policy changed to correspond with the new idea. To demonstrate more convincingly that the scholarly community actually changed policy makers' causal ideas, we need to find pointed evidence, such as contact between members of the scholarly community and French leadership, confirmation that the writing of scholarly community members circulated in government circles, and reference to the ideas of these academics in conversation with policy makers.

To find such evidence, I conducted twenty-five interviews in France among leaders of multilateral Francophone agencies and French government officials, as well as with members of the strategic scholarly community and other NGOs.[16] The central question that I posed to all of them was "What language do you think should be used for primary education in Francophone Africa?" Remarkably, I found a uniform response. All agency respondents – French government officials, as well as officials of la Francophonie – answered that African languages should be used in primary schools. This is a dramatic consensus. And it contradicts opinions of French officials a generation earlier.

Brian Weinstein, probably the first to study la Francophonie on a comparative scale (Weinstein 1976), was generous enough to lend me his field notes from 1972 to 1973. He had traveled to several member countries of la Francophonie, interviewing Northern and Southern leaders about their views on this new international entity. His notes reveal the views of French elites and government officials toward local languages in the 1970s, with which I could establish a baseline for comparison. The French ambassador to Haiti at that time, Bernard Dorin, illustrated official French opinion. It was a matter of course that French should be the language of instruction from the beginning of school. To the idea that Haiti's government was considering making local Creole even a subject in school, he worried: "If that is done, it will be a threat to French." Dorin emphasized his concern that French remain and expand as a "langue

---

[16] Agence Intergouvernementale de la Francophonie, Haut Conseil de la Francophonie, Direction Générale de la Coopération et du Développement, Direction Générale de la Langue Française, Agence Parlementaire de la Francophonie.

maternelle."[17] One French academic interviewed by Weinstein believed that French was a factor of unity in African countries and would "eventually eliminate African languages to become [a] 'mother tongue.'"[18] Another suggested that the "great danger was that some [African] governments wanted to cut their elites off from the outside world and were doing so by insisting on the teaching of the African languages in schools."[19] These interviews show the prevailing opinion of French officials and elites regarding African languages: They were a threat to French and should be discouraged in education.

But thirty years later, this sentiment had shifted entirely. One of the most forceful advocates for the use of local languages was a former French ambassador and current head of the French government's Service de la Francophonie, Michel Vandepoorter. With no prompting, he asserted the imperative that African languages be used in school; one of the main reasons was easier subsequent French acquisition. When I asked whether there were any "pockets of resistance" within the Ministry of Foreign Affairs, he answered, "It isn't even debated. It is intuitive. It is part of France's larger goal toward diversity."[20]

The direct link to the scholarly community surfaced when I asked why. All but one of the agency members I interviewed offered the rationale that easier French acquisition was the main reason African languages should be used in schools. That is, children will learn French better if they begin in their first language. This is not a self-evident relationship, and it demonstrates exposure to the writing and advocacy of the scholarly community. All agency respondents thought that within their agency, opinion on this issue had changed over time. Most were able to date the change to a precise moment: Eight placed it between 1990 and 2000. At the heart of my purpose, when asked the cause of this change, nine out of fourteen attributed it to the scholars of the academic community directly by name, another referred to "scholars in the Agency," which likely was a reference to Chaudenson and CIRELFA, and two more attributed it to specific ideas given by the scholars but could not name them. Thus twelve out of fourteen, or 85 percent, of the agency officials acknowledged that the ideas of this group of scholars had influenced the ideological climate of their agency. In all cases, the respondent communicated the idea first, and then, when asked to consider its origin, pointed to members of the scholarly community. That policy makers do not refer initially to the academics indicates that they have absorbed the causal idea, rather than using the community to legitimate the policies they want to pursue.

Not surprisingly, the four members of what I am calling the strategic scholarly community that I interviewed were in agreement about the utility of African languages in education. When I asked whether they thought they themselves had

---

[17] B. Dorin, interview with B. Weinstein, Port-au-Prince, Haiti, August 17, 1972.
[18] A. Reboullet, interview with B. Weinstein, Paris, November 3, 1972.
[19] R. Cournevin, interview with B. Weinstein, Paris, November 6, 1972.
[20] M. Vandepoorter, interview by author, Paris, April 26, 2004.

influenced policy change, three out of four (Calvet, Wambach, Renard) said they believed they had; Chaudenson (who I would argue has been the most politically agitating) said he did not think he had had much effect. He has been the most pessimistic and critical of the Francophone Agency and French government action, so this may be simply a refusal to relent in his barrage, for fear the positive changes will slow.

These academics were not simply reflecting, but vigorously pushing their agenda in high political circles. When I asked Calvet whether he thought politicians were more open to his thoughts now, he said, "I don't think so. I know so." How did he know? "Because I am invited to be an expert speaker at policy-making conferences, and contacted routinely for expert opinion."[21] Anecdotally, in at least four of my interviews with French officials, when I asked who or what had changed opinion within their agencies, they pointed to a stack of papers on their desk or gestured toward their computers, explaining that they had just received another e-mailed "Note" from Chaudenson, apparently a very common occurrence.

When compared with the baseline provided by Weinstein's interviews, which revealed the overall negative opinions held by French elites about the utility of African languages, the current consensus is remarkable. My own interviews point convincingly to the primary role played by influence agents in the process of this ideational transformation.

The step from metropolitan ideology to policy outcomes in Africa is a long one. The frontlines are embassy staff in the various countries. To ascertain messages sent from France to Africa, I sent a questionnaire to French embassy aid representatives in all former French colonies in Africa. Only a few responded (and some had to be cajoled into actually admitting to a policy, rather than hiding behind the rhetoric of "We support the African government's policy"), but the answers generally confirmed my hypothesis. French officials in Africa seem to have absorbed the new idea from DGCID in Paris that local language education is helpful for the acquisition of French and thus should be promoted. In Burkina Faso, for example, to my question "What do you perceive is the French policy concerning medium of education in Burkina Faso's primary schools?" the technical adviser for education wrote in response:

Various studies conducted around the world [support] the idea that it is easier to learn in one's first language, the learning of other language (French) being easier.... I believe essentially that the current opinion of the Ministry of Foreign Affairs is to use African languages at the beginning of education to transfer progressively toward French. I also believe this view, strongly backed by quality studies, is shared by African states and other partners.[22]

---

[21] The 2002–2003 edition of *La Francophonie dans le monde* uses long extracts from Calvet and Chaudenson (OIF 2003, 77, 85).

[22] D. Mazzoleni, technical adviser, pers. comm., March 4, 2005.

The French technical adviser for Mali answered matter-of-factly: "France supports a reform program in the framework of PRODEC (Decennial Program in Education) which looks to install a bilingual education system, with the first years in national languages and a progressive introduction of French."[23] France has sent a technical adviser to assist in writing curriculum and to help manage the bilingual program. The head of French cultural cooperation in Togo supported the idea of mother tongue education, though he was more cautious in its application:

Without a doubt, teaching in mother tongues ... is always desirable, at least in the first year of education. For a child, the passage from a mother tongue to a [different] language of learning (official or national) added to the introduction to school itself must be, to say the least, difficult. Nevertheless, without a doubt pragmatism always prevails when faced with priorities.[24]

Togo is one of the few Francophone African governments not currently implementing a mother tongue experiment. Possibly this official's reluctance or "pragmatism" has inhibited communicating France's new openness wholeheartedly enough to allow a change in policy. In Senegal, the head of French cultural cooperation reported that

there is a favorable opinion at least at the level of Francophone leadership for the development of national languages....[This sentiment] is held by DGCID.... I believe effectively on a technical level that initial literacy in a national language is a good thing; it favors the further passage to French and general academic success.

The relationship between French and African languages has been described as evolving from "apartheid to partnership."[25] In an astounding shift from colonial and much postcolonial policy, the French language has been transformed from assimilator to liberator – a far distance from the homogenizer of mankind envisioned by the Jacobins (Ozouf 1988, 279). An African member of the Francophone Association of Universities observes: "Particularly in Africa, French and national languages are linked by a common destiny. The revalorization of national languages, of African culture, passes through French, which, purged of its mark of domination, has become the language of revolt and of liberty" (Aloyse-Raymond Ndiaye, cited in Renard 2002, 11). French now promises to free Africa (and the rest of the world) from the homogeneity threatened by the English language. This was not a straight and natural trajectory; it is a sea change, and the strategic scholarly community propelled the current.

---

[23] B. Maurer, technical assistant, pers. comm., April 12, 2005.
[24] M. Fenoli, Chef du Service (SCAC), pers. comm., March 17, 2005.
[25] The title and imagery used by Renard in his chapter for Chaudenson and Calvet's (2001) edited volume.

CONTRADICTORY ANGLOPHONE VOICES

In contrast, no such consensus existed in the 1990s within the Anglophone community. Recall the "elasticity" of British policy during the colonial period – a policy "fraught with much confusion of purpose and lack of resources" (Whitehead 2005, 445). This tendency continued into the independence era, as explained in the previous chapter.

Anglophone Africa is subject to a variety of influences. In contrast to la Francophonie, the Commonwealth is a loose, independent entity. Moreover, because a large portion of linguistic research written in English is from the United States (a notable exclusion from the list of Commonwealth members), one must consider all English-language research when looking at the differential impacts of ideas on Anglophone organizations and states. A combination of the multiple points of entry, a lack of singular message, and a radical frame make the impact entirely different.

While some scholarship coming out of Francophone circles mentions selected English-language works, Anglophone scholarship rarely mentions Francophone publications.[26] Anglophone research in the area of language policy, then, is not "contaminated" at all by Francophone linguistic research, thus making comparisons neater. Unlike the Francophone case, there is no coherent academic community with shared beliefs about language use in education. Instead, there are two very distinct and sharply divided groups, particularly evident in the United States. On one side, there are those bilingual education theorists who favor using mother tongues as the basis for education.[27] On the other side are those who oppose mother tongue use in favor of structured immersion programs.[28]

Importantly – and unfortunately for its impact – the message of Anglophone scholars who favor the use of mother tongues has merged with that of transnational advocates of human language rights.[29] Language rights scholars label their enterprise "critical linguistics," and understand it to entail social activism (Tollefson 2002, 4). They point to the inequalities that inevitably arise and are sustained when elites guard their advantage in language. These critical theorists see in a country's medium of instruction "the most powerful means of

---

[26] An annotated bibliography prepared for USAID's IEQ project on language and education does not list one French-language book or article, though it purports to cover language in education policy throughout Africa. Similarly, Tove Skutnabb-Kangas's 174-page bibliography of multilingualism and linguistic human rights (http://www.tove-skutnabb-kangas.org/en/Tove-Skutnabb-Kangas-Bibliography.html) did not list any of the Francophone authors in the scholarly community in the mid-2000s. But see Fardon and Furniss 1994.

[27] Collier 1987; Cummins 1979, 1991; Ramirez et al. 1991; Krashen 1996; August and Hakuta 1997; Greene 1998.

[28] Baker and de Kanter 1981; Porter 1990; Rossell and Baker 1996; Glenn 1997.

[29] Skutnabb-Kangas and Cummins 1988; Tollefson 2002; Skutnabb-Kangas 2000; Phillipson 1992, 2000; de Varennes 1996; Skutnabb-Kangas and Robert Philippson 1994; Phillipson and Skutnabb-Kangas 1999.

maintaining and revitalizing a language and culture" and "a key means of power (re)distribution and social (re)construction" (Tollefson and Tsui 2004, 2). In Anglophone scholarship on language and education, then, researchers are divided, and those who advocate mother tongue education are identified with the radical messages that criticize English linguistic hegemony. This is not an attractive frame.

The divergent recommendations and polemical writing emanating from English-language sources have created a very indecisive climate of action regarding mother tongue education. Unlike la Francophonie, which entered the 1990s with a common policy on local languages, the Anglophone world shares no such consensus. This is evident in statements from the Commonwealth itself, in British bilateral policies, and in policies of the Anglophone-oriented World Bank.

The Singapore Declaration of Commonwealth Principles (1971) contains no discussion of languages, except to observe that the Commonwealth includes people from different "races, languages and religions."[30] Neither the Harare Commonwealth Declaration, nor the Millbrook Commonwealth Action Programme on the Harare Declaration (1995) mentions language at all, save to note a shared English language (Harare Commonwealth Declaration, paragraph 3). These three statements are considered the foundation of Commonwealth policy, and none even remotely touches the language issue. English language education did appear to be a priority in the early years of the Commonwealth, and the first in a series of specialist education conferences (Makerere, Uganda, 1962) centered on the need for training staff to teach English as a second language (Brown 2003, 10). Since then, however, the Commonwealth has not made language policy an issue of "major concern."[31] Partly this may be explained by the fact that educational exchange and cooperation in the Commonwealth are most developed at the tertiary level, where virtually all students already share a competency in English.

Though the quality of English in Africa is generally considered very poor, a careful reading of the biennial Reports of the Commonwealth Secretariat reveals no mention in any of them of language as an area of activity or concern. Unlike the *Etat de la Francophonie* publications in the 1990s, the Commonwealth Reports do not expend any ink assessing numbers of English speakers, language teaching methods, or language policies in member states. The Conference of Education Ministers' Halifax Communiqué recognized the need to address the subject of indigenous languages versus English in education but made no attempt to formulate a Commonwealth policy.[32] The subsequent Education

---

[30] *Declaration of Commonwealth Principles*, "Who We Are/Key Declarations."

[31] P. H. Williams, Hon. Secretary of the Commonwealth Consortium for Education, phone interview by author, July 23, 2004.

[32] "Ministers noted that in societies where a non-indigenous language is used as the medium of instruction, it tended to detract from the cultural sensitivity of their education systems, impair access and stifle creativity. They emphasised the value of educational systems that are inclusive

Ministers' Conference produced the Edinburgh Communiqué and Action Plan (October 30, 2003), which, contrary to this recommendation, contains no reference to language use in education. Within the Commonwealth Secretariat, it is now the "Social Transformation Programmes Division" that oversees the Education Programme. On the Secretariat's Web site advertising its accomplishments in education, activities in Cameroon are highlighted:

As one of the few members of the Commonwealth with a strong Francophone influence, a particular feature of Cameroon's primary and secondary education is the thrust to develop the teaching and learning of English. Visits to schools reveal "Commonwealth Clubs" in which teachers encourage the use of the English language in learning about the other members of the Commonwealth, and signs which encourage the use of English (and reduced use of "Pidgin"!) albeit on specific school days. . . . Cameroon school children are encouraged to appreciate and respect their own indigenous cultural practices such as dance and community drama.[33]

Given a prime opportunity for advertising innovative use of Cameroonian languages in education, the Commonwealth chooses to focus instead on the learning of English.

This silence on the language-in-education issue was echoed in my interviews. I spoke with current and former directors of education in the Commonwealth, the secretary for the Commonwealth's Consortium for Education, officials at the British Council, and former and current chief education officers at the Department for International Development (DFID). All of them expressed reluctance to take a firm stand on a policy about language use in education, saying it was an issue for individual states to decide. The current director of education in the Commonwealth, Henry Kiluba, when asked directly about a Commonwealth policy on language use in education, responded:

There is no policy on language of education. It is not part of the recommendations coming from the Commonwealth. All countries use the English language as the medium of instruction, plus some use local languages. The Ministers did discuss this issue at the last conference [Edinburgh], but there was no consensus statement. They did not mandate this office to work on the issue.[34]

The former head of education at the Commonwealth (now chief of education at UNICEF), Cream Wright, agrees that the Education Office had no expressed language policy. He recalls receiving a letter during his tenure asking whether the Commonwealth planned to comment on Ghana's decision to switch to English-only instruction. He reported that "I responded I thought it was a government

and culturally sensitive, but which at the same time ensured that learners retained a capacity to be part of an open global society. *They requested the Commonwealth Secretariat to study these issues further and report them at their next meeting.*" Halifax Communiqué, paragraph 9 (my emphasis).

[33] http://www.thecommonwealth.org/Templates/STPDInternal.asp?NodeID=37690.

[34] H. Kiluba, telephone interview by author, July 29, 2004.

issue, not one the Commonwealth should take a position on."[35] He quickly added, however, that while there is no official policy, if countries asked the Commonwealth Secretariat for technical advice on using local languages, they could probably expect to get some help. But there are no specialists on language at the Secretariat. And "there was always money to support a country if it wanted to teach English." The secretary of the Commonwealth Consortium for Education, Peter Williams (who also previously held the post of head of education at the Commonwealth Secretariat), confirmed that language has not been an issue of major concern in the Commonwealth. The Commonwealth itself has no particular policy. It believes in diversity, respecting the policies of governments. "It would never take a stand saying it is better to teach in English or in the vernacular."[36]

The bilateral relationship between the former metropole and African Commonwealth members is equally ambiguous in its policy recommendations. At the British Council, officials explained that their standard pedagogy for teaching English did not include use of local languages.[37] The acting director of the English Language Teaching Group of the British Council said that they worked primarily with postsecondary students or graduates in their Future Leaders program. When they work with the Ministries of Education on pedagogical innovations, it usually involves technology, and if the government has decided that the best way to learn English is through the vernacular, they will support them in that. "But we don't have a partisan view as to whether it's good or bad....We wouldn't preach to governments," he insisted.[38]

The major bilateral funding arm of the United Kingdom, the Department for International Development (DFID), also refrains from firm recommendations in this area. Myra Harrison, former chief education officer at DFID, herself a strong advocate of local language use in education, confirmed that DFID did not have an explicit policy, though implicitly she thought it favored the use of local languages.[39] Desmond Bermingham, current chief education officer at DFID, concurred. "There is no hard and fast line," he said. However, "most advisors are persuaded by the case for using home languages."[40] By what were they persuaded? I asked. Was there a common body of literature or a prominent study that he thought most education advisers had read? He answered no. It is a general impression that has simply been absorbed. Whatever their individual opinions on the utility of local languages, however, officials are not pushing them in a concerted way. Dr. Bermingham concluded that DFID's policy is not

[35] C. Wright, telephone interview by author, August 3, 2004.
[36] P. Williams, telephone interview by author, August 2, 2004.
[37] J. Holliday, telephone interview by author, August 4, 2004; D. Newstead, telephone interview by author, August 5, 2004.
[38] J. Jacobson, telephone interview by author, August 13, 2004.
[39] M. Harrison, pers. comm., March 28, 2004.
[40] D. Bermingham, telephone interview by author, August 18, 2004.

necessarily laissez-faire, but "you can't go in and dictate to a government what it should do." This sentiment has resulted in a de facto laissez-faire policy.

Part of this ambivalence on the part of Britain and other Commonwealth members emerges from the peculiar history of South Africa and the legacy of apartheid that separated groups by language (Kashoki 2003). Regardless of the pedagogical attributes of mother tongue education, it is tinged with the racism of apartheid and cannot escape this connotation as easily as the "newly discovered" mother tongue language option in Francophone Africa.

Finally, if we discuss external influences on African countries, we must include the World Bank. Though of course its membership is global, an American has led it since its inception.[41] Along with the predominance of American members on its board, U.S. financial contributions, its headquarters' location, and a general perception of a U.S.-led entity speak to its Anglophone orientation. This agency has been relatively silent on the issue of languages as well. The only explicit policy statement emerging from the World Bank before the mid-2000s appeared in a study by Nadine Dutcher (1982), who, after surveying several experimental programs, came to the conclusion that early mother tongue education was a good idea. Yet, since her recommendation, there has been a steady resistance to take a firm position on this sensitive issue. The bank's 1988 Report *Education in Sub-Saharan Africa* acknowledges that mother tongue education is efficacious. Nonetheless,

the policy regarding the language of instruction – whether and when to use the national language or an African language – must be derived by African governments themselves on the basis of political as well as economic imperatives. For most African countries a central objective of primary education is that pupils emerge orally fluent and literate in the national language. Fluency in the national language may help to promote political stability and build national unity as well as serve economic purposes. (World Bank 1988, 44)

Thus, even though acknowledging the pedagogical virtues of mother tongue education, it poses this method as potentially conflicting with the ultimate goal of achieving fluency in a national (e.g., European) language. Thus, there has been a steady resistance to take a firm position on this sensitive issue.[42] Ali Mazrui (1997) went so far as to accuse the bank of destroying the future of African languages in education. Jean Moulton, consultant to the World Bank on matters of education, reports that "the most frequent, visible, and controversial

---

[41] Current World Bank President Jim Yong Kim was born in South Korea but is a naturalized American citizen.

[42] Birgit Brock-Utne (2001, 122) reports a conversation with Makha N'Dao of the World Bank in Niger in April 1998, in which N'Dao told her that the World Bank "never involved itself in decisions that had to do with the choice of language of instruction" and then suggested that donors such as GTZ or the Swiss, "who often accuse the World Bank of being arrogant and setting tough conditions, were doing this themselves, forcing a certain national language policy on a country like Niger."

innovation in curriculum components has been the introduction of local languages for instruction in the early grades" (2003, 25). In personal correspondence, Moulton recalled an experience working in Mali, where Malians were very angry because the World Bank did not want to bother supporting Malian efforts to introduce mother tongue education. Since then, she says, the World Bank has begun warming to the use of local languages in education.[43]

Only very recently is it possible to discern pockets of support for mother tongue education emerging from the World Bank. Adrian Verspoor, writing the World Bank's Education Sector Assistance Strategy, advocates local language use but cites its difficulties.

Students learn better when taught in their mother tongue. Studies have shown consistently that students learn to read and acquire other academic skills faster in their own language [UNICEF 1999].... Studies of bilingual pilot programs in Mali and Niger suggest that children taught in their mother tongue learn a second language more quickly than children taught in a language other than that spoken at home [ADEA 1999].... However, much of the evidence from mother-tongue pilots is tentative and derived from questionable methodology. These pilots urgently need stronger monitoring and evaluation.... Language of instruction issues are also often politically and culturally contentious.... Governments will also have to consider the demand for education in European languages, which many parents see as opening doors to further education and professional employment. In sum, instructional policies must begin with local language and culture to improve students' performance, especially in the early grades. But successful implementation will also require an effective strategy for transition to a second language of instruction. (2001, 36–37)

Note that the referents he cites are Francophone countries. ADEA (the Association for the Development of Education in Africa), which joins donors and ministers of education from across Africa and is tied institutionally to the World Bank and UNESCO, has been influential in beginning to merge the Francophone and Anglophone bodies of research at the international level. Significantly, ADEA is headed by Mamadou Ndoye, the former minister for basic education in Senegal, who, as will be discussed later in the chapter, was central in activating Senegal's mother tongue program. More recent World Bank documents appear to take a less stringent adverse position, beginning to realize the obvious: a "major breakthrough," according to the (Francophone) scholar Hassana Alidou (2006, 31).

If a global norm explanation were doing the work, we would see similar outcomes across the board. In fact, this was my initial hypothesis when I first observed Cameroon's increasing attention to its languages in 2002. At that time, I assumed UNESCO's international advocacy and research in the field of minority language promotion were bearing fruit. But in each country I visited, while UNESCO was supposedly at the forefront of language promotion efforts, the organization turned out to be relatively impotent. Cameroon had no problem

---

[43] J. Moulton, telephone interview by author, January 13, 2004.

ignoring UNESCO recommendations supporting local language use for a long time. The UNESCO regional representative in Yaounde fairly barked me out of his office when I suggested that UNESCO might try to press for any particular policy in Cameroon. "UNESCO is made up of member countries," he retorted. "How could it try to impose anything on itself?"[44] UNESCO staff members in Senegal conceded that while UNESCO *does* try to push an agenda on issues such as HIV/AIDS or the Girl Child,[45] it does very little aside from encouragement and research on the issue of languages.[46] Thus, for language policy, UNESCO draws attention to the subject of mother tongue education only by financing research, but self-consciously does not pressure government. Because it antici-pates the potentially divisive results, it is reluctant to propose a suggestion.[47] In Ghana, UNESCO is ready to assist if asked, but it respects the unique policies of each member state, maintaining a policy of "noninterference." The secretary-general for Ghana's National Committee for UNESCO reported: "If it becomes necessary that language becomes an issue, [UNESCO] will aid, but member states have to request the funding from a platform of agreement. Since Ghana is not unanimous about its policy, it won't be requesting assistance in this area."[48] Contrary to what international language rights advocates would like to believe, the global normative influence on Africa is relatively weak. Instead, states are motivated more by a specific message emanating from their former metropole.

So we see that the ideas about language policy circling in the Anglophone and Francophone environments are radically different. France recently has decided that promoting local languages in education forms an important part of its cultural strategy, while the United Kingdom and the World Bank are ambivalent on the issue. Whereas until the early 1990s, France overtly encouraged Francophone Africa to use only French in primary schools, after that turning point, the message changed. The goal remains French-language acquisition, but the strategy is different. French leadership has recently become convinced by a community of scholars that children learn a second language better when they begin in their mother tongue. The apparent concession to the place of indigenous languages in education is actually a means to facilitate African students' learning of French. Particularly at the Etats Généraux for Francophone Education on the "Teaching of and in French" in Libreville (Gabon) in 2003, Northern and

---

[44] P. Mpayimana, director, Education Division, UNESCO, interview by author, Yaounde, October 2, 2002.

[45] R. Thwing, SIL director, told me that there is plenty of money from UNESCO if you are working on literacy in the North, where you can put it under the category of girls' education (interview by author, Yaounde, October 4, 2003).

[46] S. Benoit and M. Simiti, UNESCO, interview by author, Dakar, March 19, 2003.

[47] S. Benoit and M. Simiti, UNESCO, interview by author, Dakar, March 19, 2003.

[48] J. Kusi-Achampong, secretary-general, Ghana National Committee for UNESCO, interview by author, Ghana, April 16, 2003.

African members of la Francophonie highlighted the use of national languages as an integral part of the teaching of French.[49]

In contrast, there has been no such agreement reached within the Anglophone world. According to linguist Alamin Mazrui:

The question that preoccupied the British colonial administrators and missionaries – which language was most suited to learning in early childhood education – has virtually disappeared from current African debates on English as a medium of instruction and its implications for the acquisition of knowledge in other subjects in general. The situation affirms once again the triumph of "English only" ideology and policy in education in many British ex-colonies in Africa. (Mazrui 2002, 272)

The linguist and World Bank consultant Nadine Dutcher complained that even at the 2000 World Education Forum in Dakar there was no mention of the language issue in the plenary sessions of the conference.

It is shocking that the international dialogue on Education for All has not confronted the problems children face when they enter school not understanding the medium of instruction, when they are expected to **learn** a new language at the same time as they are learning **in** and **through** the new language. **The basic problem is that children cannot understand what the teacher is saying!** We believe that if international planners had faced these issues on a global scale, there would have been progress to report. However, instead of making changes that would lead to real advancement, the international community has simply repledged itself to the same goals, merely moving the target ahead from the year 2000 to 2015. (Dutcher 2004, 8, emphasis in original)

Messages to Africa from the Anglophone world about language in education are mixed: U.S. voices are divided, Britain's message is ambivalent, and the World Bank has notoriously vacillated in its policy prescriptions. The Francophone scholarly community differs markedly in its consensus and its strategic framing. The human rights element has not overshadowed the education focus in their writing, and the literature has not taken on the polemical tone that much of the Anglophone scholarship has adopted. In fact, the pitch has lowered from the earlier writing, and the authors arresting the attention of French policy makers have focused more on the pragmatic elements of local language use for development purposes and second language acquisition. These linguists present their interest in language not for its own sake, but as an instrument – of development, of education, and of French expansion.

An epistemic community usually emerges in the natural sciences on issues such as environment. Because this is a *social* scientific issue, it is not surprising that scholarly opinions are fragmented. The remarkable phenomenon is the cohesiveness of the Francophone linguistic research community. There are two reasons for this: framing and context. Francophone scholars have packaged their advice to policy makers as a means of bolstering French linguistic

---

[49] Supplement to *Journal de l'Agence intergouvernementale de la Francophonie* n. 32, April–May–June 2003.

aspirations. Rather than challenging the ultimate aim of French language expansion, they provide an alternate means of arriving at this goal. A side benefit is the preservation of African languages, but these languages do not compete with French for ultimate dominance. In contrast, the English-speaking academic communities advocating multilingual education have merged with linguistic rights activists, who preach a radical, uncompromising message about the inherent right of all to their respective languages. Challenging English hegemony forms the basis of this critique, a message unpalatable to most Anglophone policy makers.

A lack of compelling frame may reflect a different crisis. The disappearance of tiny languages or poor academic performance does not galvanize the same response as the potential reduction of a once-dominant power's cultural influence worldwide. Thus, an important difference is the global linguistic setting and its impact on the sense of crisis perceived by each metropole. France is trying to reverse a global language decline, while Britain and the United States can simply ride the rising tide. This influences the urgency of their motivation to listen to the prescriptions for change offered by scholarly communities. Thus, the first changed opportunity was a common shift in ideas among Francophone policy makers who controlled education funding to Africa. This message is especially influential for bureaucrats in the African Ministries of Education. With new funding and a wide scope for experimentation in local languages based on a pedagogical rather than a cultural rationale, these civil servants were much more open to persuasion from a second force: domestic advocates.

EXPANDED DOMESTIC POSSIBILITIES

A significant factor altering bureaucrats' preferences was the availability of materials in local languages. But languages do not speak for themselves; they need advocates. This section explains the expansion of written languages and their promoters particularly in the Francophone cases.

Languages must be written to be used in schools. Of the more than 2,000 languages in Africa, about 730 have a written form.[50] Not surprisingly, the larger languages were transcribed first, and so nearly 90 percent of citizens in African states have a written form for their mother tongue.[51] Thus, while well over 1,000 languages remain unwritten, these are generally for very small groups of speakers in each country. As described in Chapter 2, the first to write languages in Africa were missionaries, primarily Protestant, but also Catholic,

---

[50] Drawn from Grimes 1996, 2000, 2005 and Lewis 2009, which indicated the earliest date of Scripture portions, if they existed, for each language. The date of first Scripture portion is a proxy for date of written language, since the Scripture was usually the first piece of written material that would be available for circulation and potential literacy use.

[51] Calculated from Lewis 2009 by summing a current estimate of number of speakers for each written language as a proportion of the total current population estimate of all countries combined.

who were concerned with reaching their potential converts with a message they could understand in their own language. Missionary linguists continue to work actively on language translation in virtually every country in Africa. Of course, there are also indigenous linguists, working with missionaries, with other NGOs, and often for their own governments, to put their countries' languages into writing.

The work done by these facilitators makes the adoption of a pro–local language policy possible by providing the linguistic infrastructure necessary to build an education program. They provide orthographies, dictionaries, grammar books, reading materials, and sometimes even teacher training in local languages. Often, if a private translating organization is large enough, it has already put in place the blueprint and pilot of a literacy program that simply needs expansion. These are groups I call "evidentiary communities." A government faced with a decision about whether or not to introduce local languages in its education system will obviously have much less reason to resist if it sees a ready foundation of materials available in local languages. In the absence of a written language for a particular group of speakers, it is necessary to use another language as their medium of instruction. The cost-benefit analysis changes, however, when a language is written. It provides a necessary, even if not sufficient, condition for the use of the language in education.

The linguists serve two functions. First, they reduce setup costs for establishing and widening language use. Second, they create demand where there may not have been one before – cultivating a constituency that will use the resources they produce. Their research and, in the case of missionaries, evangelization efforts increase the demand for language resources among its speakers.

An evidentiary community thus enables government to enact language policy on the foundation of their linguistic research. Though their work inherently exerts pressure toward language recognition, this pressure has not necessarily been heeded by governments in the past. Their voices became much more important within Francophone Africa after France communicated its changed strategy. Their influence in Anglophone Africa is more ambiguous. To show the widening scope for policy choice pushed by local advocates, I begin by showing the situation of language transcriptions across the continent. Recall from Chapter 2 the marked delay of written languages in Francophone Africa, compared with British, Portuguese, Belgian, and noncolonized areas. *Outside* Francophone Africa, missionary transcription efforts began very early, and large portions of the population soon had a written language. By 1930, 73 percent of the populations under British control had their language in written form, 67 percent of populations under "other" administration, but only 40 percent of the populations in French-controlled Africa had a written form of their language. Figure 4.3 shows the cumulative proportions of the population previously under French, British, or other control that had their languages in written form.

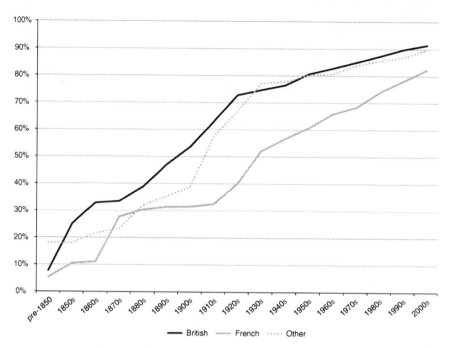

FIGURE 4.3. Population with a Written Language, by Colonizer. *Source:* I used the year Bible portions were transcribed as a proxy for availability of a written language. These dates and population figures (adjusted) were gathered from Grimes (1996, 2000) and Lewis (2009).

Of course, this did not mean these populations had *access* to these written materials; it only shows that materials were written in languages that covered a certain proportion of the population at successive periods. Activity in British territories began early and achieved the majority of transcriptions prior to 1930. It is only in the recent period – 1980 to 2000 – that we see the gap finally beginning to close in the Francophone areas. The figure reveals that it took until the late 1980s for the same percentage of the population in Francophone Africa to have a written language as the rest of Africa did in the 1930s.

This graph points to a critical factor in understanding part of the reason for the distinction in language policy in former French and British colonies. If by 1960, only 61 percent of the population of French territories had a written language, compared with 80 percent or more in British and other territories, it is perhaps not surprising that local languages were not used in education. Robert Armstrong in his 1968 seminal volume on language in developing areas writes: "To this day, not even a beginning has been made for the preparation of the teachers and pedagogic materials that would be necessary for enforcing the use of an indigenous national language in any West African country" (1968, 231). To be sure, this is an effect as well as a potential cause. British colonial policy, following practice in mission schools, extended the use of local languages to government schools, so there was certainly a demand for the written languages in these areas. In contrast, French colonial policy prohibited local language use in education, making the work of missionary translators less necessary for official purposes.

The direction of causality after independence is clearer. Despite the choice by most Francophone African governments not to use local languages in education, transcription activity by language NGOs continued to increase exponentially. As explained in Chapter 2, missionaries have long been recognized as important players in the early period of ethnic construction and mobilization (Young 1965; Comaroff and Comaroff 1991; Posner 2003, 127–146). This study shows that missionaries maintain a very central role. They, along with other language NGOs, are providing transcription for numerous unwritten languages, creating materials that facilitate their use in classrooms, and acting as advocates to bureaucrats and the public about the benefits of mother tongue education. Across Africa, one language NGO in particular has grown in importance: the Societé Internationale Linguistique (SIL),[52] a missionary affiliate of Wycliffe Bible Translators. Starting with only a few workers in Nigeria and Ghana in the 1960s, the organization grew to four hundred expatriate staff across Africa in the early 1980s, and jumped to eight hundred members by 1987. The number increased to nine hundred during the 1990s and held steady, as local workers are now trained in favor of adding expatriate staff.[53] Nonetheless, this is an extraordinary expansion of expatriate workers in the last twenty years, made possible by dramatic increases in financing from churches in the United States and Canada. Contributions to Wycliffe Bible Translators (SIL parent) nearly doubled in the 1990s from $67 million in 1990 to $120 million in 2002.[54]

Recent transcription activity by SIL linguists and other language NGOs has contributed to the current readiness of some governments to use local languages in their education systems. More important than just the number of languages is their demographic significance. Those places that are transcribing languages to cover large portions of their populations are undertaking new education efforts. The more recently transcription activity has occurred, the more likely a country is to use the languages in education. Countries that increased their language use in education had gained written languages for an average of 14 percent of their population since 1980. Countries that did not change their language policy gained a written language for an average of 5 percent of their population. And countries that reduced their use of local languages in education had only gained written material for 2 percent of their population since 1980.

---

[52] Originally the Summer Institute of Linguistics.
[53] G. Sweetman, pers. comm., March 13, 2004.
[54] D. Unruh, pers. comm., February 11, 2004. Also Wycliffe Bible Translators, Inc., "Combined Statement of Activities for the Year Ended September 30, 2002."

The recent transcription activity has two effects. First, it makes available many languages that previously were not written, changing the cost of using these languages. It is a necessary condition. Second, recent transcription suggests that there is also activity, or *advocacy*, by linguists for the languages that they are transcribing. This provides part of the "push" that motivates change, and the following section reveals its presence in Senegal and absence in Ghana.

The large comparative trends in historical transcription activity among British, French, and "other" regions of Africa, combined with this more specific analysis of the relationship between timing and scale of translation and propensity toward local language use, add to our understanding of the graphs shown at the beginning of the chapter. We see that the "French factor" has two causal pathways – ideas and transcription. Messages from the metropole have changed, allowing room for experimentation in countries within France's sphere of influence. And because they were later to begin than in British areas, it is in former French colonies that the most current transcription activity is occurring and that we see the greatest increase in local language use. Language NGOs are having a facilitating effect on governments who are faced with a choice of whether or not to use local languages in education.

The following regression (Table 4.1) is supportive of my claims. It probes for the causes of the change over the period of interest: 1990–2010. One needs to control first for the initial level of language use. The regression in the previous chapter showed the French dummy variable to be negatively significant for the intensity of language use at independence. If one did not control for the initial level in the following regression, the French coefficient would be 1.31 (.76) and the British -1.21 (.76), both significant and directly opposite the independence findings. When controlling for initial level and population size (model not shown), both colonial dummies lose their significance, though they remain in the predicted direction. Model 1 includes the variables that were important in the independence regression, fractionalization and the literacy rate, but neither affects changes in intensity of language use.

I add in Model 2 and Model 3 variables to check alternative explanations of democracy and government retrenchment, but these do not take any significance. In the fourth model, I test my own explanation that the percentage of the population that had a written language in 1990 contributed to the increasing intensity of language use after that date. Adding this variable brings the negative British dummy to significance and shows a large substantive impact. The final model adds a variable (and reduces the N, unfortunately) that will be explored in the next chapter – percentage of government revenue that derives from direct income taxes – which moves the French dummy to the fore and possibly provides a rationale for the negative sign on the British dummy (e.g., that it is in former British colonies that governments are deriving more of their revenue from direct income tax).

The regression supports my contentions that (1) colonial legacy matters, but opposite what historical expectations would indicate and (2) transcription is an

TABLE 4.1. *Regression: Determinants of Change in Intensity of Local Language Use, 1990–2010.* Outcome: Change in Intensity of Local Language Use in Education (-3.6 to +5)

	Model 1	Model 2	Model 3	Model 4	Model 5
Constant	−3.40	−2.85	−4.47	−5.01	−9.03
Initial intensity of local language use[a]	−.32**	−.28**	−.26**	−.31**	−.28**
	(.10)	(.09)	(.09)	(.08)	(.09)
French	.48	.50	.40	.79	1.63*
	(.75)	(.73)	(.75)	(.70)	(.99)
British	−.42	−.83	−1.13	−1.26*	−.75
	(.79)	(.70)	(.74)	(.68)	(.83)
Population (log)[b]	1.02*	.85**	.97**	.65*	.88*
	(.57)	(.42)	(.44)	(.41)	(.47)
Linguistic Fractionalization[c]	−.99				
	(1.31)				
Literacy rate[d]	−1.97				
	(1.78)				
Democracy[e]		−.51			
		(.42)			
Average GDP per capita growth 1980–1990[f]			.041		
			(.10)		
Percentage population with a written language, 1990[g]				3.36**	6.89**
				(1.3)	(2.87)
Percentage government revenue from income tax[h]					−.060**
					(.03)
N	49	49	46	49	34
AdjR²	.33	.34	.30	.41	.45

Standard errors in parentheses.

* Significant at .1 level.

** Significant at .05 level.

[a] ILLED 1989; 0 to 10.

[b] World Bank, WDI.

[c] Scale: 0 to 1. Language speakers calculated from Lewis 2009. I created a linguistic fractionalization index using Rae's formula: $1 - \Sigma g_i^2$, where g_i is the proportion of the population in language group *i*. Adapted from Gary Cox (1997, 205).

[d] Scale: 0 to 1. ADEA 1999 and UNESCO 1994.

[e] Autocracy = 1, Intermediate = 2, Democracy = 3 (adapted from Marshall and Jaggers's *Polity IV* database; Cape Verde, Sao Tome and Principe, and Seychelles assigned comparable scores from Freedom House; average 1990–2000).

[f] World Bank, WDI.

[g] Scale: 0 to 1. Bible portions as proxy for written language. Calculated from Grimes 1996 and 2000, Lewis 2009.

[h] Scale: 0 to 1. World Bank, WDI (taxes on income, profits, and capital gains as percentage of government revenue) average 1990–2010.

important facilitator in decisions made to use local languages in education. It also seems to cast doubt on rival explanations, such as demographics, democracy, or government retrenchment.

A regression can only demonstrate broad trends, however, and the small N makes findings relatively fragile. It is within cases that we can detect the mechanisms that combine to produce complex outcomes. The following section will show that "opportunity mechanisms" – a new message from France, language materials, and advocacy networks – are evident in Senegal, while they are absent in Ghana. Cameroon is discussed in a separate chapter.

OPPORTUNITIES FOR POLICY CHANGE IN SENEGAL AND GHANA

Senegal decided in 2001 to introduce six national languages into its education system. This was prompted by a new permissiveness communicated by France and transcription for large portions of its population, along with advocacy provided by local language NGOs. Ghana made a decision the same year to suspend its long-term mother tongue medium in schools. This resulted from opposite forces: an ambivalent message from its donors, a smaller proportion of its population affected by new language transcription, and a lack of general advocacy efforts on the part of NGOs.

This section will detail the differing opportunities within these two countries – particularly the newly transcribed languages and vigorous advocacy for their use in Senegal, versus a more static transcription in Ghana and much less public promotion.

Recall from Chapter 2 the different starting points of these two independent states. Senegal was the heart of colonial French West Africa, boasting more secondary graduates than the other territories and demonstrating France's assimilating, elite-oriented vision for education. Senegal's first president, Léopold Senghor, maintained the French-only medium of education policy at independence. "We are spiritual sons of France ... and good Africans don't break their family ties, they merely loosen them."[55] Partially because Senghor, a poet, was himself interested in languages (Senghor 1983, 11) he commissioned the study of the six major languages of Senegal by linguists at the University of Dakar.[56] He did envision their use in education in the far future – perhaps one hundred years hence (Senghor 1983, 12) – and even authorized a small, experimental program primarily in Wolof in a handful of classrooms in 1979.[57] This experiment was abandoned after two years, and the French-only policy

---

[55] "The Will to Nationhood" speech (1962), cited in Mansour 1993, 121.

[56] Decree No. 71–566 of May 21, 1971 Relative to the Transcription of National Languages. CLAD (Centre de Linguistique Appliquée de Dakar) at the University of Dakar.

[57] Several experimental classes in Wolof, Serer, and Pular medium were scheduled to begin in October 1977, but only three classes had begun in Wolof by 1979 and one in Serer by 1980. Dumont 1983, 197 (note 2), 266.

continued in full force. Senghor's ideas reflected la Francophonie's interest in *description* and preservation only, rather than practical use. At independence, with only Wolof and a few small cross-border languages transcribed,[58] less than half the population had a language that was written. By 1980, the languages of only about 60 percent of the population had written form.[59] Since 1980, however, three major languages (Pulaar, Diola, and Malinke) have received written form with an accompanying literature, adding more than 30 percent more of the population that could anticipate mother tongue literacy.

In Senegal, the majority of school-aged children are not attending formal school. Because of this, NGOs recognized the potential for their influence in nonformal education. The most significant NGO in this sector was ADEF (Association for the Development of Education and Training in Africa),[60] formed by a group of educators in 1992 to tackle the dire problem of illiteracy. They understood the limits of government activities and proposed to make their own contribution. Since such a large percentage of Senegal's school-aged children languished outside the formal education system, the field was ripe for private initiative. ADEF-Africa was born, and one of its lasting, notable achievements was the creation of Écoles Communautaires de Base (ECB) – Community Foundation Schools. These schools used the mother tongue as the medium of instruction, with French as the second language, until the third year, when French was phased in as the language of instruction. They had tremendous effects. ADEF presented results from its success in educating children in ECB schools through the medium of their mother tongue at the government education conference in Kolda (1993) and again at St. Louis (1995). Though the evaluations were not systematic and consisted primarily of teachers' accounts of student performance, the powerful message came through clearly. The former minister Ndoye reports: "We showed that in three years, pupils in the ECBs performed equal to or better in French than did their counterparts who had had six years of French."[61] As ADEF proved its success teaching children through the medium of their mother tongue outside the formal education system, its materials and methods were eventually used as templates for the formal sector.

To implement local language programs, it is essential to have public support. Surveys conducted in Senegal and Ghana revealed a striking difference (see Appendix B, Language Surveys, for description). In response to the question "Do you think students should begin education in their mother tongue?" Senegalese were nearly twice as likely as Ghanaians to be supportive. The results have much to do with the "sensitization'" conducted by language NGOs. In Senegal, the government has taken an active role, as described later, but SIL also indirectly contributes to public persuasion. For example, SIL has been vital for

[58] Wolof 1873 (38%), Mandinka 1837 (6.5%), Pular 1929 (1.5%), Jola Kasa 1961 (.4%) ≈ 46%.
[59] Above plus Mandjak 1968 (1%), Serer 1979 (10.2%), Upper Guinea Crioulo 1979 (1%) ≈ 59%.
[60] Association pour le Développement de l'Éducation et de la Formation en Afrique.
[61] M. Ndoye, executive director, ADEA, telephone interview by author, April 20, 2005.

the transcription of small languages such as Saafi-Saafi. Alioune Dione, a Saafi-Saafi speaker, had been a transcriber for a German linguist working on the Saafi-Saafi language at the University of Dakar in the late 1970s. Dione began teaching literacy in his language to people from his village in 1983. When the SIL linguist Hilbrand Dextran arrived in the area in 1987, it was easy for him to pick up where the earlier linguist had left off by enlisting Dione's help. SIL paid for teaching seminars conducted by Dione, and for his transport and meals; it also financed all materials for literacy training. In 1988, the Saafi-Saafi Language Committee began with Dextran, Dione, two academics from the university, and three other Saafi-Saafi speakers. In 1989, SIL officially hired Dione to lead literacy training among the Saafi. And it had a noticeable impact. My surveys from this language area revealed that virtually *every* respondent preferred that children begin education in their mother tongue.[62]

The government's Direction of Literacy and Basic Education (DAEB) began with basic SIL materials.[63] Importantly, in the mid- to late 1990s, a flush of money appeared to finance the development of educational materials in local languages that would be used in the nonformal sector. All codified languages could qualify for this support, and more than one hundred titles were printed in the six official languages between 1998 and 1999 (Ministère de l'Enseignement 2001, 13). The office charged with promoting local languages in the Ministry of Education (DPLN) now lists a total of more than 1,930 titles written in twenty-four Senegalese languages.[64]

Similarly, ADEF saw the importance of sensitizing parents to the utility of local language in *nonformal* education and transferred this idea to the formal program. In Senegal, where there was initially no official support for the use of African languages in education, externally funded initiatives grew up to experiment with local languages in private or nonformal schools. Their success could then be displayed to the government for emulation in the public school system. Senegal's significant recent transcription activity extended a new written language to large portions of the population. In addition, consistent, well-funded private initiatives demonstrated the effectiveness of mother tongue education, as well as laid the infrastructure (e.g., training programs and materials) that would support an official program in the future. Perhaps most importantly, these NGOs contributed to the sensitization of individual communities in ways that a heavy-handed government could not – motivating people to take pride in their languages and convincing them that learning them would improve their children's future learning of French.

---

[62] I actually dropped this group of results from my sample, fearing the research assistant may have "led" the responses, but it indicates that the work of SIL-supported language committees is having a positive effect on attitudes toward language use in education.

[63] B. Diouf, director DPLN, interview by author, Dakar, February 18, 2003.

[64] More than 700 of these works are in Wolof (Direction de la Promotion des Langues Nationales 2002, 6–7).

As in the case of the scholarly community's influence on Francophone leadership, ideas do not penetrate on their own. They need a spokesperson who can package and carry the message to policy makers. In Senegal, the individuals at the center of the effort actually infiltrated the education bureaucracy. Two names inevitably arise in discussions of mother tongue education in Senegal: Mamadou Ndoye and Mamadou Lamine Gassama. The more well-known of the two, Mamadou Ndoye, began his public career as head of the Teachers' Union. At the États Généraux held between 1981 and 1984, he headed a lobbying effort by teachers to press for the inclusion of national languages in the primary curriculum. Ndoye knew he had to prove the efficacy of the mother tongue effort. He was the instigator of ADEF, which, as described earlier, created the Écoles Communautaires de Base (ECB), schools that used the mother tongue initially as the medium of instruction.

He and other founders of ADEF met with President Abdou Diouf early on to seek his endorsement, and Diouf wrote them a letter of support, agreeing to be their first sponsor.[65] ADEF received financial support from other NGOs and several donors. These donors, particularly Canada and the World Bank, had begun to take notice of the success of the ECBs after the education conferences at Kolda and St. Louis. They began disseminating funds through a strategy known as "faire-faire." This was a decentralized method of distributing funds to recipient countries; with the money it received from donors, the state would finance NGOs to implement projects.[66] The efforts and money were still concentrated in nonformal education, but local languages were a visible and central component.

Ndoye had personally infiltrated government. In 1993, he was named minister for literacy and national languages, an office that had been created in 1991 as a marginal post for a member of the opposition.[67] When Ndoye arrived, the post was still concerned only with nonformal education. However, because of the success of the ECBs, the government added basic education to Ndoye's portfolio in 1995. Thus, he was in charge of all primary education – nonformal and formal – and he could transfer his expertise in one to the other. "Ndoye was the Minister we needed," explained an education consultant to the World Bank who had worked under Ndoye's education administration. "He pushed difficult ideas and had a positive impact."[68] Ndoye left in 1998 to become executive

[65] October 12, 1992; Letter No. 5159. Framed on the wall of the ADEF office.
[66] Programme d'Alphabétisation Intensive du Sénégal (PAIS) was started in 1993 by the Senegalese government with one thousand literacy classes using the national languages followed by the Projet d'Appui au Plan d'Action en matière d'Alphabétisation et d'Education non-Formel (PAPA), funded by the Canadian Agency for International Development in 1994. The follow-on to these projects and a new one focusing on women's education – PAPF – were funded by the World Bank after 2002 (Diallo 2010, 99–103).
[67] M. Ndoye, interview by author, Paris, April 29, 2003.
[68] A. W. Diagne, director, CAPEF, interview by author, Dakar, March 21, 2003.

secretary of ADEA, the consortium of donors to education based in Paris, but the initiatives he began continued to reverberate.[69]

Working during the same period, but less visibly, was a linguist from the University of Dakar, Mamadou Lamine Gassama. Under Ndoye's leadership, between 1993 and 1996, Gassama coordinated the effort to create an office within the ministry that would implement the mother tongue program in public schools. He recalls a meeting in 1994, when he invited a group of academics to his home informally to discuss the logistics of introducing mother tongues in education. His job was to elaborate the organizational structure of the soon-to-be-created Department for National Languages (DPLN) within the ministry, to sensitize authorities and native language speakers to the benefits of the program, and to continue to cultivate the support of teachers.[70] In 1996, Gassama became the number two technical adviser to Mamadou Ndoye and in 1998 became Ndoye's top "Technical Adviser in Linguistic Policy and Basic Education." After Ndoye left for ADEA, Gassama assumed the directorship of the newly created DPLN, under the ministry of Becaye Diop. In this capacity, he was asked to submit a proposition regarding the utility of national languages to the minister, who then transmitted the proposal for inclusion in the constitution.[71] In 2001, Gassama moved to be director of Diop's cabinet, maintaining his support of the national language program all the while.[72]

Gassama attributes his dedication to national languages to the teachers who inspired him: Arame Fal and Souleymane Faye, both linguists at the University of Dakar, who have written extensively on the need to elevate national languages.[73] I asked whether he thought it contradictory for an advocate of African languages to espouse their use in the service of French. Benefiting French was not *his* primary objective, he insisted. Using that argument is instrumental for getting support.[74] "Even if the government says it is adopting policy to help with performance in French, intellectuals should seize the opportunity. We should use all the instruments available,"[75] echoed his mentor, Arame Fal.

The creation of the DPLN was the decisive turn in Senegal, as now there is an institution for implementing the mother tongue policy. Ndoye and Gassama engaged in strategic packaging: Using mother tongues in schools benefited

---

[69] Significantly, ADEA is attached to the World Bank. With Ndoye now ADEA's executive secretary, it is not surprising that the World Bank is one of the major funding sources for the program.

[70] M. Gassama, pers. comm., letter dated July 5, 2003.

[71] Senegal's new Constitution – Section II, Article 22 – refers to the importance of national languages; the previous constitution mentioned only French as the official language.

[72] M. Gassama, pers. comm., letter dated July 5, 2003.

[73] M. Gassama, former director DPLN; former cabinet adviser to minister of education, interview by author, Dakar, February 24, 2003.

[74] M. Gassama, interview by author, Dakar, February 24, 2003.

[75] A. Fal, interview by author, Dakar, February 25, 2003 (though she is concerned about the hastiness of the reform).

French. Ndoye also used positive results to convince the government and the public. From the platform of a government ministry, he could also target the public more easily. An entire office is dedicated to "sensitizing" the public about the benefits of mother tongue education. In the new department for national languages in Senegal's Ministry of Education (which, as we saw, was created by the former head of ADEF), there is an office of communication, whose sole responsibility is to shape public opinion in favor of the new education policy: "showing people that the national languages aren't a substitute for French, but a complement."[76] The office has used a children's TV program, which airs during school vacations,[77] to emphasize the importance of mother tongue education, and the director of the department of national languages appeared on national television at least fifteen times in 2002 to talk about the benefits of the new program.[78] Therefore, significant government and private efforts have been devoted to bringing the public on board.

Ghana is a different story. The country entered independence under the lead of Kwame Nkrumah, a populist visionary who had championed the spread of mass education in the self-rule period prior to independence, and the country boasted higher-than-average primary and secondary enrollment. Nkrumah invested early in "cultural programming," setting up the Institute of African Studies at the University of Ghana and a national Arts Council "whose mission was to collect folklore traditions, promote local artists, and educate the public about Ghana's cultural heritage" (Coe 2005, 9). Previewing the country's ambivalent treatment of languages, he reoriented Ghana's schools toward English-only curriculum, while concurrently continuing to support African language development. Ghana's languages, in contrast to Senegal's, have had explicit government institutional support for use in education from before independence. The Bureau of Ghanaian Languages was established in 1951, with a mandate to produce materials – for adults and schoolchildren – in the nine (and later eleven) officially recognized languages. For the smaller languages, of which there are about fifty, there is GILLBT – the Ghana Institute of Linguistics, Literacy and Bible Translation. This organization began as SIL in 1962; most of the translators were expatriates, and Ghanaians assisted them. By 1980, this organization had transcribed nine languages in addition to the eleven managed by the government, and these transcriptions combined covered 75 percent of the Ghanaian population. Since then, there has been a "Ghanaianization" of the staff, and currently GILLBT is independent from SIL. The administration is almost entirely Ghanaian, and though there is still some Western support for translation activities, financial responsibility is being transferred to Ghanaian churches. GILLBT now has to raise local funds to support its translations. Importantly, though twelve languages have been transcribed since 1980, these only benefit an additional 6 percent of the population.

[76] M. Thiam, director of communication, DPLN, interview by author, Dakar, February 24, 2003.
[77] Oscar des Vacances.
[78] M. Thiam, director of communication, DPLN, interview by author, Dakar, February 24, 2003.

In contrast to recent production of many local language materials by the DPLN in Senegal, the Bureau of Ghanaian Languages, intended to be the sole supplier of educational materials in indigenous languages, has not printed anything for Ghana's primary schools for thirty-five years. It has published some materials for Ghanaian languages taught as subjects in secondary school, but there is literally no government-produced material available for primary schools except a 1971 booklet translated into the various official languages, called *The Way to Knowledge*. Even this is not a grammar or spelling book, but a collection of stories.[79] For the last decade, the Bureau of Ghanaian Languages has been poorly funded and has printed few materials in local languages *at all*.[80] Thus, the government could rightly claim that there were no materials available for mother tongue education. This was a technical definition of "not available," however. Several years ago, Education Minister Harry Sawyer commissioned Ghanaian language specialists to write education materials for grades one through three. The ministry received several submissions, but they remain in draft form. The government was unable to pay the printing fees, and the work came to a halt.[81] Tellingly, the bureau, which was formerly located within the Ministry of Education, is now attached to the Ministry of Culture.

The only source of new mother tongue education materials in the major languages appears to be from the German funding agency, GTZ. Though several donors are present in Ghana, GTZ is the only one of them seriously encouraging mother tongue education, according to Ghana's director of basic education.[82] In 1997, this agency began the Assistance to Teacher Education Program (ASTEP) "in cooperation within government's sound education policy," in which it produced schoolbooks in a few local languages.[83] GTZ's objective was to improve formal teacher training, since, it claimed, no methodologies existed. So GTZ created teaching methods for math and sciences, which included textbooks and teacher guides for use in teacher-training colleges. GTZ obtained about $700,000 from the World Bank to print 18,000 pupils' books in Ewe, 73,000 in Twi, and 800 teachers' guides in English for first and second grades (Andoh-Kumi 2002, 46). GTZ had produced materials that were ready for printing in the northern languages of Gonja and Dagbani and had begun work on Ga when the minister announced the reversal of policy.

In Ghana, use of local languages as media of education in schools – the prescribed policy from 1970 to 2001 – had mixed results. Often the policy was

---

[79] A. Awedoba, professor, Institute of African Studies, University of Legon, interview by author, Accra, April 3, 2003.

[80] J. C. Abbey, director, Bureau of Ghanaian Languages, interview by author, Accra, March 28, 2003.

[81] N. Klah, head of CRDD section on National Languages, GES, interview by author, Accra, April 22, 2003.

[82] E. Acquaye, director of basic education, Ghana Education Service, interview by author, Accra, April 5, 2003.

[83] K. Komarek, Ghana director, GTZ, interview by author, Accra, April 8, 2003.

implemented poorly or not at all.[84] Part of the problem was its relatively restrictive nature regarding the languages to which it applied. Only "approved" languages were to be used in schools. Gillian Hansford, SIL consultant working with GILLBT in the 1980s, reports problems that arose from this policy in the specific case of the Chumburung language (Hansford 1994, 76–84). Though GILLBT received outside funding for printing primers and anthologies of stories in Chumburung, the effort to use them to introduce the language in schools failed because there was no clear policy concerning the languages of the class-room. Chumburung was not one of the eleven official languages approved for use in schools, and the official language designated for the area was not being used. The teachers who had been trained by GILLBT pressed school officials to allow Chumburung to be taught in the slot marked for vernacular languages. Unfortunately, "among education authorities, there was disagreement as to which Ghanaian language could be taught legitimately, and a ban was placed on the teaching of Chumburung literacy in schools until such time as the current educational policy was clarified or reviewed" (Hansford 1994, 79–80).

Because of these restrictions in primary schools, GILLBT has focused mostly on adult literacy and collaborates with the adult, nonformal education depart-ment in the Ministry of Education. The underlying hope of GILLBT in its language transcription efforts is that the government will increase the number of languages approved in education if it decides to resume its mother tongue language policy.[85]

As described earlier, the most important recent producer of materials in large local languages for primary schools is GTZ. Critically, it began operating under the umbrella of Ghana's existing permissive policy. Therefore, it did not focus its efforts on ensuring that the materials penetrate into the schools. Understandably, it assumed that the use of the materials was assured because of the supportive government policy. As we will see, this existing policy reduced the perception of urgency and made advocacy efforts appear unnecessary.

Unlike ADEF or SIL in Senegal, GILLBT in Ghana was spatially removed from the capital – its headquarters was in Tamale, a two-day bus ride from Accra. It worked primarily with smaller languages and with adult literacy. Because the government-sponsored Bureau of Ghanaian Languages was sup-posed to be working on producing materials for primary education, GILLBT did not involve itself much in this area. The more active language organization, GTZ, began recently to supply local language materials for government use. But because of the existing supportive policy toward mother tongue education, it did not see a need to convince the government or public of the benefits of using local languages in education.[86]

---

[84] IEQ/Ghana Final Report: The Implementation of Ghana's School Language Policy (2001).

[85] S. Fembeti, communications director, GILLBT, interview by author, Accra, March 26, 2003.

[86] K. Komarek, director GTZ Ghana, interview by author, Accra, April 8, 2003. In fact, GTZ had used Ghana as a model to convince other countries to adopt its program.

My surveys showed that support for mother tongue education is about half as high in Ghana as in Senegal: 25 percent versus 47 percent.[87] I argue that this is because in Ghana, the language NGOs are sending mixed messages to the public, or they are not interacting with them at all. Though the public affairs coordinator in Accra insisted that GILLBT supported mother tongue education, an unsolicited letter I received from two former missionaries who were helping me to conduct surveys revealed that this sentiment is not shared by all:

We believe English (or French in French-speaking African countries) should be taught from the beginning in primary school. The examinations are so difficult at the end of primary, junior secondary and senior secondary. If English is delayed, it would be very difficult to cover everything on the syllabus. Also, for most children, if they had a vernacular language in the school, it would not be their mother tongue. As you can see from the surveys, *many* languages are spoken in our region of Northern Ghana. In urban areas, this is even more the case. So which language would be taught in the school? It would still be somebody else's language for most students. So why not get to English which is the examination language[?].[88]

In addition to a lack of consensus among missions, the language NGOs attached to the government did not engage in active advocacy. GTZ worked directly with the Ghanaian Ministry of Education, had little contact with the populations using the materials it produced, and did not engage in any sensitization of parents. It understandably believed the long-standing policy of government support for language use in education assured the policy's continuation.

Unlike in Senegal, Ghana's languages enjoyed official support in schools for thirty years. As a linguist admitted to me in an interview, linguists grew complacent. They did not think to advocate the benefits of mother tongue education, and they only came out strongly in support of it *after* the government changed the policy.[89] It appears that some urgency is necessary, and in Senegal, this was provided by prior suppression of languages. In Ghana, there was no perceived need to convince the government or the public that the use of local languages was a good policy, since the policy was already in place.

In Ghana, the government appears to have crowded out private efforts. Because only "official languages" were allowed to be used in schools, GILLBT could not experiment with the materials it produced for smaller languages in schools. And the Bureau of Ghanaian Languages was not producing materials in larger languages. GTZ, the only externally funded language NGO, was working to provide materials in the large languages in partnership with the government, but did not see the need to ensure an infrastructure for its

---

[87] Appendix B has interview questions. See Mfum-Mensah 2005, 80, for findings of similarly negative attitudes in Northern Ghana.

[88] Letter received from Baptist missionaries in the Northern region, May 2003.

[89] K. Andoh-Kumi, director of Language Centre, University of Legon, interview by author, Accra, March 30, 2003.

diffusion. No private networks had been established to cultivate or sustain public interest in such a program.

In contrast to the policy change in Senegal, Ghana's reversal of policy did not take any sustained effort at persuasion. It simply required persons in high positions. Christopher Ameyaw-Akumfi has been described as the singular instigator of the policy. Trained as a zoologist in the United States, his expertise was in science and higher education. He had been director-general of Ghana's Education Service under President Rawlings, and he became minister of education under President Kufuor. His collaborator, Christine Churcher, minister for primary, secondary, and girls' education, received a degree in English and history at University of Ghana and later taught English at secondary school. Aside from Cabinet position, she represented the Cape Coast as a minister of Parliament.

The combination of the two in the highest positions of education authority enabled the policy to be changed in a heartbeat. Ameyaw-Akumfi announced the cabinet decision on the Parliament floor on February 28, 2002. There was no debate until five months later. Though the president had earlier appointed a commission to make recommendations regarding the future of Ghana's education policies, these recommendations were not scheduled to come out until the summer of 2002, well after he announced the change of policy. Dismantling a program is much easier than building one. The ministers in Ghana personally believed there was a crisis in the education system that could only be solved by the elimination of local languages as media of instruction. They anticipated little objection except perhaps from a few intellectuals and GTZ. And they were right. Ghana's major donors did not react. And the public supported the policy change. This was because there had been little sustained effort in favor of local language education by an evidentiary community.

In contrast to active French involvement in language policy in Senegal, British officials appear not to want to be involved at all. A conversation with Donald Taylor, education adviser at DFID in Ghana, confirmed a lack of engagement on this issue. He said that DFID is "not closely involved with anything to do with language policy" in Ghana, and as far as a policy from Britain, DFID has "no particularly strong line." Taylor had met with the minister of education but had not discussed the language policy. At the time of our conversation, he had been in Ghana for a year, and during this time, at the monthly donor meetings, to his recollection donors had not discussed language policy at all.[90]

Anglophone donors' concern with mother tongue education is extremely muted on the ground. When Ghana's education minister announced his decision to change the mother tongue policy at the donors' meeting, no one but Germany objected.[91] The World Bank, USAID, UNESCO, and DFID had nothing to

---

[90] D. Taylor, education adviser, DFID Ghana, telephone interview by author, April 22, 2005.
[91] J. S. Djangmah, Dzorwulu, interview by author, Accra, April 11, 2003.

say.[92] Since Germany provides less than 5 percent of Ghana's aid, the government seemed unconcerned about flouting its contributions to mother tongue education. The EU, at the urging of Germany, was the only major donor to write a letter of criticism.[93] Obviously, the government knew that it would not lose support of any of its major donors with its change in policy.

Ghanaian ministers, in response to a query about what they perceive donor messages to be, insist that this is beside the point. They are anxious to appear unconstrained by the influence of outsiders. Christine Churcher, when I asked whether she worried that Ghana may be giving up donor money by changing the policy, insisted that it is "not for donors to tell us what to do."[94] Christopher Ameyaw Akumfi answered, "The decision was taken at the Cabinet level . . . it is not proper for donors to dictate our policy."[95]

The language situation in these cases thus differs markedly. In Senegal, active recent transcription of languages over the last twenty years has given an additional 30 percent of the population the possibility of education in their mother tongue. Ghana, by contrast, started with a higher overall percentage of the population having access to written materials but has only added another 6 percent of its population in the last twenty years. Recent transcription activity is much more marginal. We see a profusion of materials available across the spectrum of local languages in Senegal, whereas in Ghana, the only recent publications, by GTZ, are for a few major languages. Though transcribed languages and available materials are a necessary condition for the use of local languages in schools, education bureaucrats will only be convinced if they actually see positive results of their use. In Senegal, the results were demonstrated by the NGOs involved; in Ghana, this step apparently did not seem necessary, given the prior policy of official support for mother tongue education.

CONCLUSION

For a leader to take a new direction in policy, potential obstacles need to be removed. In this chapter, I explained how the two obstacles that had previously hindered Francophone African governments from considering a policy change favoring local languages – French ideology and lack of available language materials – were overcome in the 1990s. With a supportive international context and a facilitating domestic environment, mother tongue education became conceivable. This affected particularly bureaucrats in ministries of education and parents, who might have provided resistance. An evidentiary community in

[92] E. Acquaye, director of basic education, Ghana Education Service, interview by author, Accra, April 5, 2003.
[93] Letter from Ambassador Stefan Frowein to Mr. Yaw Osafo Maafo, minister of finance, October 1, 2001. K. Komarek, GTZ, interview by author, Accra, April 8, 2003, and W. Osafo, education specialist, USAID, interview by author, Accra, April 7, 2003.
[94] C. Churcher, interview by author, Accra, April 17, 2003.
[95] C. A. Akumfi, interview by author, Accra, April 24, 2003.

Senegal consciously persuaded civil servants and the public with these altered possibilities. This was also true in Cameroon, the topic of detailed study in Chapter 6. The opposite was the case in Ghana. Bureaucrats heard contradictory messages from donors, neither they nor parents were "sensitized" systematically by language activists, and new transcription was not occurring for large portions of the population.

International norms clearly did not affect all states evenly. As will be discussed in the next chapter, the bargaining explanation depends on agitation by regional language elites for promotion of their languages. Because there were no such actors pressing for local language medium in education in Senegal, the adoption of such a policy demands an alternative explanation. In this case (as in Cameroon), determined individuals worked to persuade policy makers that such a policy would improve student performance. Importantly, they and the NGOs that supported and reinforced their efforts also worked to cultivate a public willingness to accept such a policy change. Because Ndoye and his successor, Gassama, actually assumed leadership positions in the Senegalese government, they were able to continue their sensitization campaign from a public platform and with government resources. A malleable public and tireless persuasion were the keys to dampening any potential opposition. The new policies that favored local languages, however, were only possible because of a supportive attitude on the part of France, former colonizer and continuing ideational authority in Senegal. The new ideology in the metropole offered a way to meld rhetoric in support of African languages with the continued goal of eventual French language acquisition, and both pragmatic African politicians and French donors could be satisfied.

Ghana points convincingly to important contrasts. The general public appears much less malleable, and it does enter the bargaining equation in opposition to local language use in education. This situation arises from the absence of several factors that were present in the Senegalese cases. First, there was no individual working tirelessly to prove that a mother tongue program could be successful. An understandable lack of urgency resulted from a policy that had existed on paper for so long. Second, the government maintained the larger languages as its own domain, off-limits to missionary transcription work, and those missionaries working on the remaining smaller languages were not actively engaged in changing public opinion. In fact, there is evidence that some were themselves suspicious of the mother tongue language policy. The one NGO with an interest in local language use in schools (GTZ) was involved at a high level, interacting with the government, rather than concerning itself with public opinion on the ground. Third, the message received by Ghana from Britain and the United States, its two largest donors, was ambivalent: lip service to the cultural value of mother tongues, but bottom-line interest in the teaching of English. The astute politician and the ministers he appointed in the education sector would not fear a backlash from donors, and they could anticipate increased public support by reverting to an English-only policy. In this situation as well, there were no regional language elites pushing for local language use in schools, but they were not replaced by other actors, as was the case in Senegal. Absent were a tireless local advocate, a facilitating nongovernmental infrastructure, and a strong message from the metropole that favored local languages.

Though opportunities arose because of an open international environment and available materials, political leaders required more than a smoothed path to policy change. They needed political incentives. This, I argue, was provided by the pressures in the 1990s toward democratization in Africa.

5

Incentives for Policy Change

Ruler Strategies for Maintaining Power

As the climate for introducing local languages into education has become more welcoming, and NGOs facilitate this with their materials and advocacy, obstacles to adopting such a policy have been dramatically reduced. But why would leaders decide to go down this path? Most leaders undertake policies that will keep them in power. I submit that what may appear to be concessions to minority groups may instead be viewed from a ruler's perspective as a way to maintain control. If changed ideas on the part of influential partners and increased availability of materials in local languages alter leaders' *opportunities* to use local languages in education, a changing political context gives them different *incentives*. As rulers face pressures to democratize and decentralize, policies favoring local language education can become a strategy through which they attempt to maintain power by fragmenting potential opposition. Though not all leaders have singularly power-seeking motives, it is not implausible that this may drive some of their acquiescence in policies that increase the use of local languages in education. While of course we can never be certain of personal motives, this chapter will show that this is a more likely explanation than one that attributes the policy change to genuine political opening or to bargaining with political rivals.

This chapter will explore the moves toward democracy over the past two decades in Africa and juxtapose these with increasing levels of local language use in education. It will argue paradoxically that in many cases this may not be a reflection of liberalizing governments concerned with minority rights and representation, but a tool of desperate leaders attempting to maintain their hold on power. Whether this strategy will indeed restrain opposition or instead backfire – either by provoking violence or by undermining hegemonic control – is a question that will be posed in Chapter 7.

Though the upward trend in the use of African languages corresponds with overall increases in the continent's level of democracy in the 1990s, it is not in fact those states that are improving their democracy scores that are increasing their use of local languages. Democracy *does*, however, play an important role by serving to change the calculations of leaders considering the importance of language use in education. If, as described in Chapter 3, African independence leaders quickly abandoned their effort toward a single, unifying language and instead opted for indifference, the advent of multiparty democracy in the 1990s presented them with a potential motivation for deliberate policy choice. I suggest that they are beginning to see multilingualism as a political resource. The preferences of leaders who want to maintain power are shifting subtly from ambivalence to active interest in multilingual policies. This chapter first will describe the setting from the 1990s to the present. It will then show that alternative explanations of democracy and bargaining do not in fact account for the local language policies we observe. Instead, complementing the opportunities described in the previous chapter, particularly in Francophone Africa, local language policies appear logical given incentives provided by new electoral calculations. Elsewhere, variation can largely be explained with institutional configurations and economic trajectories. This chapter first looks at all states in Africa and then more specifically at Senegal and Ghana. The next chapter concentrates on the single case of Cameroon.

DEMOCRACY AND MULTILINGUAL EDUCATION

Many African leaders at independence justified single party or military rule by pointing to the potential for fragmentation within their borders. Having now squandered their credibility by leading their states into economic and political crisis, current leaders have no alternative but to accept at least the façade of elections. As the third wave of democracy swept over Africa in the 1990s, the question of constituent identities within states once again emerged.

In the last two decades, more than 70 percent of African states made changes away from autocracy, even if not necessarily arriving to full democracy.[1] Initial enthusiasm gave way quickly to pessimism, as scholars lamented the ability of authoritarian leaders to retain power and manipulate the "democratic" system to their advantage (Carothers 1997, 2002; Diamond and Plattner 1999; Ottaway 2003; Diamond 2008; Plattner 2010). Contradicting these pessimists, however, are a few new optimists, who see the potential for the exercise of elections in themselves – even if flawed – to induce greater political liberties within African states (Lindberg 2006, 2009; Harbeson 2008). Andreas Schedler recently compiled a general inventory of how electoral authoritarian regimes use democratic institutions to reinforce their rule. Yet he is hopeful about the

---

[1] Changes in Freedom House scores (average civil liberties and political rights) from 1990 to 2008 showed 71% of states moving toward greater freedom, while the remaining 29% either made no change or became less free.

possibility (even if not the probability) that these institutions may erode authoritarian stability (Schedler 2010, 77).

Arend Lijphart's influential work on consociationalism has made power sharing almost axiomatic in considerations of institutional change in multiethnic societies (Lijphart 1977 and 2007). Across Africa, national conferences in the 1990s were predicated on the participation of all parties and social groups, and virtually all postconflict settlements in Africa in the last decade have contained provisions for power sharing (Mehler 2009, 471). Lijphart's ideal type of consociationalism includes cultural autonomy and group recognition, recommendations that dovetail nicely with the concern of international organizations and activists with cultural and linguistic rights. Therefore, one would expect that this pressure toward inclusive democracy would play a role in the increasing attention to local languages in education. As the regression in the previous chapter demonstrated, however, level of democracy is not significant in predicting the increasing intensity of language use in education. Since the N was so small, however, it may be that the regression is not capturing the phenomenon adequately.

This first section of the chapter looks more closely at the relationship between regime type and propensity to recognize local languages in education systems. It finds first that democracies are not more likely to use local languages in education, and, second, while liberalization seems to be associated with increased local language use, the quality of democracy deteriorates after this policy change much more frequently than in those regimes reducing the use of local languages or making no policy change at all.

The optimists mentioned would lead one to believe that it is movements toward democracy on the continent that are motivating more minority sensitive legislation. Amy Liu (forthcoming; and Liu et al. 2011) makes this point explicitly about a global set of cases. The causal mechanisms are logical: Increased attention to civil liberties and an electoral calculus that aims to draw more voters into the fold push leaders to offer language rights to minorities. But her regression reveals that Africa is an outlier, not conforming as neatly as other regions to the hypothesis (Liu forthcoming: table 3). I look in this section for evidence (1) that democratic states are more likely to have minority language provisions and (2) that liberalizing countries are increasing their level of minority language recognition more than countries that are not making improvements in democracy. And I offer an explanation for the counterintuitive findings.

As before, I use the variable "Intensity of Local Language Use in Education" – ILLED, designed to show the commitment by governments to African language education versus foreign language education. Dividing states into Freedom House categories of Free, Partly Free, and Not Free does not reveal a positive relationship between democracy and multilingual education. Among Free states, average ILLED is 3.4; among Partly Free it is 4.6; and among Not Free it is 4.5. The most free states in 2010 actually had a slightly lower intensity of use overall than less free states.

TABLE 5.1. *Democracy and Intensity of Local Language Use in Education* (Arrow shows direction of ILLED change; first number is magnitude of change; number in parentheses gives 2010 ILLED score)

Countries That Increased ILLED 1990–2010	Democracy*	Liberalizing before Change	Regressed after Change	Countries That Decreased ILLED 1990–2010	Democracy*	Liberalizing before Change	Regressed after Change
Angola↑4 (4)	No	Yes	No	Botswana↓1.2 (6)	Yes	No	Yes
Benin↑3 (3)	No	Yes	No	Ghana↓3.6 (3.6)	Yes	Yes	No
Burkina Faso↑4.8 (4.8)	No	Yes	No	Guinea-Bissau↓3 (0)	No	No	No
Cameroon↑3 (3)	No	Yes	Yes	Kenya↓1.2 (6)	No	Yes	Yes
Chad↑1.2 (3)	No	No	Yes	Malawi↓.6 (4.8)	Yes	Yes	Yes
Cote d'Ivoire↑3 (3)	No	Yes	Yes	Mauritania↓1.2 (1.8)	No	No	No
Djibouti↑5 (5)	No	Yes	Yes	Namibia↓3 (6)	Yes	Yes	No
Ethiopia↑5 (9)	No	Yes	Yes	Somalia↓3 (6)	No	No	No
Gabon↑3 (3)	No	No	Yes	South Africa↓1.5 (6)	Yes	No	No
Guinea↑5 (5)	No	No	No	Swaziland↓1.5 (7.5)	No	No	Yes
Mali↑3 (6)	Yes	Yes	Yes	Zimbabwe↓.6 (4.8)	No	No	No
Mozambique↑5 (5)	No	Yes	Yes				
Niger↑1 (5)	No	Yes	Yes				
Senegal↑5 (5)	No	Yes	Yes				
Sudan↑2 (4)	No	No	No				
Zambia↑4 (4)	No	Yes	Yes				
	6% Yes	75% Yes	69% Yes		45% Yes	36% Yes	36% Yes

Countries That Maintained High ILLED

	Democracy*	Liberalizing in 1990s	Regressed from 2000
Burundi (9)	No	Yes	No
Congo, Dem. Rep. (5.4)	No	No	No
Eritrea (10)	No	No	Yes
Lesotho (9)	No	Yes	No
Madagascar (9)	No	Yes	Yes
Nigeria (9)	No	Yes	No
Rwanda (9)	No	Yes	No
Seychelles (9)	No	Yes	No
Sierra Leone (4.8)	No	Yes	No
Tanzania (6)	No	Yes	No
Uganda (6)	No	Yes	No
	0% Yes	82% Yes	18% Yes

Countries That Maintained Low ILLED

	Democracy*	Liberalizing in 1990s	Regressed from 2000
Algeria (1.8)	No	No	No
Cape Verde (o)	Yes	Yes	No
Comoros (o)	No	Yes	No
Congo, Republic (o)	No	No	Yes
Equatorial Guinea (o)	No	No	No
Gambia (o)	No	No	No
Liberia (o)	No	No	No
Mauritius (o)	Yes	No	No
Sao Tome & Principe (o)	Yes	Yes	Yes
Togo (o)	No	No	No
	27% Yes	36% Yes	27% Yes

*Freedom House score at the time of ILLED change or average from 1990–2010 if no change.

We are more interested, however, in the changes occurring during the democratic "opening" in Africa after the 1990s. It is therefore more appropriate to assess changes in language use against changes in democracy scores. A figure plotting changes in democracy scores and changes in local language use is inconclusive and therefore not shown. More useful is Table 5.1, which places countries into four different categories – determined by whether they increased, decreased, maintained high levels, or maintained low levels of local language use between 1990 and 2010. In this way, we can see whether democracy and liberalization are associated with changes in intensity of local language use. The table reveals that democracy is *not* in fact associated with increasing intensity of language use. There are more democracies among countries that reduced their use of local languages (45 percent) and maintained low levels of local language use (27 percent) than among those that increased it (6 percent) or maintained high levels (0 percent). *Liberalization*, however, does seem to be correlated with increasing levels of local language use. Among countries that increased the intensity of local language use, 75 percent were in the process of liberalizing in the years leading up to the change, while only 36 percent of countries reducing their levels of local language use were liberalizing in the years leading up to the change. This is an important point.

I argue, however, that this was only a superficial relationship. The shallowness of the apparent liberalization is revealed in that nearly 70 percent of all of the countries that increased their local language intensity regressed in their democracy scores in the years following the change. And this percentage should be even higher, since two of the five "nonregressors," Angola and Sudan, simply remained firmly in their nonfree categories. Only Benin and Burkina Faso seem to be genuinely liberalizing as they are increasing the intensity of their local language use. Among countries reducing the use of their local languages, only 36 percent regressed in their democracy score after the change. Countries that made no changes either way were more stable overall, only 18 to 27 percent regressing in their democracy scores after 2000.

We have found in this section, first, that democracy is not associated with increased levels of language use; in fact, one finds more democracies among countries that reduced or maintained low levels of language use. Second, while liberalization does seem to correspond with increased local language use, the deterioration of democracy after the change supports my contention that such policy concessions are not in fact evidence of real political opening.

BARGAINING: DEMOGRAPHIC AND SUBNATIONAL VARIATION

A second competing explanation is not necessarily democratic pressure, but pressure from rivals to power – a bargaining explanation. In Chapter 3, we saw that Laitin (1992) provided a general model of the bargaining between center and periphery to explain the multilingual outcomes he observed in Africa.

I hinted there that the preferences he assigns to relevant actors are not as straightforward as it may seem.

Recall that in his analysis, at independence national leaders are torn. They want unity for the country, which is easiest to achieve by continuing to advance the colonial language, but they also gain political rewards for espousing rhetoric that favors African languages. He claimed that these leaders wanted to achieve language rationalization within their countries for national unity and efficient administration. This could be achieved in two ways – either the entire country could speak a European language, or everyone could speak an African language. Their preferences over language policy, then, are mixed in terms of whether they choose a European or African language, but they all desire a unifying language. While in the heady postindependence years, many ruling parties did strongly advocate a return to African roots, including the revival of African languages in all spheres of life, few parties consistently held up language rights as a central goal. "Natural support" (Laitin 1994, 631) for indigenous national languages in populist opposition programs was not evident. And, as shown in Chapter 3, the desire for any unifying language dissipated quickly, replaced with ambivalence.

Laitin claimed that in general, bureaucrats have a clear, singular preference to maintain a European language (Laitin 1992, 94). This assures their comparative advantage, since they are among the elite that speak a European language fluently. Their expertise gives them an advantage over other claimants to their civil positions. He notes, however, bureaucrats in the Ministry of Education are exceptional because they have absorbed intellectual reasoning about the pedagogic benefits of mother tongue education (Laitin 1992, 96). I argue instead that as a result of their opposing educational experiences, these bureaucrats in fact would *not* have uniform preferences. Those educated in the British system would have absorbed the pedagogic benefits of mother tongue education, while Francophone bureaucrats did not. This changed in the 1990s. It was only with a different message from the French Ministry of Foreign Affairs, as well as the persuasive influence of local language NGOs, that these Francophone civil servants began to accept that local languages might be useful for learning French. Anglophone bureaucrats are receiving contradictory messages, and so their policy preferences are variable.

Parents of schoolchildren want their children to succeed economically, and so they normally prefer European-language education. But they are also interested in preserving their own particular language and will prefer it to a national language that is not theirs (Laitin 1994, 631). I showed in the last chapter, however, that their preferences are also malleable. We saw that many parents in Senegal have been persuaded by NGOs' sensitization efforts, as well as by government campaigns.

Finally, regional elites, though they do not figure explicitly in Laitin's game (1994, 106, 111), turn out to be necessary to the explanation for why local languages are preserved in education and regional administration. He assigns to regional elites a strong preference for preserving their own language and mobilizing their followers to press for the same privilege. This is the only way he can arrive at a *three-* rather than a two-language outcome. If language elites do not feature in his analysis, only a European language and a lingua franca would have any chance of promotion.

The bargaining explanation attributes multilingual outcomes to regional language elites who trade language concessions for political support. This implies that multilingual policies would correspond with the power of local elites. We would therefore expect to see more intense use of African languages in settings where there were no competing language groups (e.g., monolingual situations) or where there were a few significant and cohesive groups that were valuable for political support. Behind a bargaining explanation, then, are demographic configurations and subnational variation in group strength.

Demographics as a potential explanation for policy inertia was first presented in Chapter 3. In the regression looking at independence policies (Table 3.1), levels of fractionalization seemed to curb intense language use in education, but the importance of the variable declined when the extent of written languages was introduced. Rather than explaining stasis, however, it may be that the linguistic demographics of African states can explain the changes that occurred after 1990. Opposite my own explanation about the continuation of colonial influence, perhaps the weight of the past has finally lifted enough that the natural requirements of the African multilingual landscape can be met. Multilingual states can now choose the multilingual policies that fit their demographic constellation. Perhaps, as reasoned earlier, it took time for the colonial influence to dissipate, and current policies are simply a more accurate reflection of the linguistic array in each country. Before considering the dynamics of bargaining, one might reasonably assume that where there are several languages, these languages will eventually gain an alphabet, dictionary, grammar, and texts and find their way into educational use. Thus, one might expect that in countries with many languages, multilingual policies would prevail. But simple diversity, measured by fractionalization, does not reveal a relationship. Neither, it turns out, does "effective number of languages."[2] While monolingual Burundi and Rwanda continue to use their languages intensely, similarly homogeneous Sao Tome and Principe and Cape Verde do not. And though a few competing groups in Eritrea are associated with intense language use, a similar constellation in the Gambia is not. Some countries with extremely high numbers of languages are using most of them (Nigeria), while others are using none at all (Congo-Brazzaville). Testing a bargaining model with straightforward demographics, it does not appear that groups in countries with a single or a few languages are more likely to press for concessions than groups in countries with multiple languages.

But bargaining may not be this simple. Scholars have put forward several ideas about the spatial and hierarchical configuration of groups. Horowitz

---

[2] Derivation explained in Chapter 3. Inconclusive figures not shown.

points to relational size, Posner to political relevance, and Boone to autonomous power.

Donald Horowitz's foundational work, *Ethnic Groups in Conflict* (1985/2000), assumes that the most severely divided societies are found in those with two or three large groups, rather than those where one group has by far the majority, or where no group is numerically dominant. He suggests that where two or three ethnic groups command at least 20 percent of the population, consensus likely will be most difficult (Horowitz 1985, 37–38). Since language in education is thought to be one of the most contentious policies, one would expect that places with a few large language groupings would have a more difficult time reaching consensus over language policy. To see whether those countries with a certain constellation of language groups have more or less difficulty enacting multilingual education policies, I arrayed them on a scale determined by the size of the largest language(s).[3] Clustering countries by this categorization, I find that the intensity of language use is almost identical in each category.[4] There is no difference in intensity of language use on the basis of whether there is a single dominant group, two large groups, or several large groups.[5] Neither the number of groups nor their arrangement in relation to each other consistently affects a country's medium of instruction policy. The data also do not support the proposition that countries with a few large, competing groups are more prone to conflict or stasis over language policy than their counterparts with one dominant or many small groups.

Rather than a simple calculation of numbers of groups, scholars have recognized that there is a difference in their mobilization potential and cohesiveness. Dan Posner (2004, 861) constructed a "Politically Relevant Ethnic Groups" measure, in order to capture ethnicity's impact on democratic and economic performance of states in Africa more precisely. There seems little relationship, however, between this measure and the intensity of language use; correlation between PREG90 and ILLED2010 is –.19.

Finally, Catherine Boone (1995, 2003) demonstrated that variation in subnational groups' power affected the state-building strategies of the center. It may well be that the strength and cohesiveness of groups determine whether or not they are viewed as rivals and therefore enter into a bargaining relationship with the government. Boone notes that bureaucratic efficacy of the state historically

---

[3] No country in Africa has more than two language groups with 20% of the population, so I have reduced his threshold to 10%.

[4] In countries with 3+ large groups, average ILLED is 4.4; with 2 major groups, average ILLED is 4.1, and with only one major group, average ILLED is 4.7.

[5] I also looked at the size of the largest language group, which showed only the slightest effect among the most homogeneous countries. Among countries where the largest language group made up 80–100% of the population, the average ILLED score was 5.2; where the largest group made up 60–80%, average ILLED score was 3.8; where the largest group made up 40–60%, average ILLED score was 4.6; where the largest group made up 20–40%, ILLED score was 4.2; and where the largest group made up 10–20%, average ILLED score was 3.8.

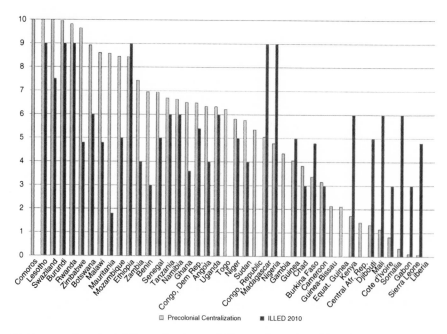

☐ Precolonial Centralization   ■ ILLED 2010

FIGURE 5.1. Precolonial Centralization and Current Intensity of Local Language Use in Education. *Source*: Gennaioli and Rainer (2007) appendix 2, table A1.

has been highest where rural interests were weakest politically. Her general theoretical framework (2003, 364–365) argues that more hierarchical rural groups would provoke more intensive state-building efforts from the center, "aimed at harnessing and manipulating local-level power relations...building spatially deconcentrated institutional apparatuses in the rural areas." This would result in power sharing where rural elites have clout but are economically dependent on the state or relative autonomy from state intervention where elites have the ability to accumulate resources independently of the state. In contrast, where regional hierarchy is absent, administrative centralization is more likely. Setting aside my argument that leaders may not want to spread a single language, this helps to understand the potential bargaining power of local power holders. Relating to language, we would expect the state to be more likely to implement standard language education when rural groups are weak and more likely to incorporate local languages in education where stronger subnational groups would pressure the state for language rights.

One way to test this is to look at the proportion of groups in a state that are "hierarchical." A measure created by the anthropologist George Murdock (1967) scores ethnic groups on their relative jurisdictional hierarchy – from centralized to fragmented. Gennaioli and Rainer (2007) have combined his measure with population proportions from *Atlas Narodov Mira* (1964) and produced a "precolonial centralization index" for most states in Africa.[6] The expectation is that the higher the proportion of centralized groupings within a country, the greater pressure they would place on the government for their languages to be used. Figure 5.1 examines this relationship. It does appear at first glance that small countries with high proportions of their populations made up of centralized groups (Lesotho, Swaziland, Burundi, Rwanda, Botswana, Zimbabwe) have relatively intense local language use. But centralized Comoros has no local language use, and Mauritania very little. Furthermore, several states with low proportions of centralized groups – Nigeria, Kenya, Mali – also have relatively high-intensity language use. From a broad perspective, local power hierarchies do not help to sort out which countries are maintaining high levels of local language use.

In sum, neither the democratic explanation nor the bargaining explanation with its demographic or subnational strength variants is sufficient to understand the intensity of local language use in Africa.

MY EXPLANATION

Valid explanations cannot be singular. Certainly there are elements of the preceding explanations in my own. Choices of language policy occur in the context of different international and local opportunities, which push outcomes in certain directions – more uniform in Francophone Africa, more varied in Anglophone. Whereas the Francophone cases mostly can be explained through the force of ideas and NGOs given in the last chapter, the variation in the other cases can be more disciplined by carefully examining the incentives that arise from a nominally democratic setting. Different demographics give general dynamics to electoral calculations; historical institutions sharpen demographic distinctions and group strength; economic circumstances widen or narrow potential bases of support.

As noted in Chapter 3, many independence leaders initially paid lip service to an African unifying language, but then quickly opted for a European language for administration, keeping the colonial education policies largely intact. Only a few ideologically driven leaders – Nyerere in Tanzania or Siad Barre in Somalia – managed to introduce a single African unifying language. There was little concerted effort in most cases to pursue a standard education policy in the way that prevailed in Europe. The context experienced by leaders differed significantly from that of European states facing constant pressure from external war. Partly as a consequence, and also because of the emphasis on trade taxes rather than direct taxes inherited from colonial rule, African leaders depended little on their citizens for a tax base, a tendency that was intensified by increasing reliance

---

[6] I am reluctant to put too much weight into this variable, but it is the only such measurement that I know of and is being used widely by economists to predict several (positive) outcomes (Fenske 2010; Nunn 2007).

on foreign aid and commodity extraction. Guyer states it succinctly: "Completely contrary to the historical sequence in Europe ... the present African leadership has to seek consent first and enforce taxation afterwards" (1992, 41). Unlike in Europe, then, military and taxation bureaucracies did not expand. Nor did much of Africa industrialize.

Consequently, it became less imperative for governments to achieve universal, standard-language education. De Swaan (1988) revealed that breaking the mediation monopoly held by local leaders was critical for national rulers to extract resources directly from their citizenry in order to fight wars in Europe. Few African leaders have had such motivation. Education could stagnate, and efforts to spread a common national language were superfluous. With no external war, moreover, there was no need for a citizen army, and therefore no pressing need to bypass local leaders to raise funds and fighters.

With democratization, however, leaders' preferences sway decisively toward multilingualism. When leaders survey their chances at electoral victory, knowing that a unifying language is not needed for war making or revenue extraction, multilingual education becomes not just something to tolerate, but an attractive option for self-preservation. Though there did not appear to be a relationship between democracy and local language use, I argue that increasing democracy overall *has* had an impact. It has changed the context for leaders' preferences over language use in education. This is counterintuitive. Donor pressure toward democratization and decentralization is inducing *less* liberal states to adopt policies favoring local language education. The new democratic framework requires that leaders search for new ways to secure their own advantage. The prospect of increased fragmentation becomes not a liability, but an asset.

The opportunities of new ideas, available materials, and advocacy of NGOs go a long way in explaining the uniformity in Francophone (and Lusophone)[7] policy choices. The incentives supplied with movement toward democracy in Africa in the 1990s affect other states differently, depending on their institutional history and economic trajectories.

Accompanying the global movement toward democracy has been a general tendency toward decentralization. Merilee Grindle (2007, ch. 1) surveys literature on decentralization, finding that political scientists were advocating decentralization for its benefits to human rights, to enhance participation and therefore strengthen democracy, and to induce better management and less corruption. Crawford and Hartmann (2008, 7–8) note that decentralization is a prevailing trend in Africa, supported by international donors and civil society organizations, as well as officially by central governments. Decentralization, even if not accompanied by real devolution, focuses attention on the representation of regions – *who* will represent them? Gaining a government position as the representative of a region certainly is a prize that may be desired by elites. Peter Geschiere argues that these two major elements of a global consensus –

---

[7] I believe the story I tell about the Francophone cases may be similar for Lusophone states.

decentralization and democratization – serve to highlight ethnic identities (Geschiere 2009). While electoral strategies latch easily onto ethnic appeals in multiethnic settings (Chandra 2004), Western donors' insistence on decentralization pushes this tendency even further. As donors privilege the local, the "penchant for 'community,' tradition, and 'chiefs' seems to be a logical consequence of the drive toward decentralization" (Geschiere 2009, 21). Chiefs, whether traditional or modern, offer a point of contact for the civil society that is so favored in donor projects. The problem arises because "chiefs" relate only to their own subjects, tending to discriminate against immigrants: "What is at stake is often less a defense of the local than efforts to exclude others from access to the new circuits of riches and power" (Geshiere 2009, 26).[8]

Robert Bates recognized more than three decades ago that modernization spurs urbanizing elites to emphasize the tradition of their rural ethnic ties in order to mediate access to the public goods that flowed from the state to cohesive groupings (Bates 1983, 158). In order to advance their position as rightful claimants to benefits of modernity (such as jobs or political office), modernizing elites found it useful to present themselves as representatives of ethnic collectivities. Similarly, elites in the current setting see the benefits that they can accrue by mediating between donors and recipients of aid. Thus instead of globalization erasing national boundaries, its democratizing and decentralizing elements serve instead to create boundaries at ever more local levels.[9]

Recall that in the bargaining explanation, regional elites played a prominent role in the multilingual "game." We saw in earlier chapters that a sensitization campaign emanating from the government and supported by local NGOs was necessary to convince the population to support multilingual education in Senegal. In Ghana, language leaders were not demanding such rights from the government, and so the policy was changed with very little local resistance. As demonstrated in the case studies to follow, not only are regional language elites more often silent on the issue of language; in many cases these language elites do not even exist.

Regional language elites are rarities that emerge only in specific situations. Laitin frequently cites Nigeria in his examples of elite activism and maintains that "specific interests in vernacular development have emerged in many states as a dialectical response to national policies promoting an indigenous lingua franca" (Laitin 1992, 114). Though he admits that the 3 ± 1 outcome is more likely in countries where "clearly bounded regions, each representing a language group, are delineated in the political process" (Laitin 1992, 114), he does not follow this thought to its logical conclusion. Where regions are *not* clearly

---

[8] This echoes a classic earlier work by Jean-François Bayart (1979), as well as more recent collaboration of Bayart, Geschiere, and Nyamnjoh (2001).

[9] See Lonsdale 2008, 311–312, for a discussion of autochthony as a strategy used by individuals to rebel against the "daily inequalities, the unpredictable inclusions and exclusions by which their states decide who is to gain from global linkages and who bear their local costs." Englebert (2009, ch. 7) notes similar responses.

bounded and delineated in the political process, the mechanism that relies on agitation by local elites is not likely to work. This is because there is no advantage for regional language elites to claim special privileges for their language group. In places outside Nigeria and Ethiopia, the only true federations in Africa, these regional elites are not a factor, and they had to be replaced by other motors promoting multilingualism. The previous chapters described the language NGOs that replaced them.

But in some cases, there *are* such elites pressuring the government for their groups' rights to language. When would we see them? Apart from the opportunities that propelled Francophone states to adopt similar policies, certain situations make it more likely that we would see elites emerge to bargain for increased or sustained use of local languages in education. Rural social organization influences how the center tries to build states. The existence or nonexistence of powerful local actors determines how states treat rural areas. In the case of language in education, rural elites only care about this policy if it brings them benefits.

It would yield benefits when a colonial legacy had promoted a limited number of local languages and federal institutions reinforced the rewards that accrued to groups on the basis of their linguistic identity. The hierarchical attributes of subnational groups would certainly interact with these colonial and institutional legacies. Where there was a single, centralized group whose language was used historically, this should continue. And it seems logical that if a smaller centralized group were selected and privileged in the early period, there would be a later backlash, with previously disadvantaged groups primed to assert their voices as soon as external support increased or internal threats decreased – as in the current nominal democratic setting.

Therefore, one would expect to see bargaining produce sustained or increased use of local languages in federations (Nigeria, Ethiopia), where there is a single, relatively centralized group (Rwanda, Lesotho), or where there is backlash against the exclusive use of a single language in a multilingual state (Malawi, Sudan). In the case of Ghana, even with a colonial legacy that promoted the use of multiple local languages in education, if there is no institutional reinforcement that produces regional elites invested in language differentiation, the government can change this policy with little resistance. And the most significant factor that may provoke a deliberate reduction in intensity of local language use is an economic one.

ECONOMICS AS A CONTRIBUTING FACTOR

A third alternative explanation – besides democracy or bargaining – that may contribute to a rise in local language education is the economic factor of state retrenchment. Many scholars have noted that the state reduced its reach in the 1990s after the debt crisis and structural adjustment that curtailed government expenditures. Education spending has been hard hit across the continent. MacLean (2011) shows in a careful study that the state retrenchment common to the continent after the 1980s has affected individual countries differently – with the main distinction between Anglophone and Francophone states. It is absolutely true that virtually all states reduced their spending on education, particularly on teachers' salaries. "The growth of the real value of average teacher salaries in Africa has been stagnant for over 30 years," says a recent UNESCO report. Teachers in Francophone Africa suffered more, however. "Thirty years ago, the average teacher salary in Francophone Africa was, in relative terms, almost twice that of teachers in Anglophone countries.... In relative terms, the average salary for teachers in these countries essentially fell by a multiple of 3 between 1975 and 2005" (UNESCO 2011, 52–53).[10] Certainly states were financially constrained, but their choice to reduce spending on education demonstrates their lack of motivation in this area.

Where the state contracts, whatever fills the space will determine the outcomes of policy. In the spirit of "privatized indirect government,"[11] Titeca and de Herdt point to the replacement of government education functions by churches and parent associations in the Democratic Republic of the Congo. They catalog the dramatic reduction in state expenditure per pupil from $159 in 1982 to $4 in 2002, a decline in teachers' salaries from $68 in 1982 to $12.90 in 2002, and a halving of the number of teachers paid by the government over the same period (Titeca and de Herdt 2011, 221). Despite this collapse in public financing, however, the number of pupils doubled, partly because of the "gradual replacement of the state education budget with higher contributions paid by parents" (Titeca and de Herdt 2011, 222). Their main point is that educational services continue to be provided, even within a hollow state. Certainly the role of nonstate providers is more visible in collapsed states, and the increase in mother tongue education in Mozambique and Angola demonstrates the power of donors concerned with mother tongue education. Often retrenchment has led to reliance on organizations outside the state; ethnic associations attempt to substitute for the state's provision of certain services. Traditional groupings actively engaged in development activities, and external material aid propel this "traditional" resurgence: "Over the last decade, foreign donors have put increased emphasis on grass-root processes, on the association of local 'stakeholders' with development projects, decentralization and the promotion of NGOs as partners in development and conflict resolution. To some extent, traditional structures of authority have benefited from this trend since they appear to outside aid agencies as readily available local counterparts with a substantial measure of authority and capacity to mobilize" (Englebert 2005, 50). Retrenchment therefore plays a role insofar as path dependency and NGOs' roles are enforced. A graph (not shown) plotting economic performance against intensity of language use, however, does not reveal state retrenchment had a uniform effect on language policy.

---

[10] The report cites Mingat and Suchaut, 2000, who suggest that this discrepancy arose because teacher salaries were indexed to those in France.

[11] Hibou 2004; Mbembe 2002; Reno 2000.

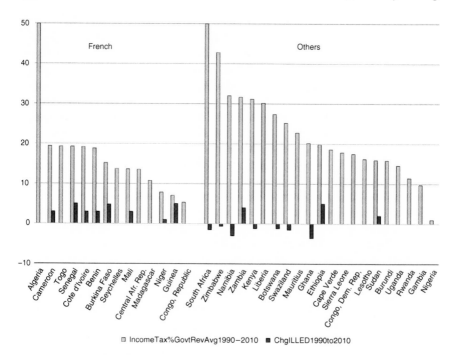

FIGURE 5.2. Tax Base and Change in Intensity of Local Language Use, 1990–2010. *Source*: World Bank WDI.

Economic trajectories matter more, however, in the other direction. Where governments begin to perceive their citizens as resources, efforts to standardize language will likely occur. This is because it becomes more important for governments to create a productive citizenry that can be taxed and to communicate directly with them to do so. Figure 5.2 shows the size of the tax base – income, profits, and capital gains – as a percentage of government revenue in the period 1990–2010, arrayed against the change in local language intensity in the same period.

First, we see that Francophone states have generally lower income tax bases than other states. Second, no matter what their tax base, all the changes among the Francophone subset of cases are in the direction of increasing intensity of local language use. This has been explained earlier with shifting opportunities. Non-Francophone states show more diversity. Outside the previous institutional and demographic configurations described previously, most of the states with wider bases of income tax collection are reducing their language intensity or making no change. Zambia appears an anomaly;[12] Ethiopia can

[12] Zambia is a difficult state to code, since the experimental mother tongue policy seems not to be enforced. The experimentation could also be explained with a high proportion of "hierarchical groups" and long historical mission activity around languages.

be explained as a federal situation, as can Sudan prior to its divide. A wider tax base seems to motivate governments to reduce the intensity of local languages used in education – or to enforce their use less – as it becomes more imperative to connect with citizens. This gives some visual corroboration to the regression results from Chapter 4.[13]

We have seen, then, that though democracy cannot explain the increase in local language intensity on its own, it does have an indirect impact on leaders' incentives. In Francophone Africa, where France is offering governments new ideas from above and language NGOs are advocating similar ones from below, a nominally democratic setting makes leaders aware that a potentially fragmentary policy may pay political dividends. Outside this relative uniformity, variations in the likelihood of regional language elites pressuring the government to maintain or expand their language privileges depend mostly on the institutional configuration of federalism and the historical treatment of subnational groups. Regional elites do not always emerge to demand language rights. This is because unlike in a situation of direct citizen taxation and conscription, their role as mediators is not threatened. The flow of goods is not upward but downward. Regional elites are interested in being the representatives for distributing goodies from the center, a common feature of federalism. Where powerful groups were privileged under colonial rule, and/or where there is federalism, we see stronger voices pressuring to keep or expand language rights as part of the institutionalization of their access to state resources.

Therefore, economic retrenchment can come into play insofar as it gives more power to private organizations – usually toward increased intensity of language use. In the opposite case, a widening tax base makes governments more aware of a need to connect with citizens through a common language, and a reduction in intensity of local languages is often the result. These different dynamics are evident in Senegal and Ghana. We see in Senegal the opportunities and incentives propelling the increase in intensity of local language education and in Ghana the lack thereof.

INCENTIVES FOR POLICY CHANGE IN SENEGAL AND GHANA

Part of the package of liberal democracy is attentiveness to minority rights. Whereas an autocratic leader might cater to the particular minority group that put him in power, liberal democratic regimes should be more sensitive to minorities in general in order to increase their potential voting base. A logical

---

[13] According to Geo-Jaja (2006, 141), Nigeria shows a "remarkably low level of effort, in fact the worst effort level of all sub-Saharan African countries" in public education spending as a percentage of government expenditure, which the author attributes to decentralization and inadequate attention by the center. This could have more to do with its narrow tax base, as we see Nigeria at the far right of Figure 5.2.

expectation is that as regimes liberalize, they are more likely to introduce policies that protect the language rights of minorities by promoting their use in schools. The cases of Senegal and Ghana, however, do not support this assumption; nor does that of Cameroon, described in the next chapter. Senegal and Cameroon instead point to a more sinister logic of semidemocratic regimes using the language of minority rights to entrench their authority, and Ghana demonstrates a more genuine democracy reducing its attention to minority language rights in favor of a unifying language as it widens its economic tax base.

Senegal's increasing intensity of local language use appears initially to correspond with its liberalization. I argue, however, that the adoption of a multilingual policy has little to do with either attracting votes or responding to pressures from regional elites for language concessions. Instead, it demonstrates well my explanation of changed ideas among policy makers and lack of sincere commitment to spreading a single language through the school system.

First, democracy is not an adequate explanation. Between 1977 and 1981, Senegal's first president, Léopold Senghor, became less autocratic, moving from –6 to –1 Polity score (Marshall and Jaggers 2009), and during that time, the government also introduced a brief mother tongue experiment. That experiment, however, was discontinued in 1982, under a regime that boasted the same score (–1), canceling the "gains" in minority language promotion. The recent introduction of local languages as media of instruction is the strongest evidence that democratizing governments will favor local languages: Between 1999 and 2000, Senegal improved its democracy score from –1 to 8. The next year, it officially introduced the local language experiment in 150 schools. Like many other Francophone states, Senegal adopted the multilingual policy as it was liberalizing. However, it is important to note that even though the first experimental classes began under the new liberal regime, the policy originated *before* the liberalization, with the 1999 decree. And importantly, though there was indeed a significant improvement in democracy from 1999 to 2002, the quality of democracy deteriorated dramatically after this. By 2008, Senegal had returned to the "not free" Freedom House category.

Second, bargaining also does not further our understanding of the policy change. As noted in the previous chapter, it was not regional power holders who pressed for rights to mother tongue education for their group. The Ministry of Education had to undertake a major public sensitization campaign to overcome resistance to the policy. If bargaining were involved, it would have occurred with potential rivals to power – Islamic notables who controlled populations in Senegal's productive groundnut region. Boone argues that even though these rural elites held powerful sway over the loyalties and political behavior of the citizens in their regions, the elites' economic privileges were only guaranteed with continuous state backing and support (1995, 23–24). They thus had no independent economic basis to challenge the state. Though they controlled the productivity and therefore the potential tax base of the countryside, it was only their intimate connections with the state that allowed them access to revenue.

The flow of resources was ultimately from the center. The privilege of controlling rural groupings did not hinge on language compatibilities, as Senegal's administrative boundaries were explicitly not along ethnic lines. Therefore, as expected, there was no mobilization by regional elites in favor of local language education.

Third, economically, Senegal's introduction of local languages does not correspond with any real state retrenchment.[14] It does reveal the power of NGOs, donors, and dedicated individuals in propelling a policy forward, rather than concerted government effort to spread a unifying language through the education system. Under colonial rule, Senegal had been the center of West African schooling, providing secondary school facilities for students across French West Africa. At independence, it stood in the ranks of Cote d'Ivoire, Togo, and Benin, boasting a much higher percentage of students in primary and secondary school than neighbors Burkina Faso, Guinea, Mali, Mauritania, and Niger (Mitchell 2007, table I1). Yet twenty years after independence, its education sector was deteriorating. When Abdou Diouf assumed the presidency in 1981, he claimed that one of his first priorities was reform of the education system. He convened a national conference to consider reform to Senegal's education sector: the General Conference on Education and Training (États Généraux), which began in January 1981. The conference deliberated for three and a half years, and the resulting documents included a recommendation to consider the use of mother tongues as media of instruction (République du Sénégal 1984, 1).

Nonetheless, these recommendations were not heeded for two decades, and the education sector continued to decline. Thirty years after independence, Senegal's adult literacy rate was less than 30 percent (ADEA 1999). In the wake of the first World Conference on Education for All (1990), the Conference of Francophone Ministers of Education began an analysis of education systems in Africa (Bernard 2003). The first wave of the study was published in 1996, comparing schooling in five Francophone African countries. The study noted that Senegal was doing 13 percent more poorly than the average of the four other countries. Simultaneously, the Monitoring Learning Achievement (MLA) project, undertaken by UNESCO-UNICEF, conducted a decade-long assessment of African countries. It published results for eleven of these countries in 2000. Overall, Senegal shared with Niger the weakest scores of students achieving desired mastery in all subjects: only 2 percent of its students were scoring 75 percent or higher on standard tests. When the bar was lowered to just minimum mastery level (achieving 50 percent or higher on standard tests), only 31 percent of Senegal's students could even claim this feat in all subjects (Chinapah 2000, 20). Statistics presented by Senegal's Ministry of Education, based on the MLA study, revealed that even when looking specifically at levels of achievement in French (disregarding science and math), fewer than 9 percent of

---

[14] GDP held steady in the $1,400–1,500 per capita range except for slight dip in the early 1990s (World Bank WDI).

students were achieving the desired level of mastery in French reading and writing, and not even half were achieving the minimum level of competency (Ministère de l'Éducation 2001, 21). Senegal's standing as the star of French West Africa had weakened precipitously.

Abdoulaye Wade assumed the presidency of Senegal in March 2000 with a renewed recognition of the need to combat illiteracy. From the beginning of his term, Wade spoke out strongly and critically about the poverty of the Senegalese education. "Our kids play with sticks, while Western kids are exposed to colors and shapes in pre-school and elementary school."[15] He vowed to focus on the very young, as opposed to the secondary education that had occupied much of Senegal's energies in previous years.

The Office for Education Planning and Reform issued a report in 2001 admitting that weaknesses in the education system stemmed partially from the fact that national languages were not being effectively used. Plans for reform included their introduction in the formal system (Ministère de l'Education Nationale 2001, 29). In my own interviews with teachers and inspectors, I often heard the refrain that introducing mother tongues is "a necessity," "absolutely essential," and that "our backwardness is because it has not been done."[16] Intellectuals corroborated that the government was introducing mother tongues for pragmatic reasons, because children are having more and more difficulty with French.[17]

We see then that despite countless donor dollars and continuing rhetoric favoring education reform, the Senegalese government had not invested seriously in spreading a common language. And the introduction of mother tongue education under a president who showed himself later not to be a true democrat casts doubt that minority rights were a real concern. I submit that at least part of the government's ambivalence toward language rationalization is its lack of sustained growth and restricted tax base – the latter providing only 19 percent of government revenue at the time of the policy change (World Bank WDI).[18] An expanding tax base would motivate a government to care more about connecting with its citizens. In the absence of these motivating factors, with pressure and financing from donors toward a mother tongue policy, the prospect of a perpetually multilingual population may have appeared less of a liability than an asset.

Ghana reveals the opposite factors at work. Its history of strong attention to cultural identities makes the reversal of its local language policy in 2001 all the more surprising. As in Senegal, democracy and bargaining do not help to explain the change, nor does state retrenchment. Instead, it was a lack of a uniform

---

[15] Recalled by M. Fall, director-adjoint, World Vision, interview by author, Dakar, February 13, 2003.

[16] I. Sy, director of G. Mbodje Elementary School, interview by author, Kaolack, March 12, 2003.

[17] I. M. Fall, professor des sciences juridiques et politiques, UCAD, interview by author, Dakar, March 20, 2003.

[18] Senegal's growth rate in the years leading up to change was negative in 6 out of 10 years in the 1990s, for an average of –.5% growth.

ideological current, which gave the government more latitude to ignore donors; weak or nonexistent regional language elites; and a widening tax base that made the spread of a common language more imperative.

First, democracy had contradictory effects on mother tongue education in independent Ghana's early years, and in the present its effects are completely opposite expectations. Nkrumah, whose administrations scored in the –8 to –9 Polity range, had a mixed policy of language instruction: English-medium schools in the capital unless the native language was necessary for comprehension, and a laissez-faire attitude that allowed the use of local languages in rural areas. When a more democratic Busia took power in 1969 (with a Polity score of 3), he restored the preindependence policy that required use of local languages in the first three years of primary school. Subsequent less democratic governments maintained the policy, a course that may either reflect inertia or contradict the idea that autocratic governments are less sensitive to minorities. And, in fact, it was the military government of Acheampong that established the School of Ghanaian Languages to train specialists. Prior to this, native speakers of a language were considered capable of teaching their language, but Acheampong believed that specialists were necessary.[19] The recent reversal of policy, moreover, completely contradicts the democratic theory: Kufuor's administration, the most democratic in Ghana's history, enacted an English-only medium policy for primary schools, apparently ignoring minority language rights. Ghanaian linguists are blunt: Two democratically elected governments (1957 and 2000) chose an English-only medium for the population, while military governments chose multilingual (Anyidoho and Kropp-Dakubu 2008, 151).

Second, bargaining also does not explain the reversal. We saw in the previous chapter that public opinion in Ghana was even more negative toward mother tongue education than in Senegal, and that there were few if any regional elites who complained when the long-standing multilingual policy was reversed.[20] Ghana's largest group, the relatively hierarchical and cohesive Akan, who enjoyed language privileges in the colonial period and after, did not organize to speak out against the policy change. Though more than capable of mounting a challenge to the government over this policy, this powerful group did not do so; nor did virtually any other language group in the country. That these powerful groups did not challenge the state over language rights was likely the result of Ghana's institutional configuration; unlike Nigeria or Ethiopia, it is not a federation. Benefits from the center do not flow to groups on the basis of their linguistic uniqueness.

---

[19] K. Agyekum, linguist, University of Legon, interview by author, Accra, April 9, 2003.

[20] The association of Ga speakers was the only language group to make a public statement after the policy change, placing an ad in the newspaper: E. Kropp-Dakubu, linguist, University of Legon, interview by author, Accra, March 31, 2003.

Finally, Ghana's economic trajectory helps to explain its policy choice. It experienced more severe retrenchment in the 1980s than did Senegal. The cocoa boom ended in 1970s, and between 1976 and 1983, government expenditures on education fell from 6.4 percent of GDP to 1.4 percent (MacLean 2002, 77). School facilities deteriorated, "and a mass exodus of health and education professionals left the country poorly staffed." Ghana's education reforms in the late 1980s were "intended to develop more practical, vocational skills that would increase local employment" rather than promoting a "brain drain" or creating "a growing group of frustrated and unemployed school dropouts" (MacLean 2002, 79). One of these education reforms was a requirement for students to take a Ghanaian language in junior secondary school and senior secondary school.

When the first batch of students who had studied under this system took tests in 1993–1995, the overall test results were not encouraging. "Less than 10 percent of those tested were deemed to have reached acceptable levels of attainment in English or mathematics" (McGrath 1999, 71). It was argued that the compulsory tests in Ghanaian languages were pulling down the average. Harry Sawyer, then minister of education, reversed the policy and made Ghanaian languages elective instead of compulsory in junior secondary school.[21] This was the first harbinger that more change was on its way.

Nonetheless, a head start in enrollment at independence gave Ghana, in contrast to Senegal, a relatively high overall literacy rate. Its pupil-teacher ratio in primary school is also better than that of its peers, averaging 31 over the period 1990 to 1998, much lower than that of most West African countries, whose ratios are above 40, and often closer to 80 or even 100.[22] But one important effect of state retrenchment was the growth of private schools in larger urban areas. National testing from 1994 to 1997 revealed that the percentage of students reaching mastery level in English was just above 6 percent in public schools, compared to nearly 69 percent in private schools (Canagarajah and Ye 2001, 8). Though Ghana as a whole has a relatively low proportion of students in private primary schools (13 percent), most of the private schools are in the capital, Accra. Here, 37 percent of students attend private schools (Canagarajah and Yet 2001, 13). Because private schools begin students in English from the first year of primary school, and these students are testing much better than their public school peers, people jump to the logical conclusion that it is the exclusive use of English that is the decisive factor in their success.

The new government of John Kufuor, which came to power at the end of 2000, pledged to tackle education as one of its highest priorities. The poor education results in public schools compared with private schools provided a ready reason to switch the medium of instruction policy. Though the Presidential

---

[21] K. Agyekum, linguist, University of Legon, interview by author, Accra, April 9, 2003.
[22] Calculated from table 5 in Canagarajah and Ye 2001, 7–8.

Commission Report on Education, like the USAID IEQ report, recommended a better application of the mother tongue policy, rather than its reversal, the government did not wait for these recommendations before it made its decision and, in fact, has not released the report to the public because the report does not support the current reversal of policy.[23]

My explanation for Ghana's shift in policy, then, rests on government latitude and economic incentives. The hands-off British colonial attitude continued through the independence period, in contrast to the continuing legacy of interventionist French colonial policy. Rather than conforming to donor directives, the government could make a maverick change. Ghana's GDP was experiencing steady growth in the years prior to the policy change in 2002 and then grew even more strongly afterward (World Bank WDI).[24] In the year of the policy change, Ghana's government was collecting 27 percent of its revenue from direct citizen contributions (higher than the 19 percent we saw in Senegal).[25] Between 1991 and 2002, it had increased its income tax as percentage of revenue by 11 percentage points, compared to 2.7 percentage points in Senegal, and its income tax as a percentage of total taxes collected had increased by 13 percentage points, compared to a slight reduction in Senegal (World Bank WDI).[26] I argue that Ghana's widening tax base caused governments to consider more seriously the potential benefits of a uniform language policy and to work more diligently to achieve it.

The Ghanaian language specialists Anyidoho and Kropp-Dakubu write that "certainly it has never been explicitly advocated that English is or should be a marker of Ghanaian identity. Nevertheless, we propose, somewhat contentiously, that the situation is developing in this direction" (2008: 144).

---

[23] *Meeting the Challenges of Education in the Twenty First Century DRAFT*, Report of the President's Committee on Review of Education Reforms in Ghana (September 2002). Though the perception of many linguists against the English-only policy is that the report unequivocally favors local languages, in fact, it does give the government some room for change: "The Committee recognizes the many advantages involved in the use of local languages as the medium of instruction [at the primary] level.... However, given the serious limitations in the implementation of this policy, such as the multiplicity of local languages, lack of teaching and learning materials in the local languages and inadequate number of local language teachers, the Committee recommends that: 1) Either the local or English language should be used as a medium of instruction at the kindergarten and lower primary as appropriate; 2) Where teachers and teaching and learning materials are available, local languages must be used as the medium of instruction" (xx–xxi). Another review more vigorously recommended local language use: Ansu-Kyeremeh et al. 2002, 146.

[24] Leading up to the policy change, growth rate was an average of 1.6% per year; in the year of the policy change, GDP growth rate was 2%, and it increased afterward.

[25] Taxes on income, profits, and capital gains as a percentage of government revenue (World Bank WDI).

[26] From 1996 (closest year available) to 2001 Senegal reduced the proportion of taxes on income, profits, and capital gains as a percentage of total taxes by –.12 percentage points.

CONCLUSION

This chapter continued the explanation put forward in the previous one. In addition to the new opportunities – ideational changes, material availability, and NGO advocacy – there are new incentives for local language education generated by a nominal democratic environment after the 1990s. But rejecting a straightforward argument about the power of democracy to force regimes into conceding to minorities to gain their support, I argue instead that these policies are not in fact granted with this calculus in mind. Because there are seldom regional elites who are asking for these privileges, and the public usually needs to be sensitized to accept them, it is just as likely that pseudodemocratic leaders see in them a means for dividing the opposition.

Senegal showed that while the intensification of local language use occurred under a liberalizing regime, the leader subsequently revealed his true, nondemocratic colors. Ghana, by contrast, restricted the intensity of local language use as it deepened its democracy. Even though Ghana's powerful language groups have been historically recognized, they did not experience the institutional entrenchment seen in federal states, which would have provided flows of resources to groupings based on their linguistic distinction. Therefore, these groups did not organize to resist a policy change reducing the use of local languages in school. The policy itself originated at the top, likely motivated by Ghana's economic growth and widening tax base, which finally convinced a government to put real effort into spreading a single language through the education system that would contribute to industrialization.

I want to be clear, however, about what this chapter is *not* saying. It is not arguing that mother tongue education is detrimental to growth. Mother tongue education was practiced before and after independence in most of Anglophone Africa, whereas it was not in Francophone Africa, and the growth rates have been uniformly higher in the former than the latter. Grier (1999) convincingly argues that this is causal. It may be, however, that the "stock" of literate citizens produced by a much denser network of mission schools across British Africa simply laid a surer foundation for economic growth, regardless of the language of instruction. Nor is this chapter claiming that mother tongue education is detrimental to democracy; some of the longest-standing (Botswana) and largest democracies (South Africa) on the continent use local languages intensely. I am only suggesting that this may be a power-seeking leader's motivation. It is important that this study moved beyond the high point of democratization in the mid-2000s. Since then, there has been a decline in quality of democracy in many states. By acceding to language rights at a low level – simply allowing them as media of instruction at primary education, for example – rulers may see the potential for perpetual fragmentation without violent extremism, a particular advantage in an environment of electoral competition.

Mahmood Mamdani foresaw that multipartyism would exacerbate ethnic tension because of the colonial legacy of harnessing custom for control: "The key to an alien power's achieving a hegemonic domination was a cultural project" (Mamdani 1996, 286). With power still organized around local custom in the postcolonial state, elections could only reinforce division. Instead of "real" nation building, states in Africa turned to show or force (Mbembe 1992; Zolberg 1968), and in these circumstances, there is little to prevent the "growth of state banditry" or the doctrine of "scapegoat communities" (Lonsdale 1981, 205). The next chapter will show these outcomes in Cameroon: A ruler under pressure for democracy increased attention to local identities in order to stabilize his rule.

6

Language, Education, and "Democratization" in Cameroon

Cameroon provided the initial question that guided this research: Why do governments of diverse states increase the intensity of their language use? Several extended research trips to the country fleshed out an answer. Previous chapters have tested this answer across all cases in Africa and within Senegal and Ghana; this one returns to the details of Cameroon. It shows that the policy change in this predominantly Francophone state was spurred by new material and ideational opportunities, in the context of new political incentives.

With 286 languages, Cameroon's diversity would seem especially problematic for a leader concerned with linguistic unity. As argued in previous chapters, however, leaders may not have placed such a high premium on unity as expected in the independence period, and ambivalence marked most governments' policies, resulting in a continuation of colonial precedent. Three changes converged in the 1990s to cause more deliberate local language policies in much of Africa, and Cameroon provides an excellent example. First, the opportunity to use many more languages presented itself, with active NGOs producing materials, personnel, and financing for such initiatives. Second, space opened for experimentation, with a permissive message communicated by France, Cameroon's most important international influence. And, finally, pressure for democratization caused President Paul Biya to recalculate his own preferences, as he realized that linguistic fragmentation might actually be of use to his own prospects for holding power.

The chapter will review briefly the language and education situation in Cameroon in its independence period. Like most Francophone states, it maintained a European language for instruction after independence. But beginning with a private project in 1981 and officially sanctioned after 1996, it began introducing local languages into its primary school curriculum. The chapter will detail the opportunities and incentives that combined to produce this policy change. Official concession to local language instruction has been a hard-fought victory for language activists. Whether this attention will marginalize groups or deepen democracy in the long run is a question that is yet to be answered. I offer some speculations drawn from Cameroon that will be further explored in the final chapter, but that remain provisional.

Of the nearly three hundred languages spoken by Cameroon's 18 million people, about half of them have ten thousand or more mother tongue speakers. This means that there are significantly large groups, but also a tremendous number of small groups. No language in Cameroon can claim more than 10 percent of the population. As described in Chapter 2, the territory of Kamerun was initially colonized by Germany but divided in 1916 between France and Britain as mandate and later trust territories. The Germans had initiated a plantation economy based in the southern coastal regions of the colony, encouraging the apparently more ambitious groups from populous regions farther north to migrate to these plantations (Konings 1993; Gardinier 1963, 519). France and Britain continued to promote this migration, which was facilitated by population densities and land shortages in the highland areas (Joseph 1977, 86–88). This movement would have lasting consequences for relations between groups.

French Cameroun achieved independence in 1960, while the southern section of British Cameroons voted in 1961 to join the former French territory in the Federal Republic of Cameroon (Delancey 1989, 37–46). French administrators had excluded the radical nationalist party, the Union des Populations du Cameroun (UPC), from contesting preindependence elections, supporting the pro-French northerner Ahmadou Ahidjo in his leadership of the country at independence (Joseph 1977, 343–345). When the southern British portion joined the Francophone regions in a federation in 1961, Ahidjo remained executive head of state, and the Anglophone side retained the relatively powerless post of prime minister.

Cameroon thus began its independent political history with a stronger role for the Francophone part of the federation, causing resentment among Anglophones about their secondary status (Awasom 2007, 152–153; Kofele-Kale 1986, 62–76). Given its varied colonial history, it had experienced greater attention to language than other French colonies. Furthering the Francophone influence, President Ahidjo moved to centralize the state with the adoption of a one-party system in 1966, followed by the wholesale replacement of the federal structure with a unitary one in 1972 (Delancey 1989, 51–54; Le Vine 1986, 23–33). Because of his preoccupation with national unity, Ahidjo was intolerant of discussions of ethnicity, banning ethnic associations, as did many African heads of state shortly after independence. Identity remained central to political considerations, however, as Ahidjo carefully maintained a balance in his cabinet and civil service of representatives from different regions of the country, rotating and reappointing them regularly to maintain their dependence on his favor.[1]

---

[1] Delancey 1989, 58–63; Takougang and Krieger 1998, 52–53; Zambo-Bilinga 1997; Kofele-Kale 1986, 57–58.

EDUCATION POLICY IN THE EARLY INDEPENDENCE PERIOD

Cameroon entered independence with higher than average enrollment rates, compared to other Francophone states, largely because of the many missionaries in the territory. In 1962, out of a population of about 6 million, 585,000 students were enrolled in primary schools and 19,000 in secondary. Two-thirds of these were in mission schools (Wilayi 2000, 6).[2] So, though approximately 41 percent of school-aged children were enrolled, the seventh highest rate in Africa – even above Anglophone high-achievers Kenya, Zambia, and Ghana (Mitchell 2007, 5, 1025) – this reflected widespread mission education activity rather than intense government interest.

Recall, however, that in the French regions of Cameroon, missions had been forbidden to teach in the vernacular, and in British areas, early vernacular policies had been reduced in the late colonial period in favor of English-only teaching. Therefore, as it attained independence, united Cameroon inherited systems on both sides that used a European language as medium of instruction.

Bernard Fonlon, cultural minister under Cameroon's first president, observed that "one of the major problems facing the leaders of almost every African country today, is how to weld this motley mass into a harmonious, homogeneous whole, how to forge this communion of thought, feeling and will of which I have been speaking; in a word, how to create national unity" (Fonlon 1969, 28). Ahidjo's rhetoric, like other independence African leaders', certainly reflected this preoccupation with nation-building. Though Fonlon often vocalized concern for lack of attention paid to Cameroon's languages, he was also pragmatic. While he advocated that languages be preserved, he supported the rationale behind the official choice of French and English, giving specific reasons for this policy (Fonlon 1969, 41–42): First, they were vehicles for modern progress and culture; second, they were languages of high technology; and, third, they were necessary for world cooperation and African unity. Cameroon's "native patrimony being so heterogeneous, so hopelessly fragmented, and none of these languages being the vehicle of science and technology, we are forced, for all our pride, to seek unity among ourselves, to seek modern development, through alien tongues" (Fonlon 1969, 49). Therefore, representing Cameroon's official policy, he contended that "the teaching of English and French together, here in Cameroon, should start right from the very first day that the child takes his seat in the infant school" (Fonlon 1969, 46).

Fonlon, as well as William Etekia Mbumua, Cameroon's minister of education between 1962 and 1974, were profoundly influenced by Léopold Senghor's

---

[2] The proportion of government-schooled children has continued to grow. By 1985, 63% of students were enrolling in public schools, and by 1998, it was 71%.

ideas of Negritude (described in Chapter 4). Senghor visited Cameroon three times between 1966 and 1973, publicly defending his ideas (Bjornson 1991, 172–173). Fonlon, as editor of *Abbia*, the country's most important cultural journal, and Etekia Mbumua advocated literary and educational projects that would allow Cameroonians to retain their "authentic African nature while adopting the scientific attitudes necessary for progress in the modern world" (Bjornson, 174). This meant embracing European languages.

The stated goal was uniform bilingualism across the country. Nevertheless, expenditure did not reflect a commitment to this goal. For East (Francophone) Cameroon the education budget was only 2.7 percent of the total government budget projected for 1961–1965. Though the twenty-year plan raised that projection to 6.8 percent (Le Vine 1964, 82), this was far below the 17 percent average reported for African government expenditure on education in the early independence period (ADEA 1999).

Cameroon, therefore, like most African states, demonstrated rhetorical pride in its linguistic heritage, accompanied by an apparent pragmatic choice in favor of a European alternative. Nonetheless, there was a lack of full-fledged effort in either direction, but rather an ambivalent continuation of colonial precedent. In the mid-1990s, however, the government officially accepted the use of several local languages as medium in a number of its primary schools. This transformation occurred because of new opportunities and new incentives.

OPPORTUNITIES FOR POLICY CHANGE

As described in Chapter 4, the opportunities for policy change were both material and ideational. In material terms, they were the transcription of new languages and production of educational resources. In ideational terms, they included a new message of openness communicated by France and the advocacy of language NGOs directed toward officials in the Ministry of Education and toward the general public.

Material Opportunities

Missionaries had written several languages in Cameroon by 1960 – eighteen, in fact[3] – but these only covered 43 percent of the population. Cameroon has a rich history of indigenous linguistic activity. As early as 1896, Sultan Njoya had created 466 ideographs for the language of Bamun, spoken in his kingdom of Foumban. Gregoire Momo also began writing the Yemba language before independence, and linguists Marcel Bôt Ba Njock and Emmanuel Sounjock

---

[3] They were, in order of transcription, Duala, Fang, Bulu, Fulfulde, Basaa, Dzodinka, Bamun, Mungaka, Mundang, Gbaya, Masana, Mbum, Medumba, Kanuri, Beti/Ewondo, Kwasio, Mafa, and Fe'fe' (Hausa is also a language spoken in Cameroon, but its early transcription date of 1857 reflects its transcription for Nigeria).

Sounjock built on early missionary foundations in the Bassa language during the first few years of independence. But the most intense activity around languages occurred after 1980.

In the late 1970s, Cameroonian linguists at the University of Yaounde began a project to standardize language orthographies. This corresponded with the arrival of the missionary group, Societé Internationale Linguistique (SIL). The first SIL linguists traveled to Cameroon from Nigeria, where their work had been disrupted by the Biafra War. The SIL director in Nigeria, John-Bendor Samuel, signed an agreement with the University of Yaounde that allowed SIL to work as a linguistic research organization. Indigenous linguists were few and poorly paid, and in a country with nearly three hundred languages to transcribe, it was only Western-supported missionaries who had the luxury of spending years perfecting the orthography of smaller languages. SIL currently employs more than one hundred language workers in Cameroon.

Central in the transformation of Cameroon's language policy is an individual named Maurice Tadadjeu. A Yemba speaker, he grew up in the West (Francophone) province of Cameroon. He attended Catholic primary school and the prestigious Collège Libermann, a Jesuit-run preparatory high school, where he distinguished himself as a youth leader. He says that the fathers at the school encouraged his leadership and the respect he already held for his language.[4] Toward the end of his schooling, the collège began to teach a few indigenous languages as subjects to reconnect students to their roots and to help them identify with the culture of other Cameroonians, and this undoubtedly influenced Tadadjeu's ideas.

After leaving the collège, Tadadjeu attended university in the United States, studying linguistics; there he was exposed to pan-Africanism in the 1970s, reinforcing pride in his language ancestry. He proposed in his 1977 dissertation at the University of Southern California a language scheme for Cameroon that would valorize indigenous languages. In this early writing, he did not highlight the potential reinforcing relationship between first- and second-language acquisition.[5] His radical contribution was to propose that virtually *all* languages in Africa could be used for education (Tadadjeu 1977, 152). This was in contrast to prevailing assumptions of linguists – French and Cameroonian – that education could only be conducted in major languages. Tadadjeu insisted that this latter view guaranteed conflict by forcing officials to decide among African languages.[6]

---

[4] M. Tadadjeu, interview by author, Yaounde, October 30, 2002.

[5] He wrote, "Many communicative skills acquired in indigenous languages may not be appropriate for a non-indigenous language" (1977, 132), though "it is possible that bilingual learners may use their previous language learning experience to approach the non-indigenous language" (135). In fact, he criticized simplistic views of the $L1 \rightarrow L2$ relationship (165).

[6] He singled out Houis (1976) for critique (see Tadadjeu 1977, 81–82), as well as a roundtable discussion at the Collège Libermann, where Cameroonian linguists tried to select certain languages

He returned to teach at the University of Yaounde, at the time that SIL was looking for an academic affiliation. He and a colleague, Emmanuel Chia, realized early the benefits offered by collaboration with the SIL missionaries and invited some of them to teach in the University of Yaounde's linguistics department. Tadadjeu was central to SIL's gaining permission to work in Cameroon, since this ensured that the missionary organization would have an academic, rather than evangelical, standing. Two of the missionaries who arrived to teach, Ursula Wiesemann and Olive Shell, had worked successfully with mother tongue education programs in Brazil and Peru, respectively. Like Tadadjeu, they were interested in transcribing and using as many languages as possible for literacy. Happily, the goals of Tadadjeu and SIL intersected. Finding common cause, these missionaries and local linguists set about codifying a host of Cameroonian languages and advocating for their use. The idea for an Operational Research Project for the Teaching of Cameroonian Languages (PROPELCA) was "collectively emitted" by Tadadjeu and his colleagues at the University of Yaounde and SIL.

The PROPELCA program began as the "Experimental Literacy Program in the Mother Tongue," a project funded through Wycliffe Bible Translators (SIL's parent organization) originally by the Canadian Agency for International Development (ACDI). Between 1981 and 1987, PROPELCA received $302,265. Of this, 66 percent was from Canada, 20 percent directly from SIL (money raised in U.S. churches), and the remainder from the University of Yaounde and the Cameroonian Ministry of Research in the form of "in-kind" donations of supervision, training, and waiving of course fees (ACDI 1987, 165–166). Canada continued funding PROPELCA through SIL until the early 1990s, after which direct SIL funds became the primary support.[7] The PROPELCA program cost approximately $50,000 per year at the outset, increased to a peak of about $200,000 in the late 1990s, and cost on average $150,000 per year in the 2000s.[8]

All of this support for SIL and accompanying indirect support for local linguists resulted in the transcription of nearly sixty languages in Cameroon between 1980 and 2010, and currently 89 percent of Cameroonians have potential access to a written language. This more than doubled the percentage of the population covered at independence. Thus, the baseline element of material opportunities was achieved. Next was the actual provision of written resources.

---

for use in education. Obviously, noted Tadadjeu, this would provoke discontent among the groups whose languages were ignored (1977, 86).

[7] In 1999, Canada resumed support, transmitting its contributions through SIL. It stopped again in the mid-2000s, and Gabriel Mba (NACALCO) says this reduced the effectiveness of the program. UNESCO is providing some new funding, and foreign and local linguists continue to work on languages and advocacy. At the highest level, La Francophonie has chosen Cameroon as one of its states to target with its ELAN program, described in Chapter 4.

[8] V. Geiger, SIL accountant, interview by author, Yaounde, October 7, 2002.

Part of the mandate of SIL translating teams is to produce – apart from the Bible – primers and basic reading materials, in order to promote literacy in the groups within which they work.[9] These foundational materials have provided the textbooks and teaching tools used in Cameroon's PROPELCA schools. Most are printed at the SIL headquarters and distributed gratis or sold for nominal fees. Sometimes the missionaries working within a language group will pay for the printing of such materials themselves. The SIL bibliography in 2001 listed 541 titles in fifty-four Cameroonian languages that were intended for literacy training in adult or primary classrooms (Ministry of Scientific and Technical Research 2001). These missionaries have designed a specific template for the transition from mother tongue to French that can be adapted quickly for any language by a teacher who is a native speaker, with only minimal training (Shell and Sadembouo 1983). Teachers can attend two-week training sessions to learn this method, usually funded by SIL.

Ideational Opportunities

In addition to material opportunities, a new ideational climate provided opportunities. There were two elements to this shift – one was a change in ideas sent from France and the other was a change in public ideas cultivated very deliberately by local NGOs.

The turn to an American organization for collaboration in a predominantly Francophone setting reflected the difficulty Cameroonian linguists had found soliciting support from France for the use of local languages in education. They might receive minimal funding for descriptive research, but the prospect of active use of these languages in French-dominated education systems was not seen favorably by the French Ministry of Foreign Affairs. Tadadjeu recounted how he was hired to do a survey of language use in several Central African countries and to make a recommendation to the Francophone Agency in the 1980s. After he proposed that African languages should be used as the basis of education, he was cut off from agency funding.[10]

This attitude has shifted dramatically. The strategy change within la Francophonie, and France in particular, led to a more permissive international environment, which was necessary for this change to be considered. The Cameroonian government could claim allegiance to a popular global agenda – support for indigenous languages – without risking the ire of the former metropole. Currently, meetings take place regularly in the Ministry of Education to discuss the PROPELCA method of teaching with Francophone Agency

[9] Dennis Malone of SIL International (2003, 332–348) describes the inexpensive and relatively short training processes required for a teacher to design and implement the basic curriculum for mother tongue education, a method practiced by SIL in most of its projects worldwide.

[10] M. Tadadjeu, NACALCO, interview by author, Yaounde, November 27, 2002.

support.[11] A report to the Ministry of Basic Education by Cameroonian representatives who had attended a conference on education held in Kinshasa noted that in the opening ceremony, officials of la Francophonie three times made the strong point that the use of national languages complements learning of French (Mbouda and Djiafeua 2005, 2). The top technical adviser to the minister of education said that France was not hindering the mother tongue policy; if there was any slowness in application, it was because a few officials in the ministry were trying to impede it.[12] When I asked the inspector-general for bilingual education whether he perceived any resistance on the part of French officials to the idea of mother tongue education, he replied that "there is a misconception that they care only about French. I believe they understand that local languages do not compete with French."[13] That there are only a few Cameroonian officials resistant to the idea reflects a sea change from two decades before. These civil servants have come on board because of the persuasive work of Tadadjeu and other linguists in concert with SIL.

SIL aimed directly to persuade the government of the utility of mother tongue education and enlist its support in spreading this method. Clinton Robinson, director of SIL in Cameroon from 1980 to 1987, recalls a cold response from Cameroonian education officials at the beginning of his tenure. SIL workers were not even allowed in the Ministry of Education. Robinson intentionally targeted only a few government ministers, inviting them to classrooms to see results, and gradually gained a warmer reception within the ministry. Currently, SIL linguists are regular visitors and respected consultants in the Ministry of Education.[14] Tadadjeu worked tirelessly to transform the opinion of government education officials – from the minister of education in the capital to divisional delegates in the provinces – as well as to alter the attitudes of political representatives.

Linguists at the University of Yaounde and SIL initially asked the Ministry of Education to collaborate on the PROPELCA program. After this first request was rejected by bureaucrats entrenched in the Francophone method, they turned instead to the Catholic Church (most of the Cameroonian leaders of the mother tongue effort were products of a Catholic school education). Tadadjeu's team approached the bishop of Bamenda to ask for a school in which to begin the PROPELCA experiment, and the bishop sent them to William Banboye (then Catholic education secretary for Bamenda), who "gave" them Catholic School (C.S.) Melim in which to try their method.

---

[11] For example, the Francophone Agency sponsored a Training Seminar on the Teaching of National Languages in Relation to French in Mons, Belgium, November 15–December 4, 2005.

[12] R. Wilayi, first technical adviser to the minister of education, MINEDUC, interview by author, Yaounde, October 28, 2002.

[13] M. Nama, telephone interview by author, April 20, 2005.

[14] C. Robinson, interview by author, Paris, April 19, 2004.

In 1984, Tadadjeu's team made a new request to the Ministry of Education, but this time it was framed in terms of the program's potential to aid in the learning of French or English. This practical rationale sounded much less subversive than their earlier cultural argument, and the ministry released a few public schools and teachers to participate. Tadadjeu had recognized the strategic potential of packaging the message in a way that was attractive to civil servants influenced by French ideology. He espoused the idea earlier than the scholarly community in France and would have to wait until the 1990s for members of that community to corroborate his message.

Therefore, PROPELCA remained a private project. A 1984 speech by Emmanuel Chia, then head of the Department of African Languages and Linguistics, explained: "It should be understood that this is a private undertaking and not a government project.... Government has so far not spent a franc in the development of any national language" (Tadadjeu 1990, 138, 141). But he and the other leaders of the mother tongue experiment knew that they would have to secure government involvement if they were to have any widespread effect. According to many commentators, 1985 marks the start of their official advocacy. Tadadjeu's team circulated a three-page memo at the CPDM (Cameroon People Democratic Movement) Party Congress in Bamenda, held in March 1985. This was the only fledgling civil society group to do so. In the resulting resolution, the ruling party included a commitment to encouraging the development of indigenous languages (Tadadjeu 1990, 224).

The private experiments in schools throughout the 1980s allowed the team to show tangible results, as ADEF had in Senegal, which further aided its efforts. At the General Conference on National Education in April 1989, George Ngango, minister of national education, spoke in favor of integrating mother tongues in public education programs, but there was as yet no concrete action on the part of the government. To overcome this resistance, language advocates had to address a "colonization of the mind" (Ngugi 1986).

I initially resisted addressing the symbolic power of language (Bourdieu 1991), wanting to stay firmly in a more "scientific" analysis. But in numerous interviews and writings about the subject, people continued to put this forward as an important concern, and it will be discussed further in the Conclusion. Using a language in an official setting gives it authority, legitimacy, and institutional dominance. The historical preference for European languages on the Francophone side after independence in the country as a whole certainly left an imprint in the average individual's mind that African languages were inferior. Explaining the obstacles to local language teaching, Tadadjeu writes, "One must sensitize the masses to the necessity of revalorizing our cultures through the teaching of our languages."[15] He bemoans the fact that one of the gravest consequences of colonization occurs at the mental, and even subconscious,

---

[15] From a discussion in Work Committee no. 6, June 15, 1978, my translation. Tadadjeu 1990, 26; also 32–33.

level: despising African culture, especially languages, by Africans (Tadadjeu 1990, 160–161). The success of PROPELCA rested on its recognition of the need to create a change in public ideas and cultivate a tight network of grassroots support.

Local linguists and SIL missionaries contributed intentionally to the organization of groups to preserve and promote their languages. In 1989, eight years after the modest start of the PROPELCA program, Tadadjeu and colleagues established the National Association of Cameroonian Language Committees (NACALCO) to manage more formally the mother tongue education effort. Most of these language committees were built on the working groups established by SIL missionaries, groups that had helped the foreign linguists with their transcription activities.[16] These were usually the outgrowth of church committees and gathered because a group wanted the Bible or hymns translated into their language. They now provide the network through which the central NACALCO office communicates, motivates, and raises grassroots support.

Numerous interviews with linguists, missionaries, and academics confirmed that it was an uphill battle to convince parents of the utility of teaching their children in mother tongues. Missionary linguists report that one of the foundational elements of linguistic research in a community is to motivate the group to value its language (Robinson 1987, 69). Reports from language committee supervisors cite "sensitization" as a major element of their work.[17] The president of the Lamnso Language Organization noted a common parental response to the suggestion of using local languages in education: "You can't write the GCE in Lamnso."[18] A Bafut Language Association leader recounted that parents saw learning Bafut in school as a deterrent to their children's learning of English.[19] Sensitizing parents is, therefore, a high priority for language committees.

---

[16] Though the link between SIL and current language committees appeared strong from my interviews with members of these committees, I sent a questionnaire to the SIL translation teams currently working in the field to get a better sense of the relationship (see Appendix B). These questionnaires asked when the SIL translating team arrived and when the language committee (if any existed in their language area) was formed. All twenty of these teams replied, and out of these responses, only one language project did not have a language committee. This was because, according to the resident linguist, the language group was composed of hunters and gatherers with little interest in formal literacy. Of the remaining nineteen, all but two formed language committees after the arrival of SIL missionaries, twelve within four years of the missionary arrival.

[17] For example, Yemba Language Committee Supervisor Pierre-Marie Akenmo reports: "From July 15th to August 11th, I went door to door to congregation members, sensitizing them to participate in language courses." He also paid for radio spots to "sensitize the public" (Akenmo 2001, 3). Bafut Language Committee Supervisor John Ambe Che reports the holding of "sensitization seminars" (Che 1999).

[18] W. Banboye, president of Nso Language Organization, interview by author, Kumbo, November 6, 2002. The GCE is the General Certificate of Education, an internationally recognized exam taken at the end of secondary school.

[19] J. Mfonyang, Bafut Language Committee, interview by author, Bafut, November 9, 2002.

For example, in 1975, the Wimbum Language Association (WILA) grew out of the Bible Translation Committee that had been established by SIL for the Limbum language a few years earlier. Emmanuel Nganga was a paid typist for the original committee, and currently he heads the association that evolved from the committee. He is also a local council member on the Ndu Rural Council, which, not surprisingly, voted to give 200,000 CFA per year to the language committee as part of its budget. Nganga speaks often at PTA meetings, assuring parents that PROPELCA is a bilingual program (rather than one ignoring English), and he has visited the divisional delegate for education three times to speak in favor of the mother tongue education policy.[20] A member of the Wimbum Language Committee said that the church always advocates that people learn to read and write Limbum so they can read Scripture and other religious material. The big problem is the parents, who cannot see how learning Limbum will help their children get a job. They want the children to learn things at school that they cannot learn at home.[21]

The Bafut Language Committee is another that grew out of a SIL translation committee. One of its aims is to raise money to help parents buy textbooks in Bafut for their children. Since Joseph Mfonyang, resident Bafut linguist, is a permanent SIL employee, he is able to raise support in the United States for projects such as the purchase of textbooks. Funds are always forthcoming. Mfonyang acknowledged that the perpetual giving of SIL does enable the committee to complain that they "can't" raise the money themselves.[22] In contrast, the language of Mungaka (Bali), which was one of the original languages translated by early missionaries in the Grassfields, is dying out because of neglect.[23] Recall from Chapter 2 that this was the single language chosen by the Basel missionaries for use in the interior. SIL decided early on not to work on this language because it already had an orthography and grammar, and likely also because of the stigma attached to it. There is now much more active advocacy around neighboring languages as a result of SIL's work, while this one remains relatively dormant.

By 1995, the PROPELCA program had been in operation for nearly fifteen years, and the results of its experimental efforts could be presented at Cameroon's États Généraux (General Conference) on Education, which was in preparation for a major reorientation of Cameroon's education law. The minister of education, Robert Mbella Mbappe, knew Tadadjeu well and gave him the opportunity to present PROPELCA activities to the general conference. Tadadjeu was one of nine presenters at the opening ceremony, and debates

---

[20] This was important when the Ministry of Education sent a questionnaire to all the divisional delegates to get their reaction to the proposed plan. E. Nganga, interview by author, Nkambe, November 5, 2002.

[21] R. Tanto, priest in Binju Catholic Church, interview by author, Nkambe, November 4, 2002.

[22] J. Mfonyang, Bafut Language Committee, interview by author, Bafut, November 9, 2002.

[23] Pastor P. Fomusoh, Presbyterian Church Bali, interview by author, Bali, November 10. 2002.

about teaching in national languages constituted a significant part of the proceedings (Ministère de l'Éducation Nationale, 1995, 20). He described the mother tongue projects that had already been put in place in the field with SIL assistance and carefully rebutted potential arguments with pragmatic appeals to second-language acquisition. In preparation for the États Généraux, the National Ministry of Education had sent a letter to provincial delegates for education, asking whether they were in favor of using local languages in schools. Tadadjeu and his team knew this was coming, so they had asked a representative of each of the language committees to visit his provincial education delegate.[24] When the responses came back to the Ministry of Education, most provincial delegates said they would support the idea.[25] Tadadjeu's proposals were adopted by the conference, and the Plenary Session's eighth recommendation was the "Introduction of national languages and cultures in the education system" (Ministère de l'Education Nationale 1995, 79). After the États Généraux, Tadadjeu's team worked within the specific nature of Cameroon's lawmaking process. They followed the draft of the law through its various stopping points, finding out who was on each committee and writing, visiting, or calling them. They would ask, "Is the national languages paragraph still in there?" And the answer was "When it left my desk, it was still there." They would not have been able to object to any changes made when the document reached the presidency, so they were very pleased when it emerged with the "language paragraph" intact.[26]

And even though the National Assembly would not have rejected the bill – it never has opposed the presidency – the NACALCO team wanted to make sure there was not negative reaction to it in assembly debates. They chose to target a total of twenty to twenty-five deputies from various parties. Etiènne Sadembo, as a representative of NACALCO, went to each of their rooms at the Hôtel des Deputés before the vote to try to defuse any potential problems. The group knew the deputies would not propose anything radical in the assembly, but they wanted to make sure there was no obstruction there.[27] After the vote, they found out there had been no objections in the discussion. It was a case of successful lobbying. Tadadjeu admits there was no argument "not because people believed in it, but because they didn't want to create waves on a sensitive issue."[28]

The Education Orientation Law that included support for national languages was passed by the legislature in 1998.[29] The lack of political bargaining is partially explained by executive domination of the legislature in Africa. For

---

[24] For example: Mba and Francis, Lamnso Language Organization members, took a letter to Northwest Divisional Delegate of Natioal Education Nyuyki Boniface Ngoran from Tadadjeu.

[25] N. Ngueffo, NACALCO, interview by author, Yaounde, November 21, 2002.

[26] M. Tadadjeu, interview by author, Yaounde, November 27, 2002.

[27] E. Sadembo, interview by author, Yaounde, December 18, 2002.

[28] M. Tadadjeu, interview by author, Yaounde, November 27, 2002.

[29] Law No. 98/004 of April 14, 1998.

the bargaining model to work, it would be necessary for a National Assembly member (a regional political player) to be able to influence policy by pressing for language rights for his constituency. In fact, in Cameroon, education policy is drafted in the Ministry of Education (part of the executive branch), revised in the Prime Ministry, reviewed at the Presidency, and approved in the National Assembly. The last step would appear an area where the public might have influence. The assembly members, however, do not even know what bills will be brought up at the assembly when they arrive for the three annual sessions.[30] If the representatives cannot prepare for discussion topics, then still less is it possible for their constituents to anticipate them and lobby. And, though the constitution makes a provision for it, no bill has ever been introduced in the assembly by representatives; they all originate in the ministries or directly from the Presidency.[31]

Tadadjeu's language association, built on SIL's language committees, created a network that persuaded by its institutionalization. The Bafut Language Association found it easier to recruit members after NACALCO had given its "Official Stamp."[32] Until the law of 1998 was passed, school inspectors worried the minister of education would ask, "Why are you allowing these local languages in your schools?" since they did not think the government knew about it. The Bafut Language Committee asked Tadadjeu and others to travel to Bamenda, where they organized a meeting of all inspectors (divisional and provincial) and gave each of them a copy of the 1998 decree.[33] The Bafut inspector of nursery and primary education has since become very supportive of PROPELCA, encouraging teachers to attend training seminars. A group from the Bafut language committee went to talk to him both before the 1998 law and after and reported that the reception was much warmer after 1998.[34] Similarly, two language committee members, Mba and Francis, brought a letter from Tadadjeu, addressed to the mayor of the Lamnso division, recommending that language committees be a budget line item in council budgets. They went to the Fon first (Fons are royal leaders of cultural groupings), then the mayor, and then to education inspectors and the divisional delegate with copies of the letter and the endorsement of each successive official.[35]

I asked Tadadjeu to elaborate on a statement he had made in his book, *Défi de Babel* that the Ministry of Education was the *maître d'oeuvre* (overseer) of the process of reform in favor of local languages. "Did you really mean that?" I asked. He admitted that even though he and his cadre were the real motivators, he could

---

[30] T. N. Lucas, member, Cameroon National Assembly, interview by author, Yaounde, December 13, 2002.

[31] E. Tawe, official French/English translator for the National Assembly, interview by author, Yaounde, November 20, 2002.

[32] J. Mfonyang, Bafut Language Committee, interview by author, Bafut, November 9, 2002.

[33] J. Ambe, supervisor, Bafut Language Association, interview by author, Bafut, November 9, 2002.

[34] J. Mfonyam, interview by author, Bafut, November 9, 2002.

[35] M. Ma'Wo Sheey, inspector for Lamnso, interview by author, Kumbo, November 6, 2002.

not say that. "You have to credit them.... Otherwise they would not let you do it. That's the hypocrisy of political discourse. You don't write always what you think. You write what would be acceptable."[36]

Tadadjeu and his team were strategic. They had to convince a public that he believed had endured a "colonization of the mind," which had long degraded local languages in favor of European ones. With SIL's financial and infrastructural support, they were systematic advocates – working with language committees where they existed, creating them where they did not, appointing committee representatives to talk to parents, teachers, and divisional education representatives. They convinced the Ministry of Education with a message that *all* languages could be used (precluding the conflict of choosing among them) and that local languages would help with French or English acquisition. And they used experimental classes to show results. They targeted bureaucratic and political leaders at all levels to enlist their support. Using the nominal endorsement of the constitution and the 1998 law, they encouraged public support and "trapped" officials into doing what they had agreed to do. Even if these officials did not fully believe what they said when allowing inclusion of a relatively vague endorsement of local language education in official documents, these statements can now be used to justify further activity.

If parents and bureaucrats were persuaded by material and ideational opportunities, what motivates rulers? I argue that in many cases it is incentives generated by the requirement for democratic institutions. While some leaders may be genuine democrats, concerned with balancing majority rule with minority protections, self-interested rulers may also perceive minority concessions as helpful in their quest to maintain their position. Even if rulers are not persuaded by the linguists' rationale or evidence, they may begin to see local education as a potential advantage in their attempt to retain electoral power. This section will show how the political climate changed in Cameroon in the 1990s, with donor and domestic pressure converging to prompt limited liberalization. This forced the government to recalculate its strategies for maintaining power. These strategies included the oft-cited fraud and intimidation of opponents, but they also began to include more subtle attempts at boundary manipulation, voter exclusion, and deliberate fragmentation of the opposition. The adoption of a multilingual education policy in this situation could appear magnanimous to outsiders and at the same time conceal more sinister intentions. While it is impossible to know the true preferences of leaders, the following evidence points to the latter interpretation.

RULER INCENTIVES FOR POLICY CHANGE

Beginning independence under the relatively autocratic leadership of Ahmadou Ahidjo, Cameroon remained autocratic under his chosen successor, Paul Biya,

---

[36] M. Tadadjeu, interview by author, Yaounde, November 27, 2002.

until the early 1990s. In 1992, when Biya allowed other parties to stand candidates in the presidential election, Cameroon improved from a Polity score of –8 to –4: still in the autocratic category, but not quite as severe. Because the government made modest overtures to opposition parties and lightened its heavy hand on the media, Cameroon was rewarded with a slightly higher score. In 1995, three years into this marginally more liberal regime, the États Généraux included local languages in the discussion of effective pedagogical practices, and the 1996 constitution contained a provision promoting the use of national languages. As described previously, the 1998 Education Orientation Law stipulated that local languages should be used as media of instruction. But this recognition of minority rights likely was not evidence of a more liberal regime. I argue that it was instead a way of dividing the opposition to ensure the ruling party's continued dominance.

When Biya assumed power, he promised to eradicate the "tribalism" of which Ahidjo had been accused as a result of his rotation of cabinet members based on region. "Cameroonians are first of all Cameroonians, before being Bamiléké, Ewondos, Foulbes, Bassas, Boulous, Doualas, Bakweris, Bayas, Massas or Makas. This means that Cameroonians are first of all Cameroonians, before being English-speaking or French-speaking, Christians, Muslims or animist," he declared to the National Assembly in 1983 (cited in Takougang 2004, 107). Nonetheless, Biya's practice of "nontribalism" increasingly favored his own group (Nkwi and Nyamnjoh 1997, 8–10). A report in the opposition newspaper *Le Messager* in 1991 found that thirty-seven of forty-seven senior prefects (administrative heads of divisions), three-quarters of directors and general managers of parastatal corporations, and twenty-two of thirty-eight high-ranking bureaucrats in the newly created office of the prime minister were from the president's clan (Takougang and Krieger 1998, 94).

Who was this "clan"? The Beti are a historically recognized group, concentrated in the Center and South provinces (Quinn 2006, ch. 1). Driven south by the nineteenth century Fulani invasion of northern Cameroon, this group has a distinctive history of migration across the Sanaga River. A map depicting the Beti group about the time of independence produced by the historian Frederick Quinn outlines their concentration around the capital of Yaounde and comprising a few language groups, such as the Eton and Ewondo (Quinn 2006, 11). Identification with this group acquired more political significance, however, and membership significantly expanded after the ascension of Biya to power (Zambo-Belinga 2005). Previously distinct groups, notably the Bulu, to whom Paul Biya belongs, are now amalgamated into a widening category of "Beti," and the reach of this grouping stretches across a remarkable span of Cameroon's central and southern territory.

As Beti boundaries have broadened, other groups have crystallized. Significant in Cameroon's political and economic landscape are the Bamiléké, another expansive group covering several distinct languages, but bound culturally by their similar allegiance to chiefdoms in the West and North West regions of Cameroon (Joseph 1977, 8). Known for their frugality and successful entrepreneurship, the Bamiléké historically have played dominant social roles as businessmen (Miaffo and Warnier 1993, 205–208). Relatively protected under Ahidjo, they felt their fortunes change after Biya's accession to power and accused his administration of "deliberate attempts to promote opportunities among Beti businessmen at their expense."[37]

Another important label is the Grassfielders. This is a geographic designation for a group in the North West Province, concentrated around the town of Bamenda; it is a loose amalgam of small chiefdoms with similar political structures (Kaberry and Chilver 1961, 357). These Grassfielders share an Anglophone identification with their counterparts in the South West Province on the basis of their common colonial heritage, and both provinces consider themselves marginalized from Cameroon's Francophone-dominated political structure, though they are divided as to how much each has suffered (Konings 2003, 36–38).

While these Bamenda Grassfielders are related culturally to the Bamiléké, they were categorized separately because of their experience with British, rather than French, administration. Both groups, however, were encouraged to migrate south to plantations under colonial rule, and they continued after independence to move frequently to urban areas throughout the territory following economic opportunities. Therefore, they are found all over southern Cameroon. In the years since the 1992 elections, the Grassfielders and the Bamiléké, along with other Anglophones from both the North West and South West Provinces, have been amalgamated under the label "Anglo-Bamis."

These distinctions have grown in salience since the early 1990s, marking boundaries of political allegiance and sometimes erupting into violent confrontation (Socpa 2006; Jua 2001). Why they have done so requires a look at the democratic opening and closing over the past two decades in Cameroon. Like that of most African countries in the mid-1980s, Cameroon's economy fell precipitously. From an average of 8 percent GDP growth between 1976 and 1986, the economy constricted an average of -4 percent per year from 1987 to 1991 (WDI). Prices for cocoa, cotton, and oil all declined, and the value of Cameroon's exports in the mid-1980s dropped by nearly half (Takougang and Krieger 1998, 98). While the Bamiléké had historically maintained close relationships with the regime because of their economic power base and because of Ahidjo's desire to pacify a region that had been a hotbed of rebellion (Konings 2002, 184), "by the late 1980s many potential investors, especially Bamiléké businessmen who had seen their domination of the economy gradually eroded in favor of businessmen from the president's Beti ethnic group, decided to utilize informal savings clubs (*tontines*) rather than put their money in [government-owned] banks" (Takougang and Krieger 1998, 100–101).

---

[37] Joseph 1977, 8–11; Takougang and Krieger 1998, 96; Jua 1993.

While Biya's 1983 speech showed his rhetoric against the dangers of tribalism, in his 1987 "manifesto," *Communal Liberalism*, he wrote that it was necessary to "encourage development of national languages" (Biya 1987, 104). This was a dramatic shift. I asked the linguist Tadadjeu whether he knew why that reference was placed in the book. He looked a bit embarrassed, but when pressed, explained that before the book was published, in 1985, there was a conference on the cultural identity of Cameroon in the Palais des Congrès. Tadadjeu presented a paper on the necessity to promote Cameroon's languages as an integral part of cultural identity. The drafter of Biya's book was at the conference. This man obviously carried Tadadjeu's ideas back to the president. "I discovered 'familiar' passages in Biya's book," said Tadadjeu with a smile. But he was not bothered. "I don't mind if people take my ideas if they agree with them!"[38]

But did this recognition of languages have a darker purpose? As opposition voices began to emerge, Biya and his top party leaders had to devise a strategy for maintaining power. Though likely there was not a coherent plan at the outset, the government adapted quickly to the constraints of democratic institutions by turning them into opportunities for control.

Under widespread international condemnation for a heavy-handed response to the launch of the Social Democratic Front (SDF) by John Fru Ndi, Biya finally legalized opposition parties in December of 1990. Immediately, the parties coalesced to press for a national conference. Biya refused. In response, opposition groups called for a nationwide strike – Villes Mortes – intended to shut down every major city and town until the government agreed to a national conference. The violence and economic strain that resulted from these "Ghost Towns" led Biya to accede to a Trilateral Conference – with members of government, opposition, and civil society representatives – but the government would not give up its sovereign prerogative to lead the proceedings (Takougang 2003, 437–438). Halfway through the meeting, SDF withdrew, leaving the opposition fragmented. Biya won international political favor for his concession, however, as a meeting in Paris just after the conference produced an aid package that had earlier been refused, allowing him the resources subsequently to renew an IMF debt renegotiation and remain solvent in the face of severe economic crisis (Takougang and Krieger 1998, 142).

Multiparty elections were finally held in 1992, first for the legislature and then for the presidency. SDF boycotted the legislative elections; as a result, the northern-based Union Nationale pour la Démocratie et le Progrès (UNDP) won most of the opposition seats. The ruling party, Cameroon People's Democratic Movement (CPDM), won just less than half of the seats in the 180-seat legislature, though it was able to cobble together a majority by allying with a small offshoot party. The official result of the single-round presidential election showed Biya with nearly 40 percent of the vote and Fru Ndi, with 36

---

[38] M. Tadadjeu, interview by author, Yaounde, November 27, 2002.

TABLE 6.1. *Legislative Election Results, 1992–2007*

Year	CPDM seats	Opposition Seats	CPDM Percentage
1992	88 (+6 MDR)	68 (UNDP) + 18 other = 86	49
1997	116	43 (SDF) + 21 other = 64	64
2002	149	22 (SDF) + 9 other = 31	82
2007	153	17 (SDF) + 10 other = 27	85

Calculated from results obtained from the Ministry of Territorial Administration and Decentralization.

percent. These results contradicted the general feeling in the country (and initial indications) that the opposition had won.[39] France was the only Western power to offer diplomatic support, but this was enough to keep Biya in power. Fru Ndi and his supporters claimed their victory had been stolen, and violence erupted in the North West Province. The regime reacted quickly, placing Fru Ndi under house arrest and declaring states of emergency in the "rebellious" regions. This was the high-water mark in the challenge to Biya's hold on political power. Observers were optimistic about the potential for democratic protagonists to prevail and praised the opposition for rising above ethnic loyalties in this initial challenge to CPDM (Krieger 1994; Ndjio 2008, 125).

Since 1992, however, this challenge has largely dissipated. Contained to less than 50 percent of legislative seats in 1992, CPDM has rebounded to win more than 80 percent in the past two elections. Table 6.1 shows the votes won by the ruling party and the opposition in each election since 1992.

Clearly, Paul Biya's party has entrenched its authority in the legislature. In 2008, Biya used this overwhelming dominance to pass a constitutional amendment that removes any limits to his terms of office. Winning again in 2012, he could be in power until 2018 or beyond.

How has he managed to turn such a volatile opposition force into putty? Of course, there are the usual explanations, such as fraud, co-optation, and intimidation (Gros 1995). The typical accusations charged at illiberal governments during elections – such as the lack of an independent electoral commission, short campaign period, government advantages in resources, and irregularities in ballot counting – are no doubt accurate and form the first layer in an autocrat's tool kit.[40] The co-optation and intimidation allowed by access to economic resources (via foreign aid and extrabudgetary oil revenues) and the political support of France form a deeper, more systemic layer that keeps the ruling party

---

[39] The National Democratic Institute's (1993) assessment of the election cites widespread fraud that led to Biya's victory, and academic observers such as Gros (1995) discuss the multiple illegal tactics necessary to keep Biya in power.

[40] Andreas Schedler (2010) has recently compiled a general inventory of how "electoral authoritarian regimes," a label for which Cameroon would qualify, use democratic institutions to reinforce their rule.

at a perpetual advantage. But to these relatively blunt tools, Biya has added more sophisticated adaptations to the constraints and opportunities of a multiparty political setting. More consequential in terms of long-term impact on the country have been the government's subtle manipulation of electoral boundaries, control of voting access, and cunning adaptation of liberal discourse to divide the opposition.

ELECTORAL DISTRICT MANIPULATION

The first such strategy is as old as elections themselves: the gerrymandering of districts.[41] Cameroon operates under a mixed electoral system, derived from the French model: The party with the majority of votes takes all seats in multi-member constituencies, and if no party receives the majority, the seats are split proportionally. Administrative divisions within Cameroon's ten provinces formed the forty-nine electoral constituencies in the first multiparty legislative election.[42] In Cameroon's 1987 census, these ten provinces varied in population from 500,000 in the South to 2.5 million in the Far North. The initial allocation of the 180 legislative seats only loosely corresponded with population size. Though the two most populous provinces (Far North and Center) received the most seats (twenty-nine and twenty-eight, respectively), Littoral and West received very different distributions (nineteen and twenty-five, respectively) with almost identical populations. The ratio of seat distribution to population highlights these discrepancies. Littoral and North have the lowest ratios, with one seat assigned per approximately 71,000 people, and South has the highest, with one seat assigned to approximately 34,000 people.[43]

The allocation of seats within districts in the provinces is even more telling, and it will be shown that Cameroon's electoral districts have progressively been redrawn to disfavor the opposition. Larger district magnitudes give more opportunities for smaller parties to gain seats, while single-member districts generally favor larger parties (Shugart and Carey 1992, 226–231). The forty-nine constituencies in 1992 varied in magnitude from one to nine seats; only four of them[44] had one seat, however, and only two[45] had more than six; the rest had an average of about four seats per district. Overall, each seat in the 1992 election

---

[41] See Lublin (1995) for an excellent discussion of the potential for "wasting" votes of a minority by packing them into majority-minority districts.

[42] These administrative divisions had formed the constituencies for the 1988 single-party elections as well.

[43] These calculations are from 1987 population figures, as it was the most recent census before the 1992 elections. Population ratios for 2007 are even more exaggerated: Littoral has 138,000 persons per seat, North 121,000, and South 58,000.

[44] These were Djerem and Faro-et-Deo in Adamawa, Nkam in Littoral, and Faro in the North, which were in fact the most lightly populated districts, ranging from 41,000 to 61,000 in population.

[45] These were Wouri in Littoral with nine seats, which encompassed Cameroon's largest city, Douala, and Mfoundi in Center with seven seats, which encompassed the capital city, Yaounde.

represented an average of 54,000 people. But distribution among districts varied widely between urban and rural areas: Rural Nkam in Littoral was allocated one seat for 41,000 people, whereas Wouri (Douala) in the same province had nine seats, translating into one seat per 93,000 people. In the Far North, seat/population ratios in multimember districts ranged from 46,000 in more rural Mayo-Kani to 77,000 in urban Diamare (Maroua). Urban populations uniformly had fewer seats than rural.

But beyond this irregularity, there were more regionally specific discrepancies. The most interesting areas to compare are the North West and South Provinces – the former the Anglophone opposition stronghold and the latter the home of the president's Beti clan. Even with the initial allocation, the South had much more electoral power per voter: Dja-et-Lobo in the South with 121,000 inhabitants elected the same number of MPs (five) as did Mezam in North West Province, which had 313,000 inhabitants. Thus, southern voters had more than twice the impact per person in the election. These district discrepancies became even more skewed over time – not just because of population growth, but because of deliberate boundary changes. By tracing the changes in district magnitude over the four elections between 1992 and 2007, this section argues that the increase from forty-nine to eighty-five districts, and particularly the creation of more than thirty single-member districts, explains to a large extent the ruling party's ability to recapture the districts it lost in 1992. Figure 6.1 shows the electoral constituencies for the 2007 elections, the solid and dotted lines indicating where new districts were created after 1992.

Following the near electoral disaster for the ruling party in 1992, a presidential decree (No. 97/061) before the 1997 elections authorized the partition of several existing districts, resulting in nine additional divisions (solid lines). Another decree in that same year (No. 97/062) created sixteen "Special Electoral Districts" (dotted lines). As a result, between 1992 and 1997, the number of districts increased from forty-nine to seventy-four, and the average magnitude decreased from nearly 4 to 2.4 seats per district. It is no coincidence that CPDM increased its seat share from 48 percent to 64 percent between 1992 and 1997.

Overall, twenty-two of the twenty-five new districts created in Cameroon between 1992 and 1997 were single-seat. CPDM won all but four of these new single-member districts in 1997. The benefit to the ruling party is clear in seat to vote share ratios: Whereas CPDM won 88 seats (49 percent of total legislature) in 1992 on 39 percent of the vote share, it won 116 seats (64 percent of total) in 1997 on 37 percent of the vote share. The government made no further boundary adjustments for the 2002 elections, though it succeeded in consolidating its gains through other methods, discussed in the next section. Another Presidential Decree (No. 2007/119) before the 2007 elections, however, authorized eleven additional "Special Electoral Districts," all of them single-seat. By the 2007 elections, then, there were eighty-five districts (compared to forty-nine at the outset of the multiparty experiment), with an average district magnitude of 2.12

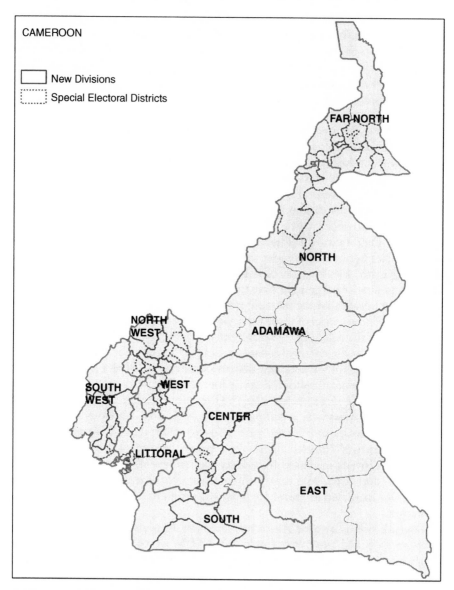

FIGURE 6.1. Cameroon: New Electoral Districts Created, 1992–2007

seats. The number of single-member districts had increased from only four in
1992 to thirty-three in 2007.

Whereas most of the divisions between 1992 and 1997 happened in the Far
North, Littoral, and South West Provinces, nearly all of the changes anticipating
the 2007 elections occurred in the North West Province. Having divided most of

the opposition with the 1997 Presidential Decrees, the 2007 laws were clearly aimed at this last bastion of resistance, the North West Province. This was the stronghold of SDF. Much could be written about the role of the opposition in bringing about its own demise – from leadership infighting to collusion. These certainly contributed to the swell in CPDM's fortunes between 1992 and 2002, and they have been well documented (Takougang 2003; Konings 2004). In contrast, I focus on the almost mechanical outcomes that occurred as a result of the institutional changes in boundary lines and seat allocation. Of course, they were magnified by a weakened opposition, but the overall institutional effects were evident in 1997, before the dissipation in opposition coherence.

The North West Province is allocated twenty seats in each election. With SDF's boycott in 1992, CPDM had won all twenty seats in five multimember districts (though turnout was only 24 percent, which reveals its weak mandate). Back in the game for the 1997 elections, SDF regained nineteen of the seats in now eight districts, losing only one to CPDM – in a new single-seat district that had been created since the last election. SDF retained these nineteen seats in 2002. The Presidential Decree before the 2007 elections, however, divided the North West Province's eight districts into sixteen; all of the new ones were single-seat, giving North West Province a total of twelve single-member districts.[46] CPDM won nine of these in 2007, losing only the three in Mezam (Bamenda) – birthplace of the SDF.[47]

The combination of initial population malapportionment and electoral district manipulation demonstrates that the CPDM learned very quickly how to use multiparty election rules to its advantage. Electoral district divisions clearly have served to increase the power of the ruling party in the National Assembly; CPDM won all but five of the thirty-three single-seat districts in 2007. In concert

---

[46] 1992 North West Province Districts (seats): Bui (4), Donga-Mantung (4), Menchum (4), Mezam (5), Momo (3); 1997 Districts (seats): Bui (4), Donga-Mantung (4), Menchum (2), Boyo (2), Mezam (3), Ngo-Ketunjia-Nord (1), Ngo-Ketunjia-Sud (1), Momo (3); 2002 Districts (same as 1997); 2007 Districts (seats): Bui-Centre (2), Bui-Ouest (1), Bui-Sud (1), Donga-Mantung (2), Donga-Mantung-Est (1), Donga-Mantung-Ouest (1), Menchum-Nord (1), Menchum-Sud (1), Boyo (2), Mezam-Centre (1), Mezam-Nord (1), Mezam-Sud (1), Ngo-Ketunjia-Nord (1), Ngo-Ketunjia-Sud (1), Momo-Est (2), Momo-Ouest (1).

[47] Mezam division encompasses Bamenda, capital of the North West Province and the home base of opposition SDF. It had five of the province's twenty seats in the 1992 elections. Because of the SDF boycott that year, however, CPDM won all five seats with a total of 8,994 votes (each parliamentary member thus represented fewer than 1,800 votes), along with all of the remaining seats in the province. Anticipating SDF's return in 1997, the first Presidential decree divided Mezam into three districts, Mezam (Bamenda) retaining three seats, and two other districts with a single-seat each: Ngo-Ketunjia-Nord and Ngo-Ketunjia-Sud. Bamenda's three-seat district contained 85,000 registered voters in 1997, single-seat Ngo-Ketunjia-Nord contained 21,000, and single-seat Ngo-Ketunjia-Sud contained 12,000. In the 1997 elections, the only seat won by CPDM in the North West Province was in Ngo-Ketunjia-Sud. The 2007 decree divided the three seats in Mezam once more – into Mezam Centre, Mezam Nord, and Mezam Sud. Unfortunately for the government, it could not dislodge SDF from this bastion, nor from neighboring Momo Est, which it had created in 2007, though it managed to win the single seat in Momo Ouest.

with this strategy, another tool was employed: restrictions on voting access. Where the opposition was strong, boundary changes were accompanied by the potentially even more effective strategy of not allowing the opposition to vote in the first place.

RESTRICTING VOTING ACCESS

Nearly five million voters registered for the 2002 election, almost one million (24 percent) more than in 1997. This was an enormous increase over the past two elections, and it was largely a result of a voter-registration campaign undertaken by the ruling party, which offered to waive the fee for people's voting cards in (largely rural) supportive regions.[48] The South West Province, for example, increased registrants by 36 percent more than population increases would predict. Newly created Lebialam district increased from 45,999 in 1997 to 71,911 registered voters in 2002.[49] But five years later, in 2007, the number of registered voters across the country had only risen by 2.5 percent from 2002, much less than population growth would predict. And the number actually decreased in many areas. This is not voter *turnout*, which decreased as well, but registration itself.

Stories of targeted disenfranchisement abound in the press and in popular discourse.[50] People recount of being denied electoral cards or being told that they had to go "home" (if they were in an urban setting) to vote. Unfortunately, there were no hard data corroborating these stories. When registration is examined as a percentage of the population, validating trends do emerge. As a percentage of the population, north westerners tend to register far less. In all four elections, north westerners registered at a rate of 20–30 percent of their population figures, whereas southerners registered at a rate of 34–49 percent of their population. These are consistently the lowest and highest registering regions, and in the 2007 election, the West and Littoral Provinces joined the North West with very low registration percentages (22 percent and 24 percent, respectively). These figures correspond with the reports of targeted disenfranchisement in opposition regions.

Because many stories of such discrimination revolve around urban voters being told to go "home," I conducted a small-scale survey to find evidence for these stories in urban areas of four different provinces: Yaounde (Center), Ebolowa (South), Douala (Littoral), and Buea (South West). To ascertain people's experiences in the last election, 160 respondents were asked simple

---

[48] Interview by author, district officer, Buea, July 15, 2009.
[49] This was likely because the single-seat district could not be divided any further, and CPDM had lost by only thirty-eight votes to SDF in 1997. With a dramatic increase in supportive voters in 2002, it won 58% of the vote in the district to recapture the seat.
[50] Fonchingong 2005, 370; Monga 2000; Geschiere 2009.

demographic information, which included their language and division of origin.[51] They were then asked whether they had obtained a voting card for the 2007 election and what that process entailed. While only suggestive because of the small sample size, the results were astonishing. Virtually all (90 percent) of Bulu and Ewondo speakers (Beti) were able to get their voting cards with no problem.[52] After receiving an affirmative response to receipt of an electoral card, the follow-up question was "How did you obtain it?" An almost uniform response among this group was some version of "I just signed up on the electoral list." In dramatic contrast, only 30 percent of the respondents who named their home origin as the North West were able to get voting cards. These would be the Bamenda Grassfielders in the earlier terminology. Examples of responses to the follow-up question of "Why?" were "My card was not seen [when I went to pick it up]" and "We went to the chieftaincy but my card was not there, and they drove us away." The West and Littoral regions, with respondents who primarily identified themselves as Bamiléké, reported from 40 to 50 percent success rates in obtaining electoral cards, and those from the South West (Anglophones) reported 43 percent.[53] Overall trends in these urban districts corroborate their stories: From 2002 to 2007, registration decreased in Cameroon's two largest cities, Yoaunde and Douala: In Mfoundi (Yaounde), it was 18 percent less than population growth would have predicted, and in Wouri (Douala), it was 26 percent less.

This strategy effectively eliminated the very voters who would have voted for the opposition. The way these cards were distributed in many cases is also telling. It is the mayor's office in a large town or the police office in a small one that distributes voting cards. Often the ward chiefs will go to register names from their neighborhood and collect all cards prior to an election. These leaders know the families in their neighborhoods and which ones would likely vote for the opposition. Many stories mentioned chiefs who did not bring back cards for everyone. Similarly, if an individual went him- or herself to the mayor's office in an urban town to register, for example, he or she would be identified by name and/or language as being from an "opposition region" and as a result would return to collect the card and discover that it "was not found." Fully half or more of all urban respondents from the West, South West, Littoral, and North West regions were not able to get voting cards. Obviously, since it is in these regions

---

[51] This was done with the help of research assistants, who spoke local languages when necessary and helped to fill out brief written surveys. Survey questions are listed in Appendix B, "Election Experience Survey."

[52] Of the four Beti who did not respond in the affirmative, two said they had not tried to get cards because they had no interest in the election, one said she had been in transition during the election, and the last was too young to vote. Obviously, anyone in this group who had wanted to obtain voting cards had no difficulty doing so.

[53] Summary: 90% from South (Beti) able to get cards; 67% Center (various groups); 50% West (Bamiléké); 43% South West (from Fako/Buea); 40% Littoral (from Wouri/Douala); 30% North West.

that the government has faced the most opposition, preventing these citizens from voting makes it unnecessary to engage in fraud on election day. Clearly, those groups not part of the Beti clan are finding disenfranchisement a stark reality. This has led to intense apathy. In nearly all conversations with the "Anglo-Bamis" conducted during the study, there was profound resignation to a lack of ability to reverse their alienated status.

When added to the electoral district manipulation, the restrictions on registration make the distribution of voters within the districts even more skewed. As noted previously, initial seat allocation was not based closely on population distribution, and in fact the average number of people per district deviated by 22 percent (up or down) from what population would have predicted. In the 1992 election, *registration* deviated by almost exactly the same amount. Since population figures are not available for the special electoral districts created in 1997 and 2007, one can look at the deviation in registered voters from what a proportional allocation of total registrants would have been. The boundary changes in 1997 raised the average deviation from 22 percent to 37 percent, and it remained the same in 2002. The deviation rose to 39 percent after the further boundary changes in 2007. The number of registrants (not even actual voters) per seat varied from nearly eighty thousand in Lebialam to fewer than ten thousand in Fako-Ouest. Simply put, electoral boundaries no longer have any relationship to population distribution at all, and they clearly have been drawn and intensified by registration restrictions to disfavor the opposition.

CONSTITUTIONAL RECOGNITION OF MINORITY RIGHTS

The effects of boundary manipulation and targeted disenfranchisement on bolstering government hegemony are immediate and observable. A third strategy involves the topic at the heart of the book – minority language policies. Beyond the gerrymandering and registration bias, the government has seized on an opportunity pressed by global human rights discourse to consolidate its authority. As discussed in the previous chapter, attention to minority rights is in vogue, and recent constitutional changes in many African countries contain provisions for decentralization (Crawford and Hartmann 2008, 7) and specific references to minority rights (Dau 2009). Cameroon is no different. Instead of protecting minorities, however, I argue that these constitutional changes actually provide a way to control them more explicitly. Other authors have pointed to the effort to divide the "Anglo-Bami" opposition with this new decentralized constitution (Njoya 2002, 269), which seems certainly to be the case. Referring to an opposition group as a bloc could be dangerous for a ruling party, as it could face a united foe. One obvious response has been to co-opt members of the opposition, discussed by several observers. Basile Ndjio makes especially poignant observations about the opposition's move from confrontation to collaboration, resulting in a "pacified democracy" with a domesticated opposition (Ndjio

2008, 142–147). But in the long term, the constitutional decentralization may impact identities in deeper ways.

Unlike the 1972 constitution, the Preamble of Cameroon's 1996 constitution declares: "The State shall ensure the protection of minorities and shall preserve the rights of indigenous populations." The 1996 constitution also outlines the new structure of decentralization, in which regional and local authorities are recognized for the first time. Article 57 (2), which relates to the newly authorized regional councils, states that elected delegates and traditional rulers "shall reflect the various sociological components of the region." Similarly, Article 57 (3) specifies that the "Regional Council shall be headed by an indigene of the Region."

The constitutional language echoes that of the electoral code introduced before the 1996 local elections, which contains a residency requirement of six months and, more critically, requires that candidates and electoral lists must reflect the sociological components of their constituency. Local representatives of the minister of territorial elections have complete discretion to decide who qualifies for that label. Both the denial of electoral cards and these requirements were arguably intended to protect "locals" from being outvoted by "strangers" (Jua 2001). As noted earlier, urban residents are often told to go home to their village of origin to vote. Since the Bamenda Grassfielders and the Bamiléké are the most dominant migrant groups, they clearly would not reflect the indigenous sociological components of the regions to which they have migrated.

Demonstrating his adaptation to these popular discourses about minorities and decentralization, Paul Biya has discovered how they can be used for political purposes. Elite ethnic associations, banned from political activity under President Ahidjo, have been resurrected since 1992. Rather than only undertaking traditional self-help and cultural development activities, these associations in the 1990s increasingly replaced political parties as major players in regional politics (Nyamnjoh and Rowlands 1998). As the ruling party has lost popular credibility and opposition parties' national reach is unclear, elite associations offer the government a potent means of mobilization and control.

The discourse of public servants and state-owned newspapers reinforces the constitutional changes (Njoya 2002, 258). After the defeat of the ruling party by the SDF in municipal elections, the (presidentially appointed) governor of the South West Province blamed it on the heavy concentration of "strangers" in the South West.[54] Geschiere notes that the journal *La Nouvelle Expression*'s May 1996 issue was devoted entirely to the topic of "minorités, autochtones, allogènes, et démocratie" (Geschiere 2009, 53). The most notable contribution was an interview with Roger Gabriel Nlep, professor of political science at the University of Yaounde, then interim rector of University of Douala – a political appointment. Professor Nlep put forward a theory of *le village electoral*, which

---

[54] *Herald*, No. 279, January 29–30, 1996, 3. Cited in Nyamnjoh and Rowlands (1998, 326).

suggested a new view of "integration" (Njoya 2002, 275). Whereas Ahidjo had stressed national integration by suppressing distinct identities, this new spin on integration indicated that people should be integrated in the place they live. Since this supposes that there is not another home area, a politician should not defend the interest of his village in another region. This rhetoric was aimed at criticizing non-"local" politicians in urban areas. Unlike Ahidjo, Nlep was locating integration at the local level. The implication was clear: "Migrants should go 'home' – to the village of origin – to vote, since they clearly feel that they belong there" (Geschiere 2009, 54).

While the immediate target of this decentralization was the "Anglo-Bamis," the overall effect of the new constitution has the potential to have a much wider impact. This is because of its provision regarding languages. Lauded by activists for its protection of Cameroon's linguistic heritage, this article highlights the importance of promoting the right of groups to be educated in their own language: Article 1(3): "The official languages of the Republic of Cameroon shall be English and French, both languages having the same status. The State shall guarantee the promotion of bilingualism throughout the country. *It shall endeavour to protect and promote national languages*" (emphasis added).

As the "language paragraph" in the 1998 Education Orientation Law, this constitutional article was promoted tirelessly by advocates of local languages. It reflects global concerns with protecting the linguistic rights of minority language groups. While these "liberal" constitutional and electoral rule changes dutifully recognized minorities and employed the recommended decentralization, this attention to the local may inadvertently feed into the government's strategy of dividing the opposition. By requiring indigenousness, these constitutional changes reinforce the outsider status of migrant "Anglo-Bamis." At the same time, those groups who were indigenous to the area may solidify their group identity around their connection to a shared language, and circles of belonging draw tighter.

In a similar process to colonial rule "fixing" populations in order to administer them, this openness to language and cultural heritage can serve to fix populations in order to preventp them from coalescing in opposition to the ruling party. While identification with ethnic or linguistic groups is not in itself inherently problematic, it lends itself exceedingly easily to political manipulation.

The 1996 constitution appeared finally to overcome its reluctance to touch the subject of national languages, largely because of the persuasive work of Tadadjeu and other linguists in Cameroon. It is conceivable, however, that the government saw in this not potential for unity as it advertized, but latent promise of division. This manipulation "works" because of the historical roots of identity validation that began under colonial rule. As Horowitz noted, labeling groups as advanced and backward put in motion comparative processes that had deep psychological consequences, making control of the state a matter not only of material access but of group worth (Horowitz 1985, chapter 5). As noted in the last chapter, Mamdani foresaw that mulitpartyism would exacerbate ethnic tension because of the colonial legacy of harnessing custom for control: "In the absence of alliance-building mechanisms, all decentralized systems of rule fragment the ruled and stabilize their rulers" (Mamdani 1996, 300).

ALTERNATIVE EXPLANATIONS

The previous section showed that though the policy change favoring local languages occurred in the context of Cameroon's liberalization, its intent was likely not to protect minority language groups or accede to their demands, thus contradicting a democracy-based explanation. Bargaining also fails to explain this phenomenon, as it rests on the importance of regional language elites, who pressure rulers to grant concessions to their language groups in return for electoral support. In Cameroon, this clearly does not match reality. Language activists are desperately trying to persuade the public, bureaucrats, and politicians that they should *want* concessions in these languages. Because it is not a widespread demand by the public, it is obviously not a strong bargaining chip for elites negotiating with rulers.

Probably the most tireless advocate for his own language whom I met was a man named William Banboye, a Lamnso' speaker. Nearly seventy-five years old, and suffering from hearing loss (our interview was conducted at a very high decibel level), this man had dedicated much of his life to promoting literacy in his language. The son of an adviser to the Fon and the product of a Catholic education, at a young age Banboye had met Phyllis Kaberry, one of the best-known anthropologists to study the culture of the Cameroonian Grassfields. When Banboye began the Nso History Society in his home in 1958, Kaberry attended periodic meetings, and in the course of their relationship encouraged him to take on the writing of the Lamnso language script. This occupied his private time, while his career led him to teaching, and then to a high position within the Catholic education bureaucracy; he became Catholic education secretary for Bamenda. This was fortunate for the promoters of PROPELCA, because, as described earlier, Banboye gave them one of the schools under his jurisdiction in 1981 as the first to participate in the experiment (this school was in his home village). He maintained his devotion to Lamnso' literacy, conducting adult literacy classes and serving as president for the Nso Language Organization since its inception. He has been active politically at a regional level – sending letters to division delegates for education and rural council members – to request their support of the mother tongue policy.

Another longtime supporter of his language in Cameroon is Joseph Mfonyang, a Bafut speaker, once a student leader at the University of Yaounde. In the early 1970s, he had worked on a grammar of Bafut, before attending a translation course offered by SIL in 1977. A British missionary, David Crozier, had also done some work on the language in the 1970s, and in 1983, Mfonyang went with Crozier to visit the Fon to request his support for the language effort. After that was secured, Mfonyang's first task was to establish a corps of people interested in their language. He wanted people to "own it."[55] Presently, the mayor of Bafut is the vice president of the Language Committee, so there is relatively strong support in this area. According to Mfonyang's brother, Samuel, who is chairman of the Bafut Language Association, a Bafut member of the national Parliament is "receptive" to their ideas, and even paid for publishing one of S. Mfonyang's speeches at the launching of the Bafut New Testament. Evidently, these advocates have seen the need to motivate political leaders to take pride in their language.

Importantly, political representatives of groups are not demanding that the government concede language rights for their followers. In Cameroon, a National Assembly member I interviewed told me that to suggest that he would bring indigenous language education for his constituents would likely be a liability in his campaign. He would never even consider offering them such a prospect.[56] Rather than political leaders spontaneously demanding language rights for their group, a few proud language speakers, such as Tadadjeu, Banboye, and Mfonyang, are trying to motivate the public to take pride in their language. This is far from the assumption that elite representatives of language groups wrest language concessions from governments.

In no sense are these political actors or ethnic entrepreneurs, who whip up identity sentiment for personal gain. Rather than self-interested political elites, the important actors are linguists and missionaries. The crux of the difference is the absence of competition. Unlike political elites, the educated linguistic elites in these cases are not competing to privilege their own language. They are not inciting ethnic sentiment in order that their own language should gain advantage over others, but rather working to persuade parents and politicians that local language education has practical benefits for European language acquisition.

Finally, economic retrenchment only partially explains the policy change in Cameroon. Government expenditures allocated to education were around 17–20 percent from 1970 to 1980. This figure dropped to 12 percent from 1986 to 1990[57] and to less than 10 percent in 2000, after which it rebounded to earlier levels (WDI). Therefore, the 1990s, the years of the policy change, did indeed experience much less government investment in education. In 1986, the Ministry of National Education began requiring annual tuition fees, whereas public schools had been free before. Government subsidies for denominational schools were reduced in 1989 and payments delayed as well in the following years (Boyle 1994, 617). As a result of this retrenchment, parent-teacher associations (APEs) were created and began raising money for building repairs and equipment (Boyle 1994, 618). Boyle argues that "the financial well-being of each school now depends on the management skills of its director and the effectiveness of its

---

[55] J. Mfonyang, Bafut Language Committee [SIL], interview by author, Bafut, November 9, 2002.
[56] T. N. Lucas, National Assembly member, interview by author, Yaounde, December 13, 2002.
[57] UNICEF cited in Boyle 1994, fn. 33, p. 616 (WDI does not provide figures for all years).

APE" (619). In addition, private schools have expanded since the late 1980s. All of this, according to Boyle, suggests the "partial retreat of the state from its near exclusive control over education" (620). As the state retreats, "Cameroonians of means are exercising their option to 'exit' and creating private institutions, while the relatively unorganized and poorer majority are struggling through APEs to maintain existing facilities" (622). With public financing for education reduced, the importance of private efforts increases. The significance of individuals like Tadadjeu and NGOs like SIL is unsurprising.

Certainly economic woes contributed to the government's concessions to multiparty competition in the 1990s. But its annual growth was greater than 2 percent at the time of the policy change and has hovered in the 1–2 percent range since. The Biya government acceded to the language policy change because of self-interested motives, but it will continue to allow outsiders to fund it. An educated, unified population is not a high priority. This is because Cameroon, like Senegal, only collects a small amount of its revenue from direct citizen taxes. From 1995 to 1998, the years of the constitutional change and the education policy change, the government collected an average of 18 percent of its revenue from income, profits, and capital gains taxes. Unlike in Ghana, its citizen taxation base was not expanding at the same time as its economy was growing; taxes on income, profits, and capital gains as a percentage of total taxes contracted by 4 percentage points from 1991 to 1998 (World Bank WDI).

CONCLUSION

This chapter returned to the place the book began – the fascinating case of Cameroon. It showed that the intensification of local language use occurred as a result of the convergence of material and ideational opportunities with electoral incentives. Nearly doubling the population that had access to a written language since 1980, foreign and local linguists produced materials and engaged in advocacy to persuade government bureaucrats and the public of the feasibility and benefits of using local languages in education. A permissive message from France allowed bureaucrats in the Ministry of Education to consider this a possibility. And the top political leadership faced new incentives in the 1990s as the state opened to multiparty elections.

Paul Biya has shown extraordinary stability facing the tumultuous waves of multiparty politics – consolidating power, rather than conceding to its diffusion. Perhaps Cameroon's uniqueness can be attributed to Biya's uncanny ability to master all of the instruments in an autocrat's tool kit. Schedler describes the "menus of manipulation" that authoritarian rulers have at their disposal,[58] and Biya has employed virtually all of them in Cameroon. Many have noted the government's banal fraud and brutal repression, as well as conniving co-optation that has reduced a once-vibrant opposition to lethargy. This chapter

---

[58] See also Gandhi and Lust-Okar 2009, 412–413.

has attempted to bring to light even more subtle strategies. Electoral boundary manipulation is particularly important, because it constrains the possibility for contingency – a hope raised by Schedler that even if abused by authoritarian regimes, representative institutions "inevitably ... contain the seeds of subversion." These institutions offer the opposition at least the *possibility* to challenge the status quo (Schedler 2010, 70). But Cameroon's malapportioned districts and targeted disenfranchisement result in institutional barriers and intense voter apathy that reduce this possibility to almost nil.

Added to this, constitutional changes that include decentralization and language rights provisions can be manipulated to divide the opposition even more. The second independence that produced constitutions incorporating decentralization and minority rights echoes the tendencies in the first independence that brought ethnic allegiances at the fore. Thus, the enthusiasm of the international community for policies that recognize the existence and rights of minority groups and languages may turn out to be less cause for praise.

While strategic autocrats might intend this policy to divide the opposition and keep themselves in power, there are alternate possibilities. One is that the cumulative effects of various attempts at division could spin out of control and end in violence, as in Cote d'Ivoire. Another possibility, however, is that local language literacy in the way envisioned by PROPELCA (using local languages to learn a national one) may contribute to confidence and communication among groups that can join together to restrain an autocratic state. The next chapter explores this possibility.

7

Language and Contention

Violence and Participation in Contemporary African Politics

This chapter marks a shift from prior chapters. Rather than investigating *why* governments choose to enact local language education policies, it begins to explore the consequences. These findings are admittedly more tentative than those in earlier chapters. The testing should be taken as suggestions for ways future research could examine the question, and they certainly are not the last word. They offer the valuable contribution, however, of looking objectively at the political consequences of a policy that is more often treated polemically – either scorned for its potential fragmentary effects or lauded for its linguistic or psychological benefits. These passionate starting points result in predictable conclusions and frequently sidestep actual political outcomes. This chapter begins from a neutral stance, taking a broad look across Africa and then narrowing to the now-familiar cases of Senegal, Ghana, and Cameroon.

Mamdani (1996) implicates the colonial legacy for harnessing custom toward the aim of control. Is the promotion of local language education in Africa permanently fragmenting the ruled and stabilizing the ruler? The previous chapter argued that this was likely the intention of Cameroon's autocratic president shaping the contours of liberal institutions to suit his own desire to retain power. Will they do so? This chapter answers a cautious no.

It does so first by looking at the role of written language in stimulating national consciousness and its dangerous derivative, violence, across a broad spectrum of cases in Africa. It then examines the effects of written languages in the more democratic settings of Senegal and Ghana. And, finally, it considers its role in the autocratic context of Cameroon. It finds that written languages and their reinforcement within the education system do not systematically affect ethnic consciousness, rebellion, or protest. Under democratic settings, it does seem that mother tongue literacy increases individuals' propensity to contact officials, and under authoritarian settings, there is some evidence that it empowers citizens better to challenge an oppressive state.

LANGUAGE, NATIONALISM, AND VIOLENCE

The work of Anderson discussed in Chapter 1 would lead one to predict that groups with a written language and printed media would become more nationalist, pressing for their state borders to correspond with the boundaries of their linguistic family. Crawford Young, in his seminal work *The Politics of Cultural Pluralism* (1976), noted that in general, African groups were not very "ideologized."[1] By this, he meant that they were not very likely to mobilize around their culture. Drawing from Deutsch (1953/1966) and from Fishman (1966), he argued that the intensity of this cultural mobilization related to the density of communication within a cultural segment and the degree to which it had acquired an ideological statement of its uniqueness. This depended much on education and the written word: "The ideologization of identity depends upon the emergence of cultural entrepreneurs, almost always associated with the rise of a professional middle class and intelligentsia; although the basis for historical mystique may exist in rich measure in the reservoir of folk tradition and myths of origin, *the move from the oral repository of the traditional elders to the written page multiplies the potential mobilization of identity*" (Young, 45, italics added). African groups' lack of a written word thus suppressed their mobilizing potential.

Such lack of ideologization, however, was not to be seen as a deficit, since when culture becomes ideologized, "the policy options of the state in coping with it are correspondingly reduced" (Young, 46). Observing Tamils in India, by contrast, Young noted that "mobilized identities alter less readily than do unmobilized ones – all the more as they become reinforced by a growing written cultural tradition of history and literary expression, widely diffused vernacular media or press, radio and film, and formally established socialization mechanisms through a school system operating in [a local language] and committed to its nurture" (Young, 121).

Young's observations about lack of ideologization in Africa were penned more than four decades ago, when only a quarter of African languages were transcribed. Now, however, half of African languages are transcribed, covering 89 percent of the continent's population.[2] And vernacular education is increasing, as shown throughout this book. Has Africa's propensity for ideologization changed with the passage of time and the increase in its written languages? As a first cut, we can look at ethnic versus national attachments among primary school attendees in the most recent round of Afrobarometer surveys. Only ten countries were chosen from among the twenty in the survey, since they

---

[1] Aside from Ganda in Uganda and Amhara in Ethiopia, "cultural ideologization has not occurred for nearly all African ethnic groups" (Young 1976, 522).

[2] Calculated from Lewis (2009). Includes only languages with more than 10,000 speakers. There were 370 languages transcribed by 1960; 727 by 2009.

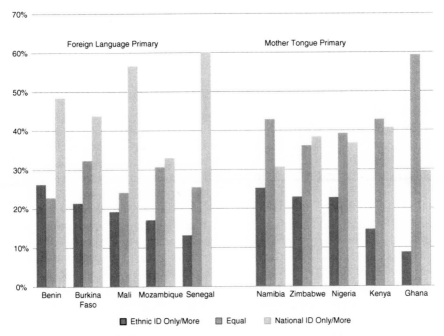

FIGURE 7.1. Ethnic/National Attachments among Primary School Attendees (*Afrobarometer 2008*)

represented the "purest" distinctions between mother tongue and foreign language education.[3]

Not surprisingly, all of the mother tongue education cases are Anglophone. The linguist Ali Mazrui posited that the recognition of chiefdoms and native rulers in Anglophone Africa helped to increase ethnic consciousness within subgroups, reducing the likelihood of an emerging national consciousness. "British approaches to colonial rule, by being culturally relative and ethnically specific, helped to perpetuate and in some cases create the kind of ethnic

---

[3] The Afrobarometer admits its bias toward Anglophone Africa and relative democracies. From among the twenty cases, in the mother tongue education category I eliminated Botswana, Lesotho, and Madagascar, since their mother tongue education corresponded with virtually the entire population, making it difficult to differentiate between ethnic and national attachments; Uganda and Malawi, since their mother tongue education was more exclusive than incorporating; Tanzania because its "mother tongue" education was more a lingua franca education; and South Africa because it differs in so many respects from other cases. In the foreign language education category, I eliminated Cape Verde, a relatively monolingual state whose ethnic/national identification would be hard to distinguish, and Liberia, whose civil war makes causal interpretation difficult. Mozambique's inclusion could be criticized for the same reason, but its much more deliberate European-language medium even throughout its civil war made it closer to the foreign language model.

consciousness which could seriously militate against nation building" (Mazrui 1983, 29). Is this demonstrated in Figure 7.1? No and yes. Immediately apparent is the fact that there is virtually no difference in ethnic attachment between states practicing mother tongue education and those practicing foreign language education. Contrary to common belief, mother tongue education does not appear to cause greater attachment to one's ethnic group. The difference is in *national* attachment. Adults who received schooling in a foreign language seem to have greater attachment to their national state than their ethnic group, whereas those who received it in a mother tongue have higher *equal* attachments. This may have as much to do with curricular content as medium of instruction, but it demonstrates that there is a third option aside from choosing either ethnic or national loyalties; citizens are capable of dividing attachments equally. Mazrui argued that as a result of this faulty nation-building, Anglophone states have been marred by greater internecine conflict than their Francophone counterparts (1983, 29). While his observation was made before more recent conflicts in Francophone Africa and was likely influenced by greater Francophone military intervention in former French territories to prevent such escalation, it is a valid question to ask whether intense mother tongue education has incubated violent or separatist tendencies over time. Does it play a role in ethnic violence?

Scholarship usually collapses ethnicity and language, labeling groups "ethnolinguistic," in recognition of the primacy of language as an ethnic marker. While casual observers usually equate ethnolinguistic fragmentation with higher violence, careful work has looked at specific configurations that lead to greater conflict. Chapter 5 discussed Horowitz's views about the size and spatial dominance of groups. Bates shows rather than ethnolinguistic diversity posing dangers, ethnic politics is most volatile when an ethnic bloc is sufficient in size to exclude others permanently from the exercise of power (1999, 26). Collier and Hoeffler (1998) similarly find the existence of one dominant group to be more dangerous for civil war outbreak, while Ellingsen (2000, 237) shows an inverted-U-shaped relationship between diversity and violence. Others have focused on institutional arrangements that provoke broader or more exclusive identification (Posner 2005). And what appears to be ethnic violence has been shown instead to depend on land scarcity, interregional inequality, and the provocation or protection provided by the state's security apparatus.[4] Laitin's overarching work *Nations, States, and Violence* discounts the role of cultural difference, economic differentials, and political discrimination in predicting violence among groups, arguing instead that the real culprit is a "weak state, unable to provide basic services to its population, unable to police its peripheries, and unable to distinguish law abiders from law breakers" (2007, 19).

Language on its own is not usually treated separately, with the notable exception of Laitin (2000), who found in a global sample that language differentiation (the distance between language families) was *not* in fact related to

[4] Boone 2007; Chaveau and Richards 2008; Berry 2009; Bakke and Wibbels 2006; Wilkinson 2004.

violence. Language grievances, because they can be accommodated within political bargaining, seem to inspire protest, rather than violence (2000, 108). This kind of testing treats language identities as rather static, however, only expecting differentiation based on size and linguistic distinction among groups.

My question is different. I want to know whether a particular language *policy* – the use of mother tongues in education – over the long term contributes to the creation of insular groups with rebellious tendencies. The mechanism would be that as groups become more "ideologized," in the words of Young, they would become more (sub)nationalist and therefore more likely to rebel against state repression and demand their autonomy. While the previous findings about ethnic attachments would cast doubt on this claim, it is important to check it empirically. To do so, I turn to the Minorities at Risk (MAR) database (2009), which catalogs all major episodes of identity-related violence from 1945 to 2006.

The relevant variables from the MAR database are summarized in Table 7.5 (at the end of the chapter), listed alongside the variables that I collected on written language history and education. Dates of transcription are noted next to each language, and the languages that have been used significantly in education prior to 2000 are also noted in bold. The shaded cells under "Rebellion" identify the groups that have engaged in substantial violence.

The first element to notice about the table is that the seventy-eight groups identified by MAR speak more than 115 languages, so there is not a perfect one-to-one correspondence between active group and language group. Among the Berbers in Algeria, for example, while most of them speak Kabyle, smaller numbers speak Tamahaq and Tachawit. But most groups are captured by a common linguistic label. And in general, with the exception of Nuba and southerners in Sudan, it does appear that the large-scale guerrilla activity and civil wars occur between groups that speak different single languages. As Somalia and Rwanda reveal, however, deadly conflicts can also erupt among members of groups speaking the same language.

A second element to notice is that virtually all the languages of these active groups are written, and about 70 percent of them were written before 1960. This is not surprising; Chapter 2 showed the scale of mission activity that spanned the continent during the colonial period. I am interested primarily in whether the fact of using a language in school increases the likelihood that the group will become violent, the mechanism being that such an institutionalized affirmation of difference results in more difficult incorporation into the state. This indeed is the rationale for many African governments' resistance to mother tongue education. But there seems no relationship. Of the fifty-one groups (not individual languages) that have experienced significant mother tongue education, fourteen of them engaged in large-scale violence (27 percent), while the large majority did not. Of the twenty-three groups that would not have experienced mother tongue education, twelve engaged in large-scale violence (52 percent). Education in one's mother tongue certainly does not appear to increase groups' chances of mobilizing violently and, in fact, seems to be correlated with less violence. In sum, many languages that are used in schools do not produce mobilized groups, and many groups whose languages are not taught in school and even some that have no written history engage in rebellious activity.

The examples that appear to conform most to the suggestion that mother tongue education coincides with potential violence are found in Ethiopia and southern Sudan. For both, the sequence of the mother tongue education and violence contradicts that contention, however. In Ethiopia, the exclusive teaching of Amharic was a grievance for the other groups, and it was only after 1994 that full-scale regional language education became available for all groups. The highest level of violence was reported among the Afar in 1989, the Oromo in 1985–1994, the Tigreans from 1989 to 1991, and the Somalis beginning in 1993. For none of the groups has the level of violence increased since the introduction of regional language education. In Sudan, mother tongue education among the southern Sudanese began much earlier, even prior to independence for many groups. But the violence escalated after the *restrictions* on this language use beginning in 1983. Other examples confirm this tendency – mobilization occurs when one language is chosen and others excluded – for instance, Chichewa in Malawi or Arabic in Algeria.

These findings resonate with the work of Horowitz and Bates, cited previously. Violent mobilization over language has to do with the potential permanent inequality that can arise if one group's language is chosen and others are not. Van de Walle demonstrates that Africa is particularly vulnerable to this entrenched inequality, given its colonial heritage of an extractive state that focused on law and order rather than development and where political power proved the quickest route to economic wealth. He argues that initial advantages for certain groups associated with the colonial regime were reinforced over time, "exacerbating the regional differences that are so striking today" (2009, 318, 320). Therefore, mother tongue education would only contribute to conflict insofar as it reinforces the privilege of a particular group that enjoyed an early head start. Where this has occurred – Sudan, Malawi, and Uganda to some extent – there have been rumblings from excluded groups. But by and large, local language education has been more inclusive than exclusive, and that is why it generally has not been linked to violence. Mother tongue education programs have normally used a language "owned" by virtually the entire population (Lesotho) or a language owned by virtually no one (Swahili in Tanzania) or have allowed for the use of most major languages in the country (Ghana, Nigeria).

This quick survey has suggested that the possession of a written language within a group does not contribute to its violent tendencies. Harpf and Gurr (2004) have highlighted risk factors for rebellion that include government repression and economic, political, or cultural grievance. Language literacy – measured by access to and education in a written language – seems unrelated to violence, except insofar as it is due to the use of one language to the detriment of others or restrictions in the use of a language that had previously been allowed.

De Swaan writes that "strife erupts when the authorities select one language among many as the medium of administration, of instruction in the schools, or even of entertainment in the media, and exclude all others from such institutional use" (2001, 60–61). Hastings's (1997) work on the role of vernacular Scripture in stimulating nationalism notes in passing that if many languages are promoted at once, their nationalizing effect may be diluted. Whereas the promotion of one language to the exclusion of others may provoke a violent backlash, the promotion of multiple languages in tandem seems to prevent such reaction. I return to this in the chapter's Conclusion.

LANGUAGE LITERACY AND POLITICAL MOBILIZATION

With mother tongue education apparently not associated with greater ethnic attachments or higher likelihood of violence, I turn to other political effects. Language communities can be viewed as a type of association that facilitates communication and sanctioning among its members. From Tocqueville to Putnam, scholars have looked to the benefits of associations – civil society – in undergirding democracy. The problem with ethnolinguistic groups, however, is that they can be insular, and theorists have criticized civil society "optimists" for not distinguishing effectively between organizations that involve bridging and those that involve bonding. Active membership in some kinds of organizations may "incubate trust through reiterated social interactions.... This may be a generalized trust if the organizations are relatively 'encompassing' and heterogeneous, and if they are pursuing collective public goals that go beyond the narrow interests of small groups of people" (Green and Preston 2001, 259). Appropriate bridging associations are parties, trade unions, major churches, and religions. "On the other hand, membership in exclusivist organizations with self-interested goals may encourage trust among their members but positively erode trust in society at large." The crux for social cohesion is "whether associations foster in their members trust in the generality of people rather than simply in other members" (Green and Preston 2001, 259). Varshney writes that "vigorous associational life, *if interethnic*, acts as a serious constraint on politicians, even when ethnic polarization is in their political interest. The more the associational networks cut across ethnic boundaries, the harder it is for politicians to polarize communities" (2001, 363, emphasis added).

Berman and Kaufman are more generally critical of the benefits of associations for democracy, since instead of supporting democracy, the presence of a dense network of associations may "corrode the foundations of the current political order" (Berman 1997, 428).[5] Therefore, while associations of literate communities speaking the same mother tongue may be more difficult for autocratic rulers to control, it does not follow that these same dense language networks facilitate a deepening of democracy. There are two separate concerns

[5] See also Berman 2003; Kaufman 2002.

with ethnic associations, then: First, ethnic associations, because of their sharp delineations, may have a difficult time connecting people across these boundaries. Second, dense interaction can be either disruptive or supportive of order. This is precisely what scholars of contentious politics reveal when they identify similar mechanisms at work in nationalism, revolution, and democratization. While democratization is generally viewed positively, nationalism and revolution can be dangerous. All undermine existing order. I return to the idea of bridging across groups in the following section, but here I want to focus specifically on the effects of mother tongue education in democratic settings. Is it undermining or facilitating for democracy?

I look in the following section at the effects of institutionalization of language groupings through mother tongue education in democratic settings. First, has it resulted in more exclusive identification? Second, has it had any effect on democratic participation – in the form of protest, contacting representatives, or voting? Proponents of mother tongue education would expect positive effects through the mechanism of language associations that bind language communities together, allowing them to share information, act in unison, and develop confidence to contact national representatives. On the other hand, detractors would expect such parochial associations to promote withdrawal from national politics and for members to communicate less with national representatives, relying on their immediate group instead.

I return to the cases of Senegal and Ghana, which conveniently are included in Afrobarometer surveys, to see whether mother tongue education has impacted identification and political participation. Because education levels are widely believed to have a strong impact on reducing particularistic attachments and increasing participation,[6] I hold this contributing variable constant and look only at respondents who had some primary education but not beyond. This is particularly useful for my study, since it is among this population that I would expect to see the greatest divergence as a result of mother tongue education. Most languages listed in Ghana's survey were used in primary schools before 2001; none of the languages in Senegal was used until after 2001. Adults questioned in 2008 would be products of these earlier systems. Since English becomes the medium in most secondary schools and higher in Ghana, students exposed to this education would have an experience closer to that in Senegal, potentially diluting the effect of mother tongue education.

The following section will look at two main questions, drawing from the Afrobarometer survey. First, does the history of a written language, or its use as a medium of education, influence ethnic versus national identification? Second, does the use of a language as medium of instruction in school influence the likelihood of political participation by members of the group? It finds, somewhat surprisingly, that written language and mother tongue education have little

---

[6] This correlation is maintained from "old" modernization theorists (Lerner 1958; Lipset 1960; Almond and Verba 1965) to new (Mattes and Bratton 2007).

effect on nationalist attitudes. It is not individuals speaking languages with a long written history, but individuals from small groups with *recently* transcribed languages who show greater ethnic attachment. The use of a language in school does not influence groups' propensity to protest, but it does seem to have positive effects on other participatory behaviors and attitudes.

WRITTEN LANGUAGE AND ATTACHMENT (SENEGAL AND GHANA)

To gauge whether a history of written language influences ethnic or national identification, I looked at the 2008 round of the Afrobarometer survey in Ghana and in Senegal. Question 82 asked about people's attachment to their ethnic group or the nation as a whole, probing to see whether they identified only with their ethnic group, more with the ethnic group than the nation, equally between their ethnic group and the nation, more with the nation than the ethnic group, or only with the nation. As noted previously, I look only within respondents who attended primary school and not beyond. Because at the most general level, it is expected that groups with a long literate tradition can be more easily mobilized, and group size certainly would affect their attachment, I divide respondents into four categories – the largest group with a long written tradition; other large groups with long written traditions; small groups with long written traditions; and small groups with short written traditions. The expectation is that groups with a longer history of a written language would feel more attachment to their ethnolinguistic group than those with no written language. The size of the group is a contradictory factor, since the largest group likely feels some ownership of the state, while large groups generally may feel more politically powerful, but smaller groups may have more ability to cultivate solidarity. In any case, the written history expectation is not borne out with the survey responses in either country. Figures 7.2a and b illustrate these findings.

In neither case is it true that languages with a long written history create stronger ethnic attachments among members. Instead, it is small groups with recently transcribed languages that exhibit greater ethnic attachments, while a long history of a written language in any group size instills higher *national* attachment. The largest groups in both cases – Akan and Wolof – do exhibit higher national attachments than average. Overall, therefore, instead of the expected relationship of a long written tradition to create stronger ethnic attachments, it seems a more recent written tradition within smaller groups actually produces this outcome.

If a long history of a written language does not increase one's ethnic attachment, does exposure to the use of languages as media of instruction do so? It seems logical that even if languages are written, if citizens are not exposed to them systematically, their effects would be muted. To judge this, I compare Ghana's respondents, who were likely exposed to their language in school, with Senegal's, who were likely not. Again I limit the sample to those respondents who only attended primary school. Figure 7.3 shows the distinction.

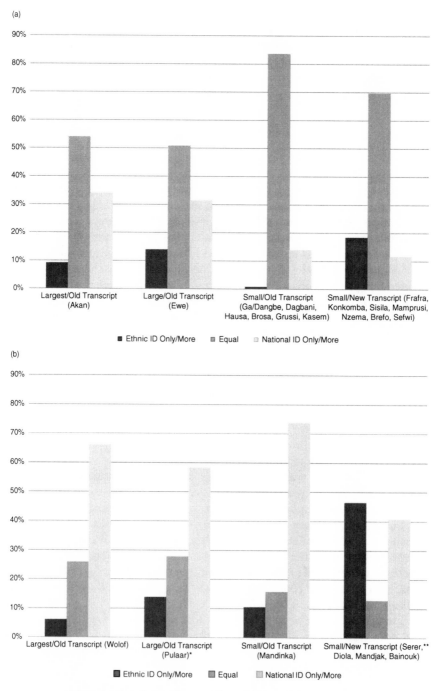

FIGURE 7.2. Ethnic/National Attachment (Group Size and Written History): (a) Ghana and (b) Senegal (*Afrobarometer 2008*)

*Pulaar could be classified as a "large new." The Afrobarometer survey collapses Pular and Toucouleur, the former a small group (also called Futa Jalon) whose language was

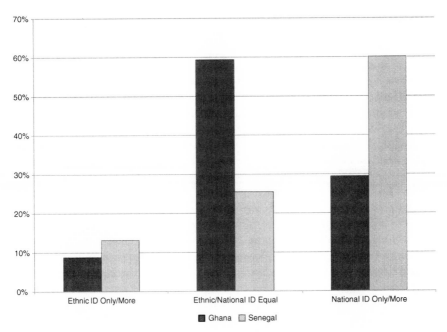

FIGURE 7.3. Ethnic/National Identification among Primary School Attendees, Ghana and Senegal (*Afrobarometer 2008*)

Ghana's mother tongue education in primary school does not seem to have produced citizens more attached to their ethnic identities than their national ones, though it did produce citizens with greater equal attachments. Senegal's foreign language education resulted in citizens that are more nationally focused, mirroring the dichotomy between Anglophone and other states demonstrated in Figure 7.1.

The bottom line is that Senegalese not exposed to their languages in school exhibit somewhat *more* ethnic attachment than do Ghanaians, contrary to what one would expect given the long history of local language education in the latter. But beyond identification, we are curious about the effect of mother tongue education on political participation.

CAPTION FOR FIGURE 7.2. (cont.)
written in 1929, and the latter a large group whose language (also called Peuhl/Pulaar) acquired a Latin script only in 1982. Nonetheless, because of the long history of Ajami writing associated with Pulaar, I kept it as an "old" language.
**Serer could be classified as "large new," since it falls just below my threshold of 10 percent. In any case, its recent (1979) writing supports my claim that more recent writing has more potent mobilizing potential.

WRITTEN LANGUAGE AND MOBILIZATION IN A DEMOCRATIC SETTING (SENEGAL AND GHANA)

Citizens mobilize for a variety of reasons, some demographic (age, gender, education level), some circumstantial (economic grievance, government repression). Mattes and Bratton thoroughly mine the Afrobarometer data to determine where we might expect to find effective mobilization for transitions to democracy. They find foremost that a "sustainable democracy requires citizens to *demand* democracy" (2007, 192). Demand, they find, is a product mostly of history and cognition – a country's history of electoral competition and citizens' cognition of the procedural benefits of democracy through education and media.

Also looking cross-nationally at Afrobarometer results, MacLean finds, somewhat in contradiction to the preceding claim, that it is not urban, wealthier, educated citizens who are more politically active, but the rural poor. In this careful study, she finds that "it is the Africans who live in rural areas and who are more impoverished, who more frequently use public services and also engage and participate in politics most often" (2011, 1230). She argues that the key mechanism is experience with public services. These encounters with a declining quality of publicly provided health and education services, which were perceived as universal entitlements, have mobilized greater citizen participation and engagement. "The gap between their popular expectations and their everyday experience mobilized them to participate more frequently in politics at all levels to voice their complaints. In contrast, those who had withdrawn and were providing for themselves outside of the state-provided social welfare system had become less involved with the state on an everyday basis and less active in demanding its accountability" (2011, 1256–1257). Given Ghana's notable growth after 1995 and the turning of many urban citizens to private provision of public goods, this explanation seems plausible.

Common to both studies is concern about public disengagement. Mattes and Bratton found that since more than half the citizens interviewed were psychologically disengaged from politics, and a similar proportion possessed low levels of political information, the solution was to "enlarge the pool of cognitively sophisticated citizens" through greater access to formal education and independent news media (2007, 204). MacLean believed the disengagement may be a response to disappointed expectations, rather than lack of awareness. While the present study cannot answer that question, it can look at whether mother tongue education plays a role in political engagement.

To try to control for the most important factors identified, I concentrate only on primary school attendees in rural areas. Outside of voting,[7] political participation is demonstrated by joining others to raise an issue or to protest publicly. More related to personal efficacy is contacting elected representatives. There are

---

[7] Voting percentages overall were almost equal in the 2008 round, at 81% for Ghana and 79% for Senegal.

TABLE 7.1. *Group Participation – Senegal and Ghana (Afrobarometer 2008)*

	Join Others to Raise an Issue*		
	Never Would (Percentage)	Would If Had the Chance (Percentage)	Have Once or More (Percentage)
Ghana	10	36	53
Senegal	2	28	68
	Attend a Demonstration*		
	Never Would (Percentage)	Would If Had the Chance (Percentage)	Have Once Or More (Percentage)
Ghana	43	51	6
Senegal	65	25	10

* Among rural respondents who had attended primary school but not more.

TABLE 7.2. *Individual Contacting – Senegal and Ghana (Afrobarometer 2008)*

	Contact Local Government Representative*	
	Never Have (Percentage)	Have Once or More (Percentage)
Ghana	60	38
Senegal	72	25

* Among rural respondents who had attended primary school but not more.

two survey questions in 2008 that touch on the first way of participating (23b and 23c) and one probing the second dimension (25a).

First, comparing Ghana and Senegal, Table 7.1 reveals that Senegalese show more willingness to join others to raise issues. Slightly more of them have actually demonstrated publicly, though more Ghanaians say they would if they had the chance.

Mother tongue education in Ghana apparently did not increase either inclination toward open political participation. I would attribute both of these higher tendencies in Senegal, however, to its colonization by strike-prone France and its history of a relatively open political system. As will be discussed in the case of Cameroon, it may not be plausible to consider open political protest in a context of repression. But clearly mother tongue education seems not to have a strong effect. Perhaps more telling for citizens' sense of personal ability to effect change through official political channels is their tendency to contact local government representatives (see Table 7.2).

Here, we see that rural citizens who had attended primary school in Ghana are somewhat more likely to have contacted their local government councillor in the last year. Since the majority of those citizens surveyed had received mother

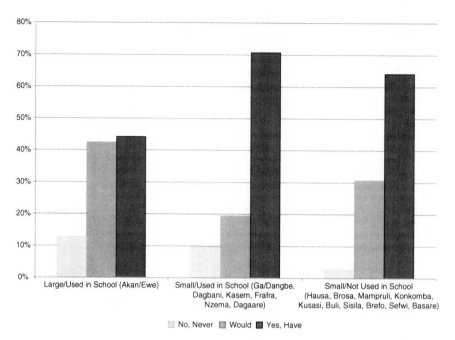

FIGURE 7.4. Join Others to Raise an Issue (Group Size and Language Use in School), Ghana (*Afrobarometer 2008*)
Among rural respondents who had attended primary school but not more.

tongue education in Ghana, overall, this lends some support to the expectation that citizens exposed to mother tongue education are participating more through contacting their representatives.

Not all of them did experience mother tongue education, however. Recall in the previous chapter that Ghana only authorized that eleven of its languages be used in schools. Because the 2008 survey included relatively detailed information about respondents' languages, it is possible to look more deeply to see whether there is a difference in participation rates between those who have actually been exposed to mother tongue education and those who have not. I hypothesize that smaller groups in general will be more likely to join together and contact representatives – because of either greater grievances or greater ease of acting collectively – so I separate out the larger groupings of Akan and Ewe speakers. We can then compare small groups who likely had mother tongue education and small groups who did not.

When it comes to joining others to raise issues, Figure 7.4 shows that small groups in general are more likely to do so, and those exposed to mother tongue education slightly more than those not. This gives some support to the contention that mother tongue education facilitates political participation. When we look at contacting government officials, however (Figure 7.5), the distinction remains between large and small groups, but the small groups *without* mother tongue education seem more likely to do so.

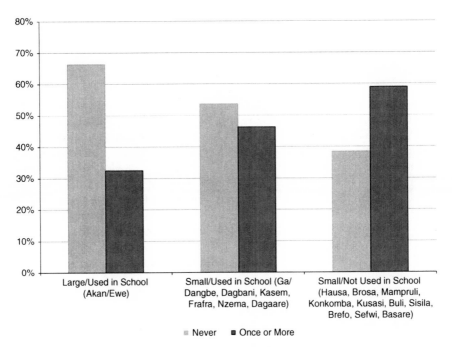

FIGURE 7.5. Contact Government Councillor (Group Size and Language Use in School), Ghana (*Afrobarometer 2008*)
Among rural respondents who had attended primary school but not more.

As I suggested in the last chapter, mother tongue education has been rather patchily applied in Ghana. The government has maintained the eleven official school languages within its domain, however, keeping them out of the hands of foreign language NGOs. These NGOs have worked instead among smaller groups. All of the "Small/Not Used in School" languages have written form, and most have active NGOs working and organizing among them. Mampruli, for example, in Ghana's Northern Region, though not an official government language, is reported by *Ethnologue* to have forty-eight literacy workers and to be used in twenty primary, ten junior secondary schools, and three secondary schools. This means that those labeled "Small/Not Used in School" are in fact the very languages that are being activated by the private efforts of NGOs.

Stepping back to consider Senegal and Ghana's comparative experience once again contributes to our understanding. Senegal has a much higher number of unschooled/informally schooled[8] citizens in its sample than Ghana. If we look only at these citizens in Senegal, we see that their tendency to protest is even higher than that of their primary schooled co-citizens, while rates of contacting

---

[8] Nonformal education is any education outside a formal primary school curriculum; it may include Koranic schooling or adult literacy classes. See Kuenzi (2011, 12–13) for a discussion of its benefits.

representatives are almost identical. These high levels of political participation seem unusual among unschooled populations. Michelle Kuenzi provides one answer in her careful study of Senegal's experience with nonformal education. She estimates that by 2001, about a quarter of Senegal's adults had been exposed to nonformal education programs (Kuenzi 2011, 65); she found that those adults who had been exposed to these nonformal education programs exhibited much more community participation in the form of contacting officials and joining and leading community groups, along with a whole range of democratic actions and attitudes (Kuenzi 2011, table 5.1, 85–87). And, importantly, nonformal education increased community participation even more strongly than did formal education (106). She attributes this in no small part to the fact that the nonformal education was conducted in local languages (136). Therefore, though Senegal had a large percentage of the population outside the formal education system, a substantial proportion of these had been touched by local language literacy nonetheless.

In the same way, in Ghana, it is members of groups whose languages have more recently been transcribed – not the eleven "approved" Ghanaian languages with longer written histories – who demonstrate a greater tendency to contact local representatives, indicating that perhaps the informal work of adult literacy in these smaller languages has just as many if not more participatory repercussions than local language use in schools. The inefficacy of the local language education, particularly in rural areas, has indeed been one of the main criticisms of Ghana's mother tongue program. Most of these small languages have active language committees and adult literacy programs supported by NGOs. It seems that it is this active promotion of *literacy*, not necessarily formal education, in mother tongues that may be the decisive factor for political participation.

We end this section, then, with some contrary findings. First, neither the length of time a language has been written nor its use in school influences groups' violent mobilization. These also have no impact on individuals' propensity for ethnic versus national identification. In fact, members of groups whose languages have been written more recently seem to have stronger attachments to that language. Comparing the relatively democratic contemporary settings of Ghana and Senegal, Ghana's long history of education in mother tongues did not seem to increase its citizens' likelihood of participation in the form of protest, but it did elevate citizens' likelihood of contacting representatives. Smaller groups with recently transcribed languages in Ghana, however, showed an even higher propensity to contact representatives.

The comparison of Senegal and Ghana, both relatively democratic settings, suggests that mother tongue literacy is not associated with more negative tendencies (ethnic particularism or destabilizing protest) and that it may have some positive participatory benefits, in terms of contacting representatives. Both point to the existence of even finer-grained distinction within "mother tongue education" settings. Literacy in one's mother tongue need not result from formal schooling, and it may be that the attention and advocacy provided by language NGOs do more to further participatory tendencies in some cases. To explore the preferences of people differentially exposed to mother tongue literacy, we turn again to Cameroon.

WRITTEN LANGUAGE AND MOBILIZATION IN AN AUTHORITARIAN SETTING (CAMEROON)

An ongoing debate in recent Africanist literature is whether informal traditional structures have contributed to democratization. Early analysts argued that as states repressed formal participatory structures, people shifted efforts into informal organizations (women's associations, ethnic associations, credit clubs) – which "have directly improved people's welfare and by sapping the government's legitimacy may even have laid the groundwork for political liberalization."[9] Bratton and van de Walle disagree, saying it is only the more formal institutions – trade unions, human rights organizations, and especially parties – that can "force recalcitrant governments into amending constitutions and calling elections, and appear to populations as plausible alternatives to the government in power" (1994, 489).

This takes us back to the thorny issue of segmented civil society discussed at the outset. Whereas it is possible to imagine associations among language groups deepening democracy by giving people opportunities, practice, and confidence for participation, it is equally plausible that these strong associations could divide groups. In an autocratic setting, it seems especially necessary to develop alternative sites of power. "If one conceives of civil society as resistance, neutralization of the state and re-appropriation of power ... then the resurgence of tradition may also be construed as a manifestation of civil society" (Englebert 2005, 53). In an authoritarian setting, language-based associations may provide venues for the practice of participation and communication that informs a more critical society. A literate community may therefore prove more resistant to the penetration of a new ideology or to top-down control. Darden and Grzymala-Busse studied the durability of postcommunist transitions in Eastern Europe and showed that populations with high proportions schooled in a vernacular language were more likely to resist communist ideology (2006). Their nationalist schooling had produced shared memories and standards that could oppose state indoctrination.

Charles Tilly's synthesis on democracy provides some insight. Democracy is a historically rare outcome – the product of intense struggle and established only when citizens are able to restrain rulers. This restraint is not automatic and can only occur when citizens have something of interest to rulers – manpower, resources, or votes. Individuals do not interact directly with a state, but are

---

[9] Cited in Bratton and van de Walle (1994, 489), referring to, among others, Chazan 1982 and Bayart, Mbembe and Toulabor 1991.

usually enclaved in smaller groupings, reached by the ruler through intermediaries. These smaller groupings Tilly has labeled "trust networks." Tilly acknowledges that trust networks can segment political life and serve parochial interests, rather than contributing to the general good. He argues, however, that even these segmented groups may be necessary first steps toward the eventual purpose of cross-category coalitions. Evidence is in South Africa, where state appointment of chiefs, which created categorical inequality, ended up stimulating resistance through cross-category coalitions (2007, 131). Tilly's definition of democracy is relatively equal, broad *consultation* of the state with citizens (2007, 13–15). Before citizens can be consulted, they must be able to communicate their preferences within their group and to the ruler. Communication and therefore the language of instruction become a central concern.

A written language and vernacular education produce group solidarity and literacy. But because of the emphasis in many African countries on using the mother tongue to teach a European language, these more literate and active communities may actually be able to join across categories to engage, restrain, and resist the state – the ideal democracy-enhancing features of civil society under an authoritarian regime. Successful social movements necessarily involve shifts in scale, coordination at higher levels of the polity (Tilly and Tarrow 2007, 94). Contentious episodes require contact between groups at higher levels in order to overcome their segmentation. Tilly argues that "formal organizations are significant in establishing social contacts across conventional social boundaries, inducing large-scale interdependencies in mobilizations that might otherwise remain isolated" (2007, 294). Democracy requires reducing particularistic ties between groups and their leaders, connecting whole categories to the state.

So why might local language literacy help in this? Language associations are not usually led by traditional leaders or those with symbolic authority. They are more often initiated by "regular" members of a group, educated or entrepreneurial citizens who have forged ties with foreign NGOs or other intellectuals. They provide an alternative point of contact for collective organization – an antidote to top-down control.

Cameroon is an ideal place to test the mobilizing effects of language use in education. In this section, reflecting Tilly's focus on restraint and consultation as necessary for inducing democracy, I look initially at whether groups with written languages are more likely to oppose an authoritarian state. I find in Cameroon some evidence that simple possession of a written language strengthens oppositional tendencies. A more "activated" language increases this tendency as well. On a microlevel, language literacy seems to produce citizens more critical of the regime, but not less trusting of others – a combination that bodes well for future collective contentious episodes.

To begin to probe these ideas, I turn to a site of great linguistic diversity and center of opposition – Cameroon's North West Province. I focus here because of the overwhelming effect of patrimonial politics in the society at large. I do not expect written language to increase oppositional tendencies of groups who are traditionally supportive of the regime. I only expect it to have some impact in areas that are already oppositional. Importantly, the North West region encompasses the Grassfields area, where chiefs hold great importance. Unlike in other areas within Cameroon (South West and East, for example), these chiefs were not colonial creations, and they retain ritual and economic importance.[10] Beginning in the colonial period, chiefs were officially recognized and received payment from the state. After independence, in 1966, they were incorporated into the structures of Cameroon's single party (Awasom 2005, 310). While generally chiefs of the North West Province are sensitive to the marginalization of Anglophones, Awasom notes that since the advent of multiparty elections in 1992, most of these chiefs have allied with the ruling party (Awasom 2005, 318). Geschiere observes that their involvement in party politics threatens to undermine their prestige: "Marginalized or co-opted into the new elite of the State, in both cases the chiefs can hardly present themselves as an alternative source of power" (Geschiere 1993, 169).

Awasom identifies a recent phenomenon, however, which is citizens' defiance of traditional rulers. In some cases, members of groups reacted negatively to their chiefs' alliance with the CPDM, a response that eventually served to pressure chiefs into taking a more neutral political stance. This defiance seems worth investigating from the vantage point of language development. In Boone's careful comparative work, she notes that Cote d'Ivoire differed from Senegal and Ghana because the "big men" were dependent on power and status "bequeathed from above and thus remained within the orbit of the presidents' control." This led to a stagnation of local-level political life, where local leaders did not contest the hegemony of the state (1995, 453–454). Unlike in Cote d'Ivoire, elites in the North West Province of Cameroon are strong. They lack economic autonomy, however, relying on the state's recognition and continued payment – and, not surprisingly, the regime has drawn on them as useful allies.

Cameroon's four legislative elections after 1992 provide an opportunity to examine areas of opposition. Because the major opposition party boycotted legislative elections in 1992, turnout rates are a better predictor of North West Province opposition than voting results in 1992. Participation in the North West overall was only 24 percent, compared to the average rate across Cameroon of 64 percent. In subsequent elections, however, North West Province participation was greater than or equal to the national average. Votes for the CPDM, while increasing in Cameroon as a whole because of district boundary changes and targeted disenfranchisement, as discussed in the last chapter, increased more slowly in the North West Province. Therefore, one can still detect here whether the possession of a written language has any impact on groups' voting patterns.

---

[10] Awasom 2005, 305–306; Geschiere 1993: These chiefs retained their own economic and ritual basis apart from the state because of their role in allocating land, the resilience of secret associations, and their role in credit associations (167).

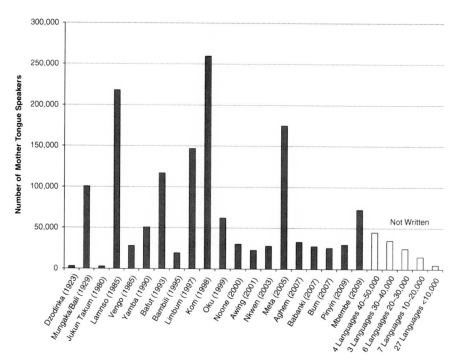

FIGURE 7.6. Written Languages of the North West Province, Cameroon. *Source:* Dates derived from various editions of *Ethnologue* – Grimes (1996, 2000) and Lewis (2009).

Of course, endogeneity may be a problem: Large, contentious language groups might demand transcription first, and so the causal story may be reversed. As will be shown, however, only a very few of the sixty-eight identified languages of the North West Province were written until recently. And it is actually not the case that the largest languages were transcribed first.

As in earlier chapters, I use Bible transcription as a proxy for date of written language.[11] The causal mechanism is that as people join language associations to become literate, they will also acquire political knowledge and practice outside the framework of traditional authority. The first sizable language to be written in this region was Mungaka, of the Bali ethnic group, used for schooling in both the German and British colonial periods and having Bible portions transcribed by 1929. The large language groupings of Lamnso and Kom have had writing systems since the 1970s, both standardized in 1979, but Bible portions were not completed in Lamnso until 1985 and in Kom until 1998. Importantly, between 1980 and 2004, each of these languages developed a body of literature – Lamnso

---

[11] Some languages were written earlier than the date of Bible portions, but the Bible usually marks the start of a body of literature.

with seventy titles and Kom with fifty-five titles (Trudell 2004, 106, 109–110). Perhaps equally important, each of these was selected as an early site of PROPELCA experimental schools (1981 for Lamnso and 1985 for Kom). This was primarily because of the importance of Catholic mission schools in both areas and the favor with which the centralized diocese looked upon the project.

In the three legislative elections following 1992, we can compare the rate of opposition voting by electoral district. I divided the sixty-eight language groups among these electoral districts for each election, reallocating as necessary with boundary changes. In each division, it was possible to gauge each language group's share of the population. Any group that had a written language at the time of the election was added to the pool of written language groups for that district. I could thereby determine what percentage of the district had a written language and compare it to the percentage of the vote that was received by the ruling party.

Despite the government's restriction of voting access and manipulation of boundaries, this allows me to see whether groups with written languages are less likely to be sidelined or co-opted by the regime. Recall from the previous chapter that the CPDM increased its seat share in the legislature consistently in the three elections after the major challenge to its dominance in 1992. The opposition appears to be decimated. Even when CPDM wins a district seat, however, opposition votes can be counted. I used the results from the three elections to ascertain where these votes were clustering, hypothesizing that a written language and the solidarity it creates might provide the means for this sustained resistance. This is because of the effects of a language committee, training, adult literacy, reading materials, meetings, and sensitization – all potentially serving to increase the ability of groups to discuss political issues among themselves and for their leaders to cooperate in common training processes. Rather than simply following the directives of their chiefs, groups who are literate in their own language may find it easier to oppose an authoritarian state. Figures 7.7a–c test this hypothesis. The dark bars show the percentage of each district's population possessing a written language, and the light bars show the percentage of that district's population that voted for the ruling party in that year's election.

I do find some evidence that groups with a written language resist state control longer. One can see that those districts with a larger percentage of their populations possessing a written language have a lower percentage of votes for the ruling party. This demonstrates citizens' potential to express opposition to their chiefs, who have in large part been co-opted by the regime. Citizens in these areas – Boyo, Bui, Mezam – seem to be resisting ruling party co-optation the longest, even in the face of electoral boundary manipulation. Discerning patterns becomes more difficult in the most recent election, as the boundary manipulation and disenfranchisement may be contributing too much noise. But groups with no written languages – in Ngo-Ketunjia-Sud and Momo Ouest, for example – seem consistently more inclined to follow their chiefs' injunctions to vote for the ruling party.

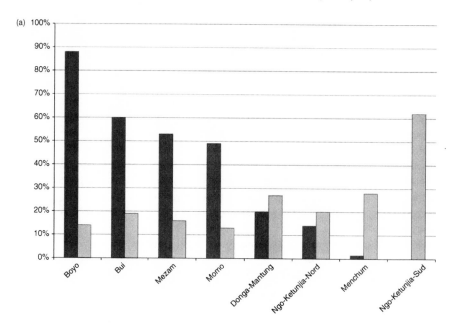

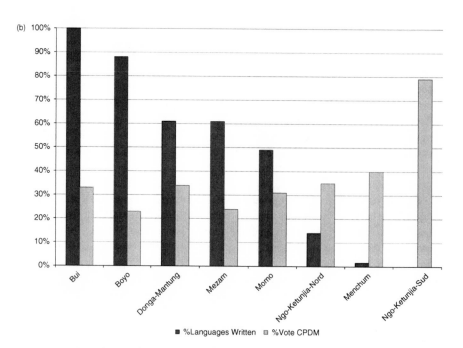

■ %Languages Written   ▨ %Vote CPDM

FIGURE 7.7. Legislative Elections North West Province, Cameroon: (a) 1997, (b) 2002, and (c) 2007.

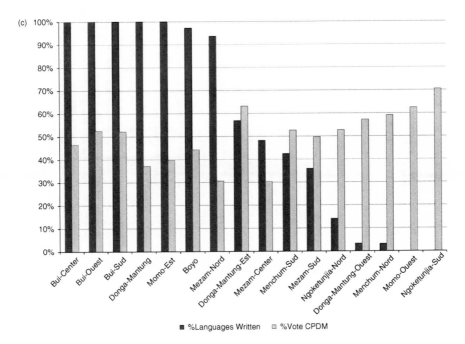

FIGURE 7.7. (cont.)

More generally across Cameroon, in the 2007 legislative elections, the constituencies that counted less than 50 percent vote for the ruling party were of two
types: first, urban centers – Douala, Maroua, Kumba, Bafoussam, and
Bamenda – with large proportions of internal migrants, groups that, as we saw
in the last chapter, have been marginalized; second, however, were districts that,
when examined more closely, encompass groups with long histories of a written
language. These were districts dominated, for example, by speakers of Fulfulde
(transcribed in 1919), Bamun (1925), Mungaka (1929), Gbaya (1933), Mafa
(1958), Mofu (1975), Gidar (1986), Psikye (1988), and Tupuri (1988).

As I came to discover, it is not simply a distinction in length of written history
but a difference as to *activation*. Some languages are written but remain dormant; others possess a body of literature, an enthusiastic language committee,
and often external support for their use in school and adult literacy. For the sixty-
eight languages, I created a numeric scale of 0–4, as a cumulative indication of the
group's possession of writing, vernacular publications, schooling, and adult
literacy programs. I then calculated for each of the thirty-four municipal districts
in the North West Province the percentage of the population that had an
activated language (Fig. 7.8). Among those districts that had 60 percent or
more of their languages that were "activated," the average vote percentage for
the CPDM was 39 percent. Among those with less than 60 percent of their

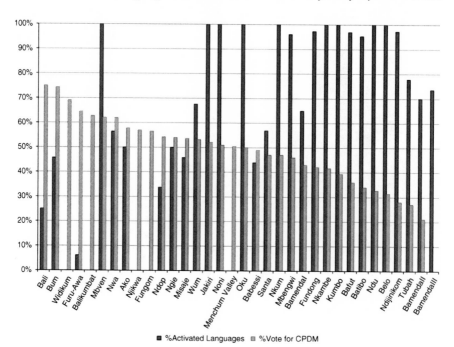

■ %Activated Languages   ▨ %Vote for CPDM

FIGURE 7.8. 2007 Municipal Council Elections in North West Province, Cameroon.

languages activated, the average vote for the CPDM was 59 percent. Clearly, there are exceptions,[12] which have been created by the co-optation efforts of the government, but overall, the districts with more language activism showed much less support for the government than those districts with inactive languages.

I believe this relates to the unique possibilities created with language associations. "Brokerage" as envisioned by McAdam, Tarrow, and Tilly (2001), has to do with reducing the relative prominence of particular ties between subjects and rulers, while connecting whole categories of the state's subject populations to agents of the state, and it is a necessary ingredient for democratization. Recall the sensitization and regular communication facilitated by an active language committee described in Chapter 4. These allow groups to speak among themselves and to other groups. The seventy-four language committees that belong to a central body – the National Association for Cameroonian Language Committees (NACALCO) – regularly communicate and receive common training through this body. The collaboration of literate community members may be a silver lining to Cameroon's dark cloud of autocratic manipulation.

---

[12] For example, a "son of Oku" was recently given a central government post, which resulted in a highly visible new road from Bamenda to Oku center, certainly influencing voting outcomes.

A Kom language development worker, when I asked him how language associations might affect people's attitudes toward other groups, answered without hesitation that they allowed for exposure and connections.[13] People running the training programs are often nonnative speakers – many foreigners, but some native Cameroonians who are teaching in the area and want to learn the Kom language. "In training sessions, we are exposed to others and hear about other groups learning their own language." This generates a sense of solidarity. In the case of Cameroon's policy change, a network of language groups acted together – influencing parents, inspectors, teachers – lobbying government representatives and finally contributing to the passage of the law. This is an example of citizens interacting with government directly. It is broadening, equalizing consultation, as rural groups gain voice. Knowledge of and interaction with others allow more critical analysis of government, as these groups are acting independently of government-controlled mobilization.

The process of identity formation is an integrative one: Groups are part of a visible national puzzle; they see themselves on a map, in relation to others, within the boundaries of Cameroon. The particular method of additive mother tongue education is central. The great flexibility of language and the ability to acquire facility in multiple languages offer wide possibilities. As Maurice Tadadjeu has advocated with unflagging zeal, Cameroonians are capable of retaining their mother tongue, mastering a regional language of wider communication, and using a European language pragmatically for national communication (Tadadjeu 1997). The PROPELCA program, as "sold" by its proponents, promises that it is not the either-or proposition that detractors fear: *either* retaining one's mother tongue *or* learning a language of wider communication. It provides for both. This additive model is a rationale heard over and over in states recently introducing mother tongue education, and it may create a basis for communication across groups, ultimately critical for democratic reform.

In addition to opposition, on an individual level, we want to know whether mother tongue education might increase the ability of citizens to restrain their rulers, an "autocracy-defying" feature, as well as a democratic imperative. Might it generate positive benefits of civil society: trust, absence of violence, peaceful protest, or "voice"? In order to gauge internal group solidarity, associational habits, and attitudes toward government and the political process, I needed to look qualitatively at comparable groups. I chose groups that were similar in most ways that might affect their political participation (e.g., size, colonial history, geographic location) except in their possession of a written language and its use in schools. I visited three pairs of groups in summer 2011. Two pairs of groups were in the Anglophone North West Province, stronghold of the country's major opposition party. The third pair was in the Center Province, near the capital of Yaounde, and presumably much more favorable toward the government.

[13] K. Godfrey, Kom language specialist, interview by author, SIL Bamenda, July 11, 2011.

TABLE 7.3. *Field Research Group Comparison*

Name of Group (British/ French Colonial Rule)	Written History of Language	Language Used in School or Adult Literacy	Vernacular Publications
Babungo (B)	Long	Yes	Yes
Nomaande (F)	Long	Yes	Yes
Mmaala (F)	Short	Yes	Yes
Bum (B)	Short	Yes	Yes (1)
Ncane (B)	None	No	No
Bamunka (B)	None	No	No

First, in the North West Province, Ngoketunjia division, the Bamunka and the Babungo live side by side. They are relatively sizable groups, 31,000 and 27,000, respectively, but the Bamunka have no written language, while the language of the Babungo (Vengo) has been written since 1985. Second, farther north in the North West Province, on either side of the Boyo and Donga-Mantung divisional boundary, there are two more groups, speaking Ncane and Bum, with about 18,000 and 25,000 members, respectively. Ncane has no formal written language, while Bum was put into writing in 2007. Finally, two groups in the Center Province, Mbam et Inoubou Division, the Mmaala and the Nomaande, live only a few miles apart, with about 10,500 and 12,000 speakers, respectively. The former has just developed a written language, while the latter has had one since 1994. Forty individuals were interviewed in each group, for a total of 240 responses.[14] Respondents had a similar range of educational backgrounds. Table 7.3 compares them on their independent variables of interest.

I purposely avoided large, established groups, targeting instead smaller groups in both Anglophone and Francophone regions and groups with varying longevity of language transcription, use in schools, adult literacy programs, and vernacular publications. These paired comparisons allowed me to assess whether groups that are exposed to their own written language are more or less likely, for example, to oppose their traditional rulers, to interact with members of groups other than their own, to engage with local administrative officers, or to participate in demonstrations against the government – all important aspects of claims making. On one hand, groups with access to their local written language might be more able to communicate with each other, and they might be more confident in evaluating and criticizing government performance. On the other hand, they might become more tightly bound, disengaged from public affairs, more interested in preserving their own heritage. Teasing out the tendencies among groups required a focused comparison.

---

[14] Appendix B details the survey, "Trust and Protest."

FINDINGS

Respondents were asked several questions to elicit their feelings of trust for others, confidence in government, and comfort with political participation. Overall, there was much less systematic differentiation between the groups than anticipated, except in two important areas, which will be discussed at the end of this section.

One did see, however, a dramatic difference between the Bamunka (with no written language) and the Babungo (with a long history of written language and its use in school). Most Bamunka trusted their elected local council, and most thought they should always obey what the Fon (chief) said. Few belonged to associations that included other language groups, many preferred that their daughters marry within the group, and almost none thought it acceptable to protest openly. This seemed the archetypical "traditional" society. In contrast, among the Babungo, most were critical of elected officials, and only half thought they should obey what the Fon said. Many more were part of associations that included other language groups, few preferred their daughters marry inside the group, and many were ready to protest openly. While actually smaller numerically, this latter group has had its language transcribed for more than twenty-five years, and one could attribute its greater "civic culture" to its experience with a written language.

The comparison between the Ncane (with no written language) and the Bum (with a recent written language) is less apparent. The majority in both groups trusted their elected local councils, though this was more pronounced among the Bum.[15] Most people in both groups did *not* think it necessary to accept what the Fon said, and they were equally positive (81–83 percent) toward their daughters marrying outside the group. A few more of the Ncane were actually part of associations (often churches) that included other language groups than were the Bum, though this could be partially explained by the exceptionally poor state of roads required to get to Bum-speaking areas. The largest difference appeared to be in their propensity to protest: Only 58 percent of the Ncane thought it acceptable to protest, while 88 percent of the Bum did. As with the Bamunka/Babungo contrast, it is the group with a written language that seems more ready to give public voice to their grievances.

Finally, the Mmaala and the Nomaande turned out to be less of a contrast than expected. Partly, this was because their experience with a written language was much more similar than initially believed. While data from SIL indicate the Nomaande language has been written since 1994, and the Mmaala language has no written form (as proxied by Bible portions), the latter in fact has recently acquired an orthography and even some vernacular publications, and it has an

---

[15] This was mirrored in voting results from 2007 municipal council elections: The ruling party CPDM earned 75% of the vote among the Bum, which gave them an obvious mandate in the council; in contrast, the CPDM only earned 54% of the vote in the Misaje council (Ncane speakers), which gave them the council, but with a much narrower margin.

especially enthusiastic local language activist who has worked with SIL for the last two years, particularly in adult literacy.[16] Therefore, among the forty respondents in each group, eighteen in each group had some experience with writing or reading their language. This was very different from the groups described earlier, where only a few within each sample had learned to read or write their language. Mmaala and Nomaande speakers were equally happy to have their daughters marry outside their groups (a frequent refrain was "A woman has no homeland"), and they were equally ambivalent in their preferences for following the Fon's directives. Unexpectedly, more (71 percent) of the Mmaala, who had only a very recent written language, believed it was acceptable to protest publicly than Nomaande (46 percent), who had a longer history of a written language.

This "protest" outcome requires some discussion. Try as I might to have my translators explain the essence well, the uneven responses revealed different understandings of the word. Some thought it meant "gathering to do things together" – a generally positive connotation; others thought it meant "acting violently" – a generally negative connotation. Roger Gould points out that the content of words like "protest" changes over time and space, preferring the term "contentious collective action." He argues that people have different "repertoires of contention," depending on what they have been exposed to: "Participants in public claim-making adopt scripts they have performed, or at least observed, before" and "Small-scale innovation modifies repertoires continuously" (Gould 2005, 138). Tilly also recognizes that innovation and learning occur in contentious politics (1997, 251). It is certainly true that memories of government repression toward organized opposition in the early 1990s condition Cameroonians' views of what is possible in the present.

While among most groups there is a strong tradition of small groups going to the chief with their grievances (e.g., four women whose corn harvests have been trampled by someone else's cow who march to the chief's residence demanding justice), it is not common parlance to talk of many people gathering to demonstrate publicly. Partly, this is because these towns are rural, and communication and coordination are much more difficult than in urban areas. But partly it is an attitude that has been reinforced by an authoritarian political system. Protest is viewed as "sticking one's neck out" or "causing chaos," and I heard often, "One shouldn't make noise." Everyone knows everyone in small villages; if you do raise a voice, you will be marked as a troublemaker, and your family will suffer. Perhaps it should not be surprising that even confident, literate citizens under an authoritarian regime are pragmatic. And this reinforces the distinction we saw in Senegal and Ghana – the former with a historically more open political system

---

[16] Evidence of this emerged when, at the end of each fifteen-minute interview I gave the respondent a coveted Bic pen as a small thank you, he volunteered that this was in order for them to learn to write their mother tongue. None of my other helpers (who were also affiliated with SIL in some way) used the occasion to further their language advocacy.

TABLE 7.4. *Field Research Results*

Group Name	Earliest Vernacular Publication	Percentage Claiming Literacy	Marry Outside Group? (Percentage)	Taxes Well Spent (Percentage)
Babungo	1976	40	85	10
Nomaande	1985	44	95	46
Mmaala	2007	44	95	65
Bum	2008	15	83	95
Ncane	None	3	78	78
Bamunka	None	5	65	71

and the latter having experienced periods of military rule, which would have dampened citizens' ability and thus propensity to protest. We need to look elsewhere for restraining attitudes.

While the findings reported earlier show less consistency than I expected, there were two strong patterns relating to language literacy. These had to do with trust toward fellow citizens and distrust of the authoritarian regime. These outcomes were related not, as initially thought, to the length of time the group had possessed a written language, but apparently to language literacy and activation. As Table 7.4 shows, the number of speakers actually claiming some exposure to reading or writing their language has some noticeable correlation with trust toward others and distrust of government. The groups with more respondents literate in their language did not display more insular attitudes; indeed, higher numbers said they would allow their daughters to marry outside the group.

Higher mother tongue literacy also had some relationship with distrust of the elected council. All six groups lived in areas where the municipal councils were dominated by the CPDM.[17] The ruling party has been increasing its control of these councils, a trend that reflects the way the regime has maintained power. Visible support (higher vote proportions for CPDM) brings a district material gains: water, roads, buildings, work contracts. So when trying to judge people's support for their local council (without asking the taboo question of which party earned their vote), I asked whether they thought the local council was using its money well. Because most people only pay the relatively trivial "tickets" collected from market sellers by the local council tax collector and equate this with the council's budget, they tend to think they are getting quite a lot for their money.[18]

---

[17] Municipal councils are elected with a hybrid majoritarian system. A party winning the majority of votes in the district can select all of the municipal councillors; only in the rare instance where there is no majority is the council split.

[18] This does not mean this is all they are paying in "taxes"; it is only the amount they are paying officially. They regularly pay police, gendarmes, and civil servants in daily transactions off the record.

More hospital beds, the construction of market stalls, repair of bridges, and invariably the new council building were named as evidence that the council was using its money well. Most seemed not to consider – or to consider it normal – that their contribution was only a small part of the overall budget, with the majority in the form of grants from the center, meaning that a large portion of the funds were being absorbed by the members of the council themselves.

Despite this overall positive view, the groups who had higher literacy in a local language were more critical of their councils. With the exception of the Bum, who almost universally reported that the local council was spending money well, given a very recently constructed bridge and market, the other groups with more literate members demonstrated more skepticism toward their elected councils. And this was not only in the "opposition" areas. The Mmaala and Nomaande are in the Central Province, a strongly supportive region for CPDM, but they were even more skeptical that their council was using the money wisely than individuals in the traditionally opposition areas.

These figures are only suggestive, of course, but they counteract the notion that mother tongue education insulates groups and lend support to the proposition that such literacy is associated with more opposition or restraint under authoritarian regimes. Why should this be? Several visits and hundreds of interviews in this area convinced me that it has much to do with language activation. Collective, contentious action requires broadening networks of cooperation through linking, brokerage, category formation, shifting object of claims, and validation of actors by external authorities. Mastery of one's own language not only gives a person confidence speaking that language, but facilitates the learning of a broader one – providing a new "repertoire of contention." By "certifying" or validating groups, the government is likely seeking to separate them. But it does not seem to have done so, at least among those I encountered.

As in the Senegalese and Ghanaian cases, the microprocess of close involvement in language groups by active locals and foreign NGOs to promote mother tongue literacy seems to have a positive impact on individuals' efficacy. Though only provisional, this finding is buttressed by others who have done work in this region. Barbara Trudell finds much evidence that mother tongue education imparts literary skills more efficiently, evokes more interaction in the classroom, and teaches English more appropriately as a second language by decreasing the disconnection between students' home and school environments. PROPELCA classes are "noisier, more participatory and less characterized by strict discipline than the English-only classes" (2005, 10). These types of psychological and behavioral attitudes seem very likely to translate into more confident and active citizens. "Activated languages" – defined as those with a written form, a language committee, vernacular publications, and either use in school or an adult literacy program – seem to provide some benefits in an authoritarian setting: They offer networks, access to broader communication, and an alternative to the patronage of traditional authorities.

CONCLUSION

This chapter aimed to evaluate the effect of written languages, and particularly their use in school, on violent mobilization, ethnic versus national attachments, and (peaceful) political participation. It found no evidence that a language's use in school increased the likelihood of violence or separatism among the language group members. It also found no evidence that a country with a tradition of mother tongue education (Ghana) had citizens with higher ethnic attachments or higher likelihood of protest than a country that had not used local languages in its education system (Senegal). Colonial models and a history of openness seemed to play more of a role in protest than mother tongue education. In these relatively democratic settings, mother tongue literacy – gained through nonformal education as much as or more than formal schooling – appeared to have positive participatory benefits, in terms of contacting representatives. But what of its effects in a nondemocratic setting?

Because of the tremendous increase in Cameroon's stock of written languages in the last twenty years, and the concurrent entrenchment of authoritarian rule, it seemed logical to conclude that there was a causal link. On the surface, it appeared that official promotion of languages in education has had the fragmentary effect of draining groups of their potency for opposition. But in the long run, it may be that this is an unreliable tool to tighten autocrats' grip on power.

The window provided by this chapter into the on-the-ground actions and views of various language groups is admittedly tentative. It reveals why simple dichotomies between mother tongue education and foreign language education are just that – too simple. There is a whole range of variation within mother tongue education itself – how many languages are used, how seriously the project is supported by government, whether outside actors are involved, and how activated language committees become. It shows the contingency of political processes and the fragility of language activism.

Tilly defines democratic government as "broad, relatively equal citizenship affording citizens considerable protection from arbitrary state action as well as significant collective control over the personnel and decisions of government" (Tilly 1997, 246). He documents the shift from making claims chiefly to local power holders to banding together and making claims on a legislature. But his context was "in the presence of a system that already made parliament the central locus of decision-making and that protected several forms of speech, association, and public deliberation" (1997, 251). This is decidedly not the case in an authoritarian setting, so it is not surprising one would not see public protest. We need to look for other indicators that may point to citizens exercising restraint over their government – voting against their traditional leaders, readiness to trust other groups, and willingness to voice suspicion of predatory councils. If we are looking for ways that authoritarianism can be constrained, a literate culture may be one route. Groups exposed to their languages in written form appear more likely to coalesce in opposition to an oppressive government.

While not praising the coercive hand of the state that turned "peasants into Frenchmen" (Weber 1976) through assimilative educational language policies and mass conscription, I had approached this study wary that leaders may exercise their coercion even through apparently liberal policies of minority recognition. I was initially skeptical of the unbridled enthusiasm of the international community for policies that recognize the existence and rights of minority groups and languages. The close look at language groups in this chapter, however, reveals a potentially fruitful result. There is some evidence that groups with a written language demonstrate more resilience against authoritarian domination. They are not, however, less trusting of other groups, a positive finding for the likelihood of national integration. Written languages and their use in school appear not to increase dangers of violence or separatist nationalism. In democratic settings, mother tongue literacy appears to increase efficacy. Under authoritarian rule, there is some evidence of heightened ability to resist and more critical attitude toward corruption. This is all very provisional, but there is no sign that mother tongue education is detrimental to broad notions of citizenship or provokes withdrawal into enclaves.

TABLE 7.5. *Relationship between Language and Rebellion*

	Group Name*	Language(s)**	Year Language Written**	Population Percentage*	Language Restriction*	Group Organization for Joint Political Action*	Protest*	Rebellion*	Separatist Movement*
Algeria	Berbers	Kabyle/ Amazigh, Tamahaq, Tachawit	1885 1948 1950	25	Sharp	Party/Militant	LargDem	PolBandit	Active
Angola	Bakongo	Kongo	1885	11	No	Party/Militant	CampTerr	CivilWar	Past
	Cabinda	Kisikongo, Yombe	1916 2005	2	No	Militant	MedDem	LargeGuerr	Active
	Ovimbundu	Umbundu	1889	37	No	Militant/Party	Symbolic	CivilWar	None
Botswana	San Bushmen	Shua, Naro	1978 1996	3	Some	Party	SmallDem	None	None
Burundi	Hutus	Kirundi	1920	85	No	Militant	SmallDem	LargeGuerr	None
	Tutsis	Kirundi	1920	14	No	Party/Militant	MedDem	LocalRebel	None
Cameroon	Bamileke	Fe'fe', Ghomala, Ngiemboon, Yemba	1960 1964 1984 2000	27	No	Umbrella Org	MedDem	None	Past
	Kirdi	Wandala, others	1988 recent	11	No	Party	None	None	None
	Westerners	Multiple, English	yes 1382	20	Sharp	Party/Militant	LargDem	LocalRebel	Active
Chad	Southerners	Mundang, Masana, Sar	1933 1934 1950	38	Some	Militant/Party	SmallDem	SmScGuer	None

TABLE 7.5. (cont.)

	Group Name*	Language(s)**	Year Language Written**	Population Percentage*	Language Restriction*	Group Organization for Joint Political Action*	Protest*	Rebellion*	Separatist Movement*
Democratic Republic of the Congo	Hutus	Kinyarwanda	1914	0.5	No	Militant	Symbolic	CivilWar	Latent
	Luba	Luba-Kasai	1913	19	No	Party	MedDem	None	Past
	Lunda, Yeke	Lunda	1914	2	No	Party	Symbolic	None	Active
	Ngbandi	Ngbandi S/N	1984/88	2	No	Umbrella Org	None	None	None
	Tutsis	Kinyarwanda	1914	0.5	No	Militant	SmallDem	CivilWar	Latent
Djibouti	Afars	Afar	1975	35	No	Party/Militant	SmallDem	CivilWar	Active
Eritrea	Afars	Afar	1975	4	No	Party/Militant	None	PolBandit	Active
Ethiopia	Afars	Afar	1975	4	No	Party/Militant	Symbolic	LargeGuerr	Active
	Amhara	Amharic	1824	25	No	Party/Militant	SmallDem	None	None
	Oromo	Oromo	1841	40	No	Party/Militant	MedDem	IntGuer	Active
	Somalis	Somali	1915	6	No	Party/Militant	Symbolic	IntGuer	Active
	Tigreans	Tigrigna	1866	7	No	Party/Militant	SmallDem	LargeGuerr	Active
Ghana	Ashanti	Akan/Fante	1859	15	No	Party	SmallDem	None	Past
	Ewe	Ewe	1858	12	No	Umbrella Org	Symbolic	None	Past
	Mossi-Dagomba	Dagbani	1935	16	No	None	Symbolic	None	None
Guinea	Fulani	Pular	1929	40	No	Party	Verbal	LocalRebel	Latent
	Malinke	Maninka	1932	30	No	Party	SmallDem	LocalRebel	None
	Susu	Susu	1869	16	No	Umbrella Org	None	None	None
Kenya	Kalenjin	Kalenjin	1912	12	No	Party	Symbolic	None	None
	Kikuyu	Gikuyu	1903	22	No	Party/Militant	SmallDem	PolBandit	None
	Kisii	Ekegusii	1929	6	No	Umbrella Org	SmallDem	None	None
	Luhya	Oluluyia	1914	14	No	Umbrella Org	SmallDem	None	None
	Luo	Dholuo	1911	13	No	Umbrella Org	SmallDem	None	None
	Maasai	Maasai	1905	2	No	Umbrella Org	SmallDem	None	None
	Somalis	Somali	1915	1	No	Umbrella Org	SmallDem	None	Past

Country	Group	Language	Year	No.					
Madagascar	Merina	Malagasy	1828	22	No	Party	LargDem	LocalRebel	None
Mali	Tuareg	Tamasheq	1953	8	Sharp	Militant	MedDem	LargeGuerr	Active
Mauritania	Black Moors	Hassaniya Arabic	recent	36	No	Party	SmallDem	None	None
	Kewri	Pulaar, Soninke, Wolof	1929, 2001	26	Some	Party/Militant	SmallDem	SmScGuer	Past
Morocco	Berbers	Tamazight, Tarifit, Tachelhit	1873, 1885, 1887, 1906	37	Sharp	Party	Symbolic	None	Latent
	Saharawis	Hassaniya Arabic	recent	1	No	Militant/Party	SmallDem	CivilWar	Active
Namibia	Basters	Afrikaans	1893	2	No	Party	Verbal	None	Active
	East Caprivians	Lozi, Tswana, Fwe, Kuhane	1922, 1830, no	4	No	Party/Militant	SmallDem	LocalRebel	Active
	Europeans	English	1382	4	Some	Party	SmallDem	None	Past
	San Bushmen	Ju/Hoan, others	1974, no	3	Informal	Umbrella Org	SmallDem	None	None
Niger	Tuareg	Tamajaq	1953	8	Sharp	Militant	SmallDem	IntGuer	Active
Nigeria	Ibo	Igbo	1860	18	No	Party/Militant	SmallDem	PolBandit	Active
	Ijaw	Izon, Ijo	1886	10	No	Militant	SmallDem	SmScGuer	Unclr
	Ogoni	Khana, etc.	1930	4	No	Party	MedDem	None	Active
	Yoruba	Yoruba	1850	21	No	Militant/Party	LargDem	PolBandit	Active
Republic of the Congo	Lari	Kilaari/ Laadi	no	8	No	Militant/Party	Verbal	CivilWar	None
	M'boshi	Mbosi	2000	12	No	Militant/Party	SmallDem	CivilWar	None
Rwanda	Hutus	Kinyarwanda	1914	85	No	Militant	None	CivilWar	None
	Tutsis	Kinyarwanda	1914	15	No	Militant	SmallDem	CivilWar	None

TABLE 7.5. (cont.)

Group Name*	Language(s)**	Year Language Written**	Population Percentage*	Language Restriction*	Group Organization for Joint Political Action*	Protest*	Rebellion*	Separatist Movement*
Senegal Diolas in Casamance	Jola-Kasa, Jola-Fogny	1961	5	No	Militant	SmallDem	SmScGuer	Active
Sierra Leone Creoles	Krio	1986	8	No	None	SmallDem	None	Past
Limba	Limba	1911	8	No	Party	Verbal	None	None
Mende	Mende	1867	30	No	Party/Militant	SmallDem	LocalRebel	None
Temne	Temne	1865	30	No	Militant	SmallDem	LargeGuerr	None
Somalia Issaq	Somali	1915	21	No	Party	Symbolic	CivilWar	Past
South Africa Asians	Hindi, Urdu	1818 1843	3	No	Party	Symbolic	None	None
Coloreds	Multiple, Afrikaans, English	yes 1893 1382	9	No	Party	SmallDem	None	None
Europeans	Afrikaans, English	1893 1382	11	Informal	Party/Militant	SmallDem	LocalRebel	Active
Xhosa	Xhosa	1833	16	No	Umbrella Org	MedDem	CampTerr	Latent
Zulus	Zulu	1848	21	No	Party/Militant	MedDem	CampTerr	Active
Sudan Darfur Black Muslims	Fur, Masalit, others	recent	7	No	Militant	MedDem	LargeGuer	Active
Nuba	Moro, Koalib, Ororo, Katcha-K-M, Laro, Ngile, Dagik, Tagoi, Tegali, Tira, Tulishi	1951 1964 1966 2003 2004 recent transcript activity	3	No	Militant/Party	Verbal	CivilWar	Active

Country	Group	Language**	Year**	Pop %	Language restriction	Group organization	Protest	Rebellion	Type of action
	Southerners	**Dinka,** **Shilluk,** Zande, Bari, Moru, Nuer, Anuak, Otuho, Taposa, Madi	1866, 1911, 1918, 1927, 1928, 1935, 1956, 1954, 2002, no	17	Sharp	Militant	SmallDem	CivilWar	Active
Tanzania	Zanzibaris	Swahili	1868	3	No	Party	MedDem	PolBandit	Active
Togo	Ewe	Ewe	1858	44	No	Party	LargeDem	CampTerr	Active
	Kabre	Kabiye	1955	15	No	Party	None	LargeGuerr	None
Uganda	Acholi	**Acholi**	1905	4	No	Militant	Symbolic	CivilWar	None
	Baganda	**Luganda**	1887	17	No	Party	SmallDem	CivilWar	Active
Zambia	Bemba	Bemba	1904	34	No	Party	SmallDem	LocReb	None
	Lozi	Lozi	1922	6	No	Party/Militant	Symbolic	LocReb	Active
Zimbabwe	Europeans	**English**	1382	0	No	Party	SmallDem	None	None
	Ndebele	**Ndebele**	1884	14	Informal	Party	SmallDem	None	Active

* Group names and population percentages from Minorities at Risk Dataset (2009). Language restriction, group organization, and type of action also from this source. Protest categories: verbal opposition; symbolic resistance; small demonstrations; medium demonstrations; large demonstrations. Rebellion categories: political banditry (sporadic); campaigns of terrorism; small-scale guerrilla activity; intermediate guerrilla activity; large-scale guerrilla activity; civil war.

** Language names and year written from Grimes (1996) and Lewis (2009); language name is bold if language was used significantly for instruction before 2000.

8

Conclusion

Political cohesion once seemed to require a standard language. As African leaders have *not* monopolized violence, collected regular taxes, expanded bureaucratic reach, or constructed a centralizing infrastructure, they have not viewed language rationalization as a critical component of their interventions. This book has explained why.

It began by showing an upward trend in the use of local languages in education. Whereas less than half of African states used local languages in education at independence, nearly 80 percent are doing so currently. The initial chapter set forth the theoretical argument about the causes of this trend. Of central interest was how such treatment of language compared to that in other historical episodes of state-building, particularly in France and Britain, where the standardization of language through compulsory primary education eventually contributed to the cohesiveness of these European nation-states.

Historically, rulers and their bureaucrats preferred a single, standard language in order to break the mediation monopoly of regional elites and approach citizens directly. Conversely, regional elites and clergy preferred local languages to retain their spheres of influence. European state-builders had three reasons for wanting to spread a single language across the territory they ruled: control, loyalty, and extraction. France provided an example of the role of war in inducing a standard language education, while Britain showed how religious rivalries and industrial dynamism could produce the same result.

The notion that language should be used to unify states followed colonizers to Africa. Chapter 2 showed that both French and British administrators sought to educate a small class of civil servants in the respective metropolitan language. Their methods differed significantly, however, with the British using local languages in early grades as part of their strategy of control, and the French proscribing African languages in favor of French from the very beginning. This, along with the greater spread of missionaries in Anglophone Africa, resulted in the transcription of many more languages in these territories.

Because of the restricted reach of education and the similar use of local inter-mediaries, however, the outcome was the same: an elite class separated from the masses by its mastery of the colonizer's language code. With their superior firepower, secure borders, and limited plans for industrialization, colonial rulers only needed a few administrative intermediaries and soldiers. No matter the colonial policy, each case demonstrated linguistic bifurcation – an incomplete penetration of a standard language and maintenance of multilingualism.

African states achieved independence at a historical moment when monolin-gualism had triumphed in the West. Chapter 3 described how many African leaders soon justified single-party and military rule with claims they were protect-ing against the dangers of ethnic and linguistic fragmentation, virtually all main-taining a colonial language in official domains. And yet the colonial bifurcation remained. Elites did not really want to share their language proficiency with competitors for their children's jobs. Overall, independence leaders in Africa found that their incentives had not much changed from those of their colonial predecessors. With protected borders, there was little need to imbue ideas of sacrifice and loyalty. With much revenue drawn from sources other than direct taxes on citizens, there was little need for breaking the mediation monopolies of elites or for gaining consent and participation. Their apathy toward languages allowed colonial legacies to continue. Even if there were a few early shifts at the whims of particular leaders, virtually all states returned to the colonial pattern of language use in education. Surveying the range of policies across the continent since independence, this chapter challenged a prevailing view that multilingual policies arose as a result of bargaining between rulers and regional elites. Nonetheless, one *does* see increasing policies favoring multilingualism in recent years. The question is, why? To explain a rise in local language education, we needed to reconsider both opportunities and incentives of rulers.

Chapter 4 explained the new opportunities that arose in the 1990s, particularly in Francophone African states. First, an alliance of indigenous linguists and foreign NGOs used a recent accumulation of written languages and evidence of their success as media of instruction to offer an alternative to African governments facing failing education systems. Second, France changed its ideas about the utility of local languages. This was because tactical scholars convinced policy makers allocating education aid to Africa that learning initially in a local language helps a child to learn French. Both of these factors opened up the space for African governments to consider using local languages in their education systems. The chapter included a cross-national regression incorporating potential compet-ing explanations for why one would see states enacting increasing local language medium policies. It confirmed that the two most important variables were colonial legacy and volume of recent language transcription. The chapter then traced these factors through the cases of Senegal and Ghana, demonstrating that the availability of written languages, persuasion by language NGOs, and a changed message from France altered the preferences of bureaucrats and parents in Senegal but not in Ghana. The argument pointed to the importance

TABLE 8.1. *Language Policy in Three Periods*

Ruler Environment	External Context	Political Context	Language Policy
18th-/19th-century European	Threat of war	Restrained autocracy	*Proactive monolingual*
Cold War African	No threat of war	Patronage autocracy	*Language ambivalence*
Post–Cold War African	No threat of war	Electoral autocracy	*Proactive multilingual*

of differing messages transmitted from Anglophone and Francophone donors, along with the centrality of transcription efforts. As Francophone bureaucrats in charge of education were persuaded by these opportunities, politicians needed a real incentive.

Naturally, African leaders would not enact policies unless they perceived doing so to be in their own interest. Chapter 5 showed that donor priorities in the 1990s emphasized democratic elections, decentralization, and human rights. Prescriptions for power-sharing arrangements were ascendant. With electoral competition becoming central to rulers' calculations, the numerical strength of the opposition began to matter. In this context, the preferences of rulers changed from ambivalence about the medium of instruction to active interest in how it might affect electoral outcomes. Facing pressure, these autocrats scoured their tool kits for strategies that would keep them in power. They began to discover that language and citizenship laws might be turned to their advantage. With no need to inspire unity for external war making and little reliance on direct taxation, leaders not only were ambivalent about standardizing their country's language, but began seeing the utility of focusing on lower level identities to ensure their own electoral victory.

Building on others who have identified decentralization as a strategy of exclusion, this chapter argued that language recognition may be viewed by rulers as a similar tool to divide an opposition. Unlike European rulers, who had a strong preference for linguistic unity, or African leaders prior to the 1990s who were ambivalent about the benefits of linguistic unity, current African leaders may see payoffs to long-term disunity. When donor pressure and domestic opportunities meet a leader whose own incentives have changed, policies promoting multilingualism are a likely result. Table 8.1 summarizes the changing incentives of leaders in three different contexts.

The wave of protests calling for immediate elections, international pressures for the same, and development policies that favored bypassing of government coffers made leaders' positions initially precarious. They needed novel tools to maintain their hold on power. In Chapter 6, Cameroon demonstrated how leaders can use electoral boundary changes and targeted disenfranchisement to marginalize an opposition. More subtly, they can adopt constitutional changes such as decentralization and minority rights provisions, including mother tongue education, to fragment opposition and secure government control. This investigation of incentives revealed leaders' learned strategic motivations under electoral competition. Today's African leaders are not threatened by mass, educated, middle-class movements, nor by external armies. They do not need to reach their citizens to stay in power. In the context of democratic institutions, the most successful strategy seems to use autochthony to exclude rather than nationalism to incorporate. It is vague enough to expand or contract as necessary, and it can provide a minimum winning coalition, excluding many from participating. It is likely that leaders believe local language education will fit well with such a divisive strategy.

In Cameroon, language recognition has been one of the tools that the long-time president, Paul Biya, has used to strengthen his authority. Nearly losing both the presidential and the legislative elections in 1992, Biya and his ruling party increased their margins of victory to more than 80 percent in the 2007 elections. This was partially achieved through the typical strategies of fraud, repression, and cooptation. But Biya's regime became more adept at using democratic institutions to its benefit. In the name of redistricting, it manipulated boundaries; in the name of decentralization, it disenfranchised voters; and in the name of linguistic rights, it fragmented opposition. Providing a prime case of authoritarian resilience, this chapter showed how apparently liberal policies such as rights to local language education can serve to entrench autocracy. Though in the short term, these tools have worked to Biya's advantage by dividing the opposition, it may be that the specific policy of language recognition in education could have contrary long-term effects.

Having shown with cross-national and case evidence the *causes* of a multilingual outcome, Chapter 7 began to examine its *consequences* as they related to violent and peaceful opposition under different regime types. Language preservation is often justified as protection of tradition, but scholars are unclear as to whether this will undermine autocracy and deepen democracy, or the reverse. Language groups can be viewed as potential sites of association, whose ability to mobilize depends much on access to a shared written code. This chapter compared actions and attitudes among groups with and without significant histories of written languages to assess their likelihood of violence and political participation. First, the assumption that local language education promotes ethnic separatism or violence was dispensed with quickly. From a larger perspective, it looked at violent mobilization of groups across contemporary Africa and found those groups with written languages or those that used them in school were no more likely to engage in violent mobilization than groups without. Second, a group's experience with a written language also seems little related to more benign ethnic attachment and peaceful protest, as evidenced by Ghana and Senegal. Here, from a more intermediate perspective using Afrobarometer surveys, it looked at ethnic attachments and participation attitudes among groups in relatively democratic settings. There was some evidence, in fact, that groups speaking smaller languages with recent transcription and informal mother tongue education were associated with stronger participatory actions. Finally, the chapter examined the consequences of local language education under authoritarianism in the single case of Cameroon. Using voting records and original survey evidence, it assessed individuals' attitudes toward others and toward government. It found that groups possessing written languages were more likely to sustain opposition to autocratic rule and groups with higher proportions of individuals exposed to their written language were more likely to criticize government. At the same time, these groups retained high levels of trust toward other groups.

These findings suggest that local language education does not have the negative outcomes that are feared and may hold some promise for both undermining authoritarianism and deepening democracy. The mechanisms have much to do with activism by local language NGOs and the efficacy it encourages among participants.

NATION-BUILDING, CITIZENSHIP, AND THE AFRICAN STATE

A major lesson of this work is that African leaders are not driven to the language rationalization that we may view as "natural." Even as global cultural norms prescribe education as an obvious government practice (Meyer et al. 1992), states' visions of rationalizing, standardizing, and social engineering through schools seem a lower priority than expected in Africa. Van de Walle notes that "the continuing failure to reach universal primary education in much of west and central Africa is striking" (2009, 322) and cites comparative education experts to show that African countries have consistently underperformed both other regions and even low-income countries in other regions in relation to outcomes such as enrollment rates and average length of schooling. This persistence of low human capital has been a consequence of low social spending (Glewwe and Kremer 2006; van de Walle 2009). African politicians have failed to achieve that ideal of an "integral state," making the postcolonial state, according to Bayart, not dissimilar to its colonial and precolonial predecessors: "It obeys a law of incompletion" (Bayart, 2009, 261). This incompleteness is evident in the limited spread of standard, official languages in states across Africa.

Figure 8.1 shows the percentage of the population in African states that currently speaks a European language. Aside from Gabon and Algeria, the remainder of the African continent has very low proficiency in any European language, reflecting low incentives for governments to spread a single official language. These two are special cases: Gabon, with population only half a million at independence, began with an unusually high number of missionaries and the highest proportion of children attending school in Francophone Africa. Its high proficiency, then, is simply a reflection of this head start. Algeria also began with a relatively high number of children enrolled, but interestingly, its official policies aimed to spread Arabic at the expense of French. Close proximity

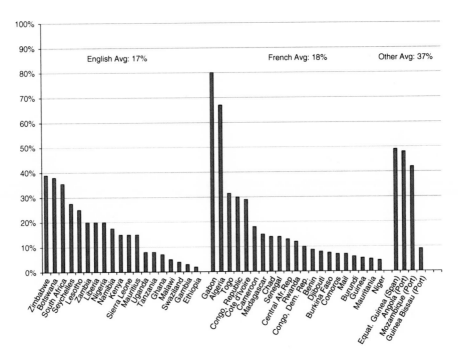

FIGURE 8.1. Portion of the Population Speaking a European Language. *Source*: Various. See Appendix A.

to France, frequent emigration and return, and more recent spread through TV programs have increased French proficiency more than deliberate government policy. Aside from these exceptions, French and English retain a relatively precarious status among African masses, with an average of less than 20 percent proficiency in any European language across the continent. We will return to this topic.

Certainly, part of this can be explained by limited means. But it also reflects state-builders' incentives. Not only is it a challenge to overcome widespread multilingualism, but it is not imperative to their maintenance of power. Inclusive citizenship is not a necessary element of African states' resilience. Though all leaders want to protect their positions, doing so may not involve the majority of the population. Mass education itself in many cases is superfluous; stratification works just fine for those at the top. We should therefore not be surprised at the extraordinary *outside* effort and investment that have been required to further universal primary education on the continent.

Despite governments' lack of effort to inculcate national sentiment through a shared language code, national cohesion has nevertheless taken hold. After more than fifty years of independence, national identities have calcified. Whether stemming from positive action or negative experience, states are now definite entities. Young observes that "although one must not prematurely presume their permanence, territorial attachments have entered the popular consciousness as one of the unreflected, assumed givens of social life. Whatever their limits, African nationalisms have evolved well beyond their roots in anti-colonial revolt" (Young 2007, 262). Early in their independence, governments did pursue the national project in a host of symbolic domains: portraits and monuments, stamps, currency, flags, parades, national anthems, holidays, identity cards, and national sports teams. These performative aspects of the state continue to mold citizens, and their cumulative effect is large.

As Chapter 3 showed, early leaders such as Ahidjo, Senghor, and Nkrumah emphasized the *nonethnic* character of these nationalisms. "Important to these nationalizing processes was the distancing of representations of the nation from ethnicity" (Young 2007, 249). This left a mark as to the realm of possible claims that could be made on the state. Brubaker, in his careful research about variation in European citizenship policies, argues that dominant "cultural idioms," "self-understandings," and "ways of thinking and talking about nationhood" (1992, 16) help explain tendencies toward assimilationist or ethnocultural citizenship policies.

But according to Young, "African nationalisms are neither civic nor ethnic.... Rather than an active and aggressive militant consciousness, it is a more passive, unreflected attachment ... 'banal nationalism.'" And a "positive attachment to the 'nation' seems often to coexist with a very negative view of the state" (Young 2007, 249). The state's minimal efforts, it seems, are reflected in citizens' response. Young is unsure these attachments will survive deteriorating and collapsing states. Englebert believes they remain a tool to claim citizenship rights in the form of "solitary nationalism" (2009, 203–5). Wedeen's findings in Yemen, however, reveal that common feelings of anger, vulnerability, even lack of government efficacy can bring people together: Nationness "can be constituted in the absence of a sovereign state, through the shared experiences of belonging to a community imagined in the breach of institutional authority" (Wedeen 2003, 707).

Cameroon's nationalism, similarly, results as much from a shared sense of skepticism about government rhetoric as a sense of real belief. Cameroonians have simply "developed a sense of being implicated in a common destiny." Though people did not necessarily accept Ahidjo's version of the national myth, "the political slogans promoted by his government became shared reference points, even when the principles behind such slogans stood in blatant contradiction to perceived reality. Whether Cameroonians supported Ajidho or reviled him, they defined themselves at least partly in response to his government and its conception of national identity" (Bjornson 1991, 126).

Common suffering under colonialism, borders secured by leaders' and donors' shared reticence to alter them, physical mapping and visualization, the power of discipline and performance in the independence period that closed the possibility of claims making on the basis of ethnic difference, and in many cases

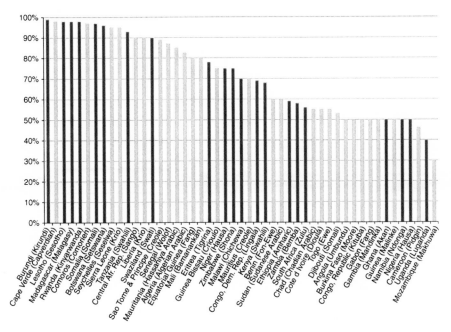

FIGURE 8.2. Portion of the Population Speaking an African Lingua Franca. *Source:* Various; see Appendix A.

collective disappointment in the recent past – all these combine to produce durable nations, even if this has nothing to do with a shared official language. Figure 8.1 implied, as is usually assumed, that African states are hopelessly fragmented. But reflecting individuals' capacities for multilingualism, the reach of major *African* languages is actually widespread. Figure 8.2 reveals that the African linguistic landscape is much less fragmented than is often perceived.

Nearly all states – forty-six of forty-nine – have a lingua franca spoken by 50 percent or more of the population. In more than half of states (twenty-six), a lingua franca is spoken by 70 percent or more, and in nearly a third (fourteen), it is spoken by 90 percent or more. Languages indeed are spreading. Many of the high proportions of lingua franca speakers occur in states where there is a single dominant group (say, more than 70 percent of the population). Language spread in these settings – Lesotho, Botswana, Comoros, Somalia – seems "natural." In many other places, however, a language is spreading where its group is much smaller. We find very dominant lingua francas in Senegal and Mali, whose largest languages are spoken as mother tongues by only 40 percent and 30 percent of the population, respectively, but they are used by more than 80 percent of the population. And we find widespread lingua francas in Sierra Leone and Tanzania – Krio and Swahili – languages that are not spoken by any but a tiny group as a mother tongue. In the first case (Tanzania), the colonial and independence government deliberately harnessed the historical dominance of Swahili, while in Sierra Leone, Krio was expressly not included in education. The spread of many African languages has occurred without the help or hindrance of governments. The light bars in Figure 8.2 show that more than half of these states have *not* used the dominant language in education. This again reveals the relative weakness of education compared to other forces propelling language spread in the African setting.

LANGUAGE POLICY AND EDUCATION IN AFRICA

Given the apparent solidity of the national idea discussed earlier, permanent multilingualism does not pose the risks to civic nationalism it may have in the past. Formal literacy and education appear not to play such a singular role in attaching one to the state as perceived from the Western experience. We have not seen language education to result in greater violence or closed identities. Avid proponents of mother tongue education present it as a cure-all – with improved educational, psychological, and democratic consequences. The present research has found its effects much more muted – largely because mother tongue education is a variable, rather than a constant. Its impact on educational achievements seems more to depend on how extensive are the resources, how activist the NGOs, and how qualified the teachers in each experiment. If pursued wholeheartedly, however, its impact could be profound. I see its potential influence in two broad areas: personal efficacy and social connection.

First involves the efficacy and confidence that arise with authentic self-awareness. I mentioned in Chapter 6 the oft-decried "colonization of the mind" through the hegemony of foreign language schooling.[1] It seems evident that validation of people's languages by those in authority – government, outsiders, or both – can only serve to increase individuals' confidence. We have seen in Chapter 7 that political participation is enhanced with civic awareness, literacy, and trust. These can be provided in many settings. But because of the retrenchment of the state from education and its falling standards, it is not surprising that the organization of community groups to support mother tongue literacy by NGOs or the extra support of classrooms and teachers toward this goal raises the efficacy of participants. Individuals involved see that outsiders are interested in *their* contributions, *their* history, *their* ideas, not only wanting to change them.

Colonial rule, particularly in Francophone Africa, left a legacy of teacher-directed education (Moloi et al. 2008). This is exacerbated when an unfamiliar

---

[1] Aside from Ngugi wa Thiong'o (1986), see useful papers in Heller and Martin-Jones (2001) that discuss how the choice of language in education categorizes groups into relations of power, a process that has important emotional effects on individuals. See also Ofori-Attah (2006), who describes the "hidden messages" inscribed in colonial education practices in Africa, which, among other effects, served to instill in learners disregard for their own customs and languages (419).

language is used, and children become twice disadvantaged – not proficient in their own *or* the foreign language (Bgoya 2001; Nishimuku 2007). Teachers talk and children listen silently. Learning must be passive, rote, and repetitious. Of course, this must be true when a completely foreign language is used. "In this context, authentic teaching and learning cannot take place. Such situation accounts largely for the school ineffectiveness and low academic achievement experienced by students in Africa" (Alidou et al. 2006, 15).

Use of "le Symbole" perpetuated inferiority associated with African languages: Students and teachers "almost unconsciously absorbed the lower status of their maternal languages" (Hale 2005, 183). Individuals sought to lose their past, become something different, don a mask. It is not necessary to accept Fanon's (1961) descriptions of the pathological responses in colonial subjects fully to recognize the psychological damage that occurred.[2] Of course, education in British Africa has been accused of mental brainwashing as well (Okoth 1993; Carnoy 1974), but it is Francophone Africa that has received the sharpest critiques. Comparing literatures that have emerged from Anglophone and Francophone African authors, Michelman argues that Francophone writers struggle with authenticity. He contrasts a passage from *Arrow of God* by Chinua Achebe with *L'enfant noir* by Camara Laye – the former able to stretch the boundaries of the English language to make it take on the character of the mother tongue, the latter less authentic because it remained within the confines of the French model (Michelman 1995, 220–221).

In British colonial Africa, "serious efforts were made by various governmental, missionary, and private organizations to foster creative writing in African languages, including the regular awarding of literary prizes. Over the years, these efforts have borne fruit and important bodies of literature have appeared in Twi, Yoruba, Hausa, Swahili, Zulu, Xhosa, Sotho and other languages spoken in areas once colonized by the British" (Michelman 1995, 218). Francophone Africa demonstrated the opposite – newspapers, prizes for writers of French, with inhibiting consequences for literacy. Moumouni noted early after independence that the distinction in literacy rates lay "not in any philanthropic tendency of English colonization compared with the French, but rather in the objectively greater possibilities of cultural development which flow from even partial use of African languages in schools" (1968, 172). While I might argue that literacy rates reflect more the density of missions in general, I concur that the Francophone pattern likely left a mark on their capacity for creativity and adaptability of language toward new models and purposes. It certainly seems to correspond with the wider variation and more policy experimentation in Anglophone Africa.

---

[2] Paulin Hountondji, in *Présence Africane*, writes "The linguistic behavior of the African, when expressing himself in French, has all the characteristics of a neurosis." The search for "linguistic perfection in French" contributes to the "intellectual's increasingly impoverished rapport with his native language" (cited in Michelman 1995, 219).

Some argue that Africans *want* Western education, with European language as part and parcel.[3] My discussions with several Africans and foreign linguists convinced me that this is an element of the colonization of the mind. People want their children to succeed. Often they express this in their preference that their children learn a European language. When they were convinced their own languages were strong enough to accomplish this goal, I found individuals to be enthusiastic in support of mother tongue education.

Mainstream literature has presented a stark choice between language rationalization and promotion of African culture. When a policy includes the use of *many* languages in schools, presumably those already spoken by the children at home or at least on the playground, it may inspire much less resistance. The divisible property of language choice in education offers the potential for rationalization and cultural preservation at the same time. Nationalists can claim victory; bureaucrats are not threatened; parents, if sensitized, are satisfied; and no regional elites are slighted. It is not necessarily as zero-sum as many observers describe it. Importantly, neither the ADEF program in Senegal nor the PROPELCA program in Cameroon is intended to overturn existing systems. "One thing PROPELCA is *not* is an attempt to establish the use of minority languages throughout the Cameroonian education system on an equal basis with English (or French)." It is purposely not aggressive (Trudell 2003, 12). Recall the distinction I made in Chapter 4 about the attractiveness of the "frame" – the idea of mother tongue education as a bridge to other foreign language acquisition in Francophone Africa, versus the more challenging rationale given by many Anglophone scholars.

Besides instilling confidence, the process of mother tongue education has opened up new opportunities for networking. Democracy arrived in Africa bearing exclusion. Young, citing Herbst, notes that citizenship is relatively restrictive in Africa and becoming more so (Young 2007, 256). Rhetoric surrounding elections in the Ivory Coast, Zambia, Eastern Congo, and, after he wrote, Kenya, demonstrates a deepening sense of barricaded borders and formalized difference. "Democratisation, even incomplete, changed the rules of politics in ways which brought ethnicity into the open" (Young 2007,

---

[3] This is evident in much of the literature of the early independence period, where Africans resisted what they perceived as inferior education in African languages. Coe writes that many educated Africans "suspected that the reason for teaching local arts, language, and customs was to keep Africans in inferior positions. Thus, they pushed for an academic education and a focus on the English language" (2002, 38). These views continue in the present, as demonstrated by leaders in Ghana, such as Christine Churcher, minister of basic education at the time of the policy change, who justified the change in Parliament by echoing common sentiment that the use of mother tongues "dumbed down" rural education: "The old policy of teaching children in the first three years in the local language is beautiful, but on the ground it is nauseating, because it is not yielding the results which would bridge the gap of inequities that we are facing as a people in this country.... It will be suicidal for us to continue with a policy which demarcates and deepens the gap between rich and poor" (Parliament of Ghana 2002, column 1660).

257–258). Echoing Geschiere, he notes how the turn toward electoral competition impacted fears of domination, desires for entitlement, relations of power between "insiders" and "outsiders." Englebert agrees that African nationalism can become exclusionary under conditions of electoral competition or fiscal tightening (2009, chapter). Leaders react by restricting citizenship laws, creating categories of indigenous and migrant, natives and foreigners. I argued in Chapters 5 and 6 that this may account for leaders' new embrace of mother tongue education as a fragmentary device.

In this setting, groups and individuals need more ways of "bridging." Somewhat nonintuitively, mother tongue education, particularly now in Francophone Africa, is framing itself in these terms. Habyarimana, Humphreys, and Posner find that ethnic identities condition actions only in certain situations, particularly through the "technology" mechanism of being able to identify and sanction coethnics: "Ethnic groups constitute social networks that make fellow group members more findable." Their study concludes that what is needed are policies promoting repeated interaction and free flow of information across group lines (2007, 719, 724).

Exclusion from decision making is cited as a particularly glaring problem, stemming from the inequalities present in many African states. Advocates of mother tongue education claim that it will enhance people's ability to participate. Wa'Njogu (2004, 70) laments the lack of serious attention to local languages apart from Swahili in Kenya:

Only through empowering these languages can the government ensure maximum participation of its populace in their sociopolitical and economic development . . . governments must ensure that their citizens get information in the languages with which they are comfortable. Governments should also ensure that their people have the freedom to express themselves in whatever language they want. It is only after establishing this line of communication and freedom that a populace can be mobilized for engaged development.

But mother tongue education will only do so if it helps with their acquisition of a linking language, and pragmatic activists are aware of this: "To ensure full participation of the masses, rigorous and deliberate efforts must be put in place to increase literacy in a multilingual model: one's native language, the national language, and a Western language" (Wa'Njogu 2004, 72). Associations promoting local language literacy provide spaces for discussion, learning, complaint, and solidarity.

The network of NGOs that have joined in Senegal and in Cameroon, with the support of outside actors, offer a model of interaction. They draw together teachers, parents, and linguists of several language backgrounds. These networks also create opportunities to force government restraint. Many of the local NGOs receive material support from foreign donors. While this support is vulnerable to changing priorities of outsiders, it is probably less fragile than relying on the whims of local magnanimity. The resources that accompany these efforts give individuals alternatives to attaching themselves to local "big men." As they say in Cameroon: "The mouth which eats does not speak" (Bayart 2009, 188). In much of Africa, the "networks in which politically mediated financial gains are redistributed are extremely narrow and do not extend down the social pyramid" (van de Walle 2009, 321). In contrast, leaders of language associations are interacting with other language organizers, with church leaders, with teachers, and with government representatives outside traditional hierarchies, connecting directly to the state but because of their relative financial independence, more able to challenge it.

Counterweights to the government are particularly difficult in Africa. The postcolonial state, observes Bayart, "represents an historical mutation of African societies ... never before, it seems, has the dominant class managed to acquire such marked economic supremacy over its subjects.... No established class of landowners could act as pivot and backbone in the process of State formation as happened in Europe" (Bayart 2009, 87, 108). Identifying and strengthening such counterweights seems a productive endeavor. Compliant behaviors in an authoritarian setting reinforce government hegemony, its symbolic power (Wedeen 1998; 2008). "Transgressive practices" by significant numbers of individuals convince others to reject "living the lie" (Kuran 1991). This will certainly be more evident where states are less coercive, as we saw in the comparison between Senegal and Ghana, but the preparation of confident, authentic citizens may incubate future protest and demand for restraint even in authoritarian regimes.

Mother tongue education, in formal or informal settings, at its best, seems to offer the potential for instilling confidence, overcoming segmentation, and paving the way for fruitful collective action. Less destructive than Weber's description of the French state turning peasants into Frenchmen (1976; see also Higonet 1980), where wedding citizens directly to the state required breaking down tradition and culture, this route aims to utilize identities that exist.

If mother tongue education offers potential confidence-building, solidarity-producing benefits, what of its educational effects? This element seems to me least clear. Given the realities in Africa, mother tongue education is converging across the board to "local language light." In Francophone Africa, local language programs will continue to be introduced in the first couple of years of education as a result of action by NGOs and a new openness in the French Ministry of Foreign Affairs. Again, these are not "aggressive" programs, but intended simply to graft on to an existing effort ultimately aimed to teach children a European language. In Anglophone Africa, path dependency will leave most programs in place, but their years may be reduced from earlier duration, given several factors: the historical tainting of "Bantu" education, rising demand for "English-only" teaching from growing groups of wealthy citizens, and the rigid framing of the mother tongue option. Whereas in Francophone Africa, educational failures can almost singularly be attributed to a French-only policy, in Anglophone Africa, failures that are probably caused by poor *application* of the policy are blamed on the mother tongue policy itself. And intense recommendations by experts are more difficult to swallow.

Kathleen Heugh – specialist on South Africa – emphasizes the importance of extended use of mother tongues, not early exit, to facilitate the acquisition of the second language. She insists that learners need six to eight years to learn a second language well enough to use it as a medium of instruction (Heugh 2008). She worries about what she notes as a convergence toward early exit transitional models, blaming it on terminological slippage on the part of experts and advisers (Heugh 2006, 62). I would argue this sleight of tongue is likely the only way the mother tongue alternative would have been adopted in Francophone states. In this setting, she warns, the "best one could hope for would be scores of between 20–40% in the [official language] by grade 12....We can now predict with some accuracy that learners in early-exit programmes and who remain in the system beyond grades 4–5 are likely to have to repeat or drop out of the system" (Heugh 2006, 69–70).[4]

"Local language light" will preserve African languages, but it may not work to its full potential toward the spread of European languages. This will be particularly true for French in Francophone Africa for two reasons: the necessary reduction in school quality because of a recent inundation of students and the low percentage of children who complete primary school.

Since the World Conference on Education for All (Jomtien 1990) and World Education Forum (Dakar 2000), there has been a massive push toward increasing enrollment in Africa in order to increase literacy rates. In 2000, the international community announced through the Dakar Framework for Action that "no countries seriously committed to education for all will be thwarted in their achievement of this goal by a lack of resources." UNESCO reports that the external flow of aid to the education sector in the region increased from US$1.1 billion in 2002 to US$2.6 billion in 2008 as a result of these commitments (UNESCO 2011, 21). The number of students in primary schools increased from 87 million to 129 million between 2000 and 2008, finally achieving average Primary Gross Enrollment rates of 100 percent (UNESCO 2011, 23).[5] There is no doubt that the rise in adult literacy in Africa, from 53 percent to 62 percent overall over the last two decades (UNESCO 2011, 16), has much to do with this massive investment by outsiders.

Because Anglophone Africa started off at a higher overall level of enrollment, however, it has only increased enrollments by an average of 16 percent since 1990, whereas enrollment in Francophone Africa has increased on average by 55 percent (World Bank WDI). In Anglophone Africa, only Tanzania and Kenya

---

[4] An interview (Bamenda, July 11, 2011) I had with the linguist Steve Walter, education specialist supervising a longitudinal study of student performance in Kom schools, also noted in passing that the improvement in achievement seems only to occur after four or five years in the program.
[5] This prompted a shift in the goal post of Education for All to *literacy*, rather than enrollment.

have seen significant enrollment increases.[6] In contrast, half of Francophone states increased enrollments by 50 percent or more, with states such as Niger, Burkina Faso, Benin, and Guinea more than doubling primary enrollments.[7] This seems to be a good thing, of course, but in classrooms that are already crowded, and with the need to recruit enormous numbers of new teachers, the quality of teaching is likely to suffer. Teaching strategies deteriorate under conditions of rapid expansion. Tendencies toward teacher-directed activities, routine, choral recitation, and emphasis on demonstrating authority are exacerbated when teachers feel insecure (Moloi 2008, 613).

Second, there is a very real difference between Anglophone Africa and Francophone Africa in the rate at which children stay in school. Whereas an average of 56 percent of school-aged children in former British colonies complete five years of primary education, only 33 percent of school-age children in Francophone Africa do so (World Bank WDI).[8] This means that even if many Francophone states are beginning to use local languages in the early years of education with a transition to French afterward, the majority of these children will never be exposed to French, because they will drop out before the transition. This is particularly true in the countries that are experimenting most intensely with local languages: Among these, none had more than 25 percent of children completing five grades of primary school. If the research cited previously is accurate – that children need six to eight years of consistent education in one language to make it practical to use that language as the foundation for another – this does not bode well for the improved learning of French.

POLICY IMPLICATIONS

So what do all of these observations mean for government policy? First, education, especially in Francophone Africa, will continue to require tenacious external investment. Given my first claim – about governments not having great incentive to spread standard education – we should not be surprised that private local and foreign, as well as official donor, efforts will be required for a long time, no matter what choice is made about the use of mother tongues in education. Policy implementation requires strong advocates and interested parties. When money dries up or people turn to other interests, then experiments stagnate. While leaders are more likely to acquiesce to persuasion in the current climate, they will not likely implement policies without strong advocacy and financing. Languages will continue to be written and preserved, promoted

---

[6] Kenya went from 56% net primary enrollment in 1990 to 82% in 2010; Tanzania from 51% in 1990 to 96% in 2010.

[7] Calculated from available data closest to 1990, compared to 2010. Niger's enrollment grew from 23% to 57%; Burkina Faso's from 31% to 63%; Benin's from 41% to 91%; Guinea's from 24% to 73%.

[8] Calculated from "Percent of Net School Enrollment" multiplied by "Persistence to Grade 5,"and because of missing data, I used averages from 1990–2000.

informally by NGOs, and governments will be content to allow others to pay for their integration. Investment in books, classrooms, and training of teachers will still have the deepest impact, regardless of education policy. The inequality in educational access that seems to be growing with decentralization of education provision in many cases could be cause for alarm. In Tilly's terms, increasing inequality "threatens democracy to the extent that its categorical relations reproduce themselves as divisions within public politics" (2000, 10). If language divisions reinforce class divisions, this effect could undermine prospects for deepening democracy.

Second, governments will become more involved with education as citizens become more important to their financial interests – as they industrialize and broaden their tax base. Chapter 5 demonstrated a low reliance in Africa on formal direct taxation. Tax systems have been narrowly based, reliant on trade and sales taxes and including enormous leakage and fraud (van de Walle 2009, 323). Since most taxing of the average citizen is informal[9] – government officials using their offices to extract resources from others – citizens' direct productivity and governments' interface with them are less of a concern than in periods of state-building elsewhere. Hanagan writes of Europe: "Throughout the last period of state transformation, rulers' needs for capital and conscripts have given populations bargaining power" (1999, 3). Rulers in Africa need populations much less.

Much as I attributed broadening standardized education to war and industrial dynamism in Europe, Migdal shows that moves toward assimilation in the United States occurred because the Civil War initiated a period of spectacular economic growth. "The need to find enough competent hands to run the complex economy meant that in the home offices of the corporations faces from 'unassimilable' groups began to appear and, indeed, be assimilated" (2004, 38). He compares this to Israel, where war played a larger role initially (2004, 39). The war of independence, with its huge number of casualties, created tremendous pressures for full Jewish mobilization and "what became a nation-in-arms." This, plus economic expansion, caused outsiders to adopt dominant group's rules "and to transform them" (2004, 39). Common to both situations is first hardening and then softening of boundaries between a dominant population and "dangerous" groups.

But in Africa, the narrowness of tax systems and the lack of mass conscription for war have prevented governments from needing to deepen citizenship. If this changes – ideally through economic mobilization rather than mass

---

[9] See, for example, Janet Roitman's discussion of the "pluralization of economic regulatory authority" in Chad and Cameroon, where states have every reason to facilitate border traffic in order to provide remuneration for military officials. "While these endeavors potentially undermine state economic regulatory authority, they also contribute to the viability of the state through the production of new rents and possibilities for redistribution among strategic military, political and commercial personalities" (2007, 191).

preparation for war – governments will become more reliant on citizens, taking a greater interest in expanding education.

Third, in the interim much language learning will necessarily occur outside the formal school system. Education expert Blommaert concludes that something is "structurally wrong with the regard to literacy in Africa" in that it is provided almost exclusively through formal education channels (1999, 4). Hobsbawm (1996) identified new technologies that were "game changers," as did Anderson (1991, 135) – technologies such as television and radio that allow people to imagine broader communities without a written text. Certainly even more translation technologies in phone and Internet applications will contribute to this imagining as well (Dor 2004). Chapter 7 pointed to the importance of nonformal education for increasing democratic participation. Large numbers of women and children, particularly in West Africa, never attend or drop out of school. The combination of a huge influx of students, low persistence, lack of capacity and training, and limitations on resources means that educational outcomes depend on creativity and working outside traditional channels. In Algeria, for example, despite the government's nearly exclusive focus on Arabic in the education system, the population is surging in its French language acquisition. Why? Because of the much more interesting cable TV shows, particularly cartoons, in French (Benrabah 2007, 205). Media will transform the linguistic landscape as much as formal education. English and French will likely remain secondary for the majority of Africans; most will see their own languages preserved indefinitely, and major African languages will spread. Multilingualism will endure, and so will national states.

CONCLUSION

Language politics are contentious – but more among academics than among average citizens in Africa. Reacting against the replication in Africa of the forced linguistic homogenization that occurred in Europe, the eminent Nigerian scholar Ayo Bamgbose rejects the assumption that the existence of multiple languages is necessarily divisive to a state, instead blaming elites for exploiting them (1991). Mazrui and Mazrui argue passionately for the preservation of African languages, even while alluding to the potential of linguistic pluralism to undermine horizontal integration (1998, 98–103). Most scholars currently writing about African languages are anthropologists and linguists. Their attention to the preservation of languages, while valuable, is hardly disinterested. An objective evaluation of the motivations for language transcription and mother tongue literacy, as well as their effects on political mobilization, is thus sorely needed. This book has attempted to be that objective voice.

It has explained the rise in local language education by looking at both opportunities and incentives. Leaders' opportunities changed for two reasons. First, influence agents within African states – notably missionary linguists and local language NGOs – made it easy for governments to consider adopting mother tongue education policies because they provided materials, programs, personnel, and evidence of mother tongue education success. Second, tactical scholars in France advocated an innovative idea to their government, offering French policy makers a new pathway to achieve France's perennial goal of linguistic *rayonnement*. They proposed that using local languages in the first years of education in Francophone African states actually helps children to learn French in the long run. Therefore, France could begin openly supporting the use of African languages in education without compromising its ultimate goal of French language expansion.

African leaders thus sit at the intersection of these forces that push toward local language education. They will not enact policies, however, unless they perceive them to be in their own interest. In the context of pressure toward democratization and decentralization, recognition of local languages can be perceived as a strategy to defend against oppositional cohesion. Their own incentives thus join with the opportunities to result in a widespread increase in local language education in virtually all Francophone African states. The reverse of official nationalisms in Europe, where dynastic rulers tried to disguise empire in "national drag" (Anderson 1991, 86), these rulers are acceding to official multilingualism, disguising exclusion in minority rights drag.

But will they achieve their goal of control? Mother tongue education policies in many states correspond with increasing authoritarian entrenchment. As a tool to consolidate their authority, the recognition of local languages in education appears to be working for autocratic leaders in the short term. And yet it may be that such divisive strategies contain seeds of their own destruction. Both because of the "natural" spread of lingua francas and because of the purposeful emphasis on using the mother tongue to teach a European language, these more literate and active communities may actually join across categories to engage, restrain, and resist the state. These are groups that have enjoyed sustained intervention by NGOs – forming language committees, engaging in adult literacy programs, writing cultural materials, facilitating integration of languages into local schools. If these pockets grow, they may produce citizens who have the confidence to participate in their own governance.

This book has provided a general model for why local language instruction has become more common in African schools. It also has assessed whether this is a beneficial or a harmful development. In the short run, it may bolster electoral authoritarianism. In the long run, such literacy may give voice to communities who can demand democratic alternatives that have thus far eluded so many African states.

Appendix A

Intensity of Local Language Use in Education

In order to compare countries' use of languages in education, I wanted to capture both the depth of their language inclusion and the breadth of their use across the school system. I therefore created a composite measure called "Intensity of Local Language Use in Education," or ILLED. This measure refines my previous coding (Albaugh 2005, 2009). I first assign a number from 0 to 5 to show the proportion of local languages that are used in each country. I then determine the extent of their use across the primary curriculum, enumerated with a 1, 1.2, 1.5, 1.8, or 2. Table A.1 lists the possible variations.

For extent of local language use, "Experimental" refers to government-authorized pilot programs, typically undertaken in 50 to 100 schools. "Moderate" and "Extensive" categories show expansions or retractions in the number of schools or years of local language use. The measurements refer to the use of languages in primary school, usually a six or seven year cycle, depending on the country. Most countries that use local languages as media of instruction do so

TABLE A.1 *Calculation of Intensity of Local Language Use in Education (ILLED)*

Proportion of Country's Languages Used (Population Covered by the Language)	Extent of Local Language Use in the Primary School System	
0 None (European language only)	1	Experimental
1 Classical Arabic	1.2	Moderate
2 Single minority language (<50%)	1.5	Extensive
3 Few languages or one major language (50–70%)	1.8	Generalized
4 Several languages or one dominant language (70–85%)	2	Exclusive
5 Most languages or one overwhelmingly dominant language (>85%)		

in the first two or three years of primary school and then transition to a European language. Some began with four or five years of local use but have reduced them to one or two; they would be coded as going from "Generalized" to "Extensive" or "Moderate." The category "Exclusive" refers to those situations where one or more local languages are used as the medium of education throughout the entire primary cycle, with the foreign language taught only as a subject.

When the language proportion figure and the extent of use figure are multiplied together, they yield a composite score between 0 and 10, with 0 indicating exclusive use of a European language and 10 indicating exclusive use of African languages in the curriculum. Table A.2 shows how each country was scored at independence, in 1990, and in 2010. The text that follows provides supporting information for this coding by country. To avoid biasing my findings, I was cautious both in assigning increased local language use to Francophone states and in reducing scores in Anglophone states over time. It could be argued, for example, that my 2010 scores for Cote d'Ivoire, Gabon, and Mauritania are too low, while those for Nigeria, Sudan, and Zambia are too high. If altered, these would point even more strongly to my hypothesis about the divergence between Francophone and Anglophone states. In the country entries that follow, I derived the language percentages in the "Languages Used" section from *Ethnologue* (Lewis 2009), adjusting for population growth, depending on when census numbers were recorded. All of the sources for the language policy information are listed in the African Language Use Bibliography, which is at the end of this appendix.

Country	Independence/1960	1990	2010
Algeria	0	1.8	1.8
Angola	0	0	4
Benin	0	0	3
Botswana	6	7.2	6
Burkina Faso	0	0	4.8
Burundi	9	9	9
Cameroon	0	0	3
Cape Verde	0	0	0
Central African Republic	0	0	0
Chad	0	1.8	3
Comoros	0	0	0
Congo, Dem. Rep.	5.4	5.4	5.4
Congo, Rep.	0	0	0
Cote d'Ivoire	0	0	3
Djibouti	0	0	5
Equatorial Guinea	0	0	0
Eritrea	10	N/A	10
Ethiopia	4	4	9
Gabon	0	0	3
Gambia	0	0	0
Ghana	0	7.2	3.6
Guinea	0	0	5
Guinea-Bissau	0	3	0
Kenya	0	7.2	6
Lesotho	9	9	9
Liberia	0	0	0
Madagascar	0	9	9
Malawi	7.2	5.4	4.8
Mali	0	3	6
Mauritania	1.5	3	1.8
Mauritius	0	0	0
Mozambique	0	0	5
Namibia	9	9	6
Niger	0	4	5
Nigeria	9	9	9
Rwanda	9	9	9
Sao Tome and Principe	0	0	0
Senegal	0	0	5
Seychelles	0	9	9
Sierra Leone	3.6	4.8	4.8
Somalia	1.8	9	6
South Africa	10	7.5	6
Sudan	1.5	2	4
Swaziland	0	9	7.5
Tanzania	4.5	6	6
Togo	0	0	0
Uganda	5.4	6	6
Zambia	5.4	0	4
Zimbabwe	4.5	5.4	4.8

Algeria

ILLED 1962	ILLED 1990	ILLED 2010	Percentage Speak French	Percentage Speak Algerian Arabic
0	1.8	1.8	67*	82.5**

LANGUAGE POLICY

Colonial French control from 1830. Until 1885, the education system was primarily for children of European settlers. In 1885, the French administrators founded a separate school system for indigenous Algerians. The French language was used exclusively in all schools. In 1938, the colonial government decreed Classical Arabic a foreign language (Benrabah 2007a, 64). The colonial authorities preferred the Kabylian (Berber) population over Arab for schooling (Benrabah 2007a, 40) and encouraged the development of the Kabylian language (as well as Algerian Spoken Arabic). There was already a literate Kabylian culture and media prior to independence.

Independence (1962) French was the medium of instruction in primary schools. Though the state wanted to transition to Arabic medium, there were so few teachers trained to teach Classical Arabic that only 7 hours of instruction was required each week (Leclerc 2010). From 1965 onward, there was a gradual process of Arabization, with Arabic replacing French as the medium for certain subjects.

Interim In 1976, the Foundation School System made French a foreign language. "Classical Arabic is the only official language of the nation.... French is regarded as a foreign language and is taught starting from the fourth year of the primary level" (Mostari 2004, 29). Another Arabization push began in 1989 and culminated in Law no. 91–05 of January 16, 1991, which required the use of Arabic in all official domains, including education. Article 4 imposed "Arabic as the unique language for all educational and administrative institutions" (Benrabah 2007a, 71). This law was intended to exclude the use of French, but it also threatened Berber groups, who had demonstrated in 1989 and did so again in 1991 (Leclerc 2010).

Current General school boycott in 1994. Berbers were pushing to include their language in public life. In 1995 the government set up a High Commission for Amazighité (Berber) identity (Leclerc 2010). In 2003, the government allowed Berber officially to be taught in schools. Also around that time, authorities began warming to introduction of French again, recognizing "ethnic and linguistic plurality as a resource for nation-building" (Benrabah 2007a, 30). Still, French and Tamazight are taught only as subjects.

Language(s) used: **Classical Arabic** (Tamazight, French as subjects)

* Benrabah (2007b, 194); Leclerc (2010).
** Benrabah (2007a, 48): 80–85%.

Angola

ILLED 1975	ILLED 1990	ILLED 2010	Percentage Speak Portuguese	Percentage Speak Umbundu
o	o	4	48*	50**

LANGUAGE POLICY

Colonial   Portuguese colonization. Teaching in Portuguese.

Independence   (1975) "At all levels of the system, the language of instruction was Portuguese" (Gorham and Duberg 1985, 271). Since 1975, many plans have been proposed to develop national languages for use in education. In 1977, the government created the National Language Institute to assist with the implementation of language policy (Roy-Campbell 2001b, 176).

Interim   The civil war made teaching in any language unproductive, and many schools were destroyed.

Current   Education Law of 2001 (Art 9) continues to prescribe Portuguese as the sole language of education in schools, though adults can receive education in national languages (Leclerc 2011). From 2005, the government began taking notice of six languages on an experimental basis with the goal of their possible future use in school: Kikongo, Kimbundu, Umbundu, Tchokwe, Ngangwela, and Kuanhama (Leclerc 2011). In 2008, Pearson Publishers, the Angolan Government, and Monteno Institute for Language and Literacy (South African NGO) undertook an initiative to introduce books in seven Angolan languages. The trial began in 120 classrooms and was to be evaluated in 2011, eventually to go nationwide up to grade 6 (Pearson 2008).

Language(s) used: **Portuguese, Umbundu (36%), Kimbundu (24%), Kikongo (6%), Cokwe (5%), Oshikwanyama (4%), Olunyaneka (3%), Ngangela (2%) ≈ 80%**

* Adegbija (1994, 11): more than 35%; Medeiros (2006): 60%. Avg. = 48%.
** Adegbija (1994, 11) 30% L1 + 20% L2 = 50%.

Benin

ILLED 1960	ILLED 1990	ILLED 2010	Percentage Speak French	Percentage Speak Fon-Ewe
o	o	3	8.8*	60**

LANGUAGE POLICY

Colonial   French colonization.

Independence (1960) French medium only.

Interim   During the Marxist revolution between 1975 and 1989, the Revolutionary Military Government decided to produce its own textbooks and national language materials, but implementation was problematic. Preschools used national languages during that time, but national languages have never been taught in primary schools (Leclerc 2010).

Current   The Cultural Charter of Benin (Law no. 91–006 of February 25, 1991) highlighted the promotion of national languages. But efforts to develop materials moved very slowly. In 2003, one school started a pilot program in Ditammari (Nelson 2004). A Ministry for Literacy and National Language Promotion was created in 2007. Meetings took place, but the project had difficulty getting off the ground. In 2010, Benin was included as one of eight countries for Project ELAN (see page 91).

Language(s) used: **French, Ditammari (2%), (others)**

* OIF (2007, 16).
** Adegbija (1994, 8).

Botswana

ILLED 1960	ILLED 1990	ILLED 2010	Percentage Speak English	Percentage Speak Setswana
6	7.2	6	38*	96**

LANGUAGE POLICY

Colonial   British colonization. Missions introduced literacy in the local languages in the early years and in English from the midprimary years (Nkosana 2008, 288). Education was relatively neglected by the colonial administration; it was provided by only four mission schools (Nyati-Ramahobo 2004, 38).

Independence (1966) From independence, there was some use of Setswana in the first three years, but lack of materials and the fact it was not subject to testing at the end of primary school meant that it was not taught well

(Molosiwa et al. 1991). But because of the "relatively low qualifications of teachers, and their inability to communicate in English, the use of Setswana was tolerated in lower grades" (Molosiwa et al. 1991, 43).

Interim   The First National Commission on Education (NCE) in 1977 recommended more and better materials, and the official policy was to teach in Setswana to grade 4 and then English thereafter (Lockhart 1985, 506).

Current   The National Commission on Education (1993) decided "in favour of the introduction of the use of English as the medium of instruction from Standard 1 by 2000." This was later amended to "English should be used as a medium of instruction from standard 2 by year 2002" (Basimolodi 2000, 145). "More resources continue to be directed towards the use of English in all social domains including education" (Nyati-Ramahobo 2004, 45).

Language(s) used: **English, Setswana (78%)**

---

* Nkosana (2008, 288): 35%; Graddol (1997, 11): 38%; Crystal (2003, 62): 40%. Avg. = 38%.
** Baker and Jones (1998, 355): 93%; Adegbija (1994, 11): 90% L1 + 9% L2 = 99%. Avg. = 96%.

Burkina Faso

ILLED 1960	ILLED 1990	ILLED 2010	Percentage Speak French	Percentage Speak Mooré
0	0	4.8	7.5*	50**

LANGUAGE POLICY

Colonial   French colonization.

Independence   (1960) French only.

Interim   The introduction of mother tongues in school was a major plank of the revolution (1979), but the initiatives stalled with the regime changes that followed.

Current   Two types of bilingual schools have been introduced since the early 1990s. First, Ecoles Bilingues, supported by Swiss NGO (Oeuvre Suisse d'Entraide Ouvriere – OSEO) and academics at the University of Ouagadougou, began using Mooré in two schools from 1994. In 2005, OSEO supported 88 schools, 212 classes, and 8,527 students in seven languages. These five-year schools target older children (older than nine) who have not enrolled in regular primary schools (Ouédraogo 2002: 14). Second, the Écoles Satellites are supported by the Ministry of Basic Education and UNICEF. Satellite schools are placed in areas that had no access to schooling; they are managed by communities, but teacher salaries are paid by the government (Alidou and Brock-Utne 2006, 119). In 2010, Burkina Faso was included as one of eight countries for Project ELAN (see page 91).

Language(s) used: **French, Mossi/Mooré (49%), Dioula (10%), Fulfulde (6%), Dagara (5%), Gulmanchema (5%), Bissa (3%), Kassem (1%), Lyélé (1%), Nuni (1%) ≈ 82%**

---

* Baker and Jones (1998, 356): 10%; OIF (2007, 17): 5%. Avg. = 7.5%.
** Baker and Jones (1998, 356): 50%; Adegbija (1994, 6): 50%.

Burundi

ILLED 1962	ILLED 1990	ILLED 2010	Percentage Speak French	Percentage Speak Kirundi
9	9	9	6*	99**

LANGUAGE POLICY

Colonial   German and Belgian colonization. The first schools were set up in 1909 by the Germans. Belgians established schools that taught in French and Kirundi.

Independence   (1962) Kirundi and French.

Interim   From 1973, the government introduced a program of "Kirundization and Ruralization." Instruction was to be given in Kirundi throughout primary. From the third year onward, French was taught as a subject (Ntawurishira 1985, 596). In 1989, French was introduced as a subject from the first year (Leclerc 2009).

Current   From the early 1990s, the school system has deteriorated, with many schools damaged or destroyed by the violence. In practice, Kirundi only serves as the language of instruction for the first four years, and French assumes that role in the final two years of primary (Halaoui 2003, 18–19). In 2010, Burundi was included as one of eight countries for Project ELAN (see page 91).

Language(s) used: **French, Kirundi (99%)**

---

* Leclerc (2009): 3–10%; OIF (2007, 17): 5%. Avg. = 6%.
** Baker and Jones (1998, 356).

Cameroon

ILLED 1960	ILLED 1990	ILLED 2010	Percentage Speak French	Percentage Speak Pidgin English
0	0	3	18*	46**

LANGUAGE POLICY

Colonial   German, French, British colonization.

Independence   (1960) English and French only.

Interim   In 1980, a mother tongue education experiment (PROPELCA) began as a joint project of linguists at the University of Yaounde and the SIL mission organization in a few private schools.

Current   The 1995 États Généraux marked beginning of government support for mother tongue education. Public schools were approved for participation in the PROPELCA experiment. The Education Orientation Law (Law no. 98/004) of April 14, 1998 declares that one of the objectives of education is the promotion of national languages (article 5.4) and promises to adapt to economic and sociocultural realities, including the teaching of national languages (article 11.1). A 2003 Ministry of Education planning document calls for use of local languages as media of instruction in public schools (Ministry of Education, 24). The number of schools in the experimental program has not grown since the early 2000s, as a result of a reduction in outside funding (Mba 2010). In 2010, Cameroon was included as one of eight countries for Project ELAN (see page 91).

Language(s) used: French, English, Fulfulde (9%), Ewondo (8%), Bulu (7%), Yemba (3%), Kom (2%), Mafa (2%), Fe'Fe'e (2%), Lamnso (2%), Meta' (1%), Makaa (1%), Bafut (1%), Gidar (1%), Dii (1%) Mofu Gudur (.6%), Mofu North (.4%), Oku (.4%) ≈ 40%

* OIF (2007, 17).
** Graddol (1997, 11) and Biloa and Echu (2008, 202): 46%; Crystal (2003, 52): 47%.

Cape Verde

ILLED 1975	ILLED 1990	ILLED 2010	Percentage Speak Portuguese	Percentage Speak Capverdian
o	o	o	*	98**

LANGUAGE POLICY

Colonial   Portuguese colonization. Use of Portuguese in the classroom (Coonan 2007, 31).

Independence   (1975) Portuguese only.

Interim   Portuguese medium. The dialectical differences in Capverdian Creole constitute the principal barrier to its officialization. Many people are afraid that the dialect of the largest island, Santiago, would dominate the others (Leclerc).

Current   Portuguese remains the language of instruction, but teachers can use Capverdian Creole for illustrations if there is a problem with comprehension (Leclerc 2011). When Manuel Viega, a linguist, was named minister of culture in 2005, new impetus was given to introducing Creole as a coofficial language with Portuguese, which would permit its introduction into education. But as of 2006, no change in the status of Creole had occurred (Coonan 2007, 130).

Language(s) used: **Portuguese**

* No reliable estimate available.
** Leclerc 2011.

Central African Republic

ILLED 1960	ILLED 1990	ILLED 2010	Percentage Speak French	Percentage Speak Sango
o	o	o	13*	90**

LANGUAGE POLICY

Colonial   French colonization.

Independence   (1960) French instruction. In 1962, all private schools were put under government control.

Interim   Since 1974, the state has attempted to introduce Sango (a Creole derived from Ngbandi) as a language of instruction in primary schools. A program was launched in 1975 – "collective promotion schools" – but it turned out to be a failure and was abandoned after two years (Leclerc 2009). French remained the language of instruction (McIntyre 1985, 658). The 1981 États Généraux on education was the basis for a 1984 law (Ordinance no. 84/031 of May 14, 1984), which stated in article 36: "Teaching is dispensed in French, the official language, and Sango, the national language" (Leclerc 2009).

Current But this ordinance has not been put into effect, and French remains the language of instruction (Leclerc 2009). Many teachers *use* Sango to explain things to students, but this is not according to official instructions. Sango is used widely by NGOs in nonformal education. As for languages other than Sango, policies have not addressed them (Leclerc 2009). Baker and Jones (1998) write that "since 1992, there has been an official policy of state bilingualism, encouraging the increasing use of Sango . . . in a variety of public spheres, including education" (357), but the current SIL director says that because of a loss of funding for language NGOs, there has been no real activity in multilingual education (Robbins 2011). A language specialist for local language organization, ACATBA, confirms that while many NGOs use Sango for adult literacy, it is not used in primary schools (Moehema 2011).

Language(s) used: **French**

---

* Leclerc (2009): 8%; OIF (2003, 16) 17.6%. Avg. = 13%.
** Baker and Jones (1998, 357): more than 90%.

Chad

ILLED 1960	ILLED 1990	ILLED 2010	Percentage Speak French	Percentage Speak Chadian Arabic
0	1.8	3	14*	55**

LANGUAGE POLICY

Colonial French colonization. French has been the language of instruction since 1900.

Independence (1960) French remained the language of instruction, but Classical Arabic was given special status as a subject.

Interim Since 1978, the government has required "obligatory bilingualism" in French and Classical Arabic (Leclerc 2010). GTZ and the Catholic Church have experimented with using three languages as medium in a few schools.

Current Starting in 2004, the government began a pilot project with five languages. The pilot project was supposed to expand to a full-scale program in 2008, but the World Bank (which was supporting most education sector reform) had ceased its funding the year before, and GTZ closed down its operations in Chad in 2008. There is still government support for the use of national languages, as evidenced by the still-existing Department for the Promotion of National Languages in the Ministry of Education (Maass 2011), and in 2010 the World Bank renewed its funding for Chad's Education Sector, which included a mother tongue component in curricular reform (World Bank 2003, 50).

Language(s) used: **French, Classical Arabic, Chadian Arabic (12%), Maba (4%), Sara (4%), Mundang (3%), Masana (2%) ≈ 25%**

---

* Leclerc (2010): 8.3%; Adegbija (1994, 6): 13%. OIF (2007, 17): 20%. Avg. = 14%.
** Adegbija (1994, 6): 13% L1 + 40% L2 = 53%; Baker and Jones (1998, 357): more than 50%; Leclerc (2010): 60%. Avg. = 55%.

Comoros

ILLED 1975	ILLED 1990	ILLED 2010	Percentage Speak French	Percentage Speak Comorien
0	0	0	7*	97**

LANGUAGE POLICY

Colonial	French colonization.
Independence	(1975) French only.
Interim	French only.
Current	In preschool and kindergarten teaching is in Comorien and French. Primary school is taught in French; secondary taught in French, with Arabic and sometimes English taught as second language (Leclerc 2009). Baker and Jones (1998: 357) report that teaching is in French.

Language(s) used: **French**

---

* OIF (2003, 16).
** Leclerc (2009).

Congo, Democratic Republic of the

ILLED 1960	ILLED 1990	ILLED 2010	Percentage Speak French	Percentage Speak Lingala
5.4	5.4	5.4	10[*]	69[**]

LANGUAGE POLICY

Colonial	Belgian colonization. Missionary and colonial schools used indigenous languages as media of instruction alongside French and Flemish/Dutch in primary. In 1958, French was made the exclusive medium in all government schools, but the many colonial-supported church or mission schools continued with the use of the vernaculars in the first three years (Bokamba 2007, 223).
Independence	(1960) French became the only language of instruction by presidential decree in 1962 (Leclerc 2009). Lingala, Swahili, Chiluba, and Kikongo were given the status of national languages and were to be taught as subjects in their regions of dominance (Bokamba 2007, 220). Implementation of the policy was sporadic, however, and the regional languages continued to be used as the medium for most subjects up to the fifth grade (Bokamba 2007, 223).
Interim	From 1972 (as part of the program of *authenticité*), the government reintroduced the four vehicular languages in primary school as media of instruction through the entire primary cycle, with French introduced as a foreign language in the third year.
Current	Currently, the four national languages are taught in the two first years of primary, and French is gradually introduced from the third year (Leclerc 2009). All secondary teaching is in French. Obviously, the war has disrupted normal school functions, and most schools lack supplies and are in disrepair. In 2010, the DRC was included as one of eight countries for Project ELAN (see page 91).
Language(s) used:	**French, Swahili (20% L2), Luba-Kasai (17%), Kikongo (5% + 12% Kituba, a Kikongo-derived creole), Lingala (4%) ≈ 40%**

[*] Leclerc (2009); OIF (2007, 17).
[**] Adegbija (1994, 7): 28% L1 + 41% L2 = 69%.

Congo, Republic of the

ILLED 1960	ILLED 1990	ILLED 2010	Percentage Speak French	Percentage Speak Kituba
o	o	o	30*	50**

LANGUAGE POLICY

Colonial   French colonization.

Independence   (1960) French only.

Interim   In 1977, a "People's School" reform project began with the backing of UNESCO, which emphasized the need to revalue national languages (Senga-Nsikazolo and Makonda 1985, 979). The language department began working on Lingala and Munukutuba (Kituba). In 1980, the Education Reorientation Law decreed that Lingala and Munukutuba were to be taught in schools. In fact, they were never used as media of instruction, but taught as subjects in certain schools. French remained the language of instruction (Renard and Peraya 1985, 10).

Current   French medium. In the mid-1990s, trends in language use showed that Lingala and Kituba (national languages) and French (official language) were increasing in use at the expense of the many mother tongues (Woods 1994, 34). The civil war actually increased the use of French, as various factions preferred to express themselves in a "neutral" language so as not to reveal their ethnic origin. After the war, Lingala gained popularity, without doubt because of the victory of Sassou-Nguesso, a Lingala speaker (Leclerc 2010). SIL director reports more interest in mother tongues each year (Robbins 2011).

Language(s) used: **French**

* OIF (2007, 17).
** Leclerc (2010).

Cote d'Ivoire

ILLED 1960	ILLED 1990	ILLED 2010	Percentage Speak French	Percentage Speak Dioula
0	0	3	29*	55**

LANGUAGE POLICY

Colonial   French colonization.

Independence   (1960) French only.

Interim   Since 1966, with the creation of the Institute of Applied Linguistics (ILA) there has been discussion of the use of national languages in education. A reform law (Law no. 77–584) of August 18, 1977 declared that "the introduction of national languages in official education should be considered a factor of national unity and of reclaiming our Ivorien cultural heritage" (Art. 67) and that the ILA "is charged with preparing for the introduction of national languages into teaching" (Art. 68) (Djité 2000, 30). But the introduction of these languages in schools depended on their codification, so French remained the language of instruction in the interim.

Current   Law no. 95–696 of September 7, 1995, Article 3, prescribed education in national languages, but rather vaguely. In 1996, an NGO (Savanne Développement) revived the idea of schooling in mother tongues and created an experimental school in Kolia, which opened for the 1996–97 school year. Preschool and first-year primary students learned through their mother tongue of Sénoufo or Malinke, followed by studies in French. In 2001, the government evaluated the Savanne Développement experiment and decided to extend it to ten other languages: Abidji, Agni, Attié, Baoulé, Bété, Guéré, Dan/Yacouba, Koulango, Mahou and Korhogo Sénoufo (N'Guessan 2001, 196). Coding is cautious, given the disruption of the war.

Language(s) used: **French, Baoulé (24%), Sénoufo (11%), Dan/Yacouba (9%), Agni (7%), Bété (6%), Guéré (4%), Attié (4%), Koulango (2%), Mahou (2%) Abidji (.6%), Malinke ≈ 70%**

---

* OIF (2003, 16): 22%; Adegbija (1994, 11) 35% L2. Avg. = 29%.

** Djité (2000, 24): 43% as of 1993; Adegbija (1994, 11): 16% L1 + 50% L2 = 66%. Avg. = 55%.

Djibouti

ILLED 1977	ILLED 1990	ILLED 2010	Percentage Speak French	Percentage Speak Somali
0	0	5	8*	53**

LANGUAGE POLICY

Colonial   French colonization. Primary education in public schools in French medium.

Independence   (1977) French medium.

Interim   French medium. French and (Classical) Arabic are coofficial languages.

Current   Law no. 96/AN of July 10, 2000, Article 5: "1) Education and training are given in official languages and national languages; 2) A decree by the Council of Ministers fixes the forms of teaching in French, in Arabic, in Afar and in Somali" (Leclerc 2009). The Ministry of Education reports that teaching in French and Arabic will be concomitant in all scholarly establishments, and that national languages will be progressively introduced (République du Sénégal, *Schema Directeur*, 31). There is a direction for national languages attached to the Prime Minister's Office, and the Ministry of Education is developing a strategy for the introduction of national languages in schools (Absieh 2005).

Language(s) used: **French, Classical Arabic, Somali (67%), Afar (23%) ≈ 90%**

* OIF (2003, 16).
** Leclerc (2009): 61%; Baker and Jones (1998, 357): 45%. Avg. = 53%.

Equatorial Guinea

ILLED 1968	ILLED 1990	ILLED 2010	Percentage Speak Spanish	Percentage Speak Fang
0	0	0	49*	80*

LANGUAGE POLICY

Colonial   Spanish colonization.

Independence   (1968) Spanish continued to be used for administration and schooling.

Interim   Equatorial Guinea asked to become a member of la Francophonie in 1989, and French was elevated to a "working language." In 1998, French became the country's "second official language" (Leclerc 2011).

Current	Spanish is the only medium in primary through secondary school (Leclerc 2011). French is the second compulsory language for secondary school students.

Language(s) used: **Spanish**

---

* Leclerc (2011): 20%; Lipski (1985, 3): 90% urban and 65% rural ≈ 77%. Avg. = 49%.
** Leclerc (2011).

Eritrea

ILLED 1993	ILLED 1990	ILLED 2010	Percentage Speak English	Percentage Speak Tigrina
10	N/A	10	2*	78**

LANGUAGE POLICY

Colonial	Occupied by Italy (1890–1941), then by the British (1941–1951). Annexed by Ethiopia in 1962. English-language schools early. Tigrina was also written and used publicly from early on. During the thirty years of conflict with Ethiopia, Eritrean languages were banned in public places. However, most Eritreans refused to speak Amharic and continued to teach their languages to their children. There was, however, significant population movement during the war, and people came into contact with Eritreans speaking different languages, with the result that there are few remaining monolingual regions in Eritrea (Leclerc 2010).
Independence	(1993) Multilingual
Interim	Multilingual
Current	Each Eritrean language (Tigrina, Tigré, Afar, Saho, Kunama, Bedawi, Bilen, Nara, Hijazi Arabic) is encouraged to be used and developed at the local level, and children receive their primary education in their mother tongue. Secondary is in Tigrina or English. In addition, each student is expected to learn one of the state languages, Tigrina or Arabic (Leclerc 2010). Literacy in English is reported fairly low among the general public (Asfaha 2009, 220). The government has blamed this on its weak English curriculum, and the ministry is currently revising the elementary curriculum so that "English lessons will be offered from the very start of elementary schooling (starting in grade 1 instead of grade 2)" (Asfaha 2009, 220).
Language(s) used:	**English, Classical Arabic, Tigrina (55%), Tigré (23%), Afar (6%), Saho (4%), Kunama (4%), Bedawi (3%), Bilen (2%), Nara (2%), Hijazi Arabic (.5%) ≈ 100%**

---

* Estimate from Asfaha (2013). A survey by Walter and Davis (2005, xxvi) among fifth grade school attendees found 15% had adequate competency in English.
** Leclerc (2010): 53% L1 + 25% L2 =78%.

Ethiopia

ILLED 1960	ILLED 1990	ILLED 2010	Percentage Speak English	Percentage Speak Amharic
4	4	9	2*	59**

LANGUAGE POLICY

Colonial No colonization (brief Italian occupation 1935–1941). Schooling introduced in 1908 in English (Heugh et al. 2007, 43). A few missionaries used mother tongues before European languages.

Independence Haile Selassie tried to unify the country by decreeing the use of Amharic only. From 1958, Amharic functioned as the medium of instruction for grades 1–6 of primary (Mekonnen 2009).

Interim After 1974, Haile Mariam Mengistu (with the influence of the Soviet Union) initiated a policy of nationalities aiming to remove Amharic from its privileged position. Education materials began to be prepared in at least four minority languages (Wagaw 1985, 1728). But there were either no written traditions in most of the languages or transcriptions only in Latin or Arabic script. Since the government wanted all to be in the Ethiopian syllabary, this was a major task (McNab 1990, 73). Until 1991, Amharic remained the language of instruction in primary schools (Heugh et al. 2007, 49).

Current Meles Zenawi introduced ethnic regionalism in order to reduce the cultural and linguistic hegemony of Amharic. The constitution of 1994 permits federal states to choose the language in which students will receive their primary education (Leclerc 2009). Current policy calls for eight years of mother tongue–based schooling. English is taught as a subject throughout primary and used as medium of instruction beginning in grade 9 (Benson 2010, 327). Amharic is to be taught as the lingua franca for communication across Ethiopia. Mekonnen (2005) reports that mother tongues are really only used exclusively in all regions in grades 1–6. In grades 7–8, mother tongues are only continued exclusively in Tigray, Amhara, and Oromiya, while English is used in the other seven regions (cited in Alidou and Brock-Utne 2006, 92).

Language(s) used: **English, Amharic (33%), Oromo (30%), Tigrina (6%), Somali (5%), Sidamo (4%), Gurage (4%), Hadiyya (2%), Afar (2%), Welaita (2%) Kambatta (1%), Kafa (1%), Silti (1%), Saho (.04%), Kunama ≈ 91%**

* Leclerc (2009).
** Leclerc (2009): 60%; Baker and Jones (1998): 28% L1 + 40% L2 =68%; Adegbija (1994, 7): 31% L1 + 40% L2 =71%; Benson (2010, 326): 27% L1 + 8% L2 =35%. Avg. ≈ 59%.

Gabon

ILLED 1960	ILLED 1990	ILLED 2010	Percentage Speak French	Percentage Speak Fang
0	0	3	80*	50**

LANGUAGE POLICY

Colonial	French colonization.
Independence	(1960) "After independence, Gabon did not encourage the use of local languages in education, but it did not forbid them either" (Leclerc 2009).
Interim	The government sponsored a linguistic atlas and descriptive projects of languages. At the beginning of the 1980s, there was renewed discussion of introducing languages into education. But French continued to be the sole medium in all schools (Leclerc 2009).
Current	The Raponda Walker Foundation created teaching manuals in local languages and has used them in several primary schools (Leclerc 2009). Since 1997, the minister of education has been convinced that "teaching in our languages is the only way to consolidate the relationship between the cultural identity and the national identity" (Leclerc 2009). The Department of National Languages was created in 1999 (Ndinga-Koumba-Binza 2007, 107). Since 2000, the minister of education has mandated a training section for mother tongue instruction in teacher training schools. It has also initiated a weekly radio program to "sensitize" the public about the value of Gabonese languages: "Our Languages, Our Culture." Language teaching remains experimental, and coding errs on the side of caution, since it is unclear how many of the languages are being used.

Language(s) used: **French, Fang (46%), Punu (11%), Njebi (9%), Myene (4%), Ikota (3%), Tsogo (2%), Mbama (1%), Vili (.3%) ≈ 76%**

* OIF (2007, 17).
** Adegbija (1994, 11): 30% L1 + 20% L2 =50%.

Gambia

ILLED 1965	ILLED 1990	ILLED 2010	Percentage Speak English	Percentage Speak Mandinka
0	0	0	3*	50**

LANGUAGE POLICY

Colonial   British colonization.

Independence   (1965) English medium.

Interim   Arabic is taught in both Koranic and public schools. Radio Gambia broadcasts news and cultural programs regularly in the main local languages (Baker and Jones 1998, 360).

Current   1988 Policy (for 1990): National languages will be the medium of instruction for grades 1 and 2 and taught as a subject from grade 3 (Ministry of Education, 17, para 4.20). It does not appear, however, that this was implemented. The constitution was suspended in 1994; the reinstated constitution declares (Art. 32) that people have the right to preserve their culture but states no specific language policy (Leclerc 2010). English is the only language used in school (Baker and Jones 1998, 360). In all sectors of education, English is the medium of instruction (Leclerc 2010).

Language(s) used: **English**

* Graddol (1997, 11); Crystal (2003, 64).
** Baker & Jones (1998, 360): 40%; Adegbija (1994, 6): 41% L1 + 19% L2 = 60%. Avg. = 50%.

Ghana

ILLED 1957	ILLED 1990	ILLED 2010	Percentage Speak English	Percentage Speak Akan
0	7.2	3.6	15*	>50**

LANGUAGE POLICY

Colonial   British colonization. The 1887 "Ordinance for the Promotion and Assistance of Education in the Gold Coast Colony" required the teaching of and in English. The 1925 Guggisberg Ordinance reversed this decree and called for the use of native languages as the medium of instruction in the first three years, after which they were replaced by English and taught as subjects (Andoh-Kumi 2002, 28).

Independence   (1957) The Nkrumah government made English the language of instruction from the first year of primary (Andoh-Kumi 2002, 28). In 1962, it chose nine languages that would be taught next to English.

Interim	The 1967 Education Review Committee (Kwapong) under the new military government reported that the English-only policy was not being followed, and in many localities, the local language was being used throughout the entire primary cycle. It recommended a return to the local language policy in Primary 1–3, with instruction in English starting from Primary 4 (Anyidoho and Knopp-Dakubu 2008, 148–149). Busia's Progress Party (1969–1972) maintained the local language policy, specifying that it should be continued for three additional years beyond the first three, if possible (Andoh-Kumi 2002, 29). Until 2001, the policy was that the Ghanaian language prevalent in the local area was to be used as medium of instruction in the first three years, with English as a subject. From the fourth year, English replaced the Ghanaian language as the medium (Andoh-Kumi 2002, 30).
Current	In 2002, the minister of education changed the policy to English only. A subsequent White Paper on Education made some allowances for the use of children's first languages in kindergarten and lower primary, though only where teachers and materials were available and the classroom language was uniform (Anyidoho and Knopp-Dakubu 2008, 150).
Language(s) used:	**English, Limited: Akan (Asante, Akuapem and Fante dialects = 42%), Ewe (11%), Dagbani (4%), Dangme (4%), Dagaare (4%), Ga (3%), Nzema (1%), Gonja (1%), Waale (.7%), Kasem (.6%) ≈ 72%**

* Graddol (1997, 11) and Crystal (2003, 62): 7%; Government Census (2000): 32%. Avg. = 15%.
** Baker and Jones (1998, 360): more than 50%; Adegbija (1994, 9): 40%; Anyidoho and Dakubu (2008, 152): more than 50%. Avg. > 50%.

Guinea

ILLED 1958	ILLED 1990	ILLED 2010	Percentage Speak French	Percentage Speak Malinke
o	o	5	5*	50**

LANGUAGE POLICY

Colonial	French colonization.
Independence	(1958). The government had decided to "adapt the structures of education to new national realities." Ten years after independence, Sékou Touré applied his policy of linguistic Africanization to schools (Leclerc 2009).
Interim	Between 1968 and 1984, the official policy was mother tongue education. After Touré's regime fell, French became the medium of education at all levels. National languages (Peul, Malinké, Soussou, Kissi, Kpelle, Toma), if they were taught at school, were subjects.

Current	New efforts to strengthen mother tongue education for primary and adult education. The Academy of Languages was renamed the Institute for Applied Linguistic Research. There is a Minister for Literacy and Promotion of National Language. Government supports revitalization of national languages in education (Leclerc 2009). There has been discussion of adapting a model from Mali in which three years of mother tongue is followed by transition to French (Yerende 2005).

Language(s) used: **French, Futa Jalon/Pular (38%), Malinke (36%), Susu (10%), Kpelle (5%), Kissi (4%), Loma (2%), Basari (.2%), Wamey (.1%) ≈ 95%**

---

* OIF (2003, 16).
** Adegbija (1994, 9): 30% L1 + 18% L2 = 48%.

Guinea-Bissau

ILLED 1974	ILLED 1990	ILLED 2010	Percentage Speak Portuguese	Percentage Speak Kiriol
0	3	0	9*	75**

LANGUAGE POLICY

Colonial	Portuguese colonization.
Independence	(1974) Portuguese medium.
Interim	In 1987, the Ministry of Education, with the assistance of Dutch Cooperation (SNV) and a Portuguese NGO (CIDAC), created experimental bilingual schools using Kiriol as the medium of instruction for the first two grades. By 1993, there were thirty experimental classes (Hovens 2002, 253). The experiment ran from 1985 to 1994, according to Benson (2010, 326), during which time "a Kiriol-Portuguese transitional bilingual model was successfully piloted by the research branch of the Ministry of Education in three remote parts of the country." But there was no subsequent reform of the Portuguese-only policy. The pilot program stopped when the funding ended (Benson 2004, 58).
Current	Portuguese only.

Language(s) used: **Portuguese**

---

* Benson (2010, 324): 8.5%; Leclerc (2009): 10%. Avg. = 9%.
** Benson (2010, 325): 50–60%; Leclerc (2009): 80%. Avg. = 75%.

Kenya

ILLED 1963	ILLED 1990	ILLED 2010	Percentage Speak English	Percentage Speak Swahili
0	7.2	6	15*	68**

LANGUAGE POLICY

Colonial British colonization. Missionary conference of 1909 agreed to use mother tongue in first three primary classes, Swahili in two middle primary classes, and English thereafter (Nabea 2009, 123). Teaching of English expanded just before independence (Bunyi 2001, 81; Nabea 2009, 125).

Independence (1963) The Education Commission Report (1964) stated: "The great majority of witnesses wished to see the universal use of the English language as the medium of instruction from Primary 1.... We see no case for assigning to [vernaculars] a role for which they are ill-adapted, namely the role of educational medium in the critical early years of schooling." Swahili is a compulsory subject in primary school. "Straight for English" from the first year of school was the New Primary Approach (Sifuna 1990, 164).

Interim The Gachathi Report (1976) reinstated the use of "catchment languages" in standards 1–3 (Mbaabu 1996, 147), though most of the recommendations were not followed (Nieuwenhuis 1996, 58). Because only a fraction of Kenya's languages were being used, "the primary school pupils end up using languages which are neither their mother tongues, nor the language of their immediate 'catchment areas'" (Mbaabu 1996, 149).

Current "The indigenous language of each region of Kenya is used as the instructional medium only in the first three years of primary school and only in linguistically homogeneous areas. In areas where there is considerable ethnic diversity, Swahili and English are used as instructional media in these first few years" (Bunyi 2001, 82). Bunyi (2007, 24) says that many teachers "rush into using English as the language of instruction right from Standard 1." Githiora (2008, 244) states that "over the years, the pressure to master English for economic advancement and Swahili for its academic value has undermined the vernaculars enough to make their teaching or use in the classroom virtually non-existent in very many cases."

Language(s) used: **English, Gikuyu (23%), Luo (14%), Kamba (13%), Luyia (8%), Kalenjin (7%), Swahili (1%) ≈ 65%**

---

* Bunyi (2007, 22): 15%; Nabea (2009, 122): "barely a quarter"; Graddol (1997, 11): 9%; Crystal (2003, 63): 8.8%. Avg. = 15%.

** Baker & Jones (1998, 361) nearly 70%; Pawlikova-Vilhanova (1996, 162): 60–70%. Adegbija (1994, 8): 5% L1 + 60% L2 = 65%; Bunyi (2007, 22): 75%. Avg. = 68%.

Lesotho

ILLED 1966	ILLED 1990	ILLED 2010	Percentage Speak English	Percentage Speak Sesotho
9	9	9	25*	98**

LANGUAGE POLICY

Colonial   British colonization.

Independence   (1966) Sesotho first, then English.

Interim   Primary education is conducted in Sesotho for the first four years and mainly in English thereafter (Maimbolwa-Sinyangwe 1985, 2999).

Current   Sesotho is language of instruction in primary 1–3; English is language of instruction in primary 4–7. "In reality, schools teach predominantly in Sesotho or switch between the two languages" (Moloi 2008, 617). English is the sole medium in secondary school, and Sesotho is a subject (Leclerc 2010). Sesotho is increasingly used in areas such as religion, politics, and broadcasting (Baker and Jones 1998, 361).

Language(s) used: **English, Sesotho (84%)**

* Graddol (1997, 11): 27%; Crystal (2003, 63): 23%. Avg. = 25%.
** Leclerc (2010): 97%; Adegbija (1994, 10): 95% L1 + 4% L2 = 99%. Avg. = 98%.

Liberia

ILLED 1960	ILLED 1990	ILLED 2010	Percentage Speak English	Percentage Speak Krio
0	0	0	20*	90**

LANGUAGE POLICY

Colonial   None.

Independence   (1847) The Lutheran Bible Society arrived in Liberia in 1969 and started the Liberia Language Institute, which is involved in literacy programs in Gola, Grebo, Kissi, Kpelle, Kra, Kru, Vai, and Vandi (Richmond 1983, 45).

Interim   The Government sponsored a National Language Program in the early 1980s, which intended to use local languages for adult education and to introduce the local languages before English in the primary schools (Richmond 1983, 43) [but] "at this writing [1983] English is the only language of instruction in the public schools" (43).

Current   With the civil war that began in 1990, there was not much done about education or languages. "The Liberian State has no apparent education policy regarding language. It does not forbid anything, but it does nothing" (Leclerc 2010). A program is under way to make use of all indigenous languages as media of instruction in early primary education (Baker and Jones 1998, 362).

Language(s) used: **English**

---

* Baker and Jones (198, 362).
** Adegbija (1994, 10): 40% L1 + 50% L2 = 90%.

Madagascar

ILLED 1960	ILLED 1990	ILLED 2010	Percentage Speak French	Percentage Speak Malagasy
o	9	9	15*	98**

LANGUAGE POLICY

Colonial — British and French colonization. Madagascar was colonized first by Britain, during which time Protestant missionaries taught in Malagasy (Johnson 2006, 685). When Madagascar was subsequently turned over to France, public schools were taught in French, though Malagasy remained in private schools.

Independence — (1960) The Malagasy Republic decided on official bilingualism of French and Malagasy. French remained the language of instruction, though Malagasy was progressively introduced as an optional subject in secondary schools (Johnson 2006, 686).

Interim — In 1975, the radical socialist regime undertook "malgasization" of the country, which included using only Malagasy in schools. Malagasy became the sole official language; there was relative isolation from French influence. The situation became explosive by 1985 and the government had to retract and allow French along with Malagasy.

Current — The Third Republic (after 1991) reintroduced French as language of instruction from the tenth class (year two of primary) (Wolhuter 2003, 32). In 2008, Madagascar decided that Malagasy would serve as the medium of instruction for grades 1–5, with French taught as a subject in the same years and gradually introduced as a medium in grades 6 and 7 (Brock-Utne and Skattum, citing Robenoro 2009, 27).

Language(s) used: **French, Malagasy (98%)**

---

* Leclerc (2011) 25%; OIF (2007, 17) 5%. Avg=15%.
** Baker & Jones (1998, 362).

Malawi

ILLED 1964	ILLED 1990	ILLED 2010	Percentage Speak English	Percentage Speak Chichewa
7.2	5.4	4.8	5*	70**

LANGUAGE POLICY

Colonial   British colonization.

Independence (1964) Several vernaculars were used initially in primary education. In 1968, the government made Chichewa (President Banda's own language) the national language and the only one to be used as medium in primary schools.

Interim   Chichewa remained the only language with official status, and it was used for instruction in standards 1–4 (with English as a subject). Standard 5 was a transitional year, in which instruction was given in both Chichewa and English, and after standard 5, all instruction was in English (Malewezi 1985, 3162).

Current   In 1996, the Ministry of Education directed that standards 1–4 should be taught through the vernaculars, with English the medium from standard 5 (Kayambazinthu 1998, 412). But since few teachers have been trained in other vernaculars, Chichewa and English remain the preferred medium of instruction in many schools (Pota 2001, 145; Kayambazinthu 1998, 412). Myra Harrison (in 2001) agrees: "It appears that the policy on language in education has not yet changed from that of the dictatorial era: Chichewa remains the medium of instruction in Grades 1 to 4, in government schools, even in areas where it is not spoken" (Samuel and Harrison 2001). Matiki (2011) reports that the initial momentum for the mother tongue policy was primarily due to the support of the external funding agency GTZ. Since this agency is no longer supporting the program, it has stalled. "Chichewa continues to be the only local language used as medium of instruction in primary school." Leclerc reports that though officially English is to begin in grade 5, in practice it often begins in grade 3, or even grade 2 for math (Leclerc 2011).

Language(s) used: **English, Chichewa/Nyanja (67%)**

* Graddol (1997, 11); Crystal (2003, 63).
** Matiki (2006, 241): 76.6%; Baker and Jones (1998, 362): 75%; Adegbija (1994, 7): 50% L1 + 10% L2 = 60%. Avg = 70%.

Mali

ILLED 1960	ILLED 1990	ILLED 2010	Percentage Speak French	Percentage Speak Bamanankan
0	3	6	7*	80**

LANGUAGE POLICY

Colonial French colonization. French used in schools and all official domains. A few missions used Malian languages, and Koranic schools used Arabic (Canvin 2007, 167).

Independence (1960) French medium, though discussion of mother tongue medium since 1962. Decree 85 PGIRM of May 26, 1967 standardized alphabets for four languages: Bambara (Bamanankan), Fulfulde, Songhay, Tamasheq.

Interim In 1978, the first four bilingual schools opened, using Bamanankan as the language of instruction. In 1982, the program was expanded to include Fulfulde, Songhay, and Tamasheq (Canvin 2007, 169). By the 1990s, there were only 104 schools involved. Many of them had regressed in the use of the mother tongue (Tréfault 2001, 235). They were phased out and replaced by a new experiment initiated by the Belgian research institute, CIAVER, in 1987: "pédagogie convergente" with one language, Bamanankan.

Current Decree 93–107/P-RM called for use of national languages in education, and from the 1994–95 school year it was supposed to be generalized to six languages. The "generalization" has reached more than 300 schools (Leclerc 2010). In 1996, Law no. 96–049 of August 23 recognized thirteen languages as national languages (Fomba and Weva 2003, 5). The languages added each year to the program were (1994–95) – Fulfulde and Songhay; (1995–96) – Soninke, Tamasheq, and Dogon; (1998–99) – Sénoufo and Bobo; (2000–01) – Mamara and Bozo; (2001–02) – Khassonke (Fomba and Weva 2003, 10). By 2005–2006, bilingual education had reached 31.6% of schools in the country (Skattum 2008, 117). Mali is one of the participants in Project ELAN (see page 91).

Language(s) used: **French, Bamanankan (31%), Soninke (9%), Fulfulde (8%), Sénoufo Mamara (7%), Dogon (5%), Tamasheq (3%), Bozo (3%), Sénoufo (3%), Songhay (2%), Khassonke (1.5%), Bobo (.2%) ≈ 73%**

* Baker and Jones (1998, 363): 5%; Skattum (2008, 98): 5–10%; OIF (2007, 17): 8.2%. Avg. = 7%.
** Canvin (2007, 158); Skattum (2008, 99).

Mauritania

ILLED 1960	ILLED 1990	ILLED 2010	Percentage Speak French	Percentage Speak Hassaniya Arabic
1.8	3	1.8	5.4*	85**

LANGUAGE POLICY

Colonial   French colonization. French medium until 1959. The education reform of 1959 allowed the use of French and Arabic as media of instruction in all schools. This was Classical Arabic, rather than Hassaniya Arabic (Leclerc 2010).

Independence   (1960) French and Classical Arabic medium.

Interim   Reforms of 1967, 1973, and 1978 reinforced the promotion of Arabic. In October 1979, a law was put into place to try to assure cultural independence from France; calling for Arabic as a language of unity for all Mauritanians; officialization of all national languages; transcription of Pulaar, Soninke, and Wolof into Latin script; creation of an Institute of National Languages; and teaching in national languages (Diallo 2000). The idea of replacing French completely with Arabic drew vigorous protest from French-speaking Mauritanians and was abandoned (Handloff 1988). Education could therefore be either in Arabic or bilingual French/Arabic. In 1982–83 the first experimental schools in Pulaar, Soninke, and Wolof began in five regions, with national languages used as the medium for all subjects for the entire primary cycle and Arabic as a subject. This experiment ended in 1988, replaced by a new method, which restricted mother tongue teaching to only the first two years with French or Arabic introduced in third year (Diallo 2000).

Current   The constitution of 1991 eliminated the official status of French. A World Bank document in 2001 reported that "while French is widely used in society and essential for highly qualified jobs, it is taught effectively only to the 5.5% of students in primary education who enroll in the bilingual stream. The rest of the students enroll either in the Arabic stream (94%) or in the local language stream (.5%), which impart poor French skills" (World Bank 2001, 3). The government in 1999 approved an education sector reform that combines the existing three education streams "into one unified stream where Arabic and French are the main languages of instruction" (World Bank 2001, 4). Diallo reports that this ended the mother tongue experiment, though Bougroum disagrees: "While official documents make no mention of the use of local languages in literacy programs ... in practice, local languages such as Wolof, Pulaar, Soninke and Hassaniya are used in literacy programmes, particularly in the South of the country" (2007, 16–17). Leclerc confirms that a few dozen local language classes continue, but coding cautiously reflects only Arabic and French medium.

Language(s) used: **French, Classical Arabic [possibly Hassaniya Arabic (92%), Pulaar (6%), Soninke (1%), Wolof (.4%)]**

---

* OIF (2007, 16).
** Baker and Jones (1998, 363) and Leclerc (2010): 80%; Adegbija (1994, 10): 87%; (Lewis 2009): 92%; Avg. = 85%.

Mauritius

ILLED 1966	ILLED 1990	ILLED 2010	Percentage Speak English	Percentage Speak Creole
0	0	0	15*	70**

LANGUAGE POLICY

Colonial   French colonization 1715–1810 – limited development of Catholic mission schools; British colonization 1810–1966 – some Protestant mission schools, but "the Catholic ethos remained dominant" (Johnson 2006, 688). The Education Ordinance of 1957 authorized the use of any appropriate language of instruction in standards 1–3. In standards 4–6, the medium of instruction was to be English (Sonck 2005, 40).

Independence   (1966) The country kept the 1957 ordinance. "Since English becomes the language of instruction as from the fourth year, however, sheer pragmatism dictates that it be introduced as early as possible" (Hookoomsing 2000, 118). Rajah-Carrim (2007, 54) reports that English was the official medium of instruction from the first year of primary school.

Interim   English is the language of government and education. The use of English from the start of primary was blamed for high failure rates in primary school. Many teachers use French instead of English in the classroom (Rajah-Carrim 2007, 54). "A large part of the population has some knowledge of French. . . . French is also the main language of the media" (Sonck 2005, 38).

Current   In 1998, the minister of education declared that young schoolchildren should be taught in their mother tongue, but little changed because of people's reluctance (Sonck 2005, 41). All children learn through a mixture of English and French at school (Sonck 2005, 42), but all school books are in English (Sonck 2005, 41).

Language(s) used: **English**

---

* Graddol (1997, 11); Crystal (2003, 63) [**French:** Baker and Jones (1998, 363): less than 10%; OIF (2007, 17): 15%. Avg. = 12.5%].
** Rajah-Carrim (2007, 51).

Mozambique

ILLED 1975	ILLED 1990	ILLED 2010	Percentage Speak Portuguese	Percentage Speak Makhuwa
0	0	5	42*	30**

LANGUAGE POLICY

Colonial Prior to independence, indigenous Mozambicans were only offered education in the first three years. If they wanted further study, students had to go to Tanzania (Stege 1985, 3438). "Metropolitan Portuguese" was the language of instruction.

Independence (1975) "Mozambican Portuguese" became the language of instruction. FRELIMO used a reinvented Portuguese, presented as "better" than the metropolitan version, as a national linguistic symbol (Stroud 1999, 350). "But never did Mozambican elites think for an instant to use African languages at school" (Leclerc 2011).

Interim During the civil war (1980–1992), opposition RENAMO advocated the use of indigenous languages, instead of Portuguese. Portuguese was reconstituted as an urban language, identified explicitly with the party in power, FRELIMO. RENAMO enforced the use of national languages in the zones it controlled (Stroud 1999, 360).

Current African "languages are still associated with authenticity and traditional values." Bilingual experiments known as PEBIMO ran from 1993 to 1997 with World Bank and UN sponsorship. They used two languages (Changana and Nyanja) to transition to Portuguese. "Following the experiment, 16 Mozambican languages were developed in preparation for their use in bilingual schooling.... A few months into the 2003 school year, ten of these languages have been introduced in individual classrooms spread throughout the provinces" (Benson 2004, 51–52). The transitional bilingual primary schooling is now offered in seventeen languages in 75 schools (out of 8,000) (Benson 2010, 328).

Language(s) used: **Portuguese, Makhuwa (16%+), Changana/Tsonga (9%), Ndawu (8%), Lomwe (8%), Sena (7%), Tshwa (6%), Chuwabu (5%), Ronga (4%), Chopi (4%), Nyanja (3%), Yao (3%), Nyungwe (2%), Makonde (2%), Tonga (2%), Tewe (1.5%), Mwani (.5%), ≈ 90%**

* Benson (2010, 238): 6% L1 + 27% L2 = 33%; Government Census (2007): 50%; Avg. = 42%.
** All Makhuwa varieties in *Ethnologue* (Lewis 2009) ≈ 30%. May be higher.

Namibia

ILLED 1990	ILLED 1990	ILLED 2010	Percentage Speak English	Percentage Speak Ndonga
9	9	6	17.5*	>50**

LANGUAGE POLICY

Colonial   German, British, South African colonization. Most children educated in their mother tongue for the first three to four years. After that, the few who had the opportunity to continue schooling switched to Afrikaans medium (Roy-Campbell 2001, 173).

Independence   (1990) The ten Namibian languages were made media of instruction for functional literacy and lower primary school, and eight of them were taught as subjects up to grade 10 (Brock-Utne 2001, 244).

Interim   A 1993 pamphlet by the Ministry of Education and Culture, *The Language Policy for Schools*, interpreted the policy as follows: "Grades 1–3 will be taught either through the Home Language, a local language, or English," opening the possibility of using English only from grade 1. "There are also those in the Ministry of Education who believe that the policy is actually promoting 'English only' and not the Namibian tongues" (Brock-Utne 2001, 309).

Current   Research conducted in 1995 in three regions showed that Afrikaans was the medium of instruction in most schools, even though most students were Khoekhoe speakers, and English is rapidly taking over from other remaining Khoekhoe schools as a medium of instruction (Brock-Utne 1997, 246). Another survey in 2000 showed that English was being used almost exclusively in the Windhoek region, which was likely indicative of other schools (Swarts 2001, 41–43). Many teachers are using the "loophole" that allows English as a medium (Swarts 2001, 46). The status of the African languages has notably diminished since independence (Leclerc 2010).

Language(s) used: **English, Ndonga/Oshivambo (43%), Nama (11%), Herero (11%), Afrikaans (5%), Tswana (1%), Few (.5%), others [13 total] ≈ 95%**

* Graddol (1997, 11): 18%; Crystal (2003, 63): 17%.
** Baker and Jones (1998, 364).

Niger

ILLED 1960	ILLED 1990	ILLED 2010	Percentage Speak French	Percentage Speak Hausa
0	4	5	4.5*	75**

LANGUAGE POLICY

Colonial   French colonization.

Independence   (1960) French only.

Interim   Systematic bilingual experimentation began in 1973 with five different mother tongues used in the first three grades and transition to French in grade 4 (Alidou et al. 2006, 52).

Current   By 1998, there were forty-two experimental schools, assisted by GTZ and USAID, using the five main languages (Hovens 2002, 253). The 1998 Law of Orientation states that the languages of instruction are French and national languages (Leclerc 2010). Niger recently decided to promote all of its eight national languages as media of instruction during the first years of school (Brock-Utne 2001, 128). Alidou and Brock-Utne (2006, 52) criticize the policy for remaining in its "'experimental' ghetto." French remains the language of instruction from the fourth year of primary and throughout secondary (Leclerc 2010). Niger is included in Project ELAN (see page 91).

Language(s) used: **French, Classical Arabic, Hausa (52%), Zarma (22%), Fulfulde (10%), Tamasheq (9%), Manga Kanuri (4%), Gourmanchéma (.4%) ≈ 98%**

---

* OIF (2007, 17) [counts both Francophones and partial Francophones; I took the midpoint]: 4.5%.
** Adegbija (1994, 6): 46% L1 + 24% L2 = 70%; Lewis (2009): 55% L1 + 25% L2 = 80%. Avg. = 75%.

Nigeria

ILLED 1960	ILLED 1990	ILLED 2010	Percentage Speak English	Percentage Speak Hausa
9	9	9	20*	50**

LANGUAGE POLICY

Colonial   British colonization. Initially English language education, but after 1926 encouraged vernacular in the first primary years, particularly Igbo, followed by Hausa, Yoruba, and Efik (Adegbija 1994, 217).

Independence   (1960) Vernacular medium in first years.

Interim	The 1977 Education Policy: "Government will see to it that the medium of instruction in the primary school is initially the mother tongue or the language of the immediate community and, at a later stage, English (Section 3:15 (4))," cited in Akinnaso 1993, 261). All students are supposed to learn one of the major Nigerian languages (Igbo, Hausa, Yoruba) as a subject up to the secondary school level. The policy of using the mother tongue for the first three years "actually happened only sporadically, and more so in Yoruba, Hausa, and Igbo areas" (Simpson and Oyètádé 2008, 188).
Current	The government recognizes twenty-seven minority local languages in education. It is typically the language of the immediate community, and not necessarily the mother tongue, that is taught. And in rural areas, local languages are often used for both lower and upper primary, while in urban areas, English is often the sole medium (Akinnaso 1993, 263). A survey conducted in 2000 revealed that in one particular minority area, 64% of primary school teachers used English in their teaching, and the remaining 36% used a combination of English and Nigerian languages, usually Yoruba, Hausa, and Igbo, rather than the immediate local language (cited in Simpson and Oyètádé 2008, 188). Adegbija reports difficulty implementing the mother tongue policy in urban areas (2007, 210) and a general shift away from the indigenous languages to English among both youth and adults (248). "Hausa, English, and Nigerian Pidgin are coming to dominate communication in informal domains where mother tongues are expected to be used, posing a serious threat to the continued transmission of many minority languages" (Simpson and Oyètádé 2008, 191). Cautious coding; the 2010 ILLED should probably be lower.

Language(s) used: **English, Hausa (18%), Yoruba (17%), Igbo (14%), [27 others] ≈ 85%**

---

* Baker and Jones (1998, 365): 20–30%; Adegbija (2007, 204): less than 20%. Avg. ≈ 20% [Crystal (2003, 52, 64): 47% including Pidgin English].
** Adegbija (1994, 11): 30% L1 + 20% L2 = 50%.

Rwanda

ILLED 1962	ILLED 1990	ILLED 2010	Percentage Speak French	Percentage Speak Kinyarwanda
9	9	9	12*	98**

LANGUAGE POLICY

Colonial	German and Belgian colonization.
Independence	(1962). French and Kinyarwanda medium.
Interim	Law no. 14/1985 of June 19, 1985, states that the first cycle of primary is dedicated to learning math, reading, and writing, all in Kinyarwanda (Article 42; cited in Leclerc 2010).
Current	Because of France's questionable role in the Rwandan genocide of 1994, and because of the influx of refugees returning from Anglophone countries, the government decided to include English as an official language along with French and Kinyarwanda. The 1996 and 2003 constitutions include all three as official languages (Leclerc 2010). Children are supposed to begin school in all three languages, and from the fourth year onward, English and French are to be the languages of instruction (Calvet 2001, 157).

Language(s) used: **French, English, Kinyarwanda (98%)**

* Leclerc (2010): 15–20%; OIF (2007, 17): 7%. Avg. = 12%.
** Leclerc (2010); Adegbija (1994, 8): 90% L1 + 8% L2 = 98%.

Sao Tome and Principe

ILLED 1975	ILLED 1990	ILLED 2010	Percentage Speak Portuguese	Percentage Speak Creole
0	0	0	*	89**

LANGUAGE POLICY

Colonial	Portuguese colonization. Portuguese medium.
Independence	(1975) Portuguese medium.
Interim	Portuguese medium.
Current	Portuguese medium. There is no place for teaching of local languages, whether Creole or Fang (Creole is not standardized, and Fang is considered a foreign language) (Leclerc 2011).

Language(s) used: **Portuguese**

* No estimate available.
** Leclerc (2010) Santoméen Creole – 85%, Principense Creole – 4%.

Senegal

ILLED 1960	ILLED 1990	ILLED 2010	Percentage Speak French	Percentage Speak Wolof
0	0	5	14*	87**

LANGUAGE POLICY

Colonial   French colonization.

Independence   (1960) French medium.

Interim   A 1971 presidential decree (no. 71566 of May 21, 1971) elevated six languages to the rank of "national languages": Wolof, Peul, Serer, Diola, Malinke, Soninke. An experiment in teaching of national languages (primarily Wolof, with one token Serer class) began in 1979. By 1981, classes had all ended.

Current   Law no. 91–22 of February 16, 1991, defining the goals of education mentions national languages vaguely: Article 6, 1: "National education is Senegalese and African: developing the teaching of national languages, privileged instruments for giving learners a living contact with their culture and rooting them in their history, it will form a Senegalese conscious of his heritage and his identity" (Leclerc 2010). An office for national languages was created in the Ministry of Education in 1999. In 2002, experiments began in 155 schools using six languages. In 2004, there were 300 schools, using six languages. Senegal is included in Project ELAN (see page 91).

Language(s) used: **French, Wolof (38%), Pulaar (27%), Serer (10%), Malinke (4%), Diola (4%), Soninke (2%) ≈ 86%**

* Leclerc (2010) 15–20%; OIF (2007, 17) 10%. Avg. = 14%.
** McLaughlin (2008, 85): close to 90%; Adegbija (1994, 9): 42% L1 + 40% L1 = 82%; Leclerc (2010): 90%. Avg. = 87%.

Seychelles

ILLED 1976	ILLED 1990	ILLED 2010	Percentage Speak English	Percentage Speak Seselwa
0	9	9	27.5*	95**

LANGUAGE POLICY

Colonial   Alternately occupied by French and British until 1810, after which Britain gained definitive possession, though Seychelles was ruled as a dependency of the Island of Mauritius, and French and Creole were allowed to be used in school and administration. From 1844 onward, teaching could be in either French or English. Until 1944 teachers usually used French or Creole in schools. In 1944, however, English became the sole language of teaching, and French was taught only as a subject.

Independence	(1976) English medium.
Interim	In 1981, Creole, which was henceforth named Seselwa, became the first national language, English the second, and French the third (Leclerc 2010). This gave official status to the teaching of Seselwa in schools alongside English and French.
Current	Seselwa is medium of instruction in the first years of primary school, with English and French as subjects. Shift from Seselwa to English as medium in last years of primary school (Rajah-Carrim 2007, 55). English becomes language of instruction in fourth year of primary and French is introduced as a subject (Sonck 2005, 47).

Language(s) used: **English, Seselwa (95%)**

* Graddol (1997, 11): 14%; Crystal (2003, 64): 41%. Avg=27.5% [**French:** OIF (2007, 17): 5%].
** Leclerc (2010).

Sierra Leone

ILLED 1961	ILLED 1990	ILLED 2010	Percentage Speak English	Percentage Speak Krio
3.6	4.8	4.8	15*	95**

LANGUAGE POLICY

Colonial	British colonization. Mende and Temne were privileged; these languages, along with Krio, were developed as languages for transitional literacy (Francis and Kamanda 2001, 233).
Independence	(1961) Sierra Leone did not have a stated language policy in 1964 (Armstrong 1968, 232). The official position between 1961 and 1978 was to continue to use English as far as possible. It was the sole medium of instruction in upper primary. Local languages Mende, Themne and Krio were unofficially used as media of instruction during early primary years (Francis and Kamanda 2001, 236–237).
Interim	In 1979, a pilot project began, using Mende, Temne, and Limba in thirty-six schools (Fyle 1994, 52). In the 1980s, the four major languages were officially infused into the primary school system as instructional media on an experimental basis (Sengova 1987, 522). Krio was added in 1984. As of the early 1990s, the pilot program had not received much support and the program had not progressed beyond the pilot stage because of lack of financing (Fyle 1994, 52).
Current	Because of its civil war from 1991 to 2002, the country's language policy has been primarily "nonintervention" (Leclerc 2009). The 1996 Basic Education Program for Primary and Secondary Education

stipulated that community languages were to be used for teaching classes 1–3 in primary school (Banya 1997, 488). The 2004 Education Act is not clear on whether these languages are subjects or media in primary school: Part II, Paragraph 2 (2) e: the system shall be designed to "introduce into the curriculum new subjects such as indigenous languages and Sierra Leone Studies which shall give and enhance a proper and positive understanding of Sierra Leone" (Government of Sierra Leone). Nishimuko implies languages are subjects (2009, 285). Leclerc says that most instruction is in English, and though languages *can* be taught, few teachers are able to do so and there are really no available manuals (Leclerc 2009).

Language(s) used: **English, Mende (28%), Temne (23%), Krio (12%), Limba (8.5%)** ≈ 70%

---

* Leclerc (2009).
** Leclerc (2009); Oyètádé and Luke (2008, 122).

Somalia

ILLED 1960	ILLED 1990	ILLED 2010	Percentage Speak English	Percentage Speak Somali
1.8	9	6	*	97**

LANGUAGE POLICY

Colonial Italian and British colonization. Elementary schools in the North used Arabic as the initial medium, introducing English in the second year; in the South, Arabic was used for the first two years, with Italian used for instruction after the second year (Cassanelli and Abdikadir 2007, 97).

Independence (1960) After independence, it was decided that English should eventually replace Italian as the medium of instruction in the third year (Cassanelli and Abdikadir 2007, 97). In 1965, the ministry decided that Arabic was an appropriate medium for all four early elementary years, and English would be used at intermediate and secondary levels (Cassanelli and Abdikadir 2007, 97).

Interim The military regime that seized power in 1969 succeeded in establishing an official (Latin) script for Somali (Warsame 2001, 347) and introduced the language into the school system in 1972 (Maimbolwa-Sinyange 1985, 4711). By 1977, "135 textbooks in the Somali language had been produced and were being used through the first year of secondary school classes, with the intention of gradually phasing out English as the medium of instruction" (Cassanelli and Abdikadir 2007, 100).

Current   No central authority has been handling education since the early
                       1990s. In Somaliland, which proclaimed independence, the
                       government has reinforced English to the detriment of Somali
                       (Leclerc 2010). In the rest of the country, the medium of instruction at
                       the primary level may be Arabic, Somali, or English. Arabic-medium
                       schools have found greater favor among parents and students
                       (Cassanelli and Abdikadir 2007, 107–108).

Language(s) used: **Arabic, Somali, English**

---

* No estimate available.
** Adegbija (1994, 6): 95% L1 + 2% L2 = 97%.

South Africa

ILLED 1960	ILLED 1990	ILLED 2010	Percentage Speak English	Percentage Speak Zulu
10	7.5	6	35.5*	56**

LANGUAGE POLICY

Colonial   Dutch and British colonization. "State education provided to 'white'
                     and some 'coloured' children was based on mother-tongue education
                     [English or Dutch/Afrikaans] for primary school and usually a switch
                     to English for Dutch/Afrikaans-speakers in secondary school during
                     the 19th century. Missionaries offered limited education for African
                     pupils and generally used mother tongue for four to six years
                     followed by English medium" (Heugh 2007, 198). Increased
                     Anglicization to 1910; dominance of English in all spheres.
                     (Kamwangamalu 2004, 202).

Independence   (1910) English and/or Dutch-Afrikaans medium. Between 1953 and
                     1979, South Africa practiced "Bantu Education," during which time
                     "the mother tongue was phased in and maintained for 8 years as the
                     primary language of learning." Strict implementation of Afrikaans
                     for half of the subjects in secondary school led to the Soweto student
                     uprising in 1976. The students wanted the option of learning English
                     instead (Brock-Utne 2001, 127).

Interim   In 1979, the Education and Training Act was passed, reducing the
                     mother tongue to four years of primary school, then allowing
                     students to choose between Afrikaans or English medium (Heugh,
                     2007, 199). Most schools opted for English (Brock-Utne 2001, 127;
                     Heugh 2008, 359–360).

Current   The 1997 constitution recognized eleven official languages, and
                     Article 29 (2) gives everyone the right to basic education in the official
                     language or languages of his choice where reasonably practicable.
                     Schools are allowed to choose their medium. Government documents

show that: 11% chose Afrikaans (mother tongue of 11.3% of school population); 51% chose English (mother tongue of 5.7% of school population); 37% chose a Bantu language (mother tongue of 83% of school population) (Webb 1999, 58, citing South African Department of Education Statistics from 1997). The revised National Curriculum Statement (2002) reduces use of the mother tongue to the end of grade 3, rather than grade 4 (Heugh 2007, 208).

Language(s) used: **English (9%), Zulu (23%), Xhosa (18%), Afrikaans (11%), Southern Sotho (10%), Sepedi [Northern Sotho] (9.5%), Tswana (8%), Tsonga (4.5%), Swati (3%), Venda (2%), Ndebele (2%) ≈ 100%**

---

* Heugh (2007, 192): up to 12% L1. Graddol (1997, 11): 25% L2; Crystal (2003, 64): L1 + L2 = 34%. Avg. = 35.5%.
** Heugh (2007, 192): no obvious lingua franca. Lewis (2009): 23% L1 + 33% L2 = 56%.

Sudan (Prior to division)

ILLED 1956	ILLED 1990	ILLED 2010	Percentage Speak English	Percentage Speak Sudanese Arabic
1.5	2	4	*	60**

LANGUAGE POLICY

Colonial British colonization. In the South, the British left education to the Christian missions. English was the official language, but six local languages were used (Bari, Dinka, Nuer, Shiluk, Luo, and Azande) (Siddiek 2010, 77). In the North, Arabic was the medium in primary school, with English as a subject.

Independence (1956) After 1965, Arabic progressively replaced English, even in higher education (Leclerc 2011).

Interim Between 1972 and 1983, there was some devolution of power to the South. In Southern schools, the policy was one of bilingualism in local languages and English. In the North, it was mother tongue and Arabic, though in urban areas, it was monolingual Arabic. But after this brief respite, local languages were again subsumed under forced Arabization (Leclerc 2011)

Current The 1998 constitution (Article 3) makes Classical Arabic the official language of the state but permits the development of local and international languages. "When schools function, children in the two first years receive instruction in their local mother tongue. After this, Arabic or English become the language of instruction" (Leclerc 2011). But many schools in the South have not functioned, and local languages regressed. During the war (1983–2005) "schools became dependent on teachers trained in East Africa, and using East African syllabuses, and though Arabic was typically taught as a subject, the vernacular languages tended to disappear from the syllabus" (James 2008, 72). When the North/South War ended in 2005, the South received some autonomy, and the new constitution of the Comprehensive Peace Agreement (CPA) promised to respect, develop, and promote national languages (Article 2.8.5), allowing any language as a medium of instruction in schools at lower levels (cited in James 2008, 65). Coding of 4 for 2010 reflects this policy. However, after 2011, when South Sudan became independent, it chose to use English as the sole medium of instruction, while the north continues to use Arabic and English only.

Language(s) used: **Classical Arabic, English [Dinka (8%), Nuer (4%), Bari (2%), Zande (2%), Shilluk (1%), Luo (.5%) ≈ 18%]**

---

* No estimate available.
** Adegbija (1994, 9) 50% L1 + 10% L2 = 60%; Leclerc (2011): 50–70%.

Swaziland

ILLED 1968	ILLED 1990	ILLED 2010	Percentage Speak English	Percentage Speak Swati
0	9	7.5	4*	90**

LANGUAGE POLICY

Colonial   British colonization. Zulu was used as medium early on, since missionaries were Zulu speaking. In the lead-up to independence, English was the primary medium of instruction.

Independence   (1968) English medium. Swati did not have a written form.

Interim   In 1978, Swati was introduced as a medium during first four years with English as a subject and then English medium thereafter (MacMillan 1989, 303).

Current   Official policy is Swati medium during first four years with English as a subject and then English medium thereafter. But this is not well implemented. A Norwegian student doing field research in 1997 in Swaziland "was struck by the fact that she found English to be the dominant language in every school setting" (Brock-Utne 2001, 126). The permanent secretary at the Ministry of Education (in interview with Brock-Utne) admitted that "he was aware of the fact that a good number of schools, especially in the towns and cities, now started with English as the language of instruction in the first grade" (Brock-Utne 2001, 125).

Language(s) used: **English, Swati (89%)**

---

* Graddol (1997, 11).
** Baker and Jones (1998, 367); Adegbija (1994, 11).

Tanzania

ILLED 1964	ILLED 1990	ILLED 2010	Percentage Speak English	Percentage Speak Swahili
4.5	6	6	8*	93**

LANGUAGE POLICY

Colonial	German and British colonization. There were English schools, Asian schools, and African schools. In African schools, Swahili was the medium in grades 1–5, English was a subject from grade 3, and English was the medium from grade 6 (Roy-Campbell 2001a).
Independence	(1964) End of Asian schools. In African schools, Swahili was medium of instruction in standards 1–5; English medium in standards 7 and 8 (Roy-Campbell 2001b, 69).
Interim	A 1967 Education Circular stated that beginning in 1968, Swahili would be the medium of education through all of primary school (not just grades 1–5). This was to take full effect by 1972–1974. English would be taught as a subject in all grades (Roy Campbell 2001b, 73).
Current	Private primary schools, using English-language medium, are a recent phenomenon in Tanzania (Yahya-Othman 2000, 73). English proficiency is deteriorating, and the government is reluctant to allow the use of Swahili as the medium of instruction past the primary level (Roy-Campbell 2001a, 275). Demand for English as language of instruction at all levels is increasing (Mohamed, 106 [citing Brock-Utne 2005]). Leclerc notes that the school law of Tanzania (2007) does not contain any mention of language.

Language(s) used: **Swahili (1%)**

* Leclerc (2010): 4.5%; Graddol (1997, 11): 10%; Crystal (2003, 64): 11%. Avg. = 8%.
** Leclerc (2010): 95%; Adegbija (1994, 7):.6% L1 + 90% L2 = 90.6%. Avg. = 93%.

Togo

ILLED 1960	ILLED 1990	ILLED 2010	Percentage Speak French	Percentage Speak Ewe
0	0	0	31.5*	55**

LANGUAGE POLICY

Colonial   German and French colonization. Mission schools under German administration privileged indigenous languages. But with French trusteeship after 1919, French became the official language and sole language of instruction (Leclerc 2010).

Independence   (1960) French medium. President Olympio made French and Ewe national languages.

Interim   President Eyadema (Kabiye speaker) launched a program of "return to authenticity." In 1978, Ewe and Kabiye appeared in schools as subjects (Leclerc 2010), while some smaller languages – Tem, Ben, and Ncem – received some support for development (Sonko-Godwin 1985, 5277).

Current   Ewe and Kabiye are used in nursery schools along with French. In primary school, teaching is in French, with Ewe and Kabiye as subjects.

Language(s) used: **French**

* Baker and Jones (1998, 368) 30%; OIF (2007, 17) 33%. Avg. = 31.5%.
** Baker and Jones (1998, 368): 60%; Essizewa (2007, 31): 60%; Adegbija (1994, 8): 44% L1 +6% L2 = 50%. Avg. = 55%.

Uganda

ILLED 1962	ILLED 1990	ILLED 2010	Percentage Speak English	Percentage Speak Luganda
5.4	6	6	8*	40**

LANGUAGE POLICY

Colonial   British colonization. Successive colonial governors advocated the teaching of Swahili, but missionaries resisted (because they were using other indigenous languages and because Swahili was associated with Islam), and the governors' efforts were thwarted (Kasozi 2000, 25). Luganda was favored because the colonial government used Buganda agents as administrators.

Independence   (1962) Local languages were used in the first years, followed by English. Luganda continued to be favored in eastern Uganda. Swahili was dropped because of opposition from missionaries and from

Luganda speakers. Swahili continued to spread among security forces and in commerce (Tembe and Norton 2008, 53).

Interim   In 1973, Idi Amin decreed that Swahili was to be the national language and the medium of instruction, but he allocated few resources to achieving the education goal. Other local languages continued to be used, particularly Luganda.

Current   A Government White Paper on Education in 1992 stated that in rural schools the medium of education should be the "relevant local language" (not necessarily mother tongue) in grades 1–4 and English from grade 5, whereas in urban primary schools, English is the medium from grade 1 (Tembe and Norton 2008, 35). In all primary schools, English and Swahili were to be compulsory subjects, with Swahili gradually emphasized. A survey by Annette Nyquist in 1998 reported: "Observations in primary schools showed that most of the teaching was done in English…The teachers I spoke to said that they were told that English should be the medium of instruction from P.1" (quoted by Brock-Utne 2001, 127).

Language(s) used: **English, Luganda (17%), Luo [Acholi-Lango] (11%), Nyoro (3%), Teso (7%), Lugbara (3%), Swahili (<1%L1 + L2) ≈ 42%**

---

* Leclerc (2010) 6%; Graddol (1997, 11) 9%; Crystal (2003, 65): 10% Avg. = 7.5%.
** Baker and Jones (1998, 368): 30% L1 + 30% L2 = 60%; Adegbija (1994, 7): 18% L1 + 20% L2 = 38%, Lewis (2009): 17% L1 + 5% L2 = 22%. Avg. = 40%.

Zambia

ILLED 1964	ILLED 1990	ILLED 2010	Percentage Speak English	Percentage Speak Bemba
5.4	0	4	20*	58**

LANGUAGE POLICY

Colonial   British colonization. Local languages used as medium of instruction to fourth grade. Four local languages selected in 1928: Cibemba, Cinyanja, Citonga, Silozi (Manchisi 2004, 2). English thereafter.

Independence   (1964) In 1966, the Ministry of Education ruled that English would be the medium of instruction from grade 1 onward (Manchisi 2004, 4).

Interim   1977 "Reform" maintained use of English from grade 1 to university (Manchisi 2004, 4).

Current   In 1996 came a new education policy: "Educating our Future/ Breakthrough to Literacy," where students were given the opportunity to learn basic reading and writing in a local language (Sampa 2001, 53). The initial project, involving 25 schools in 1998, expanded to all 4,271 schools in Zambia by 2002–2003 (Sampa 2003, 27). According to Manchisi (citing Ministry of Education 1996), the policies have not been implemented, and "the Ministry of Education has maintained English as the official medium of instruction in the early years of primary education: 'As language of instruction, English will continue to be used as the official medium of instruction, but teachers are encouraged where necessary and relevant to use the familiar language for explanations, questions and answers'" (Manchisi 2004, 6). Local languages are now used for initial literacy in the first grade, but the medium of instruction remains English, even in grade 1 (Heugh 2008, 362). English is the language of instruction, though primary instruction *can* be given in one of the six recognized languages (Leclerc 2010).

Language(s) used: English, Bemba (31%), Tonga (9%), Nyanja (7%), Lozi (5%), Lunda (4%), Kaonde (2%), Luvale (1.4%) ≈ 60%

---

* Baker and Jones (1998, 369): more than 30%; Graddol (1997, 11): 11%; Crystal (2003, 65): 19.5% Avg. = 20%.

** Adegbija (1994, 10) 31% L1 + 25% L2 = 56%; Baker and Jones (1998, 369): 60%. Avg. = 58% [but Posner (2005, 121 fn34): 40%].

Zimbabwe

ILLED 1980	ILLED 1990	ILLED 2010	Percentage Speak English	Percentage Speak Shona
4.5	5.4	4.8	39*	75**

LANGUAGE POLICY

Colonial British colonization, then white minority rule. "More than half the African schools, which were mission schools, provided only three years of primary education" (Roy-Campbell 2001, 160). These schools used Shona and Ndebele for the first three years, with English thereafter (Roy-Campbell 2001, 162). Statutes Laws of 1966 and 1973 say that "English should be used for instruction in all schools" and "instruction in an indigenous language could be authorised to expedite the acquisition of English" for six months (1966 document) or twelve months (1973 document) (Nkomo 2008, 352).

Independence (1980) "Although since 1980 there have been efforts to minimize the use of English in teaching and examinations, the English medium continues to be used alongside Shona" (Roy-Campbell 2001, 163).

Interim "English is the official language and the prescribed teaching medium. Use of a non-English vernacular is permitted only during the early primary stage. At least one of the two main African languages must be taught in all government schools" (Atkinson 1985, 5643). The 1987 Education Act required that children must be taught in Shona or

Ndebele (or an approved minority language) during the first three years of education.

Current   In the mid-1990s, among smaller language groups, resentment of the exclusive recognition of Shona and Ndebele grew, while Ndebele also feared domination by Shona (Nkomo 2008, 357). The 2002 Amendment to 1987 Education Act allowed for teaching of six minority languages in primary schools (Nyika 2008, 461). But English may be used as medium from the very beginning and often is (Nkomo, 356). The embassy reports that English is the medium; local languages are subjects. Most teachers, pushed by parents, prefer to use English from the beginning of school to assure the competence of their students in English (Leclerc 2009).

Language(s) used: **English, Shona (66%), Ndebele (10%), Ndau (5%), Kalanga (4%), Nyanja (4%), Tonga (.8%), Lozi (.7%), Tswana (.4%) ≈ 91%**

---

* Graddol (1997, 11): 28%; Crystal (2003, 65): 49%. Avg. = 39%.
** Nyika (2008, 459); Adegbija (1994, 11).

Language Policy Bibliography

Absieh, Abbi Ibrahim, Minister of National Education, telephone interview by author, 27 April 2005.

Adegbija, Efurosibina. 2007. "Language Policy and Planning in Nigeria." In *Language Planning and Policy in Africa, Vol 2*, edited by Robert Kaplan and Richard Baldauf, Jr. Clevedon: Multilingual Matters.

Adegbija, Efurosibina. 1994. *Language Attitudes in Sub-Saharan Africa*. Clevedon: Multilingual Matters.

Aguila, André, Director SIL-Burkina Faso, pers. comm., 9 November 2004.

Akinnaso, F. Niyi. 1993. "Policy and Experiment in Mother-Tongue Literacy in Nigeria." *International Review of Education* 39 (4):255–85.

Alidou, Hassana, and Birgit Brock-Utne. 2006. "Experience I – Teaching Practices – Teaching in a Familiar Language." In Alidou et al. "Optimizing Learning and Education in Africa – the Language Factor: A Stock-taking Research on Mother Tongue and Bilingual Education in Sub-Saharan Africa." Working Document prepared for use at ADEA Biennial Meeting, Libreville, Gabon, March 27–31, 2006.

Alidou, Hassana et al. 2006. "Optimizing Learning and Education in Africa – the Language Factor: A Stock-taking Research on Mother Tongue and Bilingual Education in Sub-Saharan Africa" Working Document prepared for use at ADEA Biennial Meeting, Libreville, Gabon, March 27–31, 2006.

Andoh-Kumi, Kingsley. 2002. "Language of Instruction in Ghana (Theory, Research, and Practice)." Language Centre, University of Ghana-Legon, IEQ-Ghana.

Anyidoho, Akosua, and M. E. Kropp Dakubu. 2008. "Ghana: Indigenous Languages, English, and an Emerging National Identity." In *Language and National Identity*, edited by Andrew Simpson, 141–57. New York: Oxford University Press.

Armstrong, Robert G. 1968. "Language Policies and Language Practices in West Africa." In *Language Problems of Developing Nations*, edited by Joshua Fishman et al., 227–36. New York: John Wiley & Sons.

Asfaha, Yonas Mesfun. 2009. "English Literacy in Schools and Public Places in Multilingual Eritrea." In *Low-Educated Adult Second Language and Literacy Acquisition*, edited by I. van de Craats and J. Kurvers, 213–21. Utrecht: LOT Netherlands Graduate School of Linguistics, Occasional Series, 15.

Asfaha, Yonas Mesfun, Linguist, University of Asmara, pers. comm., 29 September 2013.

Atkinson, N. 1985. "Zimbabwe: System of Education." In *The International Encyclopedia of Education*, edited by Torsten Husen and T. Neville Postlethwaite, 5643–5646. New York: Pergamon Press.

Baker, Colin, and Sylvia Prys Jones. 1998. *Encyclopedia of Bilingualism and Bilingual Education*. Philadelphia: Multilingual Matters.

Banya, Kingsley, and Juliet Elu. 1997. "Implementing Basic Education: An African Experience." *International Review of Education* 43 (5–6):481–96.

Basimolodi, Outlule Mother. 2000. "A Review of Botswana's Language Policy in Education and its Effects on Minority Languages and National Development." In *Language and Development in Southern Africa: Making the Right Choices*, edited by Richard Trewby and Sandra Fitchat, 143–158. Conference Proceedings, National Institute for Educational Development, Okahandja, Namibia, 11–13 April 2000. Namibia: Gamsberg Macmillan Publishers, Ltd.

Benrabah, Mohamed. (2007a). "The Language Planning Situation in Algeria." In *Language Planning & Policy*, Volume 2, edited by Robert Kaplan and Richard Baldauf, Jr. Clevedon: Multilingual Matters.

Benrabah, Mohamed. (2007b). "Language Maintenance and Spread: French in Algeria." *International Journal of Francophone Studies* 10 (1–2):193–215.

Benson, Carol. 2004. "Bilingual Schooling in Mozambique and Bolivia: From Experimentation to Implementation." *Language Policy* 3: 47–66.

Benson, Carol. 2010. "How Multilingual African Contexts are Pushing Educational Research and Practice in New Directions" *Language and Education* 24 (4):323–36.

Biloa, Edmond, and George Echu. 2008. "Cameroon: Official Bilingualism in a Multilingual State." In *Language and National Identity*, edited by Andrew Simpson, 199–213. New York: Oxford University Press.

Bokamba, Eyamba. 2007. "D. R. Congo: Language and 'Authentic Nationalism.'" In *Language and National Identity*, edited by Andrew Simpson, 214–34. New York: University Press.

Bougroum, M. et al. 2007. "Literacy Policies and Strategies in the Maghreb: Comparative Perspectives from Algeria, Mauritania and Morocco." *Literacy Challenges in the Arab Region*. UNESCO and Qatar Foundation.

Brock-Utne, B., Z. Desai and M. Qorro, eds. 2005. Language of Instruction in Tanzania and South Africa. Dar-es-Salaam: KAD.

Brock-Utne, Birgit. 1997. "The Language Question in Namibian Schools." *International Review of Education* 43 (2):241–60.

Brock-Utne, Birgit. 2001. "Education For All – In Whose Language?" *Oxford Review of Education* 27 (1):115–34.

Bunyi, Grace. (2001a). "Language and educational inequality in primary classrooms in Kenya." In *Voices of Authority: Education and Linguistic Difference*, edited by Monica Heller and Marilyn Martin Jones. Westport: Ablex Publishing.

Bunyi, Grace. (2007b). "The Place of African Indigenous Knowledge and Languages in Education for Development: The Case of Kenya." In *New Directions in African*

Education, edited by Dlamini, S. Nombuso, 15–40. Calgary: University of Calgary Press.

Calvet, Louis-Jean. 2001. "Les politiques linguistiques en Afrique francophone: état des lieux du point du vue de la politologie linguistique." In *Les langues dans l'espace francophone: de la coexistence au partenariat*, edited by Robert Chaudenson and Louis-Jean Calvet, 145–76. Paris: L'Harmattan.

Canvin, Maggie. 2007. "Language and Education Issues in Policy and Practice in Mali, West Africa." In *Global Issues in Languages Education and Development*, edited by Naz Rassool, 157–186. Clevedon: Multilingual Matters.

Cassanelli, Lee, and Farah Sheikh Abdikadir. 2007. "Somalia: Education in Transition." *Bildhaan: An International Journal of Somali Studies*, 7 (7):91–125.

Coonan, Patrick J. 2007. *The Language Debate in Cape Verde*. Master of Arts Thesis at the Center for International Studies of Ohio University. June 2007

Crystal, David. 2003. *English as a Global Language*, 2nd edition. Cambridge: Cambridge University Press.

Diallo, Alpha. 2000. "L'école Mauritanienne: Crise Profonde" *IQRAA: le bi-mensuel mauritanien* 7 Oct 2000 (reproduced on http://fr.groups.yahoo.com/group/flamnet/message/700)

Djité, Paulin. 2000. "Language Planning in Cote d'Ivoire: Non scholea sed vitae discimus/ We do not study for academia, but for real life." *Current Issues in Language Planning* 1 (1):11–46.

Essizewa, Komlan. 2007. "Language Contact Phenomena in Togo: A Case Study of Kabiye-Ewe Code-switching." Proceedings of the 37th Annual Conference on African Linguistics. Edited by Doris L. Payne and Jaime Pena, 30–42. Somerville, Massachussets, Cascadilla Proceedings Project.

Fomba, Cheick Oumar, and Kabule W. Weva. 2003. "La pédagogie convergente comme facteur d'amélioration de la qualité de l'éducation de base au Mali." Paper presented at the Biennial Conference of ADEA, Grand Baie, Mauritius 3–6 December 2003.

Francis, David, and Mohamed Kamanda. 2001. "Politics and Language Planning in Sierra Leone." *African Studies* 60 (2):225–44.

Fyle, C. Magbaily. 1994. "Official and Unofficial Attitudes and Policy towards Krio as the Main Lingua Franca in Sierra Leone." In *African Languages, Development and the State*, edited by Richard Fardon and Graham Furniss, 44–54. New York: Routledge.

Ghana Country Paper. Pan African Seminar/Workshop on the Problems and Prospects of the Use of African Languages in Education, 26–30 August 1996, Accra, Ghana.

Giliomee, Hermann. 2004. "The Rise and Possible Demise of Afrikaans as Public Language." *Nationalism and Ethnic Politics* 10: 25–58.

Githiora, Chege. 2008. "Kenya: Language and the Search for a Coherent National Identity." In *Language and National Identity*, ed. Andrew Simpson. 235–66. New York: University Press.

Gorham, A., and R. Duberg. 1985. "Angola: System of Education." In *The International Encyclopedia of Education*, edited by Torsten Husen and T. Neville Postlethwaite, 269–274. New York: Pergamon Press.

Government of Sierra Leone. The Education Act, 2004. 1 April 2004.

Graddol, David. 1997. *The Future of English?* UK: The British Council.

Halaoui, Nazam. 2003. "L'utilisation des langues africaines: politiques, législations et réalités." [Working Document] Paper presented at the Biennial Conference of ADEA, Grand Baie, Mauritius, 3–6 December 2003.

Hameso, Seyoum. 1997. "The Language of Education in Africa: The Key Issues." *Language, Culture and Curriculum* 10 (1):1–13.

Handloff, Robert E., ed. 1988. *Mauritania: A Country Study – Education*. Washington, D.C.: U.S. Library of Congress. http://countrystudies.us/mauritania/41.htm

Heugh, Kathleen et al. 2007. "Final Report: Study on Medium of Instruction in Primary Schools in Ethiopia." Report Commissioned by the Ministry of Education. 22 January 2007.

Heugh, Kathleen. 2007. "Language and Literacy Issues in South Africa." In *Global Issues in Language, Education and Development*, edited by Naz Rassool, 187–217. Clevedon: Multilingual Matters.

Heugh, Kathleen. 2008. "Language Policy and Education in Southern Africa." In *Encyclopedia of Language and Education*, 2nd edition, Volume 1: *Language Policy and Political Issues in Education*, edited by S. May and N.H. Hornberger, 355–67. Springer Science & Business Media.

Hookoomsing, Vinesh Y. 2000. "Language, Pluralism and Development: The Case of Mauritius." In *Language and Development in Southern Africa: Making the Right Choices*, edited by Richard Trewby and Sandra Fitchat, 109–120. Conference Proceedings, National Institute for Educational Development, Okahandja, Namibia, 11–13 April 2000. Namibia: Gamsberg Macmillan Publishers, Ltd.

Hovens, Mart. 2002. "Bilingual Education in West Africa: Does it Work?" *International Journal of Bilingual Education and Bilingualism* 5 (5):249–66.

James, Wendy. 2008. "Sudan: Majorities, Minorities, and Language Interactions." In *Language and National Identity*, edited by Andrew Simpson, 61–78. New York: Oxford University Press.

Johnson, David. 2006. "Comparing the Trajectories of Educational Change and Policy Transfer in Developing Countries." *Oxford Review of Education* 32 (5):679–96.

Kamwangamalu, Nkonko. 2004. "The Language Planning Situation in South Africa." In *Language Planning and Policy in Africa*, Vol. 1, edited by Richard Baldauf, Jr. and Robert Kaplan. Clevedon: Multilingual Matters.

Kasozi, A.B.K. 2000. "Policy Statements and the Failure to Develop a National Langauge in Uganda: A Historical Survey." *Language and Literacy in Uganda: Toward a sustainable reading culture*, ed. Kate Parry. Kampala: Fountain Publishers.

Kayambazinthu, Edrinnie. (1998). "The Language Planning Situation in Malawi." *Journal of Multilingual and Multicultural Development* 19 (5&6):369–439.

Leclerc, Jacques. *L'Aménagement Linguistique dans le Monde*. http://www.tlfq.ulaval. ca/AXL/afrique/afracc.htm. Algeria 2010, Angola 2011, Benin 2011, Botswana 2009, Burkina Faso 2009, Burundi 2009, Cameroon 2011, Cape Verde 2011, Central African Republic 2009, Chad 2010, Comoros 2009, Congo, Dem. Rep. 2009, Congo, Republic 2010, Cote d'Ivoire 2010, Djibouti 2009, Equatorial Guinea 2011, Eritrea 2010, Ethiopia 2009, Gabon 2009, Gambia 2010, Ghana 2009, Guinea 2009, Guinea Bissau 2011, Kenya 2010, Lesotho 2010, Liberia 2010, Madagascar 2011, Malawi 2011, Mali 2010, Mauritania 2010, Mauritius 2011, Mozambique 2011, Namibia 2010, Niger 2010, Nigeria 2010, Rwanda 2010, Sao Tome & Principe 2011, Senegal 2010, Seychelles 2010, Sierra Leone 2009, Somalia 2010, South Africa 2010, Sudan 2011, Swaziland 2011, Tanzania 2010, Togo 2010, Uganda 2010, Zambia 2010, Zimbabwe 2011 (Accessed Nov 2011)

Lewis, Paul M. ed. 2009. *Ethnologue: Languages of the World*, 16th edition. Dallas, TX: SIL International. http://www.ethnologue.com.

Lipski, John M. 1985? "The Spanish of Equatorial Guinea: research on la hispanidad's best-kept secret" http://www.personal.psu.edu/jml34/eg.pdf.

Lockhart, L. 1985. "Botswana: System of Education." In *The International Encyclopedia of Education*, edited by Torsten Husen and T. Neville Postlethwaite, 504–508. New York: Pergamon Press.

Maass, Antje, Mba Language Specialist, SIL-Chad, pers. comm., 7 November 2011.

MacMillan, Hugh. 1989. "A Nation Divided? The Swazi in Swaziland and the Transvaal, 1865–1986." In *The Creation of Tribalism in Southern Africa*, edited by Leroy Vail, 289–323. Berkeley: University of California Press.

Maimbolwa-Sinyange, I. M. 1985. "Somalia: System of Education." In *The International Encyclopedia of Education*, edited by Torsten Husen and T. Neville Postlethwaite, 4709–12. New York: Pergamon Press.

Maimbolwa-Sinyangwe, I. and K. Leimu. 1985. "Lesotho: System of Education." In *The International Encyclopedia of Education*, edited by Torsten Husen, and T. Neville Postlethwaite, 2998–3002. New York: Pergamon Press.

Malewezi, J. C. 1985. "Malawi: System of Education." In *The International Encyclopedia of Education*, edited by Torsten Husen and T. Neville Postlethwaite, 3160–65. New York: Pergamon Press.

Manchisi, P. C. 2004. "The Status of the Indigenous Languages in Institutions of Learning in Zambia: Past, Present and Future." *African Symposium* 4 (1).

Matiki, Alfred. 2006. "Literacy, Ethnolinguistic Diversity and Transitional Bilingual Education in Malawi." *The International Journal of Bilingual Education and Bilingualism* 9 (2):239–54.

Matiki, Alfred, pers. comm., 7 Nov 2011.

Mba, Gabriel. "PROPELCA Statistics 2010." Personal comm., 1 November 2010.

Mbaabu, Ireri. 1996. *Language Policy in East Africa: A Dependency Theory Perspective.* Nairobi, Kenya: ERAP.

McGregor, Gordon P. "National Policy and Practice in Language and Literature Education: Some Reflections from Afar." In *Language and Literacy in Uganda: Toward a sustainable reading culture*, edited by Kate Parry. Kampala: Fountain Publishers.

McIntyre, S. S. (1985). "Central African Republic: System of Education." In *The International Encyclopedia of Education*, edited by Torsten Husen and T. Neville Postlethwaite, 655–58. New York: Pergamon Press.

McLaughlin, Fiona. 2008. "Senegal: The Emergence of a National Lingua Franca." In *Language and National Identity*, edited by Andrew Simpson, 79–97. New York: Oxford University Press.

McNab, Christine. 1990. "Language Policy and Language Practice: Implementing Multilingual Literacy Education in Ethiopia" *African Studies Review* 33 (3):65–82.

Medeiros, Adelardos. (2006) "Portuguese in Africa." http://www.linguaportuguesa.ufrn.br/en_3.4.a.php.

Mekonnen, Alemn Gebre Yohannes. 2009. "Implications of the Use of Mother Tongues versus English as Languages of Instruction for Academic Achievement in Ethiopia." In *Languages and Education in Africa: A Comparative and Transdisciplinary Analysis*, Birgit Brock-Utne and Ingse Skattum, 189–200. Oxford: Bristol Papers in Education: Comparative and International Studies.

Mfum-Mensah, Obed. 2005. "The Impact of Colonial and Post-colonial Ghanaian Language Policies on Vernacular Use in Schools in Two Northern Ghanaian Communities." *Comparative Education* 41 (1): 71–85.

Ministère de l'Éducation Nationale, République de Djibouti. *Schema Directeur: Plan d'Action de l'Éducation (2001–2005)*. Table Ronde Sectorielle sur l'Éducation, Djibouti 9–11 October 2000.

Ministry of Education [Cameroon]. *Plan d'action national EPT Cameroun*. Yaounde, 2003. Available at: http://portal.unesco.org/education "Education Plans & Policies/ Africa/Cameroon."

Ministry of Education, Youth, Sports and Culture, Republic of the Gambia. *Education Policy 1988–2003*. Sessional Paper No. 4 of 1988. 8 November 1988.

Moehema, Elisée, Linguist, ACATBA, pers. comm., 14 November 2011.

Mohamed, Hashim Issa, and Felix Banda. 2008. "Classroom Discourse and Discursive Practices in Higher Education." *Journal of Multilingual and Multicultural Development* 29 (2):95–109.

Moloi, Francina et al. 2008. "Free but Inaccessible Primary Education: A Critique of the Pedagogy of English and Mathematics in Lesotho." *International Journal of Educational Development* 28: 612–21.

Molosiwa, A., N. Ratsoma, and J. Tsonope. 1991. "A Comprehension Report on the Use of Setswana at all levels of Botswana's Education System." *International Review of Education* 37: 1.

Mostari, Hind Amel. 2004. "A Sociolinguistic Perspective on Arabisation and Language Use in Algeria" *Language Problems & Language Planning* 10 (1):25–44.

N'Guessan, Jérémie Kouadio. 2001. "École et langues nationales en Côte d'Ivoire: dispositions légales et recherches." In *Les langues dans l'espace francophone: de la coexistence au partenariat*, edited by Robert Chaudenson and Louis-Jean Calvet, 177–203. Paris: Institute de la Francophonie L'Harmattan.

Nabea, Wendo. 2009. "Language Policy in Kenya: Negotiation with Hegemony." *The Journal of Pan African Studies* 3 (1):121–38.

Ndinga-Koumba-Binza, Hugues Steve. 2007. "Gabonese Language Landscape: Survey and Perspectives." *South African Journal of African Languages* 27 (3):96–116.

Nelson, Todd, Director, SIL Togo-Benin, pers. comm., 21 October 2004.

Nieuwenhuis, F. J. 1996. *The Development of Education Systems in Postcolonial Africa*. Pretoria: HSRC.

Nishimuko, Mikako. 2009. "The Role of Non-Governmental Organizations and Faith-Based Organizations in Achieving Education for All: The Case of Sierra Leone." *Compare: A Journal of Comparative and International Education* 39 (2):281–95.

Nkomo, Dion. 2008. "Language in Education and Language Development in Zimbabwe." *Southern African Linguistics and Applied Language Studies* 26 (3):351–61.

Nkosana. Leonard. 2008. "Attitudinal Obstacles to Curriculum and Assessment Reform." *Language Teaching Research* 12 (2):287–312.

Ntawurishira, L. 1985. "Burundi: System of Education." In *The International Encyclopedia of Education*, edited by Torsten Husen and T. Neville Postlethwaite, 596–600. New York: Pergamon Press.

Nyati-Ramahobo, 2004. "The Language Situation in Botswana." In *Language Planning & Policy*, Volume 1, edited by Robert Kaplan and Richard Baldauf, Jr. Clevedon: Multilingual Matters.

Nyika, Nicholus. 2008 "'Our Languages are Equally Important': Struggles for the Revitalization of Minority Languages in Zimbabwe." *Southern African Linguistics and Applied Language Studies* 26 (4):457–70.

Oeuvre Suisse d'Entraide Ouvrière. *Des Enfants du Burkina Faso Apprennent à Lire, à Compter et à Ecrire en Deux Langues.* (n.d.) (12 March 2005). [Now Solidar Suisse: http://www.solidar.ch/education-bilingue-1.html]

OIF. 2007. *Etat de la Francophonie dans le Monde 2006–2007.* Paris: Nathan.

Ouédroaogo, Mathieu Rakissouiligri. 2002. "L'Utilisation des Langues Nationales dans les Systeme Educatifs en Afrique" *IIRCA-UNESCO* Bulletin 4 (4):December.

Oyètádé, B. Akìntúndé and Victor Fashole Luke. 2008. "Sierra Leone: Krio and the Quest for National Integration." In *Language and National Identity*, edited by Andrew Simpson, 122–40. New York: Oxford University Press.

Pawlikova-Vilhanova, Viera. 1996. "Swahili and the Dilemma of Ugandan Language Policy." *Asian and African Studies* 5 (2):158–70.

Pearson, 2008. "Pearson Introduces Native Language Textbooks in Angola" (http://www.pearson.com/about-us/feature-sotories/feature-story-archive/?i=98) 24 November 2008.

Pota, P. P. 2001. "Classroom Experiences in Teaching Through Chichewa or English in a Predominantly Ciyao Speaking Area." In *Cross-border Languages Within the Context of Mother Tongue Education*, edited by Joachim F. Pfaffe. University of Malawi: Center for Language Studies.

Rajah-Carrim, Aaliya. 2007. "Mauritian Creole and Language Attitudes in the Education System of Multiethnic and Multilingual Mauritius." *Journal of Multilingual and Multicultural Development* 28 (1):51–71.

Renard, Raymond, and Daniel Peraya. 1985. *Langues Africaines et Langues d'Enseignement: Problematique de l'Introduction des Langues Nationales dans l'Enseignement Primaire en Afrique.* Paris: Didier Erudition.

République du Sénégal: Commission Nationale de Reforme de l'Education et de la Formation. [Etats Généraux] *Rapport Général Annexe IIE: L'Introduction des langues nationales dans le système éducatif.* Dakar, Senegal, 5 August 1981–6 August 1984.

République du Sénégal: Ministère de l'Enseignement Technique, de la Formation Professionnelle, de l'Alphabétisation et des Langues Nationales: Direction de la Promotion des Langues Nationales. *Schema Directeur de la Mise a l'Essai de l'Introduction des Langues Nationales à l'École Élémentaire.* Dakar, Senegal, August 2002.

Richmond, Edmun B. 1983. *New Directions in Language Teaching in Sub-Saharan Africa: A Seven-Country Study of Current Policies and Programs for Teaching Official and National Languages and Adult Functional Literacy.* Washington, D.C.: University Press of America.

Robenoro, Irene. 2009. "National Language Teaching as a Tool for Malagasy Learners' Integration into Globalisation." In *Languages and Education in Africa: A Comparative and Transdisciplinary Analysis*, edited by Birgit Brock-Utne and Ingse Skattum, 175–188. Oxford: Bristol Papers in Education: Comparative and International Studies.

Robins, Larry, Director, SIL-Central Africa Group, pers. comm., 7 November 2011.

Roy-Campbell, Zaline M. 2001(a). "Globalisation, Language and Education: A Comparative Study of the United States and Tanzania." *International Review of Education* 47 (3–4):267–82.

Roy-Campbell, Zaline Makini. 2001(b). *Empowerment Through Language: The African Experience – Tanzania and Beyond.* Trenton: Africa World Press, Inc.

Sampa, Francis. 2001(a). "Zambian New Breakthrough to Literacy (NBTL) Within the Framework of Zambian Language Policy and the Primary Reading Program." In

Cross-border Languages Within the Context of Mother Tongue Education, edited by Joachim F. Pfaffe. University of Malawi: Center for Language Studies.

Sampa, Francis. 2003(b). "Country Case Study: Republic of Zambia" Doc 5.B. ADEA Biennial Meeting – Grand Baie, Mauritius. December 3–6, 2003.

Samuel, John, and Myra Harrison. 2001. *Toward an Education Strategy for Save the Children UK: Report of a Desk Study into Language Issues and Early Childhood Education in the Southern African Region*, November.

Senga-Nsikazolo, V., and A. Makonda. 1985. "Congo, Republic of: System of Education." In *The International Encyclopedia of Education*, edited by Torsten Husen and T. Neville Postlethwaite, 975–80. New York: Pergamon Press.

Sengova, Joko M. 1987. "The National Languages of Sierra Leone: A Decade of Policy Experimentation." In *Sierra Leone 1787–1987: Two Centuries of Intellectual Life*, edited by Murray Last and Paul Richards, 519–29. Manchester: Manchester University Press.

Siddiek, Ahmed Gumaa. 2010. "Language & Education as Factors of Sustainable Relation between the Northern and Southern Sudan Post-Secession." *Research Journal of International Studies* 17 (November): 68–87.

Sifuna, Daniel N. 2008. *Development of Education in Africa: The Kenyan Experience*. Nairobi: Initiatives Publishers.

Simpson, Andrew, and B. Akìntúndé Oyètádé. 2008. "Nigeria: Ethno-linguistic Competition in the Giant of Africa." In *Language and National Identity*, edited by Andrew Simpson, 172–98. New York: Oxford University Press.

Skattum, Ingse. 2008. "Mali: In Defence of Cultural and Linguistic Pluralism." In *Language and National Identity*, edited by Andrew Simpson, 98–121. New York: Oxford University Press.

Sonck, Gerda. 2005. "Language of Instruction and Instructed Languages in Mauritius. *Journal of Multilingual and Multicultural Development*. 26 (1):37–51.

Sonko-Godwin, P. 1985. "Gambia: System of Education." In *The International Encyclopedia of Education*, edited by Torsten Husen and T. Neville Postlethwaite, 1986–89. New York: Pergamon Press.

Stege, C. T. 1985. "Mozambique: System of Education." In *The International Encyclopedia of Education*, edited by Torsten Husen and T. Neville Postlethwaite, 3438–40. New York: Pergamon Press.

Stroud, Christopher. 1999. "Portuguese as Ideology and Politics in Mozambique: Semiotic (re)Constructions of a Postcolony." In *Language Ideological Debates*, edited by Jan Blommaert, 343–80. New York: Mouton de Gruyter.

Swarts, Patti. 2001. "Language Policy Implementation in Namibia: Realities, Challenges and Politics." In *Language and Development in Southern Africa: Making the Right Choices*, edited by Richard Trewby and Sandra Fitchat, 38–51. Namibia: Gamsberg Macmillan Publishers.

Tembe, Juliet, and Bonny Norton. 2008. "Promoting Local Languages in Ugandan Primary Schools: The Community as Stakeholder." *The Canadian Modern Language Review* 65 (1):33–60.

Tréfault, Thierry. 2001. "Bambara et française à l'école malienne: la recherche de la complémentarité." In *Les langues dans l'espace francophone: de la coexistence au partenariat*, edited by Robert Chaudenson and Louis-Jean Calvet. Paris: Institut de la Francophonie/L'Harmattan.

Wagaw, T. G. 1985. "Ethiopia: System of Education." In *The International Encyclopedia of Education*, edited by Torsten Husen and T. Neville Postlethwaite, 1723–29. New York: Pergamon Press.

Walter, Stephen, and Patricia Davis. 2005. *Eritrea National Reading Survey*. Dallas, TX: SIL International.

Warsame, Ali A. 2001. "How a Strong Government Backed an African Language: The Lessons of Somalia." *International Review of Education* 47 (3–4):341–60.

Webb, Vic. 1999. "Multilingualism in Democratic South Africa: The Overestimation of Language Policy," *International Journal of Educational Development*, 4–5:351–66.

Wolhuter, C. C. et al. 2003. "Learning from South-South Comparison: the Education Systems of South Africa and Madagascar." *South African Journal of Education* 23 (1):29–35.

Woods, David. "Changing Patterns of Language Utilization in the Republic of Congo." *African Languages and Cultures* 7 (1):19–35.

World Bank. 2003. "Chad – Education Sector Reform Project (PARSET)" Project Appraisal Document, Report No. 23797. 14 February 2003.

World Bank. 2001. "Project Appraisal Document on a Proposed Credit in the Amount of SDR39.1 Million to the Islamic Republic of Mauritania for an Education Sector Development Program." *Report No. 22529-MAU.* 26 September 2001.

Yahya-Othman, Saida. 2000. "What Language, and for Whose Education?" In *Language and Development in Southern Africa: Making the Right Choices*, edited by Richard Trewby and Sandra Fitchat, 70–85. Namibia: Gamsberg Macmillan Publishers, Ltd.

Yerende, I. Eva. 2005. "Ideologies of Language and Schooling in Guinea-Conakry: A Post-Colonial Experience." In: *Languages of Instruction for African Emancipation: Focus on Postcolonial Contexts and Considerations*, edited by Birgit Brock-Utne and Rodney K. Hopson, 199–230. Dar es Salaam: Mukuti na Nyota.

Appendix B

Language Surveys

A. SIL LANGUAGE TEAM E-MAIL QUESTIONNAIRE – **Cameroon**
(October 2002) – sent to 20 teams

I introduced myself as a researcher and told them I had received their e-mail addresses and permission to ask these questions from SIL director.

1) Do you know the approximate year of the first missionary arrival to your language area?
2) Do you know when the first SIL team arrived?
3) Do you know when/if a Language Committee was formed?
4) Do you know when the first written materials appeared in this language (primers, newsletters, songs, Bible portions, etc. written by yourselves or prior language researchers)?

B. LANGUAGE ATTITUDES SURVEY – **Cameroon (319), Senegal (219), Ghana (155) = 693 valid surveys between September 2002 and April 2003**

In Cameroon, surveys were administered in twelve towns, seven Francophone (Bafia, Ombessa, and Yaounde in the Center Province; Banjoun, Batcham, Dschang, and Mbouda in the West Province) and five Anglophone (Bafut, Bali, Bamenda, Kumbo, and Nkambe in the North West Province). In Senegal, they were administered in three quartiers of Dakar, in Nguekoh (Petit Côte region), two quartiers of Thiès (Central Region) and Kaolack (Central Region, inland). In Ghana, the surveys were administered in two quartiers of Accra, in Sogakope (Volta Region), and Tamali (Northern Region). They were conducted in a public setting – a market or a downtown street – and respondents were selected at random: every fourth stall, office, or dwelling, for example. I supervised the collection of surveys in Cameroon, Senegal, and Accra, Ghana. I trusted them to trained research assistants in Sogakope and Tamali, Ghana, because I was seven months pregnant and did not feel it safe to travel these distances.

Respondents were assured the survey was anonymous. Research assistant translated if respondent did not speak English or French. We wrote answers on sheet if respondent preferred.

288

Sex_____ Age _____
Education level achieved: __none __primary __secondary __post-secondary
Province of Birth _____
Occupation _____

1) What is the first language you spoke at home?
2) Some have proposed that children should be taught in their mother tongue for the first years of primary school and then transition to English [French]. Do you think this is a good idea? Why or why not?
3) Would you prefer your own child begin primary school education in the mother tongue or in English [French]?

C. ELECTION EXPERIENCE SURVEY – Cameroon (July 2009) – 40 surveys each in Yaounde (Center Province), Ebolowa (South Province), Douala (Littoral Province), and Buea (South West Province).

Respondents were assured the survey was anonymous. Research assistant translated if respondent did not speak English or French. I wrote answers on sheet if respondent preferred.

Sex: M F
Age: _____
Education: __ None __Primary __Secondary __High School __University
Division of Origin: _____
Mother Tongue Language: _____
Did you vote in the last election (2007)? _____Yes _____No

YES, I voted	NO, I did not vote
Did you have an electoral card?	**Why did you not vote?**
___Yes	____ No interest in election
What did you have to do to obtain your card?	____ Difficulty registering (explain):
	____ Did not receive electoral card (explain):
___No	
Why did you not have a card?	____ Difficulty voting (explain):
	____ Other reasons:
Did you have any problems voting? Explain:	

Overall, do you think you had a fair opportunity to vote in the 2007 election?

D. TRUST AND PROTEST SURVEY – Cameroon (June 2011) – 40 surveys each in Misaw, Babungo, Nkanchi, Fonfouka (North West Province), Ediolomo, and Tchekos (Center Province)

Respondents were assured the survey was anonymous. Research assistant translated if respondent did not speak English or French. I wrote answers on sheet if respondent preferred.

Sex: M F
Age ___ <20 ___ 20–30 ___ 31–40 ___ 41–50 ___ 51–60 ___ >60
Education: ___None ___Primary ___Secondary ___High School ___ University
Occupation _____
Mother Tongue: _____
Can you read or write it? ___ Yes ___ No

1) Do you meet regularly with any groups that include people that speak other languages?
2) Would you encourage your daughter to marry someone from outside your language group?
3) If you had any money to save, where would you put it? (Government Bank, Credit Association, *njangi*, Home)
4) Do you think you should always accept what the chief in this area tells you to do?
5) If someone stole something from you, who would you report this to?
6) Do you think the local Government Council uses its money well?
7) When you are unhappy about something in the village, do you think it is acceptable to join others to protest publicly?

General Bibliography

Abernethy, David B. 1969. *The Political Dilemma of Popular Education: An African Case*. Stanford, CA: Stanford University Press.

ACDI (Agence Canadienne de Développement International). 1987. "Programme des ONG–alphabetisation experimentale en langue maternelle." *Rapport Final*, June 1987.

Actes du Sommet de Dakar. 1989. *Le Projet francophone: enjeux et défis*. Paris: ACCT.

ADEA (Association for the Development of Education in Africa). 1999. *Statistical Profile of Education in Sub-Saharan Africa* (SPESSA): http://www.adeanet.org/spessa99/.

Afolayan, Adebisi. 1976. "The Six-Year Primary Project in Nigeria." In *Mother Tongue Education: The West African Experience*, edited by Ayo Bamgbose, 113–34. Paris: UNESCO.

Agence Française de Développement (n.d.): Note de Communication Publique d'Opération: Initiative Ecole et Langue Nationale en Afrique (ELAN). Paris: Agence Française de Développement.

AIF. 2000. *Pour une nouvelle stratégie linguistique de l'AIF*. Paris: AIF.

AIF. 2001. *Education et Langues. 30 Ans de Programmes de Coopération à l'Agence Intergouvernementale de la Francophonie, Bilan Critique: 1970–2000*. Paris: AIF.

Akenmo, Pierre-Marie. 2001. "*Rapport Trimestriel d'Activités: Mois de juillet-aôut-sept 2001, Yemba Language Committee*." Yaounde: NACALCO Library.

Akinnaso, F. Niyi. 1993. "Policy and Experiment in Mother-Tongue Literacy in Nigeria." *International Review of Education* 39: 255–85.

Albaugh, Ericka A. 2005. "The Colonial Image Reversed: Advocates of Multilingual Education in Africa." Ph.D. Diss., Duke University.

Albaugh, Ericka A. 2007. "Language Choice in Education: A Politics of Persuasion." *Journal of Modern African Studies* 45: 1–32.

Albaugh, Ericka A. 2009. "The Colonial Image Reversed: Language Preferences and Policy Outcomes in African Education." *International Studies Quarterly* 53: 389–420.

Albaugh, Ericka A. 2011. "An Autocrat's Toolkit: Adaptation and Manipulation in 'Democratic' Cameroon." *Democratization* (Special Issue) 18: 388–414.

Alesina, Alberto, Reza Baqir, and William Easterly. 1999. "Public Goods and Ethnic Divisions." *Quarterly Journal of Economics* 114: 465–90.

Alesina, Alberto, Arnaud Devleeschauwer, William Easterly, Sergio Kurlat, and Romain Wacziarg. 2003. "Fractionalization." *Journal of Economic Growth* 8: 155–94.

Alexandre, Pierre. 1972. Languages and Language in Black Africa. Translated by F. A. Leary. Evanston, IL: Northwestern University Press.

Alidou, Hassana et al. 2006. "Optimizing Learning and Education in Africa – the Language Factor: A Stock-Taking Research on Mother Tongue and Bilingual Education in Sub-Saharan Africa." Working Document prepared for use at ADEA Biennial Meeting, Libreville, Gabon, March 27–31, 2006.

Amin, Julius. 1994. "Continuity and Change in Cameroon's Education: The Case of West Cameroon." *Journal of Asian and African Studies* 29: 248–59.

Amissah, Peter, Kingsley Andoh-Kumi, Samuel Asare Amoah, Albert Awedoba, Fiifi Mensah, Eric Wilmot, and Shirley Miske. 2001. *IEQ2/Ghana Final Report: The Implementation of Ghana's School Language Policy.* IEQ Project, American Institutes of Research, 15 Nov 2001. http://www.ieq.org/pdf/IEQ2Ghana_finalrpt.pdf.

Anderson, Benedict. 1991. *Imagined Communities: Reflections on the Origins and Spread of Nationalism.* New York: Verso.

Andoh-Kumi, Kingsley. 2002. *"Language of Instruction in Ghana (Theory, Research, and Practice)."* Language Centre, University of Ghana-Legon, IEQ-Ghana.

Andrews, Edward. 2009. "Christian Missions and Colonial Empires Reconsidered." *Journal of Church and State* 51: 663–91.

Ansu-Kyeremeh, Kwasi, Leslie Casely-Hayford, J. S. Djangmah, James Nti, and Francois Orivel. 2002. *Education Sector Review: Final Team Synthesis Report.* Accra: Ministry of Education.

Anyidoho, Akosua, and M. E. Kropp Dakubu. 2008. "Ghana: Indigenous Languages, English, and an Emerging National Identity." In *Language and National Identity in Africa*, edited by Andrew Simpson, 141–157. New York: Oxford University Press.

Armstrong, Robert G. 1968. "Language Policies and Language Practices in West Africa." In *Language Problems of Developing Nations*, edited by Joshua Fishman et al., 227–36. New York: John Wiley & Sons.

August, Diane, and Kenji Hakuta, eds. 1997. *Improving Schooling for Language-Minority Children: A Research Agenda.* National Research Council. Washington, DC: National Academy Press.

Awasom, Nico Fru. 2007. "Language and Citizenship in Anglophone Cameroon." In *Making Nations, Creating Stranger*, edited by Sara Dorman, Daniel Hammett, and Paul Nugent, 145–60. Boston: Brill.

Awasom, Nicodemus Fru. 2005. "Traditional Rulers, Legitimacy and Shifting Loyalties: The Case of North West Chiefs in Cameroon." In *Tradition and Politics: Indigenous Political Structures in Africa*, edited by Olufemi Vaughan, 305–26. Trenton: Africa World Press.

Baker, Colin. 1988. *Key Issues in Bilingualism and Bilingual Education.* Clevendon: Multilingual Matters.

Baker, Keith, and Adriana de Kanter. 1981. *Effectiveness of Bilingual Education: A Review of the Literature.* Washington, DC: Office of Planning and Budget, U.S. Department of Education.

Bakke, Kristin, and Erik Wibbels. 2006. "Diversity, Disparity, and Civil Conflict in Federal States." *World Politics* 59: 1–50.

Bamgbose, Ayo. 1976. *Mother Tongue Education: The West African Experience.* London: Hodder and Stoughton.

Bamgbose, Ayo. 1991. *Language and the Nation: The Language Question in Sub-Saharan Africa.* Edinburgh: Edinburgh University Press.

Bamgbose, Ayo. 2004. "Language of Instruction Policy and Practice in Africa." Paris: UNESCO. http://www.unesco.org/education/languages_2004/languageinstruction_africa.pdf.

Bates, Robert. 1983. "Modernization, Ethnic Competition and the Rationality of Politics in Contemporary Africa." In *State Versus Ethnic Claims: African Policy Dilemmas*, edited by Donald Rothchild and Victor Olorunsola, 152–71. Boulder: Westview Press. Originally published in "Ethnic Competition and Modernization in Contemporary Africa." *Comparative Political Studies* (January 1974).

Bates, Robert. 1999. "Ethnicity, Capital Formation, and Conflict." Center for International Development (CID) at Harvard University Working Paper #27. Cambridge, MA.

Bayart, Jean-François. 1979. *L'Etat au Cameroun*. Paris: Presses de la Fondation Nationale des Sciences Politiques.

Bayart, Jean-François. 1986. "Civil Society in Africa." In *Political Domination in Africa: Reflections on the Limits of Power*, edited by Patrick Chabal, 109–25. New York: Cambridge University Press.

Bayart, Jean-François. 2009. *The State in Africa: The Politics of the Belly*, 2nd edition (English) Cambridge: Polity.

Bayart, Jean-François, Achille Mbembe, and C. Toulabor. 1991. *La Politique par le Bas en Afrique*. Paris: Karthala.

Bayart, Jean-François, Peter Geschiere, and Francis Nyamnjoh. 2001. "J'étais là avant: Problématiques de l'Autochtonie" et "Autochtonie, Démocratie et Citoyenneté en Afrique". *Critique Internationale* 10:126–95, 177–94.

Bell, David A. 1995. "Lingua Populi, Lingua Dei: Language, Religion, and the Origins of French Revolutionary Nationalism." *The American Historical Review*. 100: 1403–37.

Benrabah, Mohamed. 2007. "Language Maintenance and Spread: French in Algeria." *International Journal of Francophone Studies* 10: 193–215.

Berman, Sheri. 1997. "Civil Society and the Collapse of the Weimar Republic." *World Politics* 49: 401–29.

Bernard, J. M. 2003. "Eléments d'appréciation de la qualité de l'enseignement primaire en Afrique francophone: Programme d'Analyse des Systèmes Educatifs de la CONFEMEN" (Study of Burkina Faso, Cameroun, Côte d'Ivoire, Madagascar and Sénégal). Paper prepared for the Biennial Conference of ADEA. Grand Baie, Mauritius, December 2–4.

Berry, Sara. 2009. "Property, Authority and Citizenship: Land Claims, Politics and the Dynamics of Social Division in West Africa." *Development and Change* 40: 23–45.

Bertz, Ned. 2007. "Educating the Nation: Race and Nationalism in Tanzanian Schools." In *Making Nations, Creating Stranger*, edited by Sara Dorman, Daniel Hammett, and Paul Nugent, 161–180. Boston: Brill.

Betts, Raymond. 1961. *Assimilation and Association in French Colonial Theory: 1890–1914*. New York: Columbia University Press.

Bingle, E. J., and Sir Kenneth Grubb. 1957. *World Christian Handbook*. New York: Friendship Press.

Biya, Paul. 1987. *Communal Liberalism*. London: Macmillan.

Bjornson, Richard. 1991. *The African Quest for Freedom and Identity: Cameroonian Writing and the National Experience*. Bloomington: Indiana University Press.

Block, Steven A. 2001. "Does Africa Grow Differently?" *Journal of Development Economics* 65: 443–67.

Blommaert, Jan. 1999. "Language in Education in Post-Colonial Africa: Trends and Problems." Paper presented at the International Conference on Language in Education in Post-Colonial Societies, City University of Hong Kong (April).

Blonde, Jacques. 1979. "L'Enseignement du Français et l'Introduction des Langues Nationales à l'Ecole." *Realités Africaines & Langue Française*. Centre de Linguistique Appliquée de Dakar 9: 20–41.

Boone, Catherine. 1995. "Rural Interests and the Making of Modern African States." *African Economic History* 23: 1–36.

Boone, Catherine. 2003a. *Political Topographies of the African State: Territorial Authority and Institutional Choice*. New York: Cambridge University Press.

Boone, Catherine. 2003b. "Decentralization as Political Strategy in West Africa." *Comparative Political Studies* 36: 355–81.

Boone, Catherine. 2007. "Property and Constitutional Order: Land Tenure Reform and the Future of the African State." *African Affairs* 106: 557–86.

Bourdieu, Pierre. 1991. *Language and Symbolic Power*. Cambridge, MA: Harvard University Press.

Boyle, Patrick M. 1996. "Parents, Private Schools, and the Politics of an Emerging Civil Society in Cameroon." *Journal of Modern African Studies* 34: 609–22.

Brass, Paul. 1991. *Ethnicity and Nationalism*. New Delhi: Sage.

Bratton, Michael, and Nicolas van de Walle. 1997. *Democratic Experiments in Africa: Regime Transitions in Comparative Perspective*. New York: Cambridge University Press.

Brock-Utne, Birgit. 2001. "Education for all – in whose language?" *Oxford Review of Education* 27: 115–34.

Brown, Lalage, ed. 2003. *Education in the Commonwealth: The First 40 Years*. London: Commonwealth Secretariat.

Brubaker, Rogers. 1992. *Citizenship and Nationhood in France and Germany*. Cambridge, MA: Harvard University Press.

Brubaker, Rogers. 1996. *Nationalism Reframed: Nationhood and the National Question in the New Europe*. Cambridge: Cambridge University Press.

Bruk, S. I., and V. S. Alencenko. 1964. *Atlas Narodov Mira*: USSR: Glavnoe upravlenie geodezii i kartografii Gosudarstvennogo geologiceskogo komiteta.

Bruthiaux, Paul. 2002. "Hold Your Courses: Language Education, Language Choice, and Economic Development." *TESOL Quarterly* 36, 3 *Language in Development*: 275–96.

Bunyi, Grace. 2001. "Language and Educational Inequality in Primary Classrooms in Kenya." In *Voices of Authority: Education and Linguistic Difference*, edited by Monica Heller and Marilyn Martin Jones. Westport, CT: Ablex.

Callaghy, Thomas M. 1987. "The State as Lame Leviathan: The Patrimonial Administrative State in Africa." In *The African State in Transition*, edited by Zaki Ergas, 87–116. New York: St. Martin's Press.

Calvet, Louis-Jean. 1993. "Francophonie et géopolitique." In *Le français dans l'éspace francophone, description linguistique et sociolinguistique de la francophonie {1993 I et 1996 II}*, edited by Didier de Robillard, Michel Beniamino, and Claudine Bavoux, 483–495. Paris: H. Champion.

Calvet, Louis-Jean. 2002. *Linguistique et colonialisme: Petit traité de glottophagie*. Paris: Payot {1974 orig.}.

Canagarajah, Sudharshan, and Xiao Ye. 2001. "Public Health and Education Spending in Ghana in 1992–98: Issues of Equity and Efficiency." *Policy Research Working Paper* 2579. Washington, DC: World Bank.

Carnoy, Martin. 1974. *Education as Cultural Imperialism*. New York: Longman.

Carothers, Thomas. 1997. "Democracy without Illusions." *Foreign Affairs* 76: 85–99.

Carothers, Thomas. 2002. "The End of the Transition Paradigm." *Journal of Democracy* 13: 5–21.

Chabal, Patrick, and Jean-Pascal Daloz. 1999. *Africa Works: Disorder as a Political Instrument.* Bloomington: Indiana University Press.

Chafer, Tony. 2002. *The End of Empire in French West Africa: France's Successful Decolonization?* New York: Berg.

Chafer, Tony. 2005. "Chirac and 'la Françafrique': No Longer a Family Affair." *Modern & Contemporary France* 13: 7–23.

Chafer, Tony. 2007. "Education and Political Socialisation of a National-Colonial Political Elite in French West Africa, 1936–47." *The Journal of Imperial and Commonwealth History* 35: 437–58.

Chandra, Kanchan. 2004. *Why Ethnic Parties Succeed: Patronage and Ethnic Head Counts in India.* Cambridge: Cambridge University Press.

Charte de Hué. 21 Oct 1997. P. 12–13. http://www.bulletin.auf.org/IMG/pdf_07_19973.pdf.

Chaudenson, Robert. 1989. *Vers une révolution francophone?* Paris: L'Harmattan.

Chaudenson, Robert. 1991. *La Francophonie: représentations, réalités, perspectives.* Paris: Diffusion Didier Érudition.

Chaudenson, Robert. 2000. *Mondialisation: la langue française a-t-elle encore un avenir?* Paris: Institute de la Francophonie: Diffusion Didier Érudition.

Chaudenson, Robert, and Louis-Jean Calvet. 2001. *Les Langues dans l'espace francophone: de la coexistence au partenariat.* Paris: Institut de la Francophonie: L'Harmattan.

Chazan, Naomi. 1982. "The New Politics of Participation in Tropical Africa." *Comparative Politics* 14 (January): 169–89.

Che, John Ambe. 1999. "Programme of Activities for 1999/2000 (Dec 27, 1999) Bafut Language Committee," Yaounde: NACALCO Library.

Chinapah, Vinayagum. 2000. *With Africa for Africa. Towards Education for All.* Pretoria: HSRC.

Clapham, Christopher, ed. 1985. *Private Patronage and Public Power.* London: Frances Pinter.

Clapham, Christopher. 1996. *Africa and the International System: The Politics of State Survival.* New York: Cambridge University Press.

Cleghorn, A., M. Merritt, and J.O. Abagi. 1989. "Language Policy and Science Instruction in Kenyan Primary Schools." *Comparative Education Review* 33: 21–39.

Coe, Cati. 2002. "Educating an African Leadership: Achimota and the Teaching of African Culture in the Gold Coast." *Africa Today* 49: 23–44.

Coe, Cati. 2005. *Dilemmas of Culture in African Schools: Nationalism, Youth, and the Transformation of Knowledge.* Chicago: University of Chicago Press.

Coleman, James. 1963. *Nigeria: Background to Nationalism.* Berkeley and Los Angeles: University of California Press.

Coleman, James, ed. 1965. *Education and Political Development.* Princeton, NJ: Princeton University Press.

Collier, Paul. 2003. "The Market for Civil War." *Foreign Policy* (May/June): 39–45.

Collier, Paul, and Jan Willem Gunning. 1999. "Why Has Africa Grown Slowly?" *Journal of Economic Perspectives* 13: 3–22.

Collier, Paul, and Anke Hoeffler. 1998. "On the Economic Causes of Civil War." *Oxford Economic Papers* 50: 563–73.

Collier, Virginia. 1987. "Age and Rate of Acquisition of Second Language for Academic Purposes." *TESOL Quarterly* 21: 617–41.

Comaroff, Jean, and John Comaroff. 1991. *Of Revelation and Revolution*. Chicago: Chicago University Press.

Commonwealth Secretariat. 1966. *Annual Report of the Commonwealth Secretary General*. London: Commonwealth Secretariat (August 26).

Commonwealth Secretariat, *Strategic Plan 2004/05–2007/08*. www.thecommonwealth. org.

Connor, Walker. 1972/1994. *Ethnonationalism: The Quest for Understanding*. Princeton, NJ: Princeton University Press.

Conseil Consultatif, OIF. 2003. *La Francophonie dans le monde 2002–2003*. Paris: Larousse.

Constitution de la République du Cameroun. 1996. January 18, 1996. Yaounde, Cameroun.

Cooper, Frederick. 2008. "Possibility and Constraint: African Independence in Historical Perspective." *Journal of African History* 49: 167–96.

Cowan, L. Gray, James O'Connell, and David G. Scanlon, eds. 1965. *Education and Nation Building in Africa*. New York: Frederick A. Praeger.

Cox, Gary. 1997. *Making Votes Count: Strategic Coordination in the World's Electoral Systems*. New York: Cambridge University Press.

Crawford, Gordon, and Cristof Hartmann. 2008. *Decentralization in Africa: A Pathway out of Poverty and Conflict?* Amsterdam: Amsterdam University Press.

Cruise O'Brien, Donal. 1991. "The Show of State in Neo-Colonial Twilight: Francophone Africa." In James Manor et al., eds. *Rethinking Third World Politics*. London: Longman.

Cumming, Gordon. 2005. "Transposing the 'Republican' Model? A Critical Appraisal of France's Historic Mission in Africa." *Journal of Contemporary African Studies* 23: 233–52.

Cummins, Jim. 1979. "Linguistic Interdependence and the Educational Development of Bilingual Children." *Review of Educational Research* 49: 222–51.

Cummins, Jim. 1991. "Interdependence of First- and Second-language Proficiency in Bilingual Children." In *Language Processing in Bilingual Children*, edited by E. Bialystok. Cambridge: Cambridge University Press.

Dah, Jonas. 1983. "Missionary Motivations and Methods: A Critical Examination of the Basel Mission in Cameroon, 1886–1914." Ph.D. Thesis, University of Basel, Switzerland.

Dakin, Julian, Brian Tiffen, and H. G. Widdowsen, eds. 1968. *Language in Education: The Problem in Commonwealth Africa and the Indo-Pakistan Subcontinent*. London: Oxford University Press.

Darden, Keith, and Anna Grzymala-Busse. 2006. "The Great Divide: Literacy, Nationalism, and the Communist Collapse." *World Politics* 59: 83–115.

Das Gupta, Jyotirindra. 1968. "Language Diversity and National Development." In *Language Problems of Developing Nations*, edited by Joshua Fishman, Charles Ferguson and Jyotirindra Das Gupta, 17–26. New York: John Wiley & Sons.

Das Gupta, Jyotirindra. 1976. "Practice and Theory of Language Planning: The Indian Policy Process." In *Language and Politics*, edited by William O'Barr and Jean O'Barr, 195–212. Sociology of Language Series #10. The Hague: Mouton.

Dau, Francesca. 2009. On African Parliaments: Constitutional and Electoral Engineering in Plural Societies. Paper presented at the *Democratization in Africa* Conference, University of Leeds, December 4–5, 2009.

Davesne, André. 1933. *La langue française, langue de civilisation en Afrique Occidentale Française*. St. Louis, Senegal: Government Printer of Senegal.

De Swaan, Abram. 1988. *In Care of the State: Health Care, Education and Welfare in Europe and the USA in the Modern Era*. New York: Oxford University Press.

De Swaan, Abram. 2001. *Words of the World*. Malden: Polity/Blackwell.

Debeauvais, Michel. 1965. "Education in Former French Africa." In *Education and Political Development*, edited by James Coleman. Princeton, NJ: Princeton University Press.

Delancey, Mark W. 1989. *Cameroon: Dependence and Independence*. Boulder, CO: Westview Press.

Deutsch, Karl. 1953/1966. *Nationalism and Social Communication*. Cambridge, MA: MIT Press.

de Varennes, Fernand. 1996. *Languages, Minorities and Human Rights*. The Hague: Assert Press.

DFID. 2011. "Multilateral Aid Review: Assessment of the Commonwealth Secretariat." https://www.gov.uk/government/uploads/system/uploads/attachment_data/file/224928/comsec.pdf.

Diallo, Ibrahima. 2010. *The Politics of National Languages in Postcolonial Senegal*. Amherst, NY: Cambria Press.

Diamond, Larry. 2008. "The Democratic Rollback: The Resurgence of the Predatory State." *Foreign Affairs* March-April: 36–48.

Diamond, Larry. 2010. "Why Are There No Arab Democracies?" *Journal of Democracy* 21: 93–104.

Diamond, Larry, and Marc Plattner. 1999. *Democracy in Africa*. Baltimore: Johns Hopkins University/National Endowment for Democracy.

Direction de la Promotion des Langues Nationales. 2002. *Etat des Lieux de la Recherche en/sur les Langues Nationales (Synthèse)*. Dakar, (July).

Djité, Paulin G. 1990. "Les langues africaines dans la nouvelle francophonie." *Language Problems and Language Planning* 14: 20–32.

Dor, Daniel. 2004. "From Englishization to Imposed Multilingualism: Globalization, the Internet, and the Political Economy of the Linguistic Code." *Public Culture* 16: 97–118.

Doxey, Margaret P. 1989. *The Commonwealth Secretariat and the Contemporary Commonwealth*. New York: St. Martins Press.

Dronen, Thomas Sundes. 2009. *Communication and Conversion in Northern Cameroon: The Dii People and Norwegian Missionaries 1934–1960*. Leiden: Brill.

Dumont, Pierre. 1983. "L'enseignement du francais langue etrangere en Afrique franco-phone." *Lengas* 14: 41–56.

Durkheim, Emile. 1922/1956. *Education and Sociology*, translated by Sherwood D. Fox. Glencoe, IL: The Free Press.

Dutcher, Nadine. 1982. *The Use of First and Second Languages in Primary Education: Selected Case Studies*. World Bank Staff Working Paper no. 504. Washington, DC: World Bank.

Dutcher, Nadine. 2004. *Expanding Educational Opportunity in Linguistically Diverse Societies*, 2nd edition. Washington, DC: Center for Applied Linguistics.

Easterly, William, and Ross Levine. 1997. "Africa's Growth Tragedy: Policies and Ethnic Divisions." *Quarterly Journal of Economics* 112: 1203–50.

Easton, Peter, Emmanuel Nikiema, and Suzanne Essama. 2002. "Developing Indigenous Knowledge in Francophone Africa." *World Bank IK Notes* 42, March 2002.

Ekeh, Peter. 1975. "Colonialism and the Two Publics in Africa: A Theoretical Statement." *Comparative Studies in Society and History* 17: 91–112.

Ellingsen, Tanja. 2000. "Colorful Community or Ethnic Witches' Brew? Multiethnicity and Domestic Conflict during and after the Cold War." *Journal of Conflict Resolution* 44: 228–49.

Englebert, Pierre. 2005. "Back to the Future: Resurgent Indigenous Structures and the Reconfiguration of Power in Africa." In *Tradition and Politics: Indigenous Political Structures in Africa*, ed. Olufemi Vaughan. Trenton, NJ: Africa World Press.

Englebert, Pierre. 2009. *Africa: Unity, Sovereignty, Sorrow*. Boulder, CO: Lynne Rienner.

Fabian, Johannes. 1983. "Missions and the Colonization of African Languages: Developments in the Former Belgian Congo." *Canadian Journal of African Studies* 17: 165–87.

Fafunwa, A. B., J. I. Macauley, and J. A. F. Sokoya, eds. 1989. *Education in the Mother Tongue: The Ife Primary Research Project, 1970–1978*. Ibadan: Nigeria University Press.

Fanon, Franz. 1961/1963. *The Wretched of the Earth*. New York: Grove Press.

Fardon, Richard, and Graham Furniss, eds. 1994. *African Languages, Development and the State*. New York: Routledge.

Fearon, James, and David Laitin. 2003. "Ethnicity, Insurgency and Civil War." *American Political Science Review* 97: 75–90.

Febvre, Lucien, and Henri-Jean Martin. 1958/1976. *The Coming of the Book: The Impact of Printing, 1450–1800*. London: Verso.

Fenske, James. 2010. "*Ecology, Trade and States in Precolonial Africa.*" unpublished mimeo.[Dept. of Economics, Univ. Oxford]

Ferguson, Charles. 1977. "Sociolinguistic Settings of Language Planning," in *Language Planning Processes*, edited by Joan Rubin, et al. New York: Mouton.

Firmin-Sellers, Kathryn. 2000. "Institutions, Context, and Outcomes: Explaining French and British Rule in West Africa." *Comparative Politics* 32: 253–72.

Fishman, Joshua, ed. 1966. *Language Loyalty in the United States*. The Hague: Mouton.

Fishman, Joshua. 1968a. "Language Problems and Types of Political and Sociocultural Integration: A Conceptual Summary." In *Language Problems of Developing Nations*, edited by Joshua Fishman, Charles Ferguson, and Jyotirindra Das Gupta, 489–98. New York: John Wiley & Sons.

Fishman, Joshua. 1968b. "Sociolinguistics and the Language Problems of the Developing Countries." In *Language Problems of Developing Nations*, edited by Joshua Fishman, Charles Ferguson, and Jyotirindra Das Gupta, 3–16. New York: John Wiley & Sons.

Fishman, Joshua A. 1971. "The Impact of Nationalism on Language Planning: Some Comparisons between Early 20th Century Europe and Subsequent Developments in South and South East Asia." In *Can Language Be Planned? Sociolinguistic Theory and Practice for Developing Nations*, edited by Joan Rubin and Bjorn Jernudd. Honolulu: University Press of Hawaii.

Fishman, Joshua. 1974. *Advances in Language Planning*. Contributions to the Sociology of Language 5. Berlin: Mouton de Gruyter.

Fishman, Joshua, Charles Ferguson, and Jyotirindra Das Gupta, eds. 1968. *Language Problems of Developing Nations*. New York: John Wiley & Sons.

Fonchingong, Charles. 2005. "Exploring the Politics of Identity." *Social Identities* 11: 363–80.

Fonlon, Bernard. 1969. "The Language Problem in Cameroon: An Historical Perspective." *Comparative Education* 5: 25–49.

Frau-Meigs, Divina. 2002. "'Cultural Exception,' National Policies and Globalisation: Imperatives in Democratization and Promotion of Contemporary Culture." *Quaderns del CAC* 14: 3–16.

Gandhi, Jennifer, and Ellen Lust-Okar. 2009. "Elections under Authoritarianism." *Annual Review of Political Science* 12: 403–22.

Gardinier, David E. 1963. *Cameroon: United Nations Challenge to French Policy*. New York: Oxford University Press.

Gardinier, David E. 1985. "The French Impact on Education in Africa, 1817–1960." In *Double Impact: France and Africa in the Age of Imperialism*, edited by G. Wesley Johnson, 333–62. Westport, CT: Greenwood Press.

Gellner, Ernest. 1983. *Nations and Nationalism*. Oxford: Blackwell.

Gennaioli, Nicola, and Ilia Rainer. 2007. "The Modern Impact of Precolonial Centralization in Africa." *Journal of Economic Growth* 12: 185–234.

Geo-Jaja, Macleans. 2006. "Educational Decentralization, Public Spending, and Social Justice in Nigeria." *Review of Education* 52: 125–48.

Geschiere, Peter. 1993. "Chiefs and Colonial Rule in Cameroon: Inventing Chieftaincy French and British Style." *Africa* 63: 2.

Geschiere, Peter. 2009. *The Perils of Belonging: Autochthony, Citizenship, and Exclusion in Africa and Europe*. Chicago: University of Chicago Press.

Geschiere, Peter, and Stephen Jackson. 2006. "Autochthony and the Crisis of Citizenship: Democratization, Decentralization, and the Politics of Belonging." *African Studies Review* 49: 1–7.

Githiora, Chege. 2008. "Kenya: Language and the Search for a Coherent National Identity." In *Language and National Identity*, edited by Andrew Simpson, 235–66. New York: Oxford University Press.

Glenn, Charles L. 1997. *What Does the National Research Council Study Tell Us about Educating Language Minority Children?* Amherst, MA: READ Institute.

Glewwe, P., and M. Kremer. 2006. "Schools, Teachers and Education Outcomes in Developing Countries." In *Handbook of the Economics of Education*, Vol. 2, edited by E. Hanushek and F. Welch, 945–1017. New York: North Holland.

Goheneix-Minisini, Alice. 2011. "Le français colonial: Politiques et pratiques de la langue nationale dans l'Empire (1880–1962)." Ph.D. Thesis. Paris, Institut d'études politiques.

Gordon, David. 2001. "Owners of the Land and Lunda Lords: Colonial Chiefs in the Borderlands of Northern Rhodesia and the Belgian Congo." *International Journal of African Historical Studies* 34: 315–38.

Gould, Roger. 2005. "Historical Sociology and Collective Action." In *Remaking Modernity: Politics, History and Sociology*, edited by Julia Adams, Elizabeth Clemens, and Ann Shola Orloff, 286–99. Durham, NC: Duke University Press.

Graham, C. K. 1971. *The History of Education in Ghana: From the Earliest Times to the Declaration of Independence*. Abingdon: Frank Cass.

Gray, J. Patrick. 1999. "A Corrected Ethnographic Atlas." *World Cultures* 10: 24–85.

Great Britain, Colonial Office. 1958. *Report to the Trusteeship Council of the United Nations.*

Green, Andy. 1997. *Education, Globalization and the Nation State.* New York: St. Martin's Press.

Green, Andy, and John Preston. 2001. "Education and Social Cohesion: Recentering the Debate." *Peabody Journal of Education* 76:247–281.

Greene, Jay. 1998. *A Meta-Analysis of the Effectiveness of Bilingual Education.* Claremont, CA: Tomás Rivera Center.

Grieg, J. C. E. 1978. "Decision-Making in Educational Administration: A Comparative Study of the Gambia and Malawi during the period 1925–1945." Ph.D. diss., Institute of Education, University of London.

Grier, Robin. 1999. "Colonial Legacies and Economic Growth." *Public Choice* 98: 317–35.

Grillo, Ralph D. 1989. "The Politics of Language in Wales, Ireland and Scotland." In *Dominant Languages: Language Hierarchy in Britain and France.* New York: Cambridge University Press.

Grimes, Barbara F. 1996. *Ethnologue: Languages of the World,* 13th edition. Dallas: SIL International.

Grimes, Barbara F. 2000. *Ethnologue: Languages of the World,* 14th edition. Dallas: SIL International.

Grindle, Merilee S., and John W. Thomas. 1991. *Public Choices and Policy Change: The Political Economy of Reform.* Baltimore: The Johns Hopkins University Press.

Grindle, Merilee. 2007. *Going Local: Decentralization, Democratization, and the Promise of Good Governance.* Princeton, NJ: Princeton University Press.

Gros, Jean-Germain. 1995. "The Hard Lessons of Cameroon." *Journal of Democracy* 6: 112–27.

Groves, Charles Pelham. 1964. *The Planting of Christianity in Africa: 1914–1954.* London: Lutterworth Press.

Guyer, Jane. 1992. "Representation without Taxation: An Essay on Democracy in Rural Nigeria, 1952–1990." *African Studies Review* 35: 41–79.

Haas, Peter M. 1992. "Introduction: Epistemic Communities and International Policy Coordination." *International Organization* 46: 1–35.

Habyarimana, James, Macartan Humphreys, Daniel Posner, and Jeremy Weinstein. 2007. "Why Does Ethnic Diversity Undermine Public Goods Provision?" *American Political Science Review* 101: 709–25.

Hagège, Claude. 1996. *Le Français, histoire d'un combat.* Paris: Michel Hagège.

Halden, Erik. 1968. *The Culture Policy of the Basel Mission in the Cameroons 1886–1905.* Lund: Berlingska Boktryckeriet.

Hale, Thomas. 2009. "The *Manifeste des Quarante-Quatre,* Francophonie, *la Françafrique* and Africa: From the Politics of Culture to the Culture of Politics." *International Journal of Francophone Studies* 12: 171–201.

Halifax Communiqué. 2000. 14th Conference of Commonwealth Education Ministers. Halifax, Nova Scotia, Canada (26–30 November 2000).

Hanagan, Michael. 1999. "Introduction: Changing Citizenship, Changing States." In *Extending Citizenship, Reconfiguring States,* edited by Michael Hanagan and Charles Tilly. New York: Rowman & Littlefield.

Hansford, Gillian F. 1994. "Using Existing Structures: Three Phases of Mother Tongue Literacy among Chumburung Speakers in Ghana." In *African Languages,*

Development and the State, edited by Richard Fardon and Graham Furniss, 76–84. New York: Routledge.

Harbeson, John W. 2008. "Promising Democratic Trajectories in Africa's Weak States." In *Africa in World Politics: Reforming Political Order*, edited by John W. Harbeson and Donald Rothchild. Philadelphia: Westview Press.

Hardy, Georges. 1917. *Une conquête morale: l'enseignement en AOF*. Paris: Armand Colin.

Harpf, Barbara, and Ted Robert Gurr. 2004. *Ethnic Conflict in World Politics*, 2nd edition. Boulder, CO: Westview Press.

Hashim, Nadra. 2009. *Language and Collective Mobilization: The Story of Zanzibar*. New York: Lexington Books.

Hastings, Adrian. 1997. *The Construction of Nationhood: Ethnicity, Religion, and Nationalism*. New York: Cambridge University Press.

Haut Conseil de la Francophonie. 1990. *Etat de la francophonie dans le monde: rapport 1990*. Paris: La Documentation française.

Haut Conseil de la Francophonie. 1994. *Etat de la francophonie dans le monde: données 1994 et 5 enquêtes inédites*. Paris: La Documentation française.

Haut Conseil de la Francophonie. 2001. *Etat de la francophonie dans le monde: données 1999–2000 et 6 enquêtes inédites*. Paris: La Documentation française.

Heller, Monica, and Marilyn Martin Jones, eds. 2001. *Voices of Authority: Education and Linguistic Difference*. Westport, CT: Ablex.

Herbst, Jeffrey. 2000. *States and Power in Africa: Comparative Lessons in Authority and Control*. Princeton, NJ: Princeton University Press.

Heugh, Kathleen. 2008. "Language Policy and Education in Southern Africa." In *Volume 1: Language Policy and Political Issues in Education. Encyclopedia of Language and Education*, 2nd edition, edited by S. May and N. Hornberger, 355–67. New York: Springer Science + Business Media.

Hibou, Beatrice. 2004. "From Privatizing the Economy to Privatizing the State." In *Privatizing the State*. New York: Columbia University Press.

Higonnet, Patrice. 1980. "The Politics of Linguistic Terrorism and Grammatical Hegemony during the French Revolution." *Social History* 5: 41–69.

Hobsbawm, Eric. 1992. *Nations and Nationalism since 1780: Program, Myth, Reality*. New York: Cambridge University Press.

Hobsbawm, Eric. 1996. "Language, Culture, and National Identity." *Social Research* 63: 1065–80.

Hornberger, Nancy, ed. 1996. *Indigenous Literacies in the Americas: Language Planning from the Bottom up*. Berlin: Mouton.

Horowitz, Donald. 1989. "Is There a Third World Policy Process?" *Policy Sciences* 22: 249–88.

Horowitz, Donald. 2000. *Ethnic Groups in Conflict*. Berkeley: University of California Press [Orig. 1985].

Houis, Maurice, and Rémy Bole Richard. 1977. *Integration des langues africaines dans une politique d'enseignement*. Paris: UNESCO/ACCT.

Hugon, Philippe. 2005. "Permanences et Ruptures de la Politique Économique de la France vis-à-vis de l'Afrique sub-Saharienne." *Modern & Contemporary France*, 13: 41–55.

Hyden, Goran. 1980. *Beyond Ujamaa in Tanzania: Underdevelopment and an Uncaptured Peasantry*. London: Heinemann.

Isichei, Elizabeth. 1995. *A History of Christianity in Africa: From Antiquity to the Present*. Grand Rapids: William B. Eerdmans.

Jackson, Robert, and Carl Rosberg. 1982a. *Personal Rule in Black Africa: Prince, Autocrat, Prophet, Tyrant*. Berkeley: University of California Press.

Jackson, Robert, and Carl Rosberg. 1982b. "Why Africa's Weak States Persist: The Empirical and the Juricial in Statehood." *World Politics* 35: 1–24.

Jackson, Robert H. 1990. *Quasi-States, Sovereignty, International Relations and the Third World*. New York: Cambridge University Press.

Johnson, Hildegard Binder. 1967. "The Location of Christian Missions in Africa." *The Geographical Review* 57: 168–202.

Johnson, Nancy Kwang. 2004. "Senegalese 'into Frenchmen'? The French Technology of Nationalism in Senegal." *Nationalism and Ethnic Politics* 10: 135–158.

Jones, Thomas-Jesse. 1925. *Education in Africa, a Study of West, South, and Equatorial Africa by the African Education Commission, under the Auspices of the Phelps-Stokes Fund and the Foreign Mission Societies of North America and Europe*. New York: Phelps-Stokes Fund.

Joseph, Richard. 1977. *Radical Nationalism in Cameroon: Social Origins of the UPC Rebellion*. Oxford: Clarendon Press.

Jua, Nantang. 1993. "State, Oil and Accumulation." In *Pathways to Accumulation in Cameroon*, edited by Peter Geschiere and Piet Konings, 131–160. Paris: Éditions Karthala.

Jua, Nantang. 2001. "Democracy and the Construction of Allogeny/Autochthony in Postcolonial Cameroon." *African Issues* 29: 37–42.

Kaberry, P. M., and E. M. Chilver. 1961. "An Outline of the Traditional Political System of Bali-Nyonga, Southern Cameroons." *Africa* 31: 355–71.

Kashoki, Mubanga E. 2003. "Language Policy Formulation in Multilingual South Africa." *Journal of Multilingual and Multicultural Development* 24: 184–94.

Kaufman, Jason. 2002. *For the Common Good? American Civic Life and the Golden Age of Fraternity*. Oxford: Oxford University Press.

Keck, Margaret, and Kathryn Sikkink. 1998. *Activists beyond Borders: Advocacy Networks in International Politics*. Ithaca, NY: Cornell University Press.

Keefer, Philip, and Stephen Knack. 2002. "Polarization, Politics and Property Rights: Links between Inequality and Growth." *Public Choice* 111: 127–54.

Kelly, Gail P. 1984. "Colonialism, Indigenous Society, and School Practices: French West Africa and Indochina, 1918–1938." In *Education and the Colonial Experience*, edited by Philip Altbach and Gail P. Kelly, 9–32. New Brunswick. NJ: Transaction Books.

Kestnbaum, Meyer. 2005. "Mars Revealed: The Entry of Ordinary People into War among States." In *Remaking Modernity: Politics, History, and Sociology*, edited by Julia Adams, Elisabeth Clemens, and Ann Shola Orloff, 249–85. Durham, NC: Duke University Press.

King, Kenneth J. 1971. *Pan-Africanism and Education: A Study of Race Philanthropy and Education in the Southern States of America and East Africa*. Oxford: Clarendon Press.

Kingdon, John. 1984. *Agendas, Alternatives, and Public Policies*. Boston: Little, Brown.

Knutsen, Anne Moseng. 2008. "Ivory Coast: The Supremacy of French." In *Language and National Identity*, edited by Andrew Simpson, 158–71. New York: Oxford University Press.

Kofele-Kale, Ndiva. 1986. "Ethnicity, Regionalism, and Political Power: A Post-Mortem of Ahidjo's Cameroon." In *The Political Economy of Cameroon*, edited by Michael Schatzberg and William Zartman, 53–82. New York: Praeger.

König, Matthias. 1999. "Cultural Diversity and Language Policy." *International Social Science Journal* 51(161): 401–408.

Konings, Piet. 1993. *Labour Resistance in Cameroon: Managerial Strategies and Labour Resistance in the Agro-Industrial Plantations of the Cameroon Development Corporation*. London: Currey/Heinemann.

Konings, Piet. 2002. "University Students' Revolt, Ethnic Militia, and Violence during Political Liberalization in Cameroon." *African Studies Review* 45: 179–204.

Konings, Piet. 2003. "Religious Revival in the Roman Catholic Church and the Autochthony-Allochthony Conflict in Cameroon." *Africa* 73: 31–57.

Konings, Piet. 2004. "Opposition and Social-Democratic Change in Africa: The Social Democratic Front in Cameroon." *Commonwealth and Comparative Politics* 42: 289–311.

Krashen, Stephen D. 1996. *Under Attack: The Case against Bilingual Education*. Culture City: Language Education Associates.

Krieger, Milton. 1994. "Cameroon's Democratic Crossroads, 1990–4." *Journal of Modern African Studies* 32: 605–28.

Kuenzi, Michelle. 2011. *Education and Democracy in Senegal*. Palgrave: Macmillan.

Kuran, Timur. 1991. "Now out of Never: The Element of Surprise in the East European Revolution of 1989." *World Politics: A Quarterly Journal of International Relations* 44: 7–48.

Laitin, David. 1992. *Language Repertoires and State Construction in Africa*. New York: Cambridge University Press.

Laitin, David. 1994. "The Tower of Babel as a Coordination Game." *American Political Science Review* 88 (3):622–35.

Laitin, David. 2000. "Language Conflict and Violence: The Straw That Strengthens the Camel's Back." *European Journal of Sociology* 41 (1):97–137.

Laitin, David. 2007. *Language, States, and Violence*. New York: Oxford University Press.

Legendre, Jacques. 2003. "Annex to the Verbal Record of 20 November 2003," Document no. 74, Sénat Session Ordinaire de 2003–2004. Avis Présenté au nom de la commission des Affaires culturelles sur le projet de *loi de finances* pour 2004, Adopté par l'Assemblée Nationale, Tome XIV "Francophonie."

Lerner, Daniel. 1958. *The Passing of Traditional Society: Modernizing the Middle East*. Glencoe, IL: Free Press.

Le Vine, Victor T. 1964. *The Cameroons from Mandate to Independence*. Berkeley: University of California Press.

Le Vine, Victor T. 1986. "Leadership and Regime Changes in Perspective." In *The Political Economy of Cameroon*, edited by Michael Schatzberg and William Zartman, 21–51. New York: Praeger.

Lewis, Paul. 2009. *Ethnologue: Languages of the World*, 16th edition. Dallas: SIL International.

Lijphart, Arend. 1977. *Democracy in Plural Societies: A Comparative Exploration*. New Haven, CT: Yale University Press.

Lijphart, Arend. 1984. *Democracies: Patterns of Majoritarian and Consensus Government in Twenty-one Countries*. New Haven, CT: Yale University Press.

Lindberg, Staffan. 2006a. *Democracy and Elections in Africa*. Baltimore: Johns Hopkins University Press.

Lindberg, Staffan. 2006b. "Opposition Parties and Democratisation in Sub-Saharan Africa." *Journal of Contemporary African Studies* 24: 123–38.

Lindberg, Staffan. 2009. *Democratization by Elections: A New Mode of Transition*. Baltimore: Johns Hopkins University Press.

Lipset, Seymour Martin. 1960. *Political Man*. Garden City: Doubleday.

Liu, Amy. Forthcoming. "Democracy and Minority Language Recognition."; Original version presented (with David Brown) at the 2010 American Political Science Association Annual Meeting, Washington, DC.

Liu, Amy, Curtis Bell, and Jennifer Gandhi. 2011. "Minority Language Recognition under Dictatorship" (paper presented at the 2011 Midwest Political Science Association Annual Meeting, Chicago, Illinois).

Lonsdale, John. 1981. "The State and Social Processes in Africa: A Historiographical Essay." *African Studies Review* 24: June/September.

Lublin, David Ian. 1995. "Race Representation, and Redistricting." In *Classifying by Race*, edited by Paul Peterson, 111–25. Princeton, NJ: Princeton University Press.

Lugard, Frederick. 1922/1965. *The Dual Mandate in British Tropical Africa*, 5th edition. London: Frank Cass.

MacKenzie, Clayton. 1993. "Demythologising the Missionaries: A Reassessment of the Functions and Relationships of Christian Missionary Education under Colonialism." *Comparative Education* 29: 45–66.

MacLean, Lauren. 2002. "Constructing a Social Safety Net in Africa: An Institutionalist Analysis of Colonial Rule and State Social Policies in Ghana and Cote d'Ivoire." *Studies in Comparative Development* 37: 64–90.

MacLean, Lauren. 2011. "State Retrenchment and the Exercise of Citizenship in Africa." *Comparative Political Studies* 44: 1238–66.

Malone, Dennis L. 2003. "Developing Curriculum Materials for Endangered Language Education: Lessons from the Field." *International Journal of Bilingual Education and Bilingualism* 6: 332–48.

Mamdani, Mahmood. 1996. *Citizen and Subject: Contemporary Africa and the Legacy of Late Colonialism*. Princeton, NJ: Princeton University Press.

Mansour, Gerda. 1993. *Multilingualism and Nation Building*. Multilingual Matters Series #91. Clevedon: Multilingual Matters.

Markovitz, Irving Leonard. 1969. *Léopold Sédar Senghor and the Politics of Negritude*. London: Heinemann.

Marshall, Monty G., and Keith Jaggers, Principal Investigators. 2003. *Polity IV Project: Political Regime Characteristics and Transitions* 1800–2002. http://www.cidcm.umd.edu/inscr/polity/.

Mazrui, Alamin. 2002. "The English Language in African Education: Dependency and Decolonization." In *Language Policies in Education: Critical Issues*, edited by Terence Wiley, 267–81. Mahwah, NJ: Lawrence Erlbaum.

Mazrui, Ali A., and Alamin M. Mazrui. 1998. *The Power of Babel: Language and Governance in the African Experience*. London: James Currey.

Mazrui, Ali. 1983. "Francophone Nations and English-Speaking States: Imperial Ethnicity and African Political Formations." *State versus Ethnic Claims: African Policy Dilemmas*, edited by Donald Rothchild and Victor A. Olorunsola, 25–43. Boulder, CO: Westview Press.

Mazrui, Ali. 1997 "The World Bank, the Language Question and the Future of African Education." *Race and Class* 38: 35–48.

Mbembe, Achille. 2002. *On Private Indirect Government*. Dakar: CODESRIA.

Mbouda, Didier, and Prosper Djiafeua. 2005. "Atelier de Formation sur la Conception et la Mise on Oeuvre des Politiques Linguistiques et Educatives pour la Promotion de l'Utilisation et l'Enseignement des Langues Nationales." *Rapport General*, Kinshasa 26–30 Septembre.

McAdam, Doug, Sydney Tarrow, and Charles Tilly. 2001. *Dynamics of Contention*. New York: Cambridge University Press.

McGrath, Simon. 1999. "Education, Development and Assistance: The Challenge of the New Millenium." In *Changing International Aid to Education: Global Patterns and National Contexts*, edited by Kenneth King and Lene Buchert. Paris: UNESCO/ NORRAG.

McIntyre, W. David. 2001. *A Guide to the Contemporary Commonwealth*. New York: Palgrave.

McKinnon, Don. 2004. "After Abuja: Africa and the Commonwealth." *Address to the Africa All-Party Parliamentary Group by Secretary General of the Commonwealth*, House of Commons, 10 Feb 2004.

McWhorter, John. 2002. *The Power of Babel: A Natural History of Language*. London: Heinemann.

Mehler, Andreas. 2009. "Peace and Power Sharing in Africa: A Not So Obvious Relationship." *African Affairs* 108: 453–73.

Meyer, Birgit. 2002. "Christianity and the Ewe Nation: German Pietist Missionaries, Ewe Converts and the Politics of Culture." *Journal of Religion in Africa* 32: 167–99.

Meyer, John W., Francisco O. Ramirez, and Yasemin N. Soysal. 1992 "World Expansion of Mass Education, 1870–1980." *Sociology of Education* 65: 128–49.

Mfum-Mensah, Obed. 2005. "The Impact of Colonial and Postcolonial Ghanaian Language Policies on Vernacular Use in Schools in Two Northern Ghanaian Communities." *Comparative Education* 41: 71–85.

Miaffo, Dieudonné, and Jean-Pierre Warnier. 1993. "Accumulation et Ethos de la Notabilité chez les Bamiléké." In *Pathways to Accumulation in Cameroon*, edited by Peter Geschiere and Piet Konings, 33–70. Paris: Editions Karthala.

Michelman, Fredric. 1995. "French and British Colonial Language Policies: A Comparative View of Their Impact on African Literature." *Research in African Literatures* 26: 216–25.

Migdal, Joel. 2004. "State Building and the Non-Nation-State." *Journal of International Affairs* 58: 17–46.

Mill, John Stuart. 1962. "Of Nationality as Connected with Representative Government." In *Considerations on Representative Government*. Chicago: Regnery {1861}.

Ministère de l'Education Nationale, Chargé de l'Enseignement Technique. 2001. "*Le Développement de l'Education: Rapport National du Sénégal*." DPRE (27 April).

Ministère de l'Education Nationale, République du Cameroun. 1995. *Rapport Général des Etats Généraux de l'Education* (Yaounde 22–27 May 1995).

Ministère de l'Education Nationale, République du Cameroun. 2001. *Annuaire Statistique* 2000–2001. Yaounde: MINEDUC.

Ministère des Affaires Étrangères. 2002. *Solidarité Influence: la coopération internationale du ministère des Affaires étrangères. DGCID Bilan 2002 et perspectives*. Paris: DGCID.

Ministry of Education, Ghana. 2000. "The Colonial Era" http://www.ghana.edu.gh/past/colonialEra.html.

Ministry of Education, Ghana. 2003. *Education Strategic Plan*. Accra, March 2003.

Ministry of Information and Culture, Republic of Cameroon. 1991. *Proceedings of the National Forum on Culture*. 23–26 August 1991, Conference Center. Yaounde, Cameroon.

Ministry of Scientific and Technical Research. 2001. *Bibliography of the World of SIL in Cameroon 1969–2001*. Yaounde: SIL.

Minorities at Risk Project. 2009. "Minorities at Risk Dataset." College Park, Canada: Center for International Development and Conflict Management. Retrieved from http://www.cidcm.umd.edu/mar/.

Mitchell, B. R. 2007. *International Historical Statistics: Africa, Asia, and Oceana 1750–2005*, 5th edition. New York: Palgrave/MacMillan.

Mokosso, Henry E. 1987. "The United Presbyterian Mission Enterprise in Cameroun, 1879–1957." Ph.D. Dissertation, Howard University. [Now published as H. E. Mokosso (2007): *American Evangelical Enterprise in Africa: The Case of the United Presbyterian Mission in Cameroon*. New York]

Moloi, Francina, Nomusic Morobe, and James Urwick. 2008. "Free but Inacessible Primary Education: A Critique of the Pedagogy of English and Mathematics in Lesotho." *International Journal of Educational Development* 28: 612–21.

Momo, Gregoire. 1997. *Le Yemba: Histoire de la langue ecrite dans le menoua*. Menoua, Dschang: CELY.

Monga, Yvette. 2000. "'Au Village!'" Space, Culture, and Politics in Cameroon." *Cahiers d'Etudes Africaines* 160: 723–49.

Moulton, Jean. 2003. "Improving the Quality of Primary Education in Africa: What Has the World Bank Learned?" Paper presented at the ADEA Biennial Meeting, Grand Baie, Mauritius, December 3–6, 2003.

Moumouni, Abdou. 1964/1968. *Education in Africa*, translated by Phyllis Nauts Ott. New York: F. A. Praeger.

Murdock, George Peter. 1967. "Ethnographic Atlas: A Summary." *Ethnology* 6: 109–236. (Plus various tables published from 1962 to 1967 in *Ethnology*). All variables corrected and loaded into an SPSS database by Joseph P. Gray. 1999. http://eclectic.ss.uci.edu/~drwhite/worldcul/SCCSarticles.htm (Explanation: http://eclectic.ss.uci.edu/~drwhite/worldcul/atlas.htm).

Mwanakatwe, J. M. 1968. *The Growth of Education in Zambia since Independence*. Lusaka: Oxford University Press.

Nabea, Wendo. 2009. "Language Policy in Kenya: Negotiation with Hegemony." *Journal of Pan African Studies* 3: 121–38.

Nadeau, Jean Benoît. 1999. "La Francophonie: Is it Franco-Phoney?" *Letters* of the Institute of Current World Affairs (20 July 1999): 1–10.

National Democratic Institute. 1993. *An Assessment of the October 11, 1992 Election in Cameroon*. Washington, DC: National Democratic Institute for International Affairs.

Ndao, Papa Alioune. 2008. "Senghor, les langues nationales et le français: problématique d'une politique francophone. In *La francophonie des "pères fondateurs,"* edited by Papa Alioune Ndao, 35–66. Paris: Karthala.

Ndjio, Basile. 2008. "Millennial Democracy and Spectral Reality in Post-colonial Africa." *African Journal of International Affairs* 11: 115–56.

Ngugi wa Thiong'o. 1986. *Decolonizing the Mind: The Politics of Language in African Literature*. London: James Currey.

Nieuwenhuis, F. J. 1996. *The Development of Education Systems in Postcolonial Africa*. Pretoria: HSRC.

Njoya, Jean. 2002. "Democratisation, Divergences Ethniques et Politisation de la Pluralité au Cameroun." *Canadian Journal of African Studies* 36: 239–80.

Nkwi Paul Nchoji, and Francis Nyamnjoh, eds. 1997. *Regional Balance and National Integration in Cameroon*. Leiden: ASC.

Nunn, Nathan. 2007. "Historical Legacies: A Model Linking Africa's Past to Its Current Underdevelopment." *Journal Of Development Economics* 83:157–75.

Nyamnjoh, Francis, and Michael Rowlands. 1998. "Elite Associations and the Politics of Belonging in Cameroon." *Africa* 68: 320–37.

Ofori-Attah, Kwabena Ei. 2006. "The British and Curriculum Development in West Africa: A Historical Discourse." *Review of Education* 52: 409–23.

Ogunsheye, Ayo. 1965. "Nigeria." In *Education and Political Development*, edited by James Coleman, 123–43. Princeton, NJ: Princeton University Press.

Okoth, P. G. 1993. "The Creation of a Dependent Culture: The Imperial School Curriculum in Uganda." In J. A. Mangan, *The Imperial Curriculum*. London: Routledge.

Ordeshook, Peter, and Olga Shvetsova. 1994. "Ethnic Heterogeneity, District Magnitude, and the Number of Parties." *American Journal of Political Science* 38: 100–23.

Organisation Internationale de la Francophonie. 2011. *ELAN: Une offre francophone vers un enseignement bilingue pour mieux réussir à l'école*. Paris: OIF.

Ottaway, Marina. 2003. *Democracy Challenged: The Rise of Semi-Authoritarianism*. Washington, DC: Carnegie.

Ouane, Adama, and Yvette Amon-Tanoh. 1990. "Literacy in French-Speaking Africa: A Situational Analysis." *African Studies Review* 33: 21–38.

Ozouf, Mona. 1984. *L'Ecole de la France: Essais sur la Révolution, l'Utopie et L'Enseignement*. Paris: Gallimard.

Ozouf, Mona. 1988. *Festivals and the French Revolution*. Cambridge, MA: Harvard University Press.

Page, John. 2012. "Can Africa Industrialise?" *Journal of African Economies*. 21 AERC Supplement 2: ii86–ii125.

Parliament of Ghana. 2002. *Parliamentary Debates*, Official Report, Tuesday, 2 July 2002: "Statements – Language Policy in Education," Column 1660.

Phillipson, Robert, and Skutnabb-Kangas, Tove. 1999. "Englishisation: One dimension of globalisation/L'anglicisation: Un aspect de la mondialisation." *AILA Review* 13: 19–36.

Phillipson, Robert, ed. 2000. *Rights to Language: Equity, Power and Education*. Mahwah, NJ: Lawrence Erlbaum Associates.

Phillipson, Robert. 1992. *Linguistic Imperialism*. New York: Oxford University Press.

Plattner, Marc. 2010. "Populism, Pluralism, and Liberal Democracy." *Journal of Democracy* 21: 81–92.

Porter, Bruce. 1994. *War and the Rise of the Sate: The Military Foundations of Modern Politics*. New York: Free Press.

Porter, Rosalie Pendalino. 1990. *Forked Tongue: The Politics of Bilingual Education*. New York: Basic Books.

Posner, Daniel. 2003. "The Colonial Origins of Ethnic Cleavages: The Case of Linguistic Divisions in Zambia." *Comparative Politics* 35: 127–46.

Posner, Daniel. 2004. "Measuring Ethnic Fractionalization in Africa." *American Journal of Political Science* 48: 849–63.

Posner, Daniel. 2005. *Institutions and Ethnic Politics in Africa*. New York: Cambridge University Press.

Poth, Joseph. 1997. *L'enseigneent d'une langue maternelle et d'une langue non maternelle. La mise en application d'une pédagogie convergente*. Mons: CIPA.

Putnam, Robert. 1993. *Making Democracy Work: Civic Traditions in Modern Italy*. Princeton, NJ: Princeton University Press.

Quinn, Frederick. 2006. *In Search of Salt: Changes in Beti (Cameroon) Society: 1880–1960*. New York: Berghan Books.

Quinn, John James, and David J. Simon. 2006. "Plus ça Change, . . . : The Allocation of French ODA to Africa During and After the Cold War." *International Interactions* 32: 295–318.

Ramirez, J. David, Sandra D. Yuen, and Dena R. Ramey. 1991. *Final Report: Longitudinal Study of Structured English Immersion Strategy, Early-Exit and Late-Exit Bilingual Education Programs for Language Minority Children*. Vols. I and II, Prepared for the U.S. Department of Education. San Mateo: Aguirre International. No. 300–87–0156.

Renard, Raymond, and Daniel Peraya. 1985. *Langues africaines et langues d'enseignement: problematique de l'introduction des langues nationales dans l'enseignement primaire en afrique*. Actes du atelier organisé à l'Université de Mons (Belgique) du 9–13 september 1985. Paris: Didier Erudition.

Renard, Raymond. 2002. "La Politique linguistique de l'organisation internationale de la francophonie dans son éspace francophone." Paper presented at the Congrès Mondiale sur les Politiques Linguistiques, 16–20 April 2002.

Reno, William. 1994. "Decaying African States and the New Regional State System." Paper prepared for the Annual Meeting of the American Political Science Association, September 3–6, 1994.

Reno, William. 2000. "Clandestine Economies, Violence and States in Africa." *Journal of International Affairs* 53: 433–59.

République du Sénégal: Commission Nationale de Reforme de l'Éducation et de la Formation. 1984. [Etats Généraux] *Rapport Général Annexe IIE: L'Introduction des langues nationales dans le système éducatif*. 5 Aug 1981–6 Aug 1984. Dakar, Senegal.

Rice, Susan and Stewart Patrick. 2008. *Index of State Weakness in the Developing World*. Washington, DC: The Brookings Institution. http://www.brookings.edu/research/reports/2008/02/weak-states-index).

Risse, Thomas, Steve C. Ropp, and Kathryn Sikkink. 1999. *The Power of Human Rights: International Norms and Domestic Change*. Cambridge: Cambridge University Press.

Risse-Kappen, Thomas. 1994. "Ideas Do Not Flow Freely: Transnational Coalitions, Domestic Structures, and the End of the Cold War." *International Organization* 48: 185–214.

Robinson, Clinton. 1987. "Alphabetisation Informelle des Adults." In *Programme des ONG: Alphabetisation Experimentale en Langue Maternelle*, edited by Agence Canadienne de Developpement International. Rapport Final, June 1987.

Rodrik, Dani. 1999. "Where Did All the Growth Go? External Shocks, Social Conflict and Growth Collapses." *Journal of Economic Growth* 4: 385–412.

Roitman, Janet. 2007. "The Right to Tax: Economic Citizenship in the Chad Basin." *Citizenship Studies* 11: 187–209.

Rossell, Christine, and Keith Baker. 1996. "The Effectiveness of Bilingual Education." *Research in the Teaching of English* 30: 7–74.

Rotberg, Robert. 2003. "Failed States, Collapsed States, Weak States: Causes and Indicators." In *State Failure and State Weakness in a Time of Terror*, edited by Robert I. Rotberg. Washington, DC: Brookings Institution Press.

Rubin, Joan, Björn Jernudd, Jyotirindra Das Gupta, Joshua Fishman and Charles Ferguson. 1977. *Language Planning Processes*. New York: Mouton.

Rukare, Enoka H. [Senior Inspector of Schools, Uganda Ministry of Education]. 1969. "Aspirations for Education in the 'New' and Free Nations of Africa." *Educational Leadership* (November): 124–28.

Sackey, J. A. 1996. "The English Language in Ghana: A Historical Perspective." In *English in Ghana*, edited by M. E. Kropp Dakubu, 127. Proceedings of the Inaugural Meeting of the Ghana English Studies Association, University College of Education, Winneba, June 13–15, 1996.

Sanneh, Lamin. 1989. *Translating the Message: The Missionary Impact on Culture.* Maryknoll, NY: Orbis Books.

Schedler, Andreas. 2010. "Authoritarianism's Last Line of Defense." *Journal of Democracy* 21: 69–80.

Schmidt, Elizabeth. 2005. *Mobilizing the Masses: Gender, Ethnicity, and Class in the Nationalist Movement in Guinea, 1939–1958.* Portsmouth, NH: Heinemann.

Seck, Ibrahima. 1993. *La stratégie culturelle de la France en Afrique: l'enseignement colonial* (1817–1960). Paris: L'Harmattan.

Senghor, Léopold. 1962. "Le français, langue de culture." *Esprit, Le français, langue vivante.* (November): 837–844.

Senghor, Léopold. 1983. "Preface." In *Le français et les langues africaines au Senegal*, by Pierre Dumont, 7–20. Paris: ACCT/Khartala.

Shell, Olive, and Etienne Sadembouo. 1983. *De la langue maternelle à la langue française, livre de transition.* PROPELCA No. 17. Yaounde: The University of Yaounde in Collaboration with SIL and CREA/ISH, 1983/1985/1988.

Shugart, Matthew Soberg, and John M. Carey. 1992. *Presidents and Assemblies.* New York: Cambridge University Press.

Simpson, Andrew. 2008. *Language and National Identity in Africa.* New York: Oxford University Press.

Skutnabb-Kangas, Tove. 1988. "Multilingualism and the Education of Minority Children." In *Minority Education: From Shame to Struggle*, edited by Tove Skutnabb-Kangas and Jim Cummins. Philadelphia: Multilingual Matters.

Skutnabb-Kangas, Tove, and Jim Cummins. 1988. *Minority Education: From Shame to Struggle.* Philadelphia: Multilingual Matters.

Skutnabb-Kangas, Tove, and Robert Phillipson. 1994. *Linguistic Human Rights: Overcoming Linguistic Discrimination.* Berlin: Mouton de Gruyter.

Skutnabb-Kangas, Tove. 2000. *Linguistic Genocide in Education or Worldwide Diversity and Human Rights.* Mahwah, NJ: Lawrence Erlbaum Associates.

Skutnabb-Kangas, Tove. 1995. "Multilingualism and the Education of Minority Children." *Policy and Practice in Bilingual Education: Extending the Foundations*, edited by O. Garcia and C. Baker, 40–62. Clevendon: Multilingual Matters.

Smith, Stephen, and Antoine Glaser. 1997. *Ces Messieurs Afrique: Des Réseaux aux Lobbies*. Paris: Caiman-Levy.

Socpa, Antoine. 2006. "Bailleurs Autochtones et Locataires Allogenes: Enjeu Foncier et Participation Politique au Cameroun." *African Studies Review* 49: 45–67.

Stark, Frank M. 1980. "Persuasion and Power in Cameroon." *Canadian Journal of African Studies* 14: 273–93.

Stone, Lawrence. 1969. "Literacy and Education in England 1640–1900." *Past & Present* 42: 69–139.

Stumpf, Rudolph. 1979. *La Politique Linguistique au Cameroun de 1884 a 1960*. Berne: Peter Lang.

Sutton, Francis X. 1965. "Education and the Making of Modern Nations." In *Education and Political Development*, edited by James Coleman, 51–74. Princeton, NJ: Princeton University Press.

Swarts, Patti. 2000. "Language Policy Implementation in Namibia: Realities, Challenges and Politics." In *Language and Development in Southern Africa: Making the Right Choices*, edited by Richard Trewby and Sandra Fitchat, 38–51. Conference Proceedings, National Institute for Educational Development, Okahandja, Namibia, 11–13 April 2000 Namibia: Gamsberg Macmillan.

Taagepera, Rein, and Matthew Soberg Shugart. 1989. *Seats and Votes: The Effects and Determinants of Electoral Systems*. New Haven, CT: Yale University Press.

Tadadjeu, Maurice. 1977. "A Model for Functional Trilingualism in Africa." Ph.D. Diss., University of Southern California.

Tadadjeu, Maurice. 1990. *Le Defi de Babel au Cameroon*. Published in collaboration with SIL, Department of Linguistics at CREA, ISH.

Tagepera, Rein, and Matthew Soberg Shugart. 1989. *Seats and Votes: The Effects and Determinants of Electoral Systems*. New Haven, CT: Yale University Press.

Takougang, Joseph, and Milton Krieger. 1998. *African State and Society in the 1990s: Cameroon's Political Crossroads*. Boulder, CO: Westview Press.

Takougang, Joseph. 2003a. "Nationalism, Democratization, and Political Opportunism in Cameroon." *Journal of Contemporary African Studies* 21: 427–45.

Takougang, Joseph. 2003b. "The 2002 Legislative Election in Cameroon: A Retrospective on Cameroon's Stalled Democracy Movement." *Journal of Modern African Studies* 41: 421–35.

Takougang, Joseph. 2004. "The Demise of Biya's New Deal: Cameroon, 1982–1992." In *The Leadership Challenge in Africa: Cameroon under Paul Biya*, edited by John Mukum Mbaku and Joseph Takougang, 95–122. Trenton, NJ: Africa World Press.

Tilly, Charles. 1992. *Coercion, Capital, and European States: AD 990–1990*. Cambridge: Blackwell.

Tilly, Charles. 2000. "Processes and Mechanisms of Democratization." *Sociological Theory* 18: 1–16.

Tilly, Charles. 2007. *Democracy*. New York: Cambridge University Press.

Tilly, Charles, and Sydney Tarrow. 2007. *Contentious Politics*. Boulder, CO: Paradigm Publishers.

Titeca, Kristof, and Tom de Herdt. 2011. "Real Governance Beyond the 'Failed State': Negotiating Education in the Democratic Republic of the Congo." *African Affairs* 110/439:213–31.

Tocqueville, Alexis de. 2000/1840. *Democracy in America*. Translated by Harvey Mansfield and Delba Winthrop. Chicago: University of Chicago Press.

Tollefson, James W. 2002. *Language Policies in Education: Critical Issues*. Mahwah, NJ: Lawrence Erlbaum Associates.

Tollefson, James W., and Amy B. M. Tsui, eds. 2004. *Medium of Instruction Policies: Which Agenda? Whose Agenda?* Mahwah, NJ: Lawrence Erlbaum Associates.

Tooley, James, Pauline Dixon, and Isaac Amuah. 2007. "Private and Public Schooling in Ghana: A Census and Comparative Survey." *Review of Education* 53: 389–415.

Tréfault, Thierry. 2001. "Bambara et francaise à l'École malienne: la recherche de la complémentarité." In *Les Langues dans l'éspace francophone: de la coexistence au partenariat*, edited by Robert Chaudenson and Louis-Jean Calvet, 227–257. Paris: L'Harmattan.

Trudell, Barbara. 2004. "The Power of the Local: Education Choices and Language Maintenance Among the Bafut, Kom and Nso' Communities of Northwest Cameroon." Ph.D. diss., University of Edinburgh.

Trudell, Barbara. 2005. "Language Choice, Education and Community Identity." *Journal of Educational Development* 25: 237–51.

Turcotte, Denis. *Lois, Règlements et Textes Administratifs sur l'Usage des Langues en Afrique Occidentale Française (1826–1959)*. Québec: University of Laval.

UNESCO. 1953. *The Use of Vernacular Languages in Education*. Monographs on Fundamental Education 8. Paris: UNESCO.

UNESCO. 1977. *Statistics of Educational Attainment and Illiteracy: 1945–1974*. Paris: UNESCO.

UNESCO. 1988. *Compendium of Statistics on Illiteracy*, No. 30. Paris: Division of Statistics, UNESCO.

UNESCO. 1990. *Compendium of Statistics on Illiteracy*, No. 31. Paris: Division of Statistics, UNESCO.

UNESCO. 1994. *Statistics on Adult Literacy: Preliminary Results of 1994 Estimations and Projections* (October). Paris: UNESCO.

Vail, Leroy. 1989. "Introduction." In *Creation of Tribalism in Southern Africa*, edited by Leroy Vail, 1–19. London: Currey; Berkeley: University of California Press.

van de Walle, Nicolas. 2001. *African Economies and the Politics of Permanent Crisis, 1979–1999*. New York: Cambridge University Press.

van de Walle, Nicolas. 2009. "The Institutional Origins of Inequality in Sub-Saharan Africa." *Annual Review of Political Science* 12: 307–27.

Varshney, Ashutosh. 2001. "Ethnic Conflict and Civil Society." *World Politics* 53: 362–98.

Verlet, M. 1986. "Les Maîtres-Mots; Langue et Pouvoir au Ghana sous Nkrumah." *Politique Africaine*, 23: 67–82.

Vernon-Jackson, Hugh O. H. 1967. *Language, Schools and Government in Cameroon*. New York: Teachers College Press.

Verspoor, Adrian. 2001. *A Chance to Learn: Knowledge and Finance for Education in Sub-Saharan Africa*. Sector Assistance Strategy. Washington, DC: The World Bank.

Walker, Jack L. 1977. "Setting the Agenda in the U.S. Senate: A Theory of Problem Selection." *British Journal of Political Science* 7: 423–45.

Wambach, Michel. 1994. *La Pédagogie Convergente à l'École Fondamentale, Bilan d'une Recherche-Action*. Ségou, République du Mali: ACCT-CIAVER.

Wa'Njogu J. Kiarie. 2004. "Language and Multiparty Democracy in a Multiethnic Kenya." *Africa Today* 50: 55–73.

Weber, Eugen. 1976. *Peasants into Frenchmen: The Modernization of Rural France 1870–1914*. Stanford, CA: Stanford University Press.

Weingast, Barry. 2005. "Persuasion, Preference Change, and Critical Junctures : The Microfoundations of a Macroscopic Concept." In *Preferences and Situations: Points of Intersection between Historical and Rational Choice Institutionalism*, edited by Ira Katznelson and Barry Weingast, 161–84. New York: Russell Sage.

Weinstein, Brian. 1976. "Francophonie: International Languages in Politics." In *Language in Sociology*, edited by Albert Verdoodt, and Rolf Kjolseth, 265–304. Institut de Linguistique de Louvain: Editions Peeters.

Weinstein, Brian. 1982. *The Civic Tongue: Political Consequences of Language Choices*. New York: Longman.

White, Bob W. 1996. "Talk about School: Education and the Colonial Project in French and British Africa 1860–1960." *Comparative Education* 32: 9–25.

Whitehead, Clive. 2005. "The Historiography of British Imperial Education Policy. Part II: Africa and the Rest of the Colonial Empire." *History of Education* 34: 441–54.

Wilayi, Richard. 2000. (Cameroon Ministry of Education). "Education in a Global Era: Challenges to Equity, Opportunities for Diversity." *Country Paper – Republic of Cameroon*. Prepared for the 14th Conference of Commonwealth Education Ministers, Halifax, Nova Scotia, Canada, November 27–30, 2000.

Wilder, Gary. 2005. *The French Imperial Nation-State: Negritude and Colonial Humanism between the World Wars*. Chicago: University of Chicago Press.

Wilkinson, Steven. 2004. *Votes and Violence: Electoral Competition and Ethnic Riots in India*. Cambridge: Cambridge University Press.

Williamson, Kay. 1980. "Small Languages in Primary Education: The Rivers Readers' Project as a Case History." In *Language in Education in Nigeria*. Vol II, ed. Ayo Bamgbose. Lagos: The National Language Center.

World Bank WDI. *World Development Indicators* http://data.worldbank.org/data-catalog/world-development-indicators

World Bank. 1988. *Education in Sub-Saharan Africa: Policies for Adjustment, Revitalization, and Expansion*. Washington, DC: The World Bank.

World Bank. 1989. *Sub-Saharan Africa: From Crisis to Sustainable Growth*. Washington, DC: The World Bank.

Wright, Sue. 2004. *Language Policy and Language Planning: From Nationalism to Globalisation*. New York: Palgrave/Macmillan.

Wurm, Stephen A. 1999. "Endangered Languages, Multilingualism and Linguistics." *Diogenes* 47: 56–65.

Yamada, Shoko. 2009. "'Traditions' and Cultural Production: Character Training at the Achimota School in Colonial Ghana." *History of Education* 38: 29–59.

Young, Crawford. 1965. *Politics in the Congo*. Princeton, NJ: Princeton University Press.

Young, Crawford. 1976. *The Politics of Cultural Pluralism*. Madison: University of Wisconsin Press.

Young, Crawford. 1983. "The Temple of Ethnicity." *World Politics* 35: 652–62.

Young, Crawford. 1994a. *The African Colonial State in Comparative Perspective*. New Haven, CT: Yale University Press.

Young, Crawford. 1994b. "Zaire: The Shattered Illusion of the Integral State." *The Journal of Modern African Studies* 32: 247–63.

Young, Crawford. 2007. "Nation, Ethnicity, and Citizenship: Dilemmas of Democracy and Civil Order in Africa." In *Making Nations, Creating Strangers: States and Citizenship in Africa*, edited by Sara Dorman, Daniel Hammett, and Paul Nugent, 241–264. Boston: Brill.

Zambo-Belinga, Joseph-Marie. 2005. "An Explanation of Electoral Attitudes in Cameroon 1990–92: Towards a New Appraisal." In *Liberal Democracy and its Critics in Africa: Political Dysfunction and the Struggle for Social Progress*, edited by Tukumbi Lumumba-Kasongo. Dakar: CODESRIA.

Index

CPSIA information can be obtained at www.ICGtesting.com
Printed in the USA
BVOW01*0038040614

355337BV00003B/60/P